THE BUSINESS OF ALCHEMY

THE BUSINESS OF ALCHEMY

SCIENCE AND CULTURE IN THE
HOLY ROMAN EMPIRE

Pamela H. Smith

PRINCETON UNIVERSITY PRESS

PRINCETON, NEW JERSEY

COPYRIGHT © 1994 BY PRINCETON UNIVERSITY PRESS

PUBLISHED BY PRINCETON UNIVERSITY PRESS, 41 WILLIAM STREET,

PRINCETON, NEW JERSEY 08540

IN THE UNITED KINGDOM: PRINCETON UNIVERSITY PRESS, CHICHESTER, WEST SUSSEX

ALL RIGHTS RESERVED

LIBRARY OF CONGRESS CATALOGING-IN-PUBLICATION DATA

SMITH, PAMELA H., 1957–

THE BUSINESS OF ALCHEMY : SCIENCE AND CULTURE IN THE HOLY ROMAN

EMPIRE / PAMELA H. SMITH.

P.   CM.

INCLUDES BIBLIOGRAPHICAL REFERENCES AND INDEX.

ISBN 0-691-05691-9

1. SCIENCE, RENAISSANCE.   2. SCIENCE—PHILOSOPHY—HISTORY.

3. HOLY ROMAN EMPIRE—HISTORY—1517–1648.   4. HOLY ROMAN EMPIRE—

HISTORY—1648–1804.   5. BECHER, JOHANN JOACHIM, 1635–1682.

I. TITLE.

Q125.2.S58   1994   306.4'5'0943'09032—DC20   93-44856   CIP

THIS BOOK HAS BEEN COMPOSED IN TIMES ROMAN

PRINCETON UNIVERSITY PRESS BOOKS ARE PRINTED
ON ACID-FREE PAPER AND MEET THE GUIDELINES FOR
PERMANENCE AND DURABILITY OF THE COMMITTEE ON
PRODUCTION GUIDELINES FOR BOOK LONGEVITY
OF THE COUNCIL ON LIBRARY RESOURCES

PRINTED IN THE UNITED STATES OF AMERICA

1   3   5   7   9   10   8   6   4   2

CONTENTS

ILLUSTRATIONS

ACKNOWLEDGMENTS

IN WRITING this book I have incurred a number of unpayable obligations, which, unlike other sorts of debts, it gives me great pleasure to acknowledge. I am especially pleased to make clear the intellectual debt I owe to Owen Hannaway, who both suggested the primary matter of this study and, by the example of his own approach to the problems of early modernity and his close readings of texts, imparted an organizing form. I am also indebted to Mack Walker, whose concept of the structure of early modern German society provided a matrix of place for the characters and ideas in the story.

As this book evolved, it benefited from the institutional support of the Department of History of Science of the Johns Hopkins University, the Program for Comparative European History at the Villa Spelman in Florence, and Pomona College. Fellowships from the Deutscher Akademischer Austauschdienst, the Forschungsinstitut of the Deutsches Museum, the Long and Widmont Memorial Foundation, and Pomona College made possible the research for this book. In connection with these fellowships, I owe thanks to Dr. Otto Mayr and Frau Nida-Rümelin of the Deutsches Museum in Munich. I am also grateful for the institutional framework provided by Professor Dr. Karin Figala and the Deutsches Museum. My doctoral dissertation, "Alchemy, Credit, and the Commerce of Words and Things: Johann Joachim Becher at the Courts of the Holy Roman Empire, 1635–82" (Johns Hopkins University, 1990), contains the original German of all passages translated here. Material from this book has appeared in different form and with a different purpose in *Patronage and Institutions: Science, Technology, and Medicine at the European Court, 1500–1750,* ed. Bruce T. Moran (Woodbridge, Suffolk: Boydell, 1991), and *Isis* 85 (1994).

Among the many people whose comments have helped me, I would especially like to thank Mario Biagioli, William Clark, Ronald Cluett, Betty Jo Dobbs, Anthony Grafton, Sharon Kingsland, Pamela Long, Christoph Meinel, Bruce Moran, Richard Olson, Orest Ranum, Lisa Rosner, Simon Schaffer, and Robert Westman.

Many wonderful hours were spent in libraries and archives in various parts of the world, but I would like to single out for special thanks the staff of the Bayrische Staatsbibliothek in Munich, the archivists of the Hofkammerarchiv in Vienna, and the very helpful staff of the library of the University in Rostock.

Intense and wonderful hours—even days—were spent too in conversation with friends, and their insights helped shape this book. David J. S. King and Mary Voss participated in most stages of this work, as did Michael Dennis, Dianne Pitman, and Jay Tribby. More recently Paula Findlen, Helena Wall,

Peggy Waller, and Elazar Barkan have provided intellectual companionship and much appreciated encouragement.

I am glad to have an opportunity to express my debt to my parents, Ronald Smith and Nancy Crenshaw Smith. Finally, I think with loving memory of my grandmother, Elisabeth Cluverius Crenshaw Working, whose love of books and storytelling, as well as her frustrated intellect, made their way to me in transmuted form. It was an impulse—not at all times fully conscious—to redeem her stymied aspirations that impelled me in the writing of this book.

Claremont, California
October 1993

THE BUSINESS OF ALCHEMY

PROLOGUE

EVOCATION

I F THERE WERE a musical interlude to introduce this text it would be the overture to an opera, a piece that could evoke the dramatic intricacies to come. We would hear the dark tones of the basso continuo, rising in crescendo, framing the drama, representing the increasing centralization of the territories of Europe and the compelling location of that center at the court of the territorial ruler. A burst of strings would signal the encroaching values of a commercial economy on the feudal, agrarian world, their bows sounding out a repeated, urgent "cash, cash, cash." The part of the winds, weaving its way around the bass frame and through the theme of the strings, related to these parts but clearly working on an internal dynamic of its own, plays the organization of knowledge. Recurring within the theme of the winds is a motif played by the horns, the relationship between words and things. Finally we hear a single voice, dancing around between the interstices of the strong bass and the themes of the higher register, connecting the disparate parts of the music. This small voice is the life of an individual. He mediates between the other voices, but he also mediates them for us. He is our link to the past.

This book is not an opera, but it does try to tie together diverse elements into a harmonious narrative. It tells the story of a single individual as well as a narrative of intellectual and cultural transformation. The voice of this book is the life of Johann Joachim Becher, spanning the last half of the seventeenth century (1635–82). Becher, who spent his life at the territorial courts of the Holy Roman Empire and who was passionately concerned with the reform of knowledge and of material life, allows us to enter into the cacophony of the past and shape it into a coherent piece. Out of his writings, the ideas expressed therein, his actions, the artifacts of his world (such as an alchemical medallion), and the narratives he told about himself and his world (such as his tale of a cunning alchemist) we may connect the various parts of the composition to delineate the parameters of his world as well as the long-term dynamics of change.

At the heart of this process of change in the early modern period was a crisis of authority. This crisis spanned an epistemological and chronological spectrum, reaching from the deep personal crisis of authority felt by a Luther or a Thomas More to Jonathan Swift's satirical *Battle of the Books*. In the intellectual realm this crisis translated into a debate about the foundations and very legitimacy of knowledge. What was the relationship of things to words? Put differently, how could knowledge acquired through the senses be legitimated and what was its relation to discursive and deductive knowledge? These questions were part of a cultural change by which a world view founded in texts and the manipulation of words was replaced by one based in natural objects and the manipulation of things.

This debate about words and things was played out in the wake of the emergence of a controversial "new philosophy" and its "new method of philosophizing." The proponents of this new philosophy claimed that, unlike their predecessors, they dealt with visible, tangible, material things (and we shall see it is significant that these things often had a commercially determinable value). Active rather than contemplative, this new philosophy was a practice, rather than a set of theories, and it flourished in such places as laboratories, theaters of nature, and cabinets of curiosities. The practitioners of the new philosophy might dispute its precise methodology and its limits, but they knew for certain that it had to do with "things": the collection of things, the observation of things, and material, visual demonstration by use of things in place of the logical demonstration by means of words.

This new method did not storm the citadels of knowledge, but slowly transformed habits of practice and thought as it became useful to a growing number of individuals and groups, as scholarly alliances formed around it, and as it provided more satisfying explanations within the new "materialistic" epistemology. It was patronized by courts, institutionalized in the academies, and gradually incorporated into an educational curriculum that had been based on the mastery of a corpus of words and texts. We can see this moment of transition at which old and new interpenetrated in a description of the "new" method pursued at the Julian Academy at Helmstedt: first, the phenomena are observed; second, their construction is noted; and, third, they are subjected to *demonstratio* from certain principles. Subject headings in the account are Aristotelian: "De corpore," "De motu," "De vacuo," "De elementis" (water, earth, air, and fire), "De meteoris," "De animalibus," and so on. In contrast, the text under these headings exemplifies the new: "De corpore" contains microscopic observations of objects such as flour and sugar. "De motu" concerns machines, while "De elementis" contains a section on a transmutation of iron into copper, and "De animalibus" lists the animals—stuffed and preserved—that have been collected by the academy. The last two subjects—"De visu" and "De auditu"— run through an assortment of instruments and their use.[1] Similar examples of this mélange of old and new could be drawn from the Royal Society, the Académie des sciences, the Academia naturae curiosorum, or the numerous collections and laboratories of new philosophers and princes all over Europe. Becher's explication and adaptation of the new philosophy illuminates this fluid cultural moment when "science" had not yet achieved its preeminent modern

---

[1] Johann Andreas Schmidt, *Theatrum Naturae et Artis. Singulis semestribus novis machinis & experimentis augendum in Academia Julia curiosis B.C.D. pandet I.A.S.D.* (Helmstedt: Georgus-Wolfgangus-Hamius Acad. Typogr., ca. 1710).

position as the sole legitimator of truth, but instead had to compete with a number of other intellectual pursuits.

Connected to the rise of this new philosophy and its emphasis on practice was a greater importance given to the knowledge of human art, as it was manifested in machines, technical processes, and the knowledge of "rude mechanics" and artisans. The progress of human art provided a model for the advance of knowledge, and technology and progress became bound up with the new philosophy. While some asserted that natural philosophy might be practiced by an artisan or by anyone who kept his eyes open, no matter what his education, others tried to limit natural philosophy to the gentleman. Thus the advent of the new philosophy both opened up possibilities for individuals who did not have an intensive text-based education that would have allowed them to call themselves learned in the old style, and resulted as well in the formation of an elite of natural philosophers who tried to distance themselves from rude mechanics.

Human art not only demonstrated the progress of the moderns over the ancients, but it was also productive of things in a way that neither theory nor practice had been before. The new philosophy claimed to involve not only theory and practice, but also to be as productive as art. Thus, the rise of the new philosophy brought on a fundamental reorganization in the scheme of knowledge. The new philosophy blurred the boundaries between what had been the separate realms of theory, practice, and art, as well as the difference that had existed between the production and manipulation of words and the production and manipulation of things. In this story of the transformation of the relationship between words and things, Johann Joachim Becher acted as an intermediary. Himself halfway between the world of artisans and that of scholars, he becomes an intermediary—both physical and intellectual—between them. Like many others of his time, he also became a go-between linking the holders of productive knowledge and the territorial ruler.

Becher's life tells us as well about the political history of the early modern period. As the territorial ruler increased his own power, he circumvented his local nobility and its grip on the revenues of the territory. Because the cost of maintaining power increased, the territorial lords began to look to commerce and the "empire of things" as a source of revenue. Although merchants had always been a source of loans and taxes for the nobility, nobles themselves did not actively take part in the commercial economy. The basis of their power and their code of values lay in feudal relationships and an economy based on the natural fruits of the land. The transformation this need for cash wrought is only one part of the very long, slow change from an agrarian society based on land, agriculture, and gift exchange to a society based on commerce and monetary exchange. Such a process of transformation, which began in late medieval society and was not completed until the industrial revolution, was nonetheless radically reshaped during the seventeenth century. Such reshaping is reflected in Becher's activities at the courts of the Holy Roman Empire, for he used natural philosophy to make commerce acceptable to his noble patrons. Thus, his texts and projects illuminate this moment of transformation in cultural values, as his employment of natural philosophy reveals some of the reasons that science came to hold a central place in the evolving modern state.

. . . . .

As the wandering son of a guild-town mother and a Lutheran pastor, Becher received a distinctive education that provided him with a model of a cycle of sustenance in the guild town on the one hand, and the potential of commerce on the other. He established himself at court as an adept in chemistry and the mechanical arts, eventually receiving the official position of court mathematician and physician. His position and activities in the court world were conditioned by his status and the knowledge associated with it. As mathematician and machine maker, Becher had a connection with and a knowledge of the mechanical arts and artisanal activity, and he exploited this in his struggle for power at court. As court physician, Becher used both the status of his position as a member of the republic of letters and his knowledge of natural processes in carrying out his projects. Becher's use of his knowledge of nature and his mechanical aptitude constitutes the substratum of this book. Becher employed his knowledge and ability as a scholar and an artisan in a variety of ways at court: first, he claimed the status of a man of theory who was competent to adjudicate and organize the knowledge of practicing artisans. Second, he drew on the association of both chemical knowledge and mechanical aptitude with a set of practices viewed as leading to "productive" knowledge. Finally, he sought to bring the results of both his knowledge of nature and the mechanical arts—productive knowledge—into the sphere of the territorial ruler.

Becher spent the majority of his life attempting to introduce commercial forms and activities into the world of the noble court. His attempt ran up against many difficulties, usually attributed by historians to a lack of "organized" and "rational" court bureaucracy and a deficiency in courtiers' understanding of the mechanisms of the market and commerce. I argue, on the contrary, that Becher's difficulties stemmed from the fact that the structure and rationality of the court was based on a different set of practices and principles than that of the commercial world. Becher's success, such as it was, was due to his ability to mediate between the two worlds. He framed his commercial projects in the traditional idiom and gesture of noble court culture, and his knowledge of natural processes as physician and alchemical adept assisted him in translating commercial values into court culture.

In elaborating the link between Becher's chemistry and commerce, I develop a second argument about the broader significance of Becher's activities. His activities embodied a vision of reform that was "material." Becher was concerned with the temporal world, with material increase, with the elevation of things over words, and with observation, practice, and experience. This concern with the observable material world characterizes the conceptual transformation from words to things of the early modern period. We may also see in it an assertion and co-option in European culture of artisanal modes of seeing and doing. Artisanal culture embodied an understanding of production, creation, and working with the hands, as well as a set of skills and techniques by which this knowledge was employed to manipulate material things. It operated from an understanding of the human relationship to the material world and the power of human art.[2] It embodied a view that humankind was capable of productive abilities similar to those of nature, for *ars imitatur naturam*: human art imitated nature.

The world of the artisans and their culture in the guild cities of the Holy Roman Empire embodied this potential for human production. The guilds that dominated these cities were powerful centers for the manufacture of valuable goods as well as centers for the reproduction of the knowledge and techniques that sustained this production. Where scholars reproduced and transferred knowledge by writing, the artisanal structures reproduced knowledge by doing and imitating. In the balance of powers that characterized the Holy Roman Empire, guild cities took on a distinctive social structure, and as such, they provided a model of self-sustaining production that imitated natural production. Nature was productive, and, through the imitation of nature by art, the world of human beings was also viewed as potentially productive. Such notions of generation possessed a religious dimension, and the city as the center of human art and production had a powerful spiritual significance: God gave humans the power to use their hands to create for themselves what previously had been supplied to them by bountiful nature in Paradise. The power of art was thus not only creative, but redemptive, for by work of the hand, humans would regain Paradise.

Commerce on the other hand was an unproductive activity, indeed a parasitical one, for merchants took advantage of deficiencies in the cycle of production in the town and on the land. Merchants were thus perceived as draining wealth from a town, and commerce was considered an unnatural activity, for merchants were viewed as producing nothing. Instead they acted as middlemen, distributing goods produced by other members of society, thus profiting from the labor of others, while doing no honest work themselves. The unnatural

[2] In helping me to shape this view, I am indebted to Owen Hannaway's direction of a 1989 seminar at the Folger Institute, Washington, D.C., entitled " 'Technologia': Language and Technical Knowledge from the Renaissance to the Enlightenment," and in particular to two of the readings for that seminar: Neil Kamil, "War, Natural Philosophy and the Metaphysical Foundations of Artisanal Thought in an American Mid-Atlantic Colony: La Rochelle, New York City and the Southwestern Huguenot Paradigm, 1517–1730" (Ph.D. diss., Johns Hopkins University, 1988); and J. A. Bennet, "The Mechanics' Philosophy and the Mechanical Philosophy," *History of Science* 24 (1986): 1–28.

offspring of this unnatural activity was money. Money was considered unnatural because it was a means of exchange that did not contain the seeds of its own regeneration. It was a means and not a fruit of labor. Money and commerce did not imitate productive nature, as agriculture and guild society did. Yet this barren, parasitical, and unnatural activity paradoxically provided surplus wealth—wealth that formed a source of power as great as the violence of arms and the force of noble rank. Merchants, while dangerous to the community because they were consuming, rather than producing, members of society, seemed nevertheless to hold a key to material increase.

. . . . .

Chapter 1 explores the background from which Becher fashioned his own identity and drew his principal ideas. It argues that he was attuned to a view of the city as a center of human production and the reproduction of productive techniques, as well as to the possibilities of commerce and mobility. Becher brought the results of his experience to the court world, and offered the court a solution to its need to create surplus wealth. His scheme combined the structure of the guild city and its "material knowledge" of human art and production with the surplus-creating capabilities of commerce. In seeking to implement his plan, he had to find a coherent structure that would combine the guild town, as a center of human production, with the commercial world, in order to make it attractive to the court.

To achieve this, Becher drew on his knowledge of the mechanical arts and of medical chemistry and alchemy. The mechanical arts—the province of the guilds—represented productive knowledge to Becher, and he attempted to capture not only the skills of individual artisans but also the productive knowledge they possessed; indeed he sought the very material understanding by which the artisan transformed raw materials into valuable goods. To express this artisanal understanding, Becher sought to formulate an unornamented "material discourse" and a method of cognition that captured the technique and knowledge of the artisan. Chapter 2 treats the period during which Becher established himself at court as *medicus* and *mathematicus*, and began to formulate this material understanding of knowledge and reform. Chapter 3 shows how Becher sought to draw material, productive knowledge, embodied in commerce, into the world of his noble patrons, while the first Interlude, in recounting a single episode, illustrates Becher's use of natural philosophy in attempting to integrate commercial values into the court world.

Alchemy and chemistry provided Becher with a language by which to represent the processes of natural creation and regeneration, and the means by which these processes could be imitated by the human hand. Becher's chemical and alchemical works were directed toward gaining knowledge about the creative principles of nature and imitating them by human art. Being both art and science, alchemy could illuminate the relationship of the artisan to his material and the productive process, as well as give the scholar a language in which to talk about this relationship and process. Alchemy thus became the vehicle by which Becher spoke to the court about production and material increase. The language of alchemy was particularly well suited to the discussion of commerce, for alchemical transmutation—the ennoblement of metals—provided an example of fabulous material increase and the production of surplus. This was especially true in Becher's theory of alchemical transmutation, which postulated that the multiplication of precious metals took place by means of consumption. Alchemy was thus a natural, virtuous activity within the compass of human art, and an accepted activity and language at the noble court. Chapter 4 makes clear the manner in which Becher used alchemy as such a language of material increase, and the second Interlude continues this theme by examining Becher's plan for an alchemical laboratory. The conflation of alchemy and politics in this plan reveals a transformative moment in the creation of the persona of the natural philosopher, as well as in the significance of industry for the actions of the territorial ruler.

In attempting to carry through this material reform, Becher became an intermediary between the court and the bearers of productive knowledge, attempting to bring their skills, knowledge, and productive potential under the control of the prince. He was not alone in this project, and a group of like-minded individuals accompanied him throughout his life, alternately assisting and hindering his schemes at court. Chapter 5 examines these men who colluded with Becher on his travels and in his intrigues. It particularly focuses on the interest evinced by Gottfried Wilhelm Leibniz in Becher, and attempts to pinpoint the source of Leibniz's fascination with Becher, as well as the common basis of their habits of thought and action in their shared world view. Like Becher, Leibniz and the other mobile individuals resided outside the town walls and sought positions at court, pursuing an understanding of the material world and of the process of creation. They were looking to capture the productive potential of art, thereby transporting the techniques and knowledge of the artisans outside that incubator of artisanal techniques, the guilds and the guild towns. By capturing their techniques and codifying the method of artisanal reproduction, this group destroyed the guild structure and ushered in a new order in which productive knowledge and the reproduction of that knowledge was taken outside the artisanal world and brought within the sphere of the state.

·   ·   ·   ·   ·

In telling the story of this transformation in the life of an individual, we must deal with the configuration of individual identity—both its creation in an individual's lifetime and its reformulation by the historian. In forming a picture of Becher's identity out of the stories he left, those he told about himself and those we can construct from these vestiges, a multitude of stories emerges. They are *only* stories in that they do not claim to represent a whole and seamless reality. They cannot, as written history never can, encompass the whole of lived experiences or all the possibilities of a past world. Entangled in the web of hindsight, the historian must narrow the multivalency of the past to render it comprehensible, without, however, doing away with the complexity of reality. We can thread our way along such a path in the narrative of Becher's life by seeking to understand the way in which he constructed his own identity out of the possibilities open to him as an actor during the years 1635 to 1682. Pierre Bourdieu, Michel Foucault, and other recent theorists have provided a vision of the extent to which the structures of power determine the possibilities open to an individual (and therefore self-identity) and have indicated how the changes in political structure in the early modern period might have affected the individual's understanding of society and self. Becher's identity was first of all shaped by the society of orders that defined the individual in the early modern period. But this hierarchy was being transformed. He was separated from the society of his parents' generation by the bloody caesura of the Thirty Years' War and by his own self-fashioned life at the courts of the Holy Roman Empire, where he spent almost two decades. The court world had a distinctive structure, hierarchy, and code of behavior, within which Becher created a space for himself and his peculiar qualifications and ideas.

While Becher negotiated the possiblities open to him within the limits imposed by the noble court, he also shaped his self-identity by his activity in the world of ideas. As a court physician, Becher regarded himself as a member of the republic of letters, and this identity was not precisely congruent with his place in the society of orders nor with his place as a servant of noble princes. The republic of scholars relied upon the past for its self-definition and legitimacy in a way that in our own day is irretrievably gone (despite all the talk of the canon). Dead languages provided an identity for anyone learned (or even half-learned as was Becher). And although the ancient authorities were long gone, many scholars felt a greater affinity to them than to their own contemporaries of a different social order. Moreover, the *universitas* of scholars—the republic of letters—possessed a set of ideals and conventions that in some ways worked in opposition to the hierarchical structure of the noble court. Although Becher could only take part in public life as a courtier of the territorial ruler, he nonetheless looked to the republic of scholars as an alternative model, where learning could make possible an independent life. And he looked to the Dutch Republic as a place where money could make such a life possible.

Becher also used his knowledge of nature and his adherence to the new philosophy to form his self-identity. He was one of a group of more or less liminal individuals—many of whom were interested in natural philosophy—who took advantage of the fluidity of their society to seek new sorts of authority.

Their claims to legitimacy presupposed a new vision of knowledge and learning; one associated with a new type of person who had little time or training. Such men often called themselves "natural philosophers." The new vision of knowledge was exemplified in the shift from polymathic and pansophic encyclopedias—arranged "systematically" with one subject flowing seamlessly into the next—to newly published tomes organized alphabetically. Such encyclopedias were especially useful to the curious man in a hurry, who did not have time to work his way methodically through such a systematic text and wanted his knowledge "torn into tiny pieces."[3] In 1637, Samuel Hartlib alluded to such a change when he stated that "From Descartes and gentlemen such as he it will be difficult to get an opinion on the pansophism of Comenius. Usually they are too lazy for that. They do not allow themselves that much time, unless one provokes them."[4]

Becher was one such *homo novus*. A restless, mobile man, he trumpeted his new ideas, but simultaneously grafted them onto traditional (or merely legitimate) notions. Like others of his day, he vacillated between viewing change as necessary, promising a hope of redemption, and as harboring a potential for chaos.[5] Thus he embraced change only within established models and always for the purpose of facilitating "order." At the same time, his vision of reform relied upon the future in a new way. Because he led a public life, in the service of the common good, Becher concerned himself with material increase in the world around him and, in the process, began to view *fortuna* as controllable by human agency. Religious resonances still inhered in his vision, however, as they did in the work of a Lutheran pastor who collected numbers of births and deaths in Breslau over a five-year period, then sent his careful tables to Leibniz, noting that perhaps they would demonstrate something about God's Providence, but might also be helpful in combating superstition.[6] Becher's project for the reform of his world had at its base a belief in the future that only begins to be typical of European society in the early modern era, but in Becher's day that future still resonated with the meaning of a very different sort of salvation.

Thus, Becher's life was the conjunction of a present spent in the courts of the Holy Roman Empire, a past of classical scholarship, and, in a new way, a

---

[3] Johann Hübner, 1712, quoted in Gotthardt Frühsorge, *Der politische Körper. Zum Begriff des Politischen im 17. Jahrhundert und in den Romanen Christian Weises* (Stuttgart: J. B. Metzlersche Verlagsbuchhandlung, 1974), p. 204.

[4] Hartlib, 1637, quoted in Wilhelmus Rood, *Comenius and the Low Countries* (Amsterdam: Van Gendt, 1970), p. 124.

[5] David Harris Sacks, *The Widening Gate: Bristol and the Atlantic Economy 1450–1700* (Berkeley: University of California Press, 1991), p. 352, distinguishes between these two views of change in the early modern period. Merchants especially suffered from the tension engendered by the need for security and the desire for expansion (pp. 358–59).

[6] Hans Schmitt-Lermann, *Der Versicherungsgedanke im deutschen Geistesleben des Barock und der Aufklärung* (Munich: Kommunalschriften-Verlag J. Jehle, 1954), p. 55.

future. He not only drew from that distant past, the Holy Roman Empire's immediate political present, but also projected a vision of society (although not always seamless and coherent) onto the future. Finally, however, Becher's identity was shaped by his own particular experiences of life, and by his employment of those diverse and sometimes incoherent elements in a kind of bricolage.

. . . . .

In this book, I have attempted to explain Becher's actions and texts in terms of the significance they would have had to his contemporaries and to himself. Thus I sought to examine Becher and his world not as it has usually been considered as part of a fairly linear history of economic thought and scientific development. Rather I regard the central categories of these histories—the market, economic thought, and, most of all, science—not as stable identifiable units through history, but rather as discourses or sets of practices that human individuals constructed for particular purposes at specific moments. The figure of Johann Joachim Becher also exists, however, in the story of our modern culture—that is, he represents something of significance to the modern world. And I have tried, particularly in the last chapter, to understand the ambiguous place to which our culture assigns Becher. An example of this ambiguity can be found in the work of the historian of chemistry, J. R. Partington:

> Becher is an obscure writer. . . . he was quarrelsome and vain, and was more successful with theories than with experiments. . . . He believed firmly in alchemy, and his "proof" that Solomon was an alchemist is a good specimen of his mentality. . . . his whole outlook shows the influence of the Neoplatonic ideas and confused thinking of Paracelsus, e.g. his belief that minerals as well as plants and animals have a sort of life and grow in the earth from seeds.[7]

For Partington, Becher developed concepts that more systematic, scientific characters would use in the onward progress of scientific knowledge. The modern view of cumulative, nonpersonal (or objective), scientific knowledge can be read in Partington's history of Becher's place in chemistry.

Similarly, the author of a recent history of economic thought writes that the notion of consumption, or "consumption spending" as he calls it, was of central importance for Becher:

> Consumption spending . . . formed, as the other side of the coin, so to speak, the incomes of the community. . . . Indeed Schumpeter described as "Becher's Principle" the proposition that one man's expenditure is another man's income. This is one of those fundamental truisms, . . . [and] it was, among others, Quesnay and

[7] J. R. Partington, *A History of Chemistry*, 4 vols. (London: Macmillan, 1961), 2:638–39.

Keynes who used it as a starting point. Schumpeter even goes so far as to suggest that Becher was one of the most important forerunners of Keynes.[8]

In a sense, these two histories of Becher's place in chemistry and economic thought must be read as primary sources, from which we can draw meaning and understand the parameters and categories of our own world.

The significance invested in "objectivity," "science," and "social mobility" has increased since the seventeenth century, and historians now "find" the seeds of these defining and meaningful concepts in Becher's thought. Ironically, Becher was entrapped within the rhetoric and the culture of the new philosophy that he himself had helped to create and propagate. After his death, the new philosophy eventually relegated his projects and curiosities to the trivial and banal realm of Madame Tussaud's and the occult. Today the mention of a curiosity cabinet evokes the bizarre stuffed alligator hanging from the ceiling, and alchemy evokes hocus-pocus. Such activities lost their meaning because the new philosophy, which took for granted the progress of knowledge, became established. Until recently, the historians who recounted this progress of knowledge displaced these pursuits—sometimes even Becher himself—to the status of "mere curiosities" in a story of great men and great theories. In this book, however, I have attempted to convey a sense of the complexity (indeed, messiness) of the transformation out of which science emerged and by which Becher's notions came to be curiosities.

[8] Terence Hutchison, *Before Adam Smith: The Emergence of Political Economy, 1662–1776* (Oxford: Basil Blackwell, 1988), p. 93.

ONE

PROVENANCES

Becherus Medicus, homo ingeniosus, sed polypragmon . . .
(Leibniz to Jakob Thomasius, September 1669)

B
Y HIS PAIRING of "ingeniosus" and "polypragmon," Gottfried Wilhelm Leibniz attempted to capture Johann Joachim Becher's spirit and temper. While Leibniz celebrated Becher's innate cleverness, he believed that his restlessness brought down odium upon him.[1] In the seventeenth century, *polypragmon* usually had negative connotations, suggesting that someone was overly busy, restless, and a busybody. It was, however, sometimes used in a positive sense to signify someone curious after knowledge. Its Latin equivalent, *curiosus*, was also frequently used at the time, and it too possessed both the positive sense of eager inquisitiveness (especially about the material world) and a negative one of weakness of will arising from too great a reliance upon the senses, as well as of overbusyness, ranging even to spying (figure 1).[2]

Such multivalent restlessness appears typical of Johann Joachim Becher (figure 2). A polymath, he published works on chemistry, politics, commerce, universal language, didactic method, medicine, moral philosophy, and religion. Becher was a man of deeds as well as of words, and, in the service of the most important princes of the German territories, he proposed and carried out many mechanical, chemical, and commercial projects.

A sketch of Becher's life illustrates well the diversity of activity that was an expression of his restlessness.[3] What little we know of Becher's early life is gleaned from his own published works. His birth in 1635 to Lutheran parents in the free imperial city of Speyer is confirmed in city records, but from that time

---

[1] In a letter to Lambert van Velthuysen in which he compared Becher to other German scholars, Leibniz remarked that he was "a man of the greatest ingenuity, but not a little restless, which has brought down ill-will upon him everywhere." 6/16 April 1669, Gottfried Wilhelm Leibniz, *Sämtliche Schriften und Briefe*, ed. Preussische Akademie der Wissenschaften et al. (Darmstadt: Otto Reichl et al., 1923–), ser. 2, vol. 1, pp. 39–40.

[2] See Hans Blumenberg, *Die Legitimität der Neuzeit*, 2d ed. (Frankfurt a.M.: Suhrkamp, 1988), and Gotthardt Frühsorge, *Der politische Körper. Zum Begriff des Politischen im 17. Jahrhundert und in den Romanen Christian Weises* (Stuttgart: J. B. Metzlersche Verlagsbuchhandlung, 1974), pp. 193–205.

[3] I summarize Becher's life in the following sketch. This summary will be expanded and reference will be made to appropriate sources in the chapters that follow.

Figure 1. *The Spy or Excessive Curiosity,* wood-panel
carving, by Francesco Pianta the Younger (1630?–1692).
The spy is masked and accompanied by a lantern and
winged boot. Scuola Grande di S. Rocco, Venice.

until 1655, when he appears again in documents, the portrait of the formative
years of his life is his own. He claims to have left Speyer with his mother and
brothers in 1648, the year of the signing of the Peace of Westphalia. His father
had died in 1643 and his mother had remarried. His stepfather took the boys and
their mother into foreign lands in search of a livelihood. Becher does not dwell
on these facts, for they only provide the backdrop for the more evocative
connections that he establishes in the presentation of his life, in which he
emphasizes more than once his travels and autodidacticism. From the time he
left the city of his birth in 1648, he claimed never to have attended school or
university, learning instead by the light of nature and through conversation with

Figure 2. Portrait of Johann Joachim Becher, *Mineralisches ABC,* 1723. With permission of the Huntington Library, San Marino, California.

the learned.[4] In 1654, at the age of nineteen, he published an alchemical work under the pseudonym Solinus Saltzthal.

In 1655, Becher appears in Vienna, where he titled himself mathematician to

[4] Becher provides some autobiographical information in his *Methodus didactica* (Munich: Maria Magdalena Schellin, 1668), and *Psychosophia. Das ist/ Seelen-Weiszheit* (Güstrow: Chris-

Emperor Ferdinand III.[5] He had by this time converted to Catholicism, and was apparently supplying the emperor with advice on alchemical projections and perpetual motion machinery. In 1658, Becher was in Mainz, continuing his search for patronage, and in 1660 he was finally successful, for in that year the elector and archbishop of Mainz, Johann Philipp von Schönborn, appointed him *Hofmedicus und -mathematicus* (court physician and mathematician).

Becher's status changed significantly in 1661. He moved from mechanical virtuoso to membership in an established profession, for in that year he defended a treatise on epilepsy before the faculty of medicine at the university in Mainz and was awarded the doctorate of medicine. Within the same week he became a member of the faculty of medicine, and in the next year married Maria Veronika von Hörnigk, the daughter of the Mainz professor of medicine, Ludwig von Hörnigk, who in 1663 stepped down from his position as professor in Becher's favor. For the next three years, Becher published works on medicine conforming to his professional status within the university.

In 1664, Becher moved to the court in Munich, having been named *Hofmedicus und -mathematicus* to Elector Ferdinand Maria of the Wittelsbach House of Bavaria. His wide-ranging activities in this position mainly centered on work in the laboratory and the improvement of commerce. For example, he established a laboratory at the court, began a silk manufactory in Munich, traveled to the Netherlands in 1664 to try to obtain a colony in the New World for the elector and to hire artisans for his manufactory, and created various trade companies. In 1666, while carrying out trade negotiations in Vienna, he became involved in a dispute with the imperial treasurer, Georg Ludwig von Sinzendorf, and he returned to Munich for four years.

During these four busy years, he published the majority of his books. In 1667 he published a verse version of a devotional work, which he called an "Ethics,"[6] and finished in quick succession a work on teaching Latin and didactic theory, the *Methodus didactica*; and a book of political economy, the *Politischer Discurs von den eigentlichen Ursachen deß Auf- und Abnehmens/ der Städt/ Länder und Republicken* (Political discourse about the true causes of the rise and fall of cities, territories, and republics). In 1669 he published his most important chemical work, *Actorum Laboratorii Chymici Monacensis, seu*

---

tian Scheippel, 1678). Additional clues to his early life can be found in the manuscript documents in the four folio volumes of the Becher *Nachlaß* in the Rostock University library, Mss. var. 1(1), 1(2), 1(3), and 2. Mss. var. 2 was not known to Herbert Hassinger who has provided the only biographical study of Becher of monograph length, *Johann Joachim Becher, 1635–82. Ein Beitrag zur Geschichte des Merkantilismus* (Vienna: Adolf Holzhausen, 1951). I follow Hassinger for information about Becher's family.

[5] Becher drafted several works in which he so titled himself, although there is no external evidence for this appointment.

[6] *Bona Becheri. Das ist: Handleytung zu dem Himmel/ Begreiffend den Kern der Lehre der H. H. Vätter/ und alten Weltweisen. Erstlich in Latein beschriben/ durch den Hochwürdigen Herrn D. IOANN BONA* (Munich: Johann Wilhelm Schell, 1667).

Physicae Subterraneae libri duo (Two books of the acts of the chemical laboratory of Munich, or subterranean physics), and *Moral Discurs von den eigentlichen Ursachen deß Glücks und Unglücks* (Moral discourse about the true causes of fortune and misfortune). In the same year, he spent three months in Holland negotiating for a colony in the New World from the West India Company, not, however, for the elector of Bavaria, but for Friedrich Casimir, count of Hanau. In 1670, his last year in Munich, he perfected a method of extracting iron from clay and linseed oil, that is, of extracting a metal from nonmetallic substances. He performed this process before Elector Johann Philipp in Mainz, and it excited interest as far away as the Royal Society of London. In addition to all these activities, he managed his career so successfully that in 1666 he was appointed commercial advisor to the emperor of the Holy Roman Empire, Leopold I. Although Becher held this position simultaneously with that of *medicus* and *mathematicus* to the Bavarian court, from 1666 he always titled himself "Advisor on Commerce to His Majesty, the Emperor of the Holy Roman Empire."

In 1670, Becher left Munich in order to serve the emperor exclusively. He advised the emperor on pretenders to alchemical knowledge as well as on commerical projects. He also performed a transmutation from lead to silver himself in 1675, and set up a Kunst- und Werckhaus (art and workhouse), which was to be a model manufactory, patent deposit, archive, cabinet of curiosities, and library.

In 1676 Becher set out with his brother-in-law, Philipp Wilhelm von Hörnigk, to enforce a ban on French imports imposed by the emperor on the trading cities of Germany. This trip ended his career at the Habsburg court since it provided his enemies an opportunity to make damaging accusations against him during his long absence from Vienna. Becher was accused (probably with just cause) of taking bribes, and the project ultimately failed.

Becher never returned to Vienna after this trip and spent the remaining years of his life again in the search for patronage, in northern Germany, the Netherlands, and England. In 1677 he entered the service of Duke Gustav Adolph of Mecklenburg-Güstrow in Rostock (where four volumes of Becher's pre-1678 papers still remain). In Duke Gustav Adolph's service, Becher attempted to secure the discoverer of phosphorus, Henning Brand, and his process for the icy noctiluca, but Gottfried Wilhelm Leibniz preempted Becher and lured the phosphorus maker away for the duke of Hannover. In 1678–79, Becher raised a flurry of interest among the learned of Europe when he contracted with the States General of Holland to extract gold from the beaches of the Dutch Republic. A small-scale assay of the process succeeded, but Becher left secretly for England before the large-scale probe could be carried out. In England, where he was possibly patronized by the circle around Prince Rupert of the Palatinate, Becher advised on mines in Cornwall and wrote two large works: a collection of chemical and alchemical processes[7] and a collection of failed and successful projects and inventions.[8] In these works, Becher established for posterity his own and others' priority to ideas, inventions, and chemical recipes.

Becher died at the age of forty-seven in London far from the main stage of his life's activities, but he had enjoyed a very successful career in the service of the most important political figures in the Holy Roman Empire, and he had written more than twenty books—many of which were reissued several times. And he ensured his fame after death as skillfully as he had obtained patrons in his lifetime. He left behind a set of words and actions that would be put to use in the following generations. Becher's life as a practical (active) but learned (contemplative) man became exemplary soon after his death and is expressed perfectly in the title of the first biography of Becher published in 1722: *Das Muster eines Nützlich-Gelehrten in der Person Herrn Doctor Johann Joachim Bechers*[9] (The model of a useful scholar in the person of Dr. Johann Joachim Becher).

His name and work were also used in other ways in the eighteenth century. In 1703 Georg Ernst Stahl (1660–1734) edited and republished Becher's major chemical work of 1669, the *Physica Subterranea*.[10] Stahl claimed to have used Becher's ideas in his own construction of a theory for the discipline of chemistry.[11] That theoretical construction, which has come to be known as the phlogiston theory, gave way before Antoine Lavoisier's theory of chemical change based on the theory of oxidation in the last decade of the eighteenth century. Since Stahl wrote him into the history of chemistry, Becher has had an established place in the history of science.

In the history of economic thought, too, Becher's place endures. His *Politischer Discurs* was used by the earliest teachers of *Kameralwissenschaft* (cameral science), a subject instituted at the universities of Frankfurt an der Oder and

---

[7] *Chymischer Glücks-Hafen/ Oder Grosse Chymische Concordantz und Collection/ von funffzehen hundert Chymischen Processen* (Frankfurt: Georg Schiele, 1682).

[8] *Närrische Weiszheit und Weise Narrheit: Oder Ein Hundert/ so Politische als Physicalische/ Mechanische und Mercantilische Concepten und Propositionen/ deren etliche gut gethan/ etliche zu nichts worden* (Frankfurt: Johann Peter Zubrodt, 1682).

[9] Urban Gottfried Bucher (Nuremberg and Altdorf: Johann Daniel Tauber, 1722).

[10] *Joh. Joachimi Beccheri . . . Physica subterranea profundam subterraneorum genesin, è principiis hucusque ignotis, ostendens. Opus sine pari, primum hactenus & princeps, editio novissima. Præfatione utili præmissa, indice locupletissimo adornato, sensuumque & rerum distinctionibus, libro tersius & curatius edendo, operam navavit & Specimen Beccherianum fundamentorum, documentorum, experimentorum, sujunxit Georg. Ernestus Stahl* (Leipzig: J. L. Gleditsch, 1703). Since Stahl, Becher's work has come to be known as the *Physica Subterranea*, and I shall refer to it as such.

[11] Stahl was called to the University at Halle as Professor of Medicine at its founding in 1694, where he lectured on medicine and chemistry. In 1715 he became court physician to Elector Friedrich Wilhelm of Prussia. Stahl has usually been considered a primary opponent of mechanism in medicine and chemistry in the eighteenth century as well as a leading Pietist. See *Dictionary of Scientific Biography* (New York: Scribner, 1970–), s.v. "Stahl, Georg Ernst."

Halle in the first decades of the eighteenth century. Georg Heinrich Zincke (1692–1768) edited and republished this major work written by Becher in 1668.[12] Zincke's own texts, which he claimed were based to a large extent on Becher's ideas, became part of the discipline of *Kameralistik*.[13]

Zincke sought to delineate the boundaries and subject matter for his new faculty in the university, while Stahl attempted to establish his vitalist medical theories and Pietist doctrines. Both scholars wished to create a history for their disciplines and doctrines, and they placed Becher at its center. Later generations of historians have accepted the place in history assigned to Becher by Stahl and Zincke uncritically, and, as a result, the secondary literature on Becher fits clearly into one of two stories: the story of the rise of modern chemistry,[14] or the story of the rise of modern economic thought.[15] But while historians have

---

[12] D. *Johann Joachim Bechers politischer discurs von den eigentlichen ursachen des auf- und abnehmens der städte und Länder. Oder gründliche anleitung zur stadt-wirtschaft und policey der teutschen staaten . . . neue hauptstücke von denen . . . wahrheiten des ganzen stadt-, policey- und cämmerey-, manufactur-, commercien- und haushaltungs-wesens, das erste mahl für jetzige umstände . . . brauchbarer gemacht und verbessert von d. George Heinrich Zincken* (Frankfurt and Leipzig: G. C. Gsellius, 1754).

[13] Zincke, trained in law, became perpetual *Commissarius in Policey-sachen* to Elector Friedrich Wilhelm of Prussia in the 1720s, then professor of law and cameral sciences in Leipzig in the 1740s.

[14] J. R. Partington, *A History of Chemistry*, 4 vols. (London: Macmillan, 1961–70), and Robert P. Multhauf, *The Origins of Chemistry* (New York: F. Watts, 1967), are examples of such disciplinary history, in which Becher is the source of the phlogiston theory. Allen G. Debus, *The Chemical Philosophy*, 2 vols. (New York: Science History Publications, 1977), is concerned to chronicle the fortune of Paracelsian ideas, "the chemical philosophy," in the seventeenth and eighteenth centuries. He sees Becher as one of the "chemical philosophers," along with Johann Rudolf Glauber (1603–70) and Johann Kunckel (1630/38–1703), who realized "the potential of the chemical philosophy for economic prosperity and national power" (2:426).

Christoph Meinel sees the history of chemistry in the eighteenth century not primarily as the history of a change in theory, but in the organization and alliances of chemical practices. Meinel maintains that Becher established a connection between *oeconomia* and chemistry which was strengthened and bore fruit in the eighteenth century when the first chairs of chemistry were founded in the *Kameralistik* faculties of Swedish and German universities. See his articles: "De praestantia et utilitate Chemiae. Selbstdarstellung einer jungen Disziplin im Spiegel ihres programmatischen Schrifttums," *Sudhoffs Archiv* 65 (1981): 366–89; "Theory or Practice? The Eighteenth-Century Debate on the Scientific Status of Chemistry," *Ambix* 30 (1983): 121–32; and "Reine und angewandte Chemie," *Berichte zur Wissenschaftsgeschichte* 8 (1985): 25–45.

One author who has explicitly attempted to provide an interdisciplinary approach to Becher's work is Mikulás Teich, "Interdisciplinarity in J. J. Becher's Thought," *History of European Ideas* 9 (1988): 145–60.

[15] In the extensive literature on economic thought in the early modern period, Becher along with his brother-in-law Philipp Wilhelm von Hörnigk (1638–1712) and Wilhelm von Schröder (1640–88) is considered a mercantilist or cameralist. Herbert Hassinger's biography of Becher is primarily an economic history; however, it was written with the view that mercantilism was both an economic and political practice, with the aim of centralizing all of society around the economic needs of the absolute monarch. This approach, taken first by Gustav Schmoller and his students in the late nineteenth century, is predominant in German historiography of early modern economic thought.

continued to situate Becher ever more firmly as a figure of significance in the history of chemical and economic thought, they have overlooked the context and cultural significance of Becher's actions. For, as Leibniz aptly noted, Becher was a very active man. And he was active within a certain social setting, namely, the German court society. Historians have not attempted to understand Becher's work as possessing a connecting thread, or to understand the motivation for his polymathy.[16] Becher's early champions, Stahl and Zincke, situated Becher so thoroughly within their histories that Becher as a significant figure in his own right disappeared in the retrospective vision of the stories of disciplinary development.

The use of Becher as exemplary figure is particularly clear in the history of technology. Scholars have combed the texts of the past in the search for precursors and inventors, and often they have not needed to look farther than the entertaining and well-organized collection of projects and inventions that Becher published while in England. He has consequently been named the "father" of many inventions, from gas-lighting to the planting of sugar beets in Central Europe.

Becher has also had his uses in the history of Germany. Periods of intensive study on Becher have coincided with periods of economic disaster or rising nationalist feeling. Numerous dissertations on Becher appeared in the 1920s and 1930s, at least two of which ended with a section on the relevance of Becher's ideas to their own time.[17] Becher's most recent and thorough of

---

One good example of this type of analysis of Becher is a curiously neglected book by Ferdinand August Steinhüser, *Johann Joachim Becher und die Einzelwirtschaft. Ein Beitrag zur Geschichte der Einzelwirtschaftslehre und des Kameralismus* (Nuremberg: Verlag der Hochschulbuchhandlung Krische, 1931). A recent history in this tradition is Jutta Brückner, *Staatswissenschaften, Kameralismus und Naturrecht* (Munich: C. H. Beck, 1977), and a useful guide to literature and the outlines of this approach is Erhard Dittrich, *Die deutschen und österreichischen Kameralisten* (Darmstadt: Wissenschaftliche Buchgesellschaft, 1974). The view that mercantilism was primarily an economic system persists, particularly in anglophonic literature—for example, Terence Hutchison, *Before Adam Smith: The Emergence of Political Economy, 1662–1776* (Oxford: Basil Blackwell, 1988); and Donald Cuthbert Coleman, ed., *Revisions in Mercantilism* (London: Methuen, 1969). Fruitful approaches to the history of economic thought from other disciplines have been made by Hans Maier, *Die ältere deutsche Staats- und Verwaltungslehre*, 2d ed. (Munich: C. H. Beck, 1980); Wolf-Hagen Krauth, *Wirtschaftsstruktur und Semantik. Wissenssoziologische Studien zum wirtschaftlichen Denken in Deutschland zwischen dem 13. und 17. Jahrhundert* (Berlin: Duncker & Humblot, 1984); and Ulrich Troitzsch, *Ansätze technologischen Denkens bei den Kameralisten des 17. und 18. Jahrhunderts* (Berlin: Duncker & Humblot, 1966).

[16] Hassinger treated all Becher's works, but was not seeking a unifying thread through them. Hassinger was himself mainly interested in Becher's political and economic ideas, and did not attempt to link them to his natural theory.

[17] These were Heinrich Apfelstedt, "Staat und Gesellschaft in J. J. Bechers Politischen Discursen" (Ph.D. diss., Gießen, 1926), p. 77, and Otfried Herr, "Johann Joachim Becher über das Verhältnis von Staat und Wirtschaft in seinen wirtschaftlichen Schriften" (Ph.D. diss., Heidelberg, 1936). Other dissertations were Emil Kauder, "Johann Joachim Becher als Wirtschafts und Sozialpolitiker" (Ph.D. diss., Berlin, 1924); Heinrich Jantzen, "Johann Joachim Becher als theo-

biographers, Herbert Hassinger, submitted his biography of Becher as a *Habilitationsschrift* to the university in Vienna in 1944, although the war prevented its publication until 1951.[18]

War

Becher provides an exemplum of history for these modern writers because throughout his life he pursued political and economic reform in a Germany severely damaged by war. Becher's date of birth, 6/16 May 1635, fell midway through the Thirty Years' War, which had raged through the Holy Roman Empire since 1618. Shortly before Becher's birth, the city of Speyer had been taken by the troops of Bernhard of Weimar, and, not long after, a false hope of peace appeared with the treaty between the elector of Saxony and the emperor. This treaty ended the internal war of the Reich, but the battles between foreign powers continued inside the empire for another thirteen years.

The war left the Holy Roman Empire in economic shambles, and the decline and shifts in population it caused were visible and remarked upon at the time. Later historians have calculated that the German Empire lost about a third of its population in the cities and two-fifths of the population on the land. Agriculture and trade were seriously disrupted, and many towns were left deserted through lack of population or means of sustenance. The Thirty Years' War occasioned not only economic chaos but also social and intellectual crisis. In the 1660s Becher himself said that this ostensibly "theological" conflict made "of belief a comedy," which in Germany had turned into "a slaughterhouse and tragedy."[19]

The way Becher conducted his life must be seen against this political, economic, and intellectual backdrop. Much has been written about the crisis of the seventeenth century to which this war ostensibly contributed, and while Becher's works testify that he saw no general European crisis, he did consider his immediate world, the Holy Roman Empire of the German Nation, to be in social and economic, moral, and intellectual crisis.

Becher's work must also be seen against the background of the power struggles between territorial princes that led up to the Thirty Years' War. The treaties

---

retischer und praktischer Privatökonom" (Ph.D. diss., Cologne, 1925); and A. Kolb, "Johann Joachim Becher in Bayern" (Ph.D. diss., Munich, 1941). Another example of the use to which Becher's thought has been put is the monograph of Konrad Ullrich, *Dr. Johann Joachim Becher. Der Erfinder der Gasbeleuchtung* (Munich: R. Oldenbourg, 1935). This short book opens with a copy of a letter from the Reichsleitung (Amt für Technik) of the Nazi party thanking Ullrich for the copy of his book, which he had sent to the Führer. They promised to mention Ullrich's name whenever an opportunity in connection with gas-lighting provided itself and closed with "Heil Hitler!"

[18] Hassinger, *Becher*, foreword.

[19] Johann Joachim Becher, *Moral Discurs von den eigentlichen Ursachen deß Glücks und Unglücks* (Frankfurt: Johann David Zunner, 1669), pp. 82–87.

of Osnabrück and Münster codified the increasing particularization of the German territories by ensuring the sovereignty of the prince within his territory. The resulting political and economic issues that revolved around the sovereign prince's court provide the framework for Becher's activities. The court was the center of power and patronage in the seventeenth century, and it attracted many purveyors of schemes and projects similar to Becher's. His success in obtaining court positions derived from a particular ability to speak in a language comprehensible and persuasive to the court world, and at the same time to deal effectively with the artisans necessary to carry out his projects. He became an intermediary between court and artisan. As intermediary, he proposed practical, material projects that would aid the German courts impoverished by the Thirty Years' War, but he articulated and carried out these projects in such a way that he bolstered the traditional structure and expression of power within the court society.

Becher was not an atypical figure in early modern Europe in responding to the real economic crisis in his society by projecting a scheme for ordering it. His scheme developed from models already present within political and economic discourse. He advocated reform not by denouncing established social, intellectual, and political structures, but rather by "refurbishing" them with new connecting spaces and arrangements within their walls. Employing the rhetoric and observing the conventions of established power structures, Becher attempted to contruct a new constellation of power and a new discourse that embraced political, moral, and natural philosophy.

In order to provide for the landed ruler's need of specie, Becher sought to integrate the landed ruler into the commercial exchange economy. In pursuing this goal, Becher used his position of medical doctor and advisor and his knowledge of nature to transform and conflate natural, productive, landed values and mobile, material values of the merchant and exchange. He proposed to the court a new language and vision, at the center of which stood commerce.

Commerce and the Closed Society

zwar in dem Sprüchwort heisset/ *quae ad omnes pertinent, à singulis negliguntur*, und heutiges Tags gar wenig seynd/ welche dem gemeinen Wesen zum Besten nutzliche Concepten führen.

Indeed [as it] says in the proverb, what is everyone's business is nobody's concern, and today there are very few men who put forward useful concepts that lead to the best for the community.
(*Becher*, Politischer Discurs)

On 6/16 May 1635, Johann Joachim Becher, the eldest of three sons, was born to a Lutheran pastor, a native of Wittenberg, and his wife, the daughter of an established citizen and Lutheran pastor of the free imperial city of Speyer. The crisis of war that enveloped much of the lives of Becher's parents reverberates in his own life and writings. In the social and political realm from which his mother came, the free imperial town of Speyer, the war led to a breakdown of the stable guild society through the cessation of trade, the levying of war taxes, and the resultant loss of power by the guilds. The influx of the soldiers and refugees of war also brought chaos to this closed society. A tension between the commonweal and self-interest, and between universalism and closed community characterized Becher's mother's realm.

Anna Margaretha Gauss, Becher's mother, survived her husband and apparently accompanied Becher and her other two sons through large parts of Europe in search of a livelihood. Becher reports nothing about her except that she remarried after his father died in 1643 and that her second husband was a wastrel who took them away into foreign lands. During this time, Becher claims that he had to give lessons in order to sustain his mother and brothers. When they set off on this journey, his mother had been an established member of the community, born to a family of citizens and council members in Speyer.[20]

As the daughter of a citizen of a free imperial city, Becher's mother belonged to a community society that embodied a notion of common purpose and a hostility to the unincorporated individual. The citizenry of Speyer, a town of middle size, was divided into fifteen guilds, ruled over by a patriciate drawn from members of these guilds.[21] Because Speyer was a seat of a bishopric and meeting place for the Reichskammergericht, the artisanal citizenry had to assert itself against representatives of the bishop and local nobles for control of the town. The emperor granted various special privileges to the town of Speyer, and the location of the Imperial Court of Appeals in the town allied the emperor with the town citizens against the bishop and the nobility.

A middle-sized guild town of the Holy Roman Empire had a distinctive structure and outlook that was nurtured by the balance of powers in the empire, and that resulted in the town's ability to assert its independence against the local nobility.[22] These towns had formed around the production of goods by artisanal guilds, and town government and politics were dominated by guild members. The corporate guild mentality asserted the communal good over the interest of the individual, and required that all the citizens of a city be united into corporate organizations. The ostensible goal of this community was not to provide for a single family and name but to benefit all in the community, thereby giving the

---

[20] Her father was pastor of the Augustinian church in Speyer and died in 1644, a year after his son-in-law.

[21] Johann Heinrich Zedler, *Grosses vollständiges Universal-Lexicon* (1732–50; facs. repr., Graz: Akademische Druck- und Verlagsanstalt, 1961), vol. 38, s.v. "Speier."

[22] The following view of German society in the seventeenth century draws on Mack Walker's analysis of "home town" society in *German Home Towns: Community, State, and General Estate, 1648–1871* (Ithaca: Cornell University Press, 1971).

town the power of common purpose by which it could assert itself against outside forces.[23] The town was not just a society of individuals (*Gesellschaft*) but a community (*Gemeinde*), or, as it was sometimes translated, a *universitas*. Not every person residing in a town belonged, however, to its citzenry, but only those who could be corporately represented and who had been approved by their corporate body. In a small town like Nördlingen, probably no more than half of the adult, working males between 1580 and 1700 were *Bürger*, citizens who possessed the privileges and duties of citizenship (*Bürgerrechte*). In a large city, such as Frankfurt, in 1700, about 62 to 67 percent of all inhabitants lived within *Bürger* households.[24] Overwhelmingly, these *Bürger* were drawn from the guilds and were wealthy enough to meet property requirements for citizenship. Citizenship, however, was more than a measure of economic wealth; it was also a measure of one's political position, social quality, family history, and personal dignity.

The community was organized around a notion of common purpose, which was antithetical to personal ambition and individual prominence (monetary or social), and the corporate structure enforced this. The structure and mentality of the community was hostile to noncollective elements typically residing outside the town walls or passing through the town, such as the rural landholder, the peasant, the learned man, the civil servant, the mercenary, and the merchant. These outsiders were disruptive sources of competition. In particular, merchants were seen by guildsmen as disruptive competitors, for, although some small retailer guilds selling imported goods existed, the guildsman ideally sold his goods directly from his workplace.[25] Thus the merchant was seen as an unnecessary middleman who inflated prices and who lived off the sweat of other men's brows. The merchant was not only a competitor in that he brought in outside wares that competed with the manual workers' goods, but he was also outside the collective community. The guildsman entered a tacit contract as a member of the community to supply wares of good quality in return for exclusive control of the market. The merchant took part neither in the community nor in the contract. Therefore he competed on a different level and in accordance with an entirely different set of rules that seemed to the guildsman to give him an incomparable advantage.[26] Thus the merchant was not only a competitor, but he belonged to a different world—a world in which property was not defined in terms of one's place in the community, nor in terms of land, but in

[23] See Walker, *Home Towns*, chap. 2, "The Civic Community."

[24] Christopher R. Friedrichs, *Urban Society in an Age of War: Nördlingen, 1580–1720* (Princeton: Princeton University Press, 1979), pp. 39–43. Uncounted were the wives and daughters of these *Bürger*, the "passive citizens," and their sons, the "potential citizens." The Frankfurt statistics are from Gerald Lyman Soliday, *A Community in Conflict: Frankfurt Society in the Seventeenth and Early Eighteenth Centuries* (Hanover, N.H.: Brandeis University Press, 1974), p. 40.

[25] Walker, *Home Towns*, p. 78.

[26] Ibid., pp. 120–21.

terms of movable goods and money. Movable goods and money were traditionally associated with risk, instability, vanity, selfishness, and private interest, but most of all, money wealth was considered suspect in the stable town
world by reason of its very mobility.

Merchants were not, therefore, normally part of the small-town citizenry.
They were looked upon with suspicion and excluded from town government
and community life.[27] Moreover, the merchant and his money wealth were
considered external to the town economy because they were not productive.
The town, like agriculture, was viewed as producing goods, whereas commerce involved only the consumption of others' work. Where land produced
natural fruits and the artisans in the towns produced worked goods, the merchant took from the community and gave nothing in return. The townsman
viewed merchants as taking wealth and means of sustenance from the community, for merchants took advantage of deficiencies in town production, as, for
example, in their import of luxury goods (also considered evidence of their
corrupting influence), or in the inefficient distribution of goods. If the retail
merchant was seen as a middleman who drove up prices, the large import
merchant was viewed as sucking wealth and money out of the town. This view
hinged on the fact that neither sort of merchant could claim to be productive in
the way that those engaged in agriculture and craft could. Furthermore, the
money wealth that the merchant accumulated was traditionally viewed as unnatural because it was properly a means of exchange, rather than a regenerative
resource, for "pecunia non fructificat."[28]

[27] Friedrichs, *Urban Society*, notes the small number of merchants among the Nördlingen
citizenry (5 out of 1541 in 1579), but sees it as coincidental (pp. 80–81).

[28] Trade was not regenerative like agriculture, in which the fruits of the earth were multiplied
and replenished, for it simply involved the taking of wealth from one group to enrich another. This
view had its source in Aristotle, *Politics*, 1.8.1–11.35. See Steinhüser, *Johann Joachim Becher und
die Einzelwirtschaft*, pp. 49–50, who traces the antimerchant rhetoric through scholasticism,
humanism, and Reformation literature. He quotes "pecunia non fructificat" on p. 113. Steinhüser
provides an excellent analysis of Becher's model of human society and its sources in earlier
economic structures. More recently, Wolfgang Zorn, "Humanismus und Wirtschaftsleben nördlich
der Alpen," in *Humanismus und Ökonomie*, ed. Heinrich Lutz (Weinheim: Acta humaniora, 1983),
pp. 31–60, goes over the same material, but points up some of the problems for the historian in
drawing out a consistent thread of thought on economic questions (as they are defined since Adam
Smith). Part of this problem stems from the effort to impose a theory of coherent economic system
on writers of earlier periods. These authors were usually writing in response to immediate and
single issues within an established discourse, rather than elaborating their views within a comprehensive system. Jonathan Parry, "On the Moral Perils of Exchange" and "Introduction: Money and
the Morality of Exchange," in *Money and the Morality of Exchange*, ed. J. Parry and M. Block
(Cambridge: Cambridge University Press, 1989), pp. 1–32, provides a useful overview of literature
and approaches to the subject of exchange. See also Niels Steensgaard, "The Seventeenth-century
Crisis," in *The General Crisis of the Seventeenth Century*, ed. Geoffrey Parker and Lesley M.
Smith (London: Routledge & Kegan Paul, 1979), pp. 26–56; and Stuart B. Schwartz, "The Voyage
of the Vassals: Royal Power, Noble Obligations, and Merchant Capital before the Portuguese
Restoration of Independence, 1624–1640," *American Historical Review* 96 (1991): 735–62.

By 1635 the power of the guilds that had initially enabled the cities to free themselves from territorial rule had dwindled. The movement of trade away from the empire to Antwerp and finally Amsterdam and the other maritime nations reduced trade in the empire as a whole. The Thirty Years' War destroyed the cities' productivity and their markets, while war tax levies put fatal financial strain on their treasuries. The war also greatly increased mobility in the society.[29] The increasing power of the territorial rulers and their courts resulted in a greater number of *hofbefreite* artisans, who operated outside the guilds under direct license from a member of the nobility. The artisan at the noble court was freed from guild constrictions and rules, and, as the residential seats of noble courts moved increasingly off the land and into the towns, these free artisans competed fiercely with the often already struggling incorporated guild artisans of the towns. The corporate guild structure of the towns was also eroded in the first half of the seventeenth century by the system of *Verlag*, a putting-out system in which a merchant supplied artisans with raw material, which they made into goods and sold back to him.[30]

The town society was just one of three separate worlds that coexisted in the Holy Roman Empire of the German Nation in the seventeenth century. Outside the town walls of the community-centered society of the towns lay a hierarchical world of the landed territorial prince, and a mobile and individualistic world of commerce and money.[31] Each of these worlds had its own economy, structure of power, and set of values, and each saw in the others a threat to its own stability. The community world was structured around a guild economy in which members of a reciprocally defined status worked according to a careful division of labor for a common good. Wealth resided in the ability of the community to sustain itself, and the status of an individual corresponded to his place in the community. The hierarchical world of the landed ruler, on the other

[29] See Volker Press, ed., *Städtewesen und Merkantilismus in Mitteleuropa* (Cologne and Vienna: Böhlau Verlag, 1983), a collection of essays on the status of cities and their sociopolitical infrastructures in post-1648 Germany.

[30] Friedrichs, *Urban Society*, chronicles the decline of corporatism in Nördlingen. In the late seventeenth and early eighteenth centuries, the status of artisans declined because their urban monopoly was broken down by new forms of production. This happened because the citizens' (i.e., the guilds') economic position was eroded in the Thirty Years' War and did not return to its former state before enormous war taxes were levied by the empire against the towns for the Turkish and French wars.

[31] Again, I follow Walker's analysis in *Home Towns*, esp. pp. 26–27, for this section. His label for the third mobile group is "movers and doers." I have set out the three worlds here in schematic form; I do not claim that the situation in the seventeenth-century German Empire corresponded neatly to these divisions. These divisions, however, reflected the common perception of society as separated into the *Lehr-, Nähr-, und Wehrstände*. The estate of teaching (*Lehrstand*) included individuals such as priests and scholars, who were not tied to a single locale. The *Nährstand* of sustenance-providers such as peasants and artisans was normally perceived to be tied to a particular location on the land or in the cities. The *Wehrstand*, composed of the nobility, was understood to defend the other two estates, and resided on the land.

hand, was organized around the lord, who, as father of his household, looked after the welfare of the rest of his dependents. The economy of the landed household was based on the agricultural production of the land, and, in this economy, wealth was measured by land and power, and status by honor. Lastly, the world of the large-scale merchant existed outside these societies of land and town, and in this world of exchange for monetary profit, wealth was measured in money, and status by credit.

The values of the town and of the land were both based on production for self-sustenance, and these societies were careful to conserve a balance of power by the observation of traditional rights and privileges. In contrast, the third world of commerce, which was based on taking advantage of lapses in self-sustenance in the other two worlds, depended on a suspension of the traditional rights in the court and town worlds. In Germany, the commercial world was an accepted part neither of the community world nor of the hierarchical landed society. By the seventeenth century, however, the two stable societies of town and landed wealth began to break down in the face of increased demands for money, competition in international commerce, and war, and the court began to seek additional means of hard cash.

In his political writings, Becher took over the rhetoric and self-sustaining structure of the community world, exemplified by his notion of common good as a model for territorial government,[32] and his cyclical model of sustenance and provision in society. Although he drew his model of civil society from the community world, he transformed the model in significant ways. He made the commercial activity of merchants the "soul" of his self-sustaining community, and the prince, although a "servant" of the community, came, by means of *Policey* (government ordinances), to control the community world. By drawing the community world under the control of the prince, Becher sought to make the town cycle of sustenance the basis of princely wealth. Becher thus sought to extract the goal of common purpose and the cycle of economic sustenance (which he made dependent, however, upon commercial activity) from the community world and place them under the control of the territorial ruler. He desired to retain corporate forms, such as the guilds, but to police them by requiring them to be privileged by the prince. The corporate forms and the common purpose of his mother's community world thus resounded in Becher's thought. But by drawing it into the court and commercial worlds, he ultimately helped to destroy this corporate world.

Becher left the town walls of Speyer with his mother in 1648 and became a wanderer. The citizen of no city, he joined the mobile group of individuals who threatened town stability. Becher recounted that while on his travels with his mother, he learned from merchants, and records indicate that during this time

---

[32] Walker, *Home Towns*, notes Becher's use of community rhetoric and structure on pp. 148–50, and uses Becher as a "spokesman" for the town world.

he may have resided in the large trading cities of northern Europe.[33] He drew from his experience of the world of the *Bürger*, as well as from the mobile world of commerce, in formulating a comprehensive view of society.

Commerce and the Open World

Becher's view of commerce as a productive and meliorative force in society did not come from within the town world. To understand the central place of commerce in his model of society, we must turn to the world of his father, Joachim Becher. The advent of war in the seventeenth century brought forth projects of intellectual and spiritual reform. Commerce was a significant component in these reform projects, but it was a very different notion of commerce than Becher had learned in his mother's town world.

Joachim Becher was a Lutheran pastor, perhaps educated in Strasbourg, called to Speyer as deacon in 1633 and made pastor of the church of Saint George in October 1635. Becher claimed that his father could understand ten languages by the age of twenty-eight: Hebrew, Chaldean, Samaritan, Syrian, Arabic, Greek, Latin, German, Dutch, and Italian.[34] Becher's father died at the age of thirty-seven in 1643 when Becher was eight years old, but by this time he had perhaps begun to teach his son the rudiments of Latin, and had passed on to him a glimpse of the vision that lay behind his attempt to master these languages. His learning of the ancient languages was rooted in the philological analysis of the Scriptures, a legacy of the conjunction of humanist philology and Lutheran reform, while his knowledge of the vernacular tongues, Dutch and Italian, indicates the increasing use of the vernaculars as Europe divided into separate political units. The ideal of a unified European Christendom had not quite faded, however, and the interest in language at this particular time was part of a scholarly effort to unify the different European languages as a first step toward the unity of peoples and the peace that was to follow on it. For Becher's father, the Lutheran pastor, who had been twelve years of age when the war began and who died before it ended, the search for a universalism that would lead to reform and to universal peace was particularly immediate.

We have no other indication of the elder Becher's educational and theological views than Becher's statement that his father had mastered ten languages; however, Becher possessed several lists of books, one of which set out a course of study with a distinctly Lutheran cast. Perhaps this was a Lutheran pastor's course for his son. In this course, lectures were to be heard and disputations undertaken in philology, history, Greek, and Hebrew. The student was then to proceed to a *studium sacrum*, which drew upon authors in rhetoric, oratory,

---

[33] Mss. var. 2, fol. 674r–v. See n. 106.
[34] Becher, *Methodus didactica*, p. 33.

epistolary writings, poetics, history, chronology, logic, mnemonics, and the rudiments of philosophy.[35] Mastering the corpus of ancient Latin, Greek, and Hebrew authorities and their modern commentators was the aim of this *studium*, but the reform of knowledge and of humankind's relationship with God was also a strong component. The authors included Lutheran theological reformers such as Luther, Melanchthon, Johann Heinrich Alsted, Jan Amos Comenius, as well as other reforming moderns, such as Erasmus, Vives, and Scaliger.

Becher's father belonged to the generation of reformers of learning such as Johann Heinrich Alsted and Jan Amos Comenius, from whom Becher himself would draw vocabulary and ideas while completely transforming their goals. In the early decades of the seventeenth century, Alsted published a seemingly endless number of polymathic encyclopedias. In the thousands upon thousands of folio pages contained in these weighty tomes and at the Reformed University of Herborn where he taught, Alsted instituted and extended the school reforms of Petrus Ramus.[36] Later scholars ridiculed the dusty folio volumes that represented his life's effort, but in the lands of German tongue in the first half of the seventeenth century Alsted's reform of learning was very serious business indeed.[37] It drew from Hermetic and Neoplatonic doctrines as well as from reformed religious thinkers to establish a new place for humankind in the cosmos and a new relationship between humans and God.

Jan Amos Comenius, Alsted's student at Herborn, best exemplifies the climate of intellectual and religious reform into which Becher was born and to which he would return for ideas.[38] Comenius would imitate Alsted in formulating a course of study to reform philosophy so as to accommodate the new understanding of humankind's relationship with God. Such reform was necessary as the end of history approached. Comenius had also come under the influence of another chiliastic Protestant thinker, Johann Valentin Andreae (1586–1654), a Lutheran pastor publishing just at the outbreak of the Thirty Years' War. Andreae's *Societas Christiana* promoted an individual piety akin to

[35] Mss. var. 2, fols. 17r–20v.

[36] See Walter J. Ong, *Ramus, Method, and the Decay of Dialogue* (Cambridge, Mass.: Harvard University Press, 1983), pp. 164–65, 298.

[37] On the reform of learning in central Europe, see R.J.W. Evans, *Rudolf II and His World* (Oxford: Clarendon Press, 1973); Anthony Grafton, "The World of the Polyhistors: Humanism and Encyclopedism," *Central European History* 18 (1985): 31–47; idem, *Defenders of the Text: The Traditions of Scholarship in an Age of Science 1450–1800* (Cambridge, Mass.: Harvard University Press, 1991); Erich Trunz, "Der deutsche Späthumanismus um 1600 als Standeskultur," in *Deutsche Barockforschung. Dokumentation einer Epoche*, 2d ed., ed. Richard Alewyn (Cologne and Berlin: Kiepenheuer & Witsch, 1966), pp. 147–81; and Conrad Wiedemann, "Polyhistors Glück und Ende. Von D. G. Morhof zum jungen Lessing," in *Festschrift Gottfried Weber*, ed. Heinz Otto Burger and Klaus von See (Bad Homburg, Berlin and Zürich: Verlag Gehlen, 1967), pp. 215–35.

[38] For the following portrayal of Comenius, I have drawn heavily on Hans Aarsleff's outstanding article in the *Dictionary of Scientific Biography*, 3:359–63. See also the substantial bibliography that he cites there.

pietism and the acquisition of pansophic knowledge based in part on the study of nature and of the crafts.[39] Andreae's ideas for the reform of learning show a marked similarity to those of his slightly older contemporary Francis Bacon in *The New Atlantis* and *Sylva sylvarum*, but it was probably from Andreae's writings, filtered through the works of Comenius, Samuel Hartlib, and other Protestant reformers, that the ideal of natural knowledge as an integral part of religious and material reform emerged.[40]

Forced into exile as the Catholic forces entered his native Bohemia and destroyed the community of the Bohemian Brethren among whom he was a pastor, Comenius struggled throughout his life with the first stage of a thoroughgoing reform of humankind in preparation for the Last Days. This reform centered on the school curriculum and began with the teaching of language, both because learning Latin was propaedeutic to any course of study, and because he believed that only a proper understanding of the relationship between words and things could bring about an understanding of God's revelation in the words of Scripture and the things of Creation. Learning began with the senses, especially the sense of sight; thus a study of things through vision and observation was primary. For this reason, Comenius formulated his celebrated method of teaching language by pictures, which finally resulted in the publication of his famous picture book, *Orbis sensualium pictus* (1658).[41]

Drawing on Hermetic and Paracelsian ideas, especially as formulated by Jacob Boehme, Comenius believed that God had left his signature in all the things of nature as well as in the mind of man himself. Man must therefore come to know himself as well as study the things of nature in order to read these signatures. For, as Paracelsus (1493–1541) had set forth, the seeds or signatures of the things resonated with the Platonic ideas in the mind of man to bring about true understanding and knowledge of God. The natural philosopher or physician must "overhear" and unite with the thing under study in order to gain true, natural knowledge of the object.[42]

---

[39] See John Warwick Montgomery, *Cross and Crucible: John Valentine Andreae (1586–1654)* (The Hague: Martinus Nijhoff, 1973); Felix E. Held, *Christianopolis: An Ideal State of the Seventeenth Century* (Oxford: Oxford University Press, 1916); and G. H. Turnbull, "Johann Valentin Andreaes Societas Christiana," *Zeitschrift für deutsche Philologie* 74 (1955): 151–85.

[40] Frances Yates, *The Rosicrucian Enlightenment* (London: Routledge & Kegan Paul, 1972), argues this strongly, as do Charles Webster, "Macaria: Samuel Hartlib and the Great Reformation," *Acta Comeniana* 26 (1970): 147–64, and Richard Olson, *Science Deified and Science Defied*, vol. 1 (Berkeley: University of California Press, 1982), one of the few historians of science to examine Andreae's writings closely.

[41] The literature on Comenius is vast but see Gunter E. Grimm, "Muttersprache und Realienunterricht," in *Res Publica Litteraria. Die Institutionen der Gelehrsamkeit in der frühen Neuzeit*, ed. Sebastian Neumeister and Conrad Wiedemann, 2 vols. (Wiesbaden: Otto Harrassowitz, 1987), 1:299–324, for a discussion of how this emphasis on pedagogy by means of material things was transformed in the course of the seventeenth century.

[42] Walter Pagel, *Paracelsus: An Introduction to Philosophical Medicine in the Era of the Renaissance*, 2d ed. (Basel: S. Karger, 1982), p. 51.

Like the reformers of the curriculum and of philosophy before him, Comenius sought a universal method that would enable the student to see the order of things and to understand their causes, moving the mind toward wisdom and insight. This had been the aim of Alsted's encyclopedia, but Comenius's method added millenarian components. A universal method would lead to universal knowledge—pansophia—which would overcome the fallen state of humankind and lead to the final reform.

In the face of the proliferation of vernacular books and the increasing separation of nations, a prominent feature of this universalist reform was the search for a universal language. Such a language would overcome the state of mutual ignorance and misunderstanding that had been the fate of humankind since the attempted construction of the Tower of Babel. The new universal language would make feasible a universal method of learning, and this in turn would lead to order, peace, and harmony among people.[43] The universal language of things that Comenius set forth with his book of pictures was to initiate this reform. He believed universalism had been furthered in the modern era by the invention of printing, the advances in navigation, and the increase in long-distance trade and exchange. Commerce, the exchange of things, held out a strong promise of universality.

This notion of universalism and its associated concepts continued to resonate in Becher's thinking, and, significantly, one of Becher's first works was a scheme for a universal language.[44] But he had a quite different vision of universalism and reform than that of his father's generation. For Becher, the immediacy of spiritual reform in a world ravaged by war had been replaced by the urgency for material and financial reform of the temporal world at the court of princes. The focus had shifted from the eternal sphere of God to that of his representative on earth, the prince. As a convert to Catholicism and a *créature* of the Habsburg/Catholic world, Becher manipulated the ideas of his father's world to create a new vision of the order of society. Becher remained fascinated by commerce, by ships, by travel, and by universalist undertakings, but in his hands the spiritual and cosmic meaning was muted, and the material content emphasized. The religious and millenarial significance with which these activities had been invested by Comenius and also, perhaps, by his own father continued, however, to reverberate in Becher's thought.

His father's world of the universal exchange of words and things stood in

---

[43] Allison Coudert, "Some Theories of a Natural Language from the Renaissance to the Seventeenth Century," *Studia Leibnitiana*, Sonderheft 7 (Wiesbaden, 1978): 56–118. M. M. Slaughter, *Universal Languages and Scientific Taxonomy in the Seventeenth Century* (Cambridge: Cambridge University Press, 1982), shows how a desire for order motivated the search for universal languages and taxonomies.

[44] *Character pro Notitia Linguarum Universali. Inventum steganographicum Hactenus inauditum quo quilibet suam legendo vernaculam diversas imò omnes linguas, unius etiam diei informatione, explicare ac intelligere potest* (Frankfurt: Joh. Wilh. Ammon & Wilh. Serlin, 1661).

contrast to the values of the closed town society that had been his mother's world. When Becher left the town walls of Speyer, he carried with him a legacy composed of these contrasting values, and he would draw from this legacy for understanding and ideas in the course of his life.

The Mechanical Arts

Becher states he was just thirteen years of age when his stepfather took him and his family to seek their livelihood in foreign lands in the year of the Peace of Westphalia, 1648. Perhaps his stepfather died or deserted them, for Becher said he had to become his family's sole support in foreign countries, giving lessons by day and studying at night. After they left Speyer it is unlikely that Becher had any formal course of education.[45] When he became established he recalled his course of study:

> By night I had to study and with great effort seek from books what one [feeds] to others in schools already chewed up and laid out in the best way. Often I could not understand and from a lack of books, I had to search *de novo* and by the light of nature for many theses and axioms myself, which took much time, although afterward I had learned it with greater solidity. I had to learn in a different manner: start from the fundament and go from things to words. In contrast, the schools remain only in words and do not know anything about real things. When I had to study at night, during the day I had to teach others so that I could keep not only myself but also my mother and two brothers who were abroad with me. . . . While I taught, I learned . . . for I was not over thirteen years of age.[46]

Becher claimed to have begun with the things themselves, and from this basis to have risen "by the light of nature" to understand theses and axioms. He sought a "kurtzen *Methodum*," or a "newes *expediens*" by which he could teach languages to his pupils. When he had mastered this reform of language teaching (by the light of nature and by studying other *Methodisten*), he turned to other subjects:

> I wanted to move to other studies; I set aside didactics and studied theology. When I finished that I moved to mathematics, from there to medicine, from there to chemistry, and after this, by means of mathematics, I learned various manual trades. In these I observed the artisanal practices and privileges so that I finally arrived at political and juridical study.[47]

[45] Becher does mention that he had private lessons with a teacher named Debus in the Latin school in Speyer (*Methodus didactica*, p. 69). Hassinger noted that Debus was *Konrektor* of the school in 1644 (Hassinger, *Becher*, p. 12). Becher's name does not appear on the rolls of matriculation of any universities he would have been likely to visit (Hassinger, p. 16).

[46] Becher, *Methodus didactica*, Vorrede, unpaginated.

[47] Ibid.

Becher claims to have passed from language learning, the basis of all boys' schooling, directly to theology, as the Lutheran plan in his *Nachlaß* advised. He did not tarry long, however, with his theological studies, as he moved quickly to practical concerns, and from there to politics and law. Mathematics also led him to commerce, for, from the mechanical arts, he claimed to have learned artisanal vocabulary and instruments and to have speculated about how he might produce the objects of manufacture. He learned about selling and the market, and thus came to a *scientz* of commerce:

> Because I studied mathematics and especially took pleasure in mechanical subjects, I had to do with many types of artisans, and so had to learn to understand their work, vocabulary, and instruments. I even invented various artisanal compendia, and I speculated how manufactured goods might be more easily made. After this, I went further and examined how they might be sold, and, because of this, I learned about putting-out companies. In a nutshell, I had to learn the entire art, nature, and character of merchant activity. Thus I entered into this science slowly; not suddenly without understanding, cause, or calling. Then, in addition, I did many other things, for example, I undertook long travels, I saw numerous trading cities and their government and customs, and I was employed in different commissions dealing with this material.[48]

Becher emphasized again and again the importance of mathematics and experience in his education and life:

> I cultivated the ingenuity, judgment, and memory such as God had given me in mathematics and learned thereby order. After that I studied the axiomatic methods, and besides that I have read much, listened much, experienced much, made many trials, labored much, speculated much, and I have associated with many learned people.[49]

In emphasizing mathematics, his contact with artisans, and his own experience, Becher was drawing on a Ramist tradition as mediated by Alsted and Comenius. Petrus Ramus (1515–72) believed that "natural" or "practical" reason should be allowed to guide humankind in the acquisition of knowledge, for this was the method used by the ancients, but distorted by modern scholars. Natural reasoning resided in the daily life of humankind and in its trades, such as navigation, medicine, agriculture, and bookkeeping.[50] In his search for ancient sources, Ramus found the practice of these arts more ancient than the theories

---

[48] Becher, *Politischer Discurs* (Frankfurt: Johann David Zunner, 1668), dedication, b recto.

[49] "Das *ingenium, judicium* und *memorie,* so mir Gott verliehen/ habe ich in der *Mathesi* excolirt/ und dardurch die Ordnung gelernt/ darauf habe ich mich auf die *Methodos axiomata* auffgemerckt/ über dieses habe ich viel gelesen/ viel gehört/ viel erfahren/ viel probirt/ viel laborirt/ viel speculirt/ bin auch mit viel gelehrten Leute umgangen." Becher, *Psychosophia* (the second printing [Hamburg, 1705] of the second edition of 1683 was used here, p. 316).

[50] R. Hooykaas, *Humanisme, science et réform. Pierre de la Ramée (1515–1572)* (Leiden: E. J. Brill, 1958), pp. 20–21.

of scholars. Thus his reform advocated attentiveness not only to practice itself but also to the practices of the mechanical arts.[51]

Mathematics was particularly important, not only for Ramus, but for other reformers of the trivium and quadrivium, such as Melanchthon and Rudolph Agricola, because it was the heart of the quadrivium and was seen as corresponding to the place of logic in the trivium. For Ramus, however, it became central in his intellectual and pedagogical reform, for it represented to him a way of unifying the practices of the liberal and mechanical arts, and of theory and practice.[52] Mathematics was most important for Ramus in its connection to the practices of the mechanical arts, and their utility for society. He visited the workshops of artisans in Paris and Nuremberg, and claimed to be confirmed in his opinion that mathematics was important for civil life.[53] Ramus considered Nuremberg, and Germany in general, to be a model of the practice of the mechanical arts, and the related study of mathematics. For Ramus, Germany possessed so much wealth and honor because both its cities and princes cultivated the mathematical and mechanical arts in their mining, machine making, fortification, and weapon manufacture.[54] Many other writers of the sixteenth and seventeenth centuries believed that the advancement of mathematics and the mechanical arts proved the possibility of intellectual and material progress, as well as the superiority of the moderns over the ancients.[55]

During Becher's lifetime, mathematics was very much associated with the mechanical arts and trades. John Wallis's 1690 memory of mathematics as it had existed in the 1630s in English universities illustrates this attitude in the time of Becher's youth: "For Mathematicks, (at that time, with us) were scarce looked upon as *Accademical* studies, but rather *Mechanical*; as the business of *Traders, Merchants, Seamen, Carpenters, Sur*veyors of Lands, or the like; and perhaps some *Almanak-makers in London.*"[56] In the sixteenth and seventeenth centuries mathematics came to signify both the exact science and certain

---

[51] Hooykaas makes the point that practice was both the source and the goal for Ramus (ibid., p. 30).

[52] Ibid., pp. 30–31, and chap. 10, "Apologie des mathématiques," pp. 75–90.

[53] Ibid., p. 84.

[54] Ibid., pp. 95–96. See also Bruce T. Moran, "German Prince-Practitioners: Aspects in the Development of Courtly Science, Technology, and Procedures in the Renaissance," *Technology and Culture* 22 (1981): 253–74.

[55] See Paolo Rossi, *Philosophy, Technology, and the Arts in the Early Modern Era*, trans. Salvator Attanasio (New York: Harper & Row, 1970); and Alex Keller, "Mathematical Technologies and the Growth of the Idea of Technical Progress in the Sixteenth Century," in *Science, Medicine and Society in the Renaissance*, ed. Allen G. Debus (New York: Science History Publications, 1972), 1:11–27.

[56] This example is drawn from Christoph J. Scriba, "The Autobiography of John Wallis, F.R.S.," *Notes and Records of the Royal Society* 25 (1970): 27. Mordechai Feingold, *The Mathematicians' Apprenticeship* (Cambridge: Cambridge University Press, 1984), attempts to refute this description of mathematics in 1630 by examining the teaching of mathematics at English universities at this time. His conclusion that mathematics was indeed taught does not preclude the possibility that mathematics was viewed as mechanical.

knowledge of geometrical demonstration and the practical, mechanical activity of the workshop. Mathematics was an established part of the scholar's training that would have been learned from the subjects of the quadrivium—arithmetic, geometry, music, and astronomy—but mathematics was also firmly associated with the machines and workshops of artisans.[57]

Ramus believed the union of scholarly mathematics and the practice of the mechanical arts by artisans would bring about great civic prosperity. Writing in 1730 about Nuremberg mathematicians and *Künstler* of the town's more prosperous and glorious days, Johann Gabriel Doppelmayr saw Nuremberg as exemplifying the fruitful relation existing particularly in Germany between exact mathematics and the mechanical arts. He believed Nuremberg's fame as a center of mathematical astronomy (the chosen home of the astronomer Regiomontanus), its reputation for artisanal virtuosity, and its affluence as a center of artisanal manufacture were not coincidental. Exact mathematics, the practice of the mechanical arts, and artisanal ingenuity had driven each other on to raise Nuremberg to heights of material abundance. While the *studium mathematicum* had been cultivated in Italy, it had flourished especially in Germany, and particularly in Nuremberg.[58] Because of its relationship to material progress and plenty, mathematics was invoked by artisans to establish their learned status and by scholars to demonstrate their ability to carry out in practice what they proposed in theory.

Mathematics was thus associated with the arts and with the artisanal cities seen as centers of production and prosperity. Becher's background in the guild city may well have prepared him to regard the artisanal city as a place where mathematics and the mechanical arts brought about great productivity; however, his papers and publications give no clue as to where he might have honed his mathematical and mechanical skills. His interest in the arts was in any case fully in tune with the increasing attention paid to artisanal labor since the sixteenth century. In England, John Wilkins had published *Mathematical magick* in 1648, which was concerned with practical mathematics and machines. He wrote this book for learned men, traditionally prejudiced against the mechanical arts and their

---

[57] As Ramus's views make clear, this association was already made in the sixteenth century. For evidence of this view in other settings, see also F. R. Johnson, "Thomas Hood's Inaugural Address as Mathematical Lecturer of the City of London (1588)," *Journal of the History of Ideas* 3 (1942): 94–106; Mario Biagioli, "The Social Status of Italian Mathematicians, 1450–1600," *History of Science* 27 (1989): 41–95; Alex Keller, "Mathematics, Mechanics and the Origins of the Culture of Invention," *Minerva* 23 (1985): 348–61; Rossi, *Philosophy, Technology, and the Arts*.

[58] Johann Gabriel Doppelmayr, *Historische Nachricht von den Nürnbergischen Mathematicis und Künstlern* (Nuremberg: Peter Conrad Monath, 1730), Vorrede, unpaginated. Penelope Gouk, *The Ivory Sundials of Nuremberg, 1500–1700* (Cambridge: Whipple Museum of the History of Science, 1988), examines this nexus of mathematical, mechanical, and civic prosperity in the trade of sundial making. The association of prosperity and mathematics in the free imperial cities might point to an explanation of the conjunction of social circumstances and world view that formed the particularly "northern" culture, for which Svetlana Alpers argues in *The Art of Describing: Dutch Art in the Seventeenth Century* (Chicago: University of Chicago Press, 1983).

practitioners. For this audience, he relates the story of Heraclitus in the trades-man's workshop:

> It is related of Heraclitus, that when his scholars had found him in a tradesman's shop, whither they were ashamed to enter, he told them . . . that the gods were as well conversant in such places, as in others: intimating, that a divine power and wisdom might be discerned, even in those common arts which are so much de-spised.[59]

Artisanal knowledge was separated from the realm of school knowledge by the fact that the mechanical arts were neither taught in the schools nor written down, and a certain unclean odor clung to them as the illiberal arts, for in antiquity they had been the work of slaves and the *vulgus*. The knowledge of artisans was transmitted by doing and imitation, rather than by the study of books, and artisanal guilds and guild towns constituted the means by which their knowledge and techniques were reproduced. As the power of the guilds and guild cities grew, and the arts came to be seen as the foundation of the wealth of cities and republics, scholars began to look to artisans and artisanal knowledge as productive and valuable. Juan Luis Vives, for example, encour-aged scholars not to "be ashamed to enter into shops and factories, and to ask questions from craftsmen, and to get to know about the details of their work."[60]

Johann Valentin Andreae and Francis Bacon both believed that a study of the mechanical arts would yield knowledge of nature as well as knowledge useful to the state,[61] and their thought was particularly influential in plans for the

---

[59] Quoted in J. A. Bennett, "The Mechanics' Philosophy and the Mechanical Philosophy," *History of Science* 24 (1986): 22. Wilkins here paraphrased Aristotle, *De partibus animalium*, 1.5.15–25, in which Aristotle used the example of Heraclitus in comparing the study of the eternal, unchanging divine with the study of the perishable things of the observable world. While Aristotle conceded that study of the divine was more pleasing, he maintained that because the things of nature were closer to human nature and experience, their study had its own compensations. He therefore advocated the study of all the objects of nature, no matter how small and unattractive. Aristotle wrote: "For even in the study of animals unattractive to the senses, the nature that fashioned them offers immeasurable pleasures in the same way to those who can learn the causes and are naturally lovers of wisdom. It would be unreasonable, indeed absurd, to enjoy studying their representations on the grounds that we thereby study the art that fashioned them (painting or sculpture), but not to welcome still more the study of the actual things composed by nature, at least when we can survey their causes. Therefore we must avoid a childish distaste for examining the less valued animals. For in all natural things there is something wonderful. And just as Heraclitus is said to have spoken to the visitors, who were wanting to meet him but stopped as they were approaching when they saw him warming himself at the oven—he kept telling them to come in and not worry, 'for there are gods here too'—so we should approach the inquiry without aversion, knowing that in all of them there is something natural and beautiful." Trans. D. M. Balme (Oxford: Clarendon Press, 1972).

[60] *De tradendis disciplinis* (1531), bk. 4, chap. 6, trans. Foster Watson (Totowa, N.J.: Rowman and Littlefield, 1971), p. 209. On this subject, see also Rossi, *Philosophy, Technology, and the Arts*.

[61] Paolo Rossi, *Francis Bacon: From Magic to Science*, trans. Sacha Rabinovitch (London: Routledge & Kegan Paul, 1968), and Julian Martin, *Francis Bacon, the State, and the Reform of Natural Philosophy* (Cambridge: Cambridge University Press, 1992).

"Histories of Trades" pursued by English scholars of Becher's generation.[62] Comenius's émigré associate in England, Samuel Hartlib, and his circle of like-minded Protestant reformers, were particularly active in promoting these plans. When John Dury traveled to Germany in the 1630s in pursuit of a Protestant union, he wanted not only to promote his overarching cause, but also to observe "all Inventions, and Feats of Practise in all Sciences."

> For Inventions and Industries, I will seeke for such chiefly as may advance learning and good manners in the Universities, Schooles, and Commonweales; next for such as may bee profitable to the health of the body, to the Preservation and Encrease of wealth by trades and mechanicall Industries, either by sea or Land; either in Peace or Warre.[63]

In Dury's view, the reformation of learning and of the world was to come from things: the materials out of which the artisan crafted his objects, the techniques that tried and transformed things, and the inventions that brought profit and wealth to commonwealths and republics. Samuel Hartlib brought Comenius to England in 1641/42, where his history of trades projects aroused attention among other English notables in contact with Hartlib such as Robert Boyle, William Petty, and John Evelyn. Henry Oldenburg, a fellow German émigré, fell in with Samuel Hartlib's plans, and on his travels on the Continent in the 1650s would meet with Becher in his search for mechanical knowledge. Becher would begin his career constructing perpetual motion machines, and, just as Hartlib had been eager for news of Comenius's perpetual motion schemes in the 1640s,[64] so two decades later Henry Oldenburg and Samuel Hartlib would be anxious to bring Becher to England also. By that time, however, the German war was over, the English civil war was drawing to a disappointing close for reformers like Hartlib, and a new political order was falling into place.

"Viel Erfahren"

Experience was the second important component in Becher's education: "habe ich viel gelesen/ viel gehört/ viel erfahren/ viel probirt/ viel laborirt/ viel

[62] See Walther E. Houghton, Jr., "The History of Trades: Its Relation to Seventeenth-Century Thought," *Journal of the History of Ideas* 2 (1941): 33–60; Charles Webster, ed., *The Intellectual Revolution of the Seventeenth Century* (London: Routledge & Kegan Paul, 1974), and idem, *The Great Instauration: Science, Medicine, and Reform 1626–1660* (London: Gerald Duckworth, 1975).

[63] "The Purpose and Platform of My Journey into Germany," 1631, printed in G. H. Turnbull's *Samuel Hartlib* (Oxford: Oxford University Press, 1920), pp. 10–13.

[64] See G. H. Turnbull, *Hartlib, Dury and Comenius: Gleanings from Hartlib's Papers* (London: Hodder & Stoughton, 1947).

speculirt/ bin auch mit viel gelehrten Leute umgangen."[65] He claimed to have learned "by the light of Nature," from the things themselves. Here again he echoed, especially in the way he chose to recount his education, the reformers of knowledge such as Jacob Boehme, Paracelsus, Francis Bacon, Ramus, and, closer to his own life, Comenius. His own vivid observations and experience fill his works, as for example, when discussing the efficacy of cold in halting putrefaction, he recalls the body he saw hanging from the gallows with no signs of putrefaction for an entire long winter in Sweden.[66]

In the seventeenth century, observation, experience, and the practical trials and labors of art constituted a *novus methodus philosophandi*, a new method of philosophizing.[67] This new method, which was based upon active practice and was seen to yield new knowledge, would eventually transform completely the older system of education directed toward the mastery of a corpus of authorities.[68] The mottoes of the academies that formed around the "new method of philosophizing" in the seventeenth century distilled the essence of this method. To pick only three examples, the "Nullius in verba" of the Royal Society of London expressed the members' loyalty to things, rather than words; the Accademia del Cimento's "Provando e riprovando" declared an adherence to active trial and practice; and the adoption of pseudonyms from the story of Jason and the Argonauts by the members of the Academia naturae curiosorum emphasized the active search for knowledge.

[65] "I have read much, listened much, experienced much, made many trials, labored much, speculated much, and I have associated with many learned people." *Psychosophia* (1705), p. 316.

[66] Becher, *Chymisches Laboratorium oder Unter-erdische Naturkündigung* (Frankfurt: Johann Haaß, 1680), p. 362. This work is Becher's translation of *Actorum Laboratorii Chymici Monacensis, seu Physicae Subterraneae libri duo* (Frankfurt: Johann David Zunner, 1669).

[67] One of the clearest statements of the nature of this new method and the changes it had wrought was expressed by Johann Christoph Sturm, a professor of mathematics and physics at Altdorff, in *Collegium Experimentale, sive Curiosorum in quo Primaria hujus seculi inventa & experimenta Physico-Mathematica . . . Phaenomena & effecta . . .* (Nuremberg: Wolfgang Maurice Endter & Johannes Andrea Endter, 1676), pp. xxx2 r–v. He states that the "new method of philosophizing . . . called experimental" is practiced in various societies and colleges throughout Europe.

[68] Two recent works that chronicle this transformation are Grafton, *Defenders of the Text*, and Joseph M. Levine, *The Battle of the Books: History and Literature in the Augustan Age* (Ithaca: Cornell University Press, 1991). In their very important book, Steven Shapin and Simon Schaffer, *Leviathan and the Air-Pump: Hobbes, Boyle and the Experimental Life* (Princeton: Princeton University Press, 1985), showed the new method of philosophizing was not accepted without controversy. Other recent works of note that treat the creation of this new method are Steven Shapin, "Pump and Circumstance: Robert Boyle's Literary Technology," *Social Studies of Science* 14 (1984): 481–519; Simon Schaffer, "Making Certain" (essay review of *Probability and Certainty* by B. J. Shapiro), *Social Studies of Science* 14 (1984): 137–52; Peter Dear, "Jesuit Mathematical Science and the Reconstitution of Experience in the Early Seventeenth Century," *Studies in the History and Philosophy of Science* 18 (1987): 133–75; Michael Hunter, *Establishing the New Science: The Experience of the Early Royal Society* (Woodbridge, Suffolk: Boydell, 1989); and Paula Findlen, *Possessing Nature: Museums, Collecting and Scientific Culture in Early Modern Italy* (Berkeley: University of California Press, 1994). Peter Dear, "*Totius in Verba*: Rhetoric and

This new method had its origins in the importance placed on the things of nature and on knowledge of God's Creation by authors influenced by Hermetic philosophy such as Paracelsus and Jacob Boehme.[69] These authors elevated the work of the hands and the manual worker (*Handwercker*) above the learning of books because the artisan worked with the objects and materials of nature. The *Handwerker* was more closely attuned to nature, because by his art, he imitated nature (*ars imitatur naturam*), which yielded knowledge of nature and ultimately formed a path to the understanding of God's Creation. The art of the craftsman also "reformed" nature by creating valuable objects out of the raw materials of nature. The manual labor of refining nature for human needs, common to all *Handwerck* and thought by Paracelsus to be exemplified in the refining processes of alchemy, brought about the reformation and ultimately the redemption of the world and humankind. Medicine and alchemy, above all other arts, carried out in microcosm the macrocosmic process of human redemption after the Fall.[70]

Becher notes that he too "did many trials, and labored much," and his first published work was one of alchemical medicine. In 1654, at the age of nineteen

Authority in the Early Royal Society," *Isis* 76 (1985): 145–61, presents a useful survey of the transformation in the bases of intellectual authority.

[69] Historians regarded this world view as antithetical to the new methods of natural philosophy until the scholarship of Eugenio Garin, Walter Pagel, Frances Yates, and Paolo Rossi, as well as that of the generation of scholars whom they influenced, made clear that Renaissance alchemy, and the hermetic philosophy that informed it, shaped the habits of mind and practice that formed early modern natural philosophy: Eugenio Garin, *Science and Civic Life in the Italian Renaissance*, trans. Peter Munz (New York: Doubleday, 1969); idem, *Italian Humanism: Philosophy and Civic Life in the Renaissance*, trans. Peter Munz (New York: Harper and Row, 1965); Pagel, *Paracelsus*; idem, *Joan Baptista Van Helmont: Reformer of Science and Medicine* (Cambridge: Cambridge University Press, 1982); Frances Yates, *Giordano Bruno and the Hermetic Tradition* (Chicago: University of Chicago Press, 1964); idem, *The Rosicrucian Enlightenment*; Rossi, *Philosophy, Technology, and the Arts*; idem, *Francis Bacon*; J. E. McGuire and P. M. Rattansi, "Newton and the 'Pipes of Pan,'" *Notes and Records of the Royal Society of London* 21 (1966): 108–43.

[70] On Paracelsus, see Walter Pagel, *Paracelsus*; idem, *Das medizinische Weltbild des Paracelsus. Seine Zusammenhänge mit Neuplatonismus und Gnosis* (Wiesbaden: Franz Steiner Verlag, 1962); Kurt Goldammer, *Paracelsus: Natur und Offenbarung* (Hanover: Theodor Oppermann Verlag, 1953); and Owen Hannaway, *The Chemists and the Word: The Didactic Origins of Chemistry* (Baltimore: Johns Hopkins University Press, 1975), esp. pp. 43–45. Betty J. T. Dobbs, *The Foundations of Newton's Alchemy* (Cambridge: Cambridge University Press, 1975), and *Alchemical Death and Resurrection: The Significance of Alchemy in the Age of Newton* (Washington, D.C.: Smithsonian Institution Libraries, 1990), show how these Paracelsian ideas were maintained into the seventeenth century. Debus, *The Chemical Philosophy*, provides a good introduction to the use made of the Paracelsian legacy by the new philosophers. The religious alliances of Paracelsian (al)chemists are treated in a different way by Webster, *The Great Instauration*; idem, *From Paracelsus to Newton: Magic and the Making of Modern Science* (Cambridge: Cambridge University Press, 1982); and P. M. Rattansi, "Paracelsus and the Puritan Revolution," *Ambix* 11 (1963): 24–32; but Webster's thesis that Paracelsian views were allied solely with radical religious sects should be tempered by the recent article by J. Andrew Mendelsohn, "Alchemy and Politics in England 1649–1665," *Past and Present* 135 (1992): 30–78.

he published, under the pseudonym of Solinus Salzthal of Regiomontanus, *Solini Saltzthals Regiomontani Discurs von der Großmächtigen Philosophischen Universal-Artzney/ von den Philosophis genannt Lapis Philosophorum Trismegistus.*[71] Becher often cited Paracelsus, although he distanced himself from the religious enthusiasm (and social radicalism) of Paracelsus. Becher used his references to Paracelsus, rather, to connect himself with a figure who personified the method of philosophizing practiced outside the schools and based in the experience of natural things. This method could be learned by studying the techniques and the mentality of artisans, for they had particular access to the knowledge of nature in the practice of their arts.

Respublica litterae

In describing his education, Becher was careful to balance the experience, assaying and laboring of his early life with reading, speculation, and conversation with scholars ("bin auch mit viel gelehrten Leute umgangen"). Becher was always eager to be regarded as a member of the scholarly world, even when others saw him as a "mechanick" or noted his poor Latin. He claimed to have been acquainted with many of the most famous members of the republic of scholars of his day, but the facts of his claim are less important than investigating the group of scholars with whom he chose to ally himself. In 1678, when he claimed to be retiring from court life, he counted up his famous acquaintances and found they included a small number of Jesuits, several professors at the university at Leiden, and all the most stellar names of Queen Christina's erudite court, most of whom had also spent time at Leiden.[72] Like great numbers of his countrymen,[73] Becher may have studied at Leiden, although he did not formally matriculate. While there, he probably came in contact with Cartesian ideas, which he seems to have rejected,[74] as well as with the late humanist Stoicism of Justus Lipsius and the wave of practical, political literature Lipsius left in his wake in the Netherlands and throughout Europe.

The republic of letters, like the rest of the European society of orders in the

[71] Discourse about the powerful philosophical universal medicine, called Trismegistus, stone of the philosophers, no place of publishing and no pagination, only known copy in the British Library. A manuscript of the title and foreword for this work, dated 1654, is in Mss. var. 2, fols. 266r–275v. A Latin translation was included in the sixth volume of the *Theatrum Chemicum*, ed. Johann Joachim Heilmann (Strasbourg: Eberhard Zetzner, 1661), pp. 675–94.

[72] In *Psychosophia* (1705), p. 316, Becher lists Marin Mersenne, René Descartes, Claude de Saumaise (Salmasius), Gabriel Naudé, Samuel Boschart, Nicolas Heinsius, Johann Freinsheim, Johann Heinrich Boeckler, Heinric Meibom, and Johann Scheffer.

[73] See Heinz Schneppen, *Niederländische Universitäten und Deutsches Geistesleben* (Münster: Aschendorffsche Verlagsbuchhandlung, 1960).

[74] Becher viewed Descartes as a materialist—someone who investigated spiritual matters by a method meant only for corporeal things (*Psychosophia* [1705], pp. 80–81).

seventeenth century, was changing, and this transformation is reflected in Becher's list of his scholar-*amici*. Almost all the scholars on it were in the service of a noble patron. In contrast to the previous century in central Europe, a scholar in the seventeenth century might never hold a position at a university.[75] At the beginning of the seventeenth century, many scholars believed that they no longer belonged to what had previously been an elite social order—the guild of scholars.[76] Instead they sought prestige and legitimation at the new center of active life, the noble court. This became the arena for the translation of their words and texts into practice, and provided the place where they could quite literally make their fortune. Their ideas echoed this new focal point of their lives, and, in their works, the territorial prince and his state became a necessity for social order. Thinkers as diverse as Thomas Hobbes and Justus Lipsius claimed that the body politic was dead without a prince to hold it together.[77]

In the scholars' new environment of the noble court, the Ur-question of their predecessors, the civic humanists—"how should one live one's life"[78]— became their central concern. They sought to answer it not only for themselves in their courtiers' and *Höflichkeit* manuals, but also for the whole of their society in an explosion of literature on politics, civil prudence, and *arcana imperii*. They did not proceed by a single method. Some—Bodin, Althusius, Conring—began from Aristotle's *Politics* and discussed the structure of the state, while others made their starting point the Bible, or began from the huge number of *policey-ordnungen* that had accumulated in every town and territory by the mid-seventeenth century.[79] Another route is exemplified by Lipsius, who developed a set of practical axioms of political behavior based on Roman Late Republican and Imperial writers such as Cicero, Tacitus, and Seneca (and tacitly on Machiavelli).

Becher almost never referred to the Aristotelians and their theories of state structure. He placed himself instead in the tradition of Lipsius's practical poli-

---

[75] Siegfried Wollgast, *Zur Stellung des Gelehrten in Deutschland im 17. Jahrhundert* (Berlin: Akademie-Verlag, 1984), p. 57, makes this point particularly in relation to scholars interested in natural philosophy.

[76] Wilhelm Kühlmann, *Gelehrtenrepublik und Fürstenstaat* (Tübingen: Max Niemeyer Verlag, 1982), p. 89. For a picture of the late humanist guild of scholars, see Trunz, "Der deutsche Späthumanismus," in Alewyn, *Deutsche Barockforschung*.

[77] Kühlmann, *Gelehrtenrepublik*, p. 72.

[78] Nancy S. Struever, *Theory as Practice: Ethical Inquiry in the Renaissance* (Chicago: University of Chicago Press, 1992), sees this as the overriding concern of Petrarch and the practical inquiry that he initiated.

[79] See Kühlmann, *Gelehrtenrepublik*, p. 51, for the controversy between Aristotelians and neo-Stoics, and Horst Dreitzel, *Protestantischer Aristotelismus und absoluter Staat* (Wiesbaden: Franz Steiner Verlag, 1970), pp. 162ff., on the contrast between the Aristotelians and the "Christian pragmatics." One of the best treatments of *polizei-ordnungen* is Maier, *Die ältere deutsche Staats- und Verwaltungslehre*. See also Marc Raeff, *The Well-Ordered Police State: Social and Institutional Change through Law in the Germanies and Russia 1600–1800* (New Haven: Yale University Press, 1983).

tics, as he signaled when he named among his "acquaintances" Claudius Salmasius, Johann Freinsheim, Johann Boeckler, and Johann Scheffer. The political writings of these men focused on the development of self-knowledge and Stoic self-control. Their goal was the worldly and urbane experience of the courtier (or Stoic) that brought with it an ability to act prudently, to distinguish between reality and appearance, and, most important, to develop the virtue that would permit personal triumph over *fortuna*.[80] Their writings sought to keep not only the individual but the whole of society, within the bounds of order. The seventeenth-century commentators of Aristotle, the neo-Stoics, Jesuits, the authors of novels,[81] and even playwrights[82] and poets were all caught up in the struggle for order that their concern with the political expressed. They found opportunities for practical comment and political axioms at every turn. As one poet apostrophized in 1667: "Diogenes Laertius said that many useful things concerning ruling and running a house can be taught through poetry. In the poems of Amphion and Orpheus is hidden nothing other than the possiblity of learned and decent people bringing an unwashed folk to obedience and good laws."[83]

Order was, however, acquired at a cost. The scholars of the seventeenth century, displaced and held by the golden chain of servitude, seeing their value at court calculated upon a different scale than that current in the republic of letters, clung to the freedom of will and mind that Stoicism offered. They often lamented their position at court, and the tension they felt between court privileges and the life of the mind was palpable in their work.[84] Becher would lament that at court a person was regarded for his born worth and name, rather than for his capabilities.[85] He reflected that the final cause of all civil society was to protect and serve the individual, but the less one needed this protection

---

[80] The basic text on early modern neo-Stoicism remains Gerhard Oestreich's collected essays in *Geist und Gestalt des frühmodernen Staates* (Berlin: Duncker & Humblot, 1969). Other useful works in this relation are Günter Abel, *Stoizismus und Frühe Neuzeit* (Berlin: Walter de Gruyter, 1978); Frühsorge, *Der politische Körper*; and some of the essays in Neumeister and Wiedemann, *Res Publica Litteraria*.

[81] Such as Christian Weise (see Frühsorge, *Der politische Körper*) and Duke Heinrich Julius of Brunswick. On the political novels of this period, see Arnold Hirsch, " 'Politischer' Roman und 'politische' Lebensführung," in Alewyn, *Deutsche Barockforschung*, pp. 205–66.

[82] On these political dramas, see Günther Müller, "Höfische Kultur," in Alewyn, *Deutsche Barockforschung*, pp. 182–204.

[83] "Viel nützliche Sachen von dem Regier- und Hauß-Stande können durch Poetische Lieder beygebracht werden/ saget Diogenes Laertius. Unter den Gedichten von Amphion und Orpheus, stecket nichts anders verborgen/ als daß verständige und beredte Leute ein ungeschlachtes Volck leichtlich zum Gehorsam bringen und zu guten Gesätzen gewöhnen können." G. Neumark, *Poetische Tafeln*, quoted in Kühlmann, *Gelehrtenrepublik*, p. 324.

[84] See Helmuth Kiesel, *"Bei Hof, bei Höll." Untersuchungen zur literarischen Hofkritik von Sebastian Brant bis Friedrich Schiller* (Tübingen: Max Niemeyer Verlag, 1979), and Kühlmann, *Gelehrtenrepublik*.

[85] Becher, *Psychosophia* (1705), p. 342.

the freer one would be. To prove his point, he cited both Seneca, "neminem timet, quem nemo timet" (he fears no one, whom no one fears), and Paracelsus, "Qui omnia secum portat, non indiget alieno auxilio" (he who carries all things with him needs not the aid of others).[86]

The explosion of literature on *politicis* in the seventeenth century, like the earlier humanist concern with the public, active life from which it derived, was above all a practical movement. Political action and the new philosophy were both grounded in this practice, dependent on curiosity (with all its voluptuous sensory and sensual connotations), and undertaken by a new group of men who needed to acquire knowledge quickly and put it to immediate use. These men agreed on the human ability to control *fortuna* by ingenuity, invention, and virtue, and possessed a vision of the future that comprehended the idea of human progress. They evinced, above all, an overriding belief that the visible, material world was the real world in which a material salvation would be attained. The skills necessary to the new philosopher, the scholar-courtier, and the territorial ruler would turn out to be very similar: good observation of people and circumstances,[87] collection of experience, ability to distinguish reality from appearance, and an ability to play on the unforeseen circumstances of the moment.

Consummate courtier Gabriel Harvey (1545–1630) would note that "Euerie pragmatician castes about for life, and scoures the coast to the purpose. Jt importes euerie negotiatour, discouerer, intelligencer, practitioner, and euerie wittie man continually to cast abowt, & scowre the coast. Still & still more & more."[88] In Rome, scholars interested in natural philosophy formed an Accademia dei lincei (Academy of the lynx-eyed), while a German author of political axioms quoted an Italian proverb that "the assistants of princes must have the eyes of the lynx."[89] The telescope became an emblem both of natural philosophy and political prudence in the seventeenth century.[90] Duke Heinrich Julius of Brunswick stated that he would not speculate like a philosopher, but "like a Politicus or old Aulicus about such things as I have seen and experienced myself,"[91] and Louis XIV would write that "the entire art of politics consists in playing upon circumstances."

Becher would hazard and improvise to effect a conjunction of his own

---

[86] Ibid., pp. 89–90.

[87] Norbert Elias, *The Court Society*, trans. Edmund Jephcott (New York: Pantheon, 1983), pp. 105, 113, sees this emphasis on observation as the basis of a new rationality formed not by bourgeois capitalism but by the dynamics of the court. Frühsorge, *Der politische Körper*, pp. 108–9, discusses the identification of prudence ("politische Klugheit") with careful observation.

[88] Gabriel Harvey, quoted by Frank Whigham, *Ambition and Privilege: The Social Tropes of Elizabethan Courtesy Theory* (Berkeley: University of California Press, 1984), p. xiv.

[89] Christian Georg Bessel, *Faber Fortunae Politicae, Monitis ad vitam politicam admodum necessariis & saluberrimis* (Hamburg: Johannes Naumann & Georgius Wolff, 1673), p. 252.

[90] Frühsorge, *Der politische Körper*, pp. 108–9.

[91] Kühlmann, *Gelehrtenrepublik*, p. 342 n. 80.

mechanical inclinations and practical education, the manual practice and collection of experiences in the new philosophy, the political focus of the scholars with whom he associated himself, the need for prudence in his daily life at the noble court, and the overriding need to make his work relevant to his own princely patrons.

Theoria and *Ars*

Practice, the active gathering of experience by trial, by assay, by observation, and by collection, was the work of politics and history, but also of artisans. For them it constituted an unwritten knowledge that was productive and provided for the necessary wants of humankind. The significance and potential of this sort of knowledge was exemplified for Becher, as it had been for Paracelsus, in alchemy, and was epitomized in the alchemical anecdote evoked by the tag (often quoted by Becher), "Solve mihi hunc syllogismum" (solve for me this syllogism). This anecdote recounted how a professor of philosophy had lectured to his students about the impossibility of alchemical transmutation. He brought long logical demonstrations, as well as the words of authorities, to bear on his argument. A stranger in the audience stood up, and, without entering into the disputation, called for some lead, charcoal, and a crucible, and transmuted it into gold on the spot. He handed the still-warm gold to the professor and pronounced, "Solve mihi hunc syllogismum," and left the lecture hall.[92] This anecdote (or emblem) indicates the distance between practice and theory and between their methods in the seventeenth century. The professor is stranded without a method, without principles and proofs, without even the possibility of continuing speech when confronted by the creative, productive *action* of raw *ars*.

Becher carried with him on his travels a book that makes clear the tension between theory and art at this time. *Advices from Parnassus*, by Trajano Boccalini, was first published after Boccalini died in 1613, and went through numerous editions and translations from the Italian over the next two centuries.[93] In the satiric text, Boccalini conjured up a court of Apollo on Parnassus, in which Apollo played beneficent patron to the *respublica litterae*, including the most famous scholars and teachers of the ancient world and of humanist

[92] John Ferguson, *Bibliotheca Chemica*, 2 vols. (London: Derek Verschoyle, 1954), 2:374–77, mentions the history and sources for this anecdote in his biographical sketch of Alexander Seton.

[93] Originally published as *De' ragguagli di Parnaso*, this work was printed in German in 1644, and in 1655 edited by Jesuit law professor and political writer, Christoph Besold, to whom Becher made reference in *Politischer Discurs* and *Methodus didactica*. Becher cited Boccalini's work in *Appendix Practica, über seinen* Methodum Didacticam (Frankfurt: Johann David Zunner, Munich: Sebastian Rauch, 1669), p. 39. A list of his effects entitled "Joachim Becher's things that belong on the trip" indicates that he carried Boccalini's book with him. This list is in Mss. var. 2, fols. 678r–681v, and Boccalini is mentioned on fol. 680r.

Europe. In Boccalini's missivelike series of tidings from this court, these scholars and literati, the gods of Roman mythology, and the political figures of the sixteenth and early seventeenth centuries argue, found academies, duel, make proclamations, hold court, and gossip. Boccalini's work forms a witty synopsis of the debates and concerns of the literati in the sixteenth and early seventeenth centuries. Becher probably obtained his education from precisely such works as Boccalini's, and out of them, he formed an understanding of the issues of his world and of the sphere and scope of knowledge, as well as an image of himself as an actor in the republic of letters. He would carry this understanding into his positions at the noble courts of the German Empire and use it to establish himself there.

One of the many issues Boccalini addressed in *Advices* was the relation of contemplation and action, and of theory and practice. In Advice 76 several princes have besieged Aristotle in his country house in order to force him to revoke his definition of the tyrant:

Aristotle, Prince of the Peripateticks, that he might philosophize without interruption, retir'd t'other day to his pleasant Country-seat, where he was unexpectedly besieg'd in the night by a great number of Horse and Foot under the Command of several Princes. The Enemy having with great diligence cast up their Trenches, and rais'd their Batterys, were preparing to play upon the House, and beat it about his ears. But Apollo, who had speedy advice of this great News, dispatch'd two famous Italian Satyrists, Lodovico Ariosto, and Francisco Berni, with a Detachment of Satyrick Poets to raise the Siege. They attempted it with their utmost skill, but to no purpose; for tho the Poets ply'd the Besiegers very warmly with their Vollys of Lampoon and Defamation, yet the Princes Armor was of proof against their smartest fire. Apollo therefore, seeing Force cou'd not prevail, in a tender care to the honor of the Peripatetick Philosophy in the person of its great Master, sent into the field the magnanimous and ever-glorious lover of the Learned, Frederick Feltrio Duke of Urbin, who upon a parley with those Princes, obtain'd a Truce.

When they first began to treat, the Princes complain'd grievously of Aristotle for having in his Politicks given so malicious a Definition of a Tyrant, that it included every good Prince: for if, as he had dar'd to assert, those who regard their own profit more than that of their Subjects, ought to be call'd Tyrants, in their opinion no Prince cou'd clear himself from the imputation; since no Shepherd was so fond of his Sheep as to be afraid to milk and shear 'em, and to be willing to starve himself to keep them fat. That the Stagyrite was grosly ignorant; if he did not know that Profit is the sole end of all dealing, and the whole World is but one publick Warehouse. And if the Law of Nature it self allow'd Parents to love themselves better than their own Children, with what color wou'd that Beast Aristotle oblige Princes to be fonder of others profit than their own? They added that the Literati were grown so malapert and conceited, that they took upon 'em to meddle with the deepest concerns of the State, and even prescribe Rules for Princes to govern by;

not perceiving (poor Pedants!) that Politicks are quite out of their sphere, and that none shou'd pretend to 'em but such as have been practis'd in the Government of Kingdoms, which is not to be learn'd from Philosophy, Rhetorick, and the mouldy Records of Learning. For since the Theory of Politicks can't be form'd into a System, those who have not study'd it in the Closets of great Princes, and in their Administration of State-affairs, ought never to argue upon it, unless they have a mind to make themselves ridiculous to all the world, by writing and telling things for which they deserve to be scourg'd.

These words convinc'd Duke Frederick that the Princes had good reason to be angry; wherefore he told his Friend Aristotle, he must needs revoke his antient Definition of a Tyrant, and give 'em another more to their satisfaction. The Philosopher comply'd with all his heart, and said, That Tyrants were a certain sort of strange Creatures in very antient Times, whose Race is now wholly extinct.

The Princes having obtain'd their desire, instantly rais'd the Siege and march'd home; and poor Aristotle, half dead with the Fright, return'd to Parnassus, where he confess'd to all the Virtuosi, that his Philosophical Precepts avail'd him but little against the fear of Death; and, Gentlemen, says he, if you'll be advis'd by me, mind your Books and let State Affairs alone, for 'tis impossible for you to treat upon that Subject without evident danger of incurring the Displeasure of the Great.[94]

In this inventive bit of news from Parnassus, Boccalini alluded to the hazards for the scholar at the noble court but, more significantly, to the idea that the knowledge and books of scholars were useless to the man of politics. The man of affairs needed knowledge born of the experience of practice. The pedantic rule making and system building of the scholars was wholly irrelevant to political practice, for philosophical precepts did not provide knowledge that could assist the person engaged in the active life of the forum.[95]

To understand the significance of this satiric piece for Becher, let us return to Aristotle. In the *Nicomachean Ethics*, Aristotle discusses the organization of knowledge and distinguishes among the life of enjoyment, the contemplative life and the active life. He leaves aside a lengthy discussion of the life of enjoyment as too vulgar and treats in detail the active and contemplative lives.[96]

---

[94] *Advices from Parnassus in Two Centuries* (London, 1706), pp. 128–29.

[95] In Advice 76, as in every one of Boccalini's "advices," there are several issues being addressed at once. Here, one in particular should be indicated: Boccalini's princes claim that Aristotle is ignorant of the fact that "Profit is the sole end of all dealing, and the whole World is but one publick Warehouse," which illustrates well the moral concerns raised by the nobility's need of surplus wealth, or commercial profit, in the early modern period, and the problem of finding an ancient source that could reconcile this.

[96] *Nicomachean Ethics*, 2d ed., trans. H. Rackham (Cambridge, Mass.: Harvard University Press, 1982), 1.5.1–7. My reading of Aristotle's *Nicomachean Ethics* owes much to discussion with Owen Hannaway about the relation of theory and practice in the early modern period and the importance of locating the categories of this debate in the classical corpus.

Each sphere of life had its own end, type of knowledge, and degree of certainty. The life of contemplation concerned itself with the pursuit of the unchanging and eternal good. The result of contemplation was epistemic or theoretical knowledge about the immutable objects of nature; things that existed by necessity and contained within themselves the source of their change. Theoretical knowledge was proved by demonstration in the form of syllogisms and based on certain, demonstrable principles.[97]

Practical knowledge, or *praxis*, on the other hand, concerned mutable affairs that could be directed and intervened in by humans. This knowledge was based in *action* and derived from either "things done" or "things made." The sphere of practical knowledge pertaining to things done resulted in "prudence," and was the knowledge required by rulers and men of public life. Aristotle dealt with this knowledge particularly in his practical writings on ethics, economics, and politics. Prudence could not be called a science, and was not of absolute certainty, for it could not be proved by demonstration based on certain principles, or, as Boccalini's bellicose princes said, it could not be "form'd into a System." Prudence might never be certain, but it could be used as the basis for action if it were based on experiences, or particular facts.[98] Prudence apprehended only the particular, not the general (which was the basis of theoretical knowledge), and achieved this apprehension by (often fallible) sensory perception.[99]

The practical knowledge concerning "things made" was *technē*, or art. Art did not deal with things that already existed or had come into existence of necessity; rather, art itself brought its objects into existence. Art was the only one of the three types of knowledge that was productive, for the efficient cause of its objects lay in the maker and not in the objects themselves.[100]

Science, prudence, and art were different types of knowledge for Aristotle, and his distinctions continued to be observed in the course of European thought. The Roman concern with political life in the forum focused the sphere of practical knowledge on "things done," and *praxis* came to refer to the type of knowledge necessary for a life in the service of the *respublica*. The development in the medieval universities of a course of education that focused on the systematization of the liberal arts and excluded the mechanical arts as incapable of similar ordering widened the gap between theoretical and practical knowl-

[97] Aristotle, *Nicomachean*, 6.3.2–4.

[98] Barbara J. Shapiro, *Probability and Certainty in Seventeenth-Century England* (Princeton: Princeton University Press, 1983), and Henry G. Van Leeuwen, *The Problem of Certainty in English Thought 1630–1690* (The Hague: Martinus Nijhoff, 1963), treat the seventeenth-century discussions about the relative degrees of certainty obtained by different types of knowledge, while Lorraine Daston, *Classical Probability in the Enlightenment* (Princeton: Princeton University Press, 1988), provides useful background to these debates.

[99] Aristotle, *Nicomachean*, 6.4.

[100] Ibid., 6.4.4–5.

edge. At the same time, however, the practitioners of the mechanical arts, organized in guilds, took on increasing economic importance and political power in public life.[101] The humanist reform of knowledge, reacting against the life of contemplation as exemplified for the humanists in the medieval universities, renewed the Roman perception of the value of the active life and, as Boccalini has shown us, developed a rhetorical strategy that set the life of contemplation and theory against the life of political activity and practice. Concurrently, the practical knowledge of "things made" had become a source of power and a subject of great interest to the scholars, literati, and princes in the sixteenth and seventeenth centuries.

By the seventeenth century, *praxis* still referred to the type of knowledge needed by the man of affairs, but frequently it was used to mean the *activity* of the maker of things. Practice as experience and trial began to take over from the more specific view of *praxis* as relevant to the sphere of public life. Becher and his contemporaries still recognized the basis of their division between theory and practice as resting in the separate spheres of political life and scholarly contemplation, but for Becher, "practice" increasingly denoted experience, especially the experience of artisanal manual labor that was carried out without the schooled or written learning of theory and system. Thus, he referred to the *Handwerk* of the smelter and assayer at their furnaces, or the *Proben* and trials of the chymist in his laboratory, as practice. In his lifetime, Becher would rise from the status of a practicing mechanical virtuoso to a scholar and member of the noble court and, in his rise, he would refer always to his distinctive abilities to unify theory and practice. As a practitioner claiming access to theory, Becher had a stake in this union, as did the inspector of mines, who in 1690 proclaimed that the moderns were superior to the ancients because for the ancients there "was no theory to go along with the *praxis*" ("keine Theoria nechst der Praxin vorhanden gewesen").[102]

Boccalini's princes, who called for the strict separation of *theoria* and *praxis*, claiming that *praxis* could be learned only from experience, indicate the con-

---

[101] Scholars who have investigated the increased value placed upon labor and the mechanical arts in the Middle Ages include Elsbeth Whitney, *Paradise Restored: The Mechanical Arts from Antiquity through the Thirteenth Century* (Philadelphia: American Philosophical Society, 1990); George Ovitt, *The Restoration of Perfection: Labor and Technology in Medieval Culture* (New Brunswick, N.J.: Rutgers University Press, 1987); and Jacques Le Goff, *Time, Work, and Culture in the Middle Ages*, trans. Arthur Goldhammer (Chicago: University of Chicago Press, 1980). In a very interesting article, William Newman, "Technology and Alchemical Debate in the Late Middle Ages," *Isis* 80 (1989): 423–45, finds that alchemical writers of the late medieval period associated alchemy with the power of the mechanical arts.

[102] Johann Christian Orschall, *Nutz- und sonderbahre Erfindung einer Neuen Seigerung und Ertz-Beizung* (Frankfurt and Leipzig, 1690), Vorrede, quoted in Lothar Suhling, "'Philosophisches' in der frühneuzeitlichen Berg- und Hüttenkunde: Metallogenese und Transmutation aus der Sicht montanistischen Erfahrungswissens," in *Die Alchemie in der europäischen Kultur- und Wissenschaftsgeschichte*, ed. Christoph Meinel (Wiesbaden: Otto Harrassowitz, 1986), p. 294.

tested nature of the division of knowledge in this period. In his rise from mechanic to scholar, Becher would take advantage of the changing relationship between theory and practice, and he would answer the anonymous stranger's syllogism by asserting that the union between theory and practice would make knowledge productive. Such productive knowledge would prove indispensable to the political considerations of the territorial ruler.

The alchemist's "Solve mihi hunc syllogismum" pointed up not only the active nature of art, but also the productive potential of art. Art was productive knowledge, and alchemy, as art, exemplified the possibility of material production and indicated the value of productive knowledge. Alchemy, however, also involved theoretical contemplation of immutable nature, for, as one alchemical writer expressed it, Hermes, the discoverer of alchemy, was also the inventor of all the arts *and* sciences:

> Und er ist der Hermes gewesen/ der nach der Sündflut aller Künsten und Disciplinen/ beydes der freyen und so die Handwerks Leut treiben/ der erst Erfinder und Beschreiber gewesen.[103]

> And it was Hermes, who, after the Flood, was the first inventor and articulator of all the arts and disciplines, both of the liberal arts, as well as of those which the artisans practice.

Alchemy involved art and theory and thus gave access to the worlds both of the scholar (through books) and of the artisan (through the laboratory). Becher would find it perfectly suited to his needs, for he could use it to talk to the court about the processes of artisanal creation and production.

Wanderjahre

Travel was an essential part of the artisan's indoctrination in a craft, for after his apprenticeship, he worked for different masters as a journeyman. It was also part of the university student's education before he became a master of the liberal arts. Paracelsus advocated travel as the basis of experience for the student of nature: "He who wishes to explore nature must tread her books with his feet. Writing is learnt from letters, Nature, however, [by traveling] from land to land: One land one page. Thus is the Codex of Nature, thus must its leaves be turned."[104] For Paracelsus, *Erfahrung* (experience) in fact meant "the result of traveling with open eyes."[105] Travel continued to be part of the rhetoric

---

[103] "Der güldinen Kunst die sie sonst Chymia nennen . . . verteutscht durch Philippum Morgenstern," in *Turba Philosophorum*, ed. Philipp Morgenstern (Basel: Ludwig König, 1613), pt. 2, Vorrede, Aii verso.

[104] Quoted by Pagel, *Paracelsus*, pp. 56–57.

[105] Ibid., p. 57.

of the new method of philosophizing as a source of experience. Becher traveled much, especially between 1648 and 1655. It appears that Becher and his family stopped in Bremen, Hamburg, Danzig, Stockholm, and Lübeck, before finally coming to rest in Breslau, for on a list of what seem to be his mother's effects at her death are included *attestata honoris* from these cities—testimonials to her upright standing as part of a *Bürger* family. It is perhaps not surprising that Becher attempted to construct a model of human society on the example of the guild town, when one realizes that even after his mother had left the closed community, she continued to carry the town world with her, as part of her baggage, in the form of letters of *bürgerlich* credit.[106]

Becher seems to have spent time in Stockholm where he claims to have met many of the learned philologues and philosophers at the court of Queen Christina.[107] He specifically mentions Mersenne, who died on his way back from Sweden in 1648, and Descartes, who died in Stockholm in 1650, as well as many other scholars who were in the queen's service between 1648 and 1652. Perhaps his stepfather or his mother's family had connections to the court, but even as a studious sixteen-year-old who perhaps tutored younger pupils, he could well have taken part, if only at a distance, in the scholarly debates of Christina's learned court. His totting up of these most famous members of the republic of scholars in a list at a much later date betrays his desire to show that he was part of this world from early on, although it does not prove any real converse with these scholars. Rather, a mention of his "very good acquaintance," a certain Andreas Reußner, is more in keeping with Becher's mechanical inclinations at that time. By a constant stream of correspondence, this enterprising man kept his patron, Magnus Gabriel de la Gardie—one of the most powerful men at Queen Christina's court—informed about war machines, mines, mills, medicines, silk making, and the progress of legal proceedings (all the favorite projects).[108] Becher remembered Reußner later as someone who had lost a bet and been ridiculed when he failed to draw water up through a lead syphon over the Brückenberg in Stockholm.[109]

Becher states he was in Danzig in 1650/51,[110] and a list of baggage he carried

[106] The list, entitled "der f. Mutters Sachen," was presumably a list of her possessions drawn up on her death. It is in Mss. var. 2, fol. 674r–v, and includes, besides the testimonials, a legal document from Speyer, a bill, a letter from her [?] guardians, kitchen utensils, medicaments, housewares, writing instruments, paper, a ruler, compass, dividers, bedclothes, a straw mattress, and some foodstuffs (butter, cheese, salt, ginger, vinegar, and oil).

[107] Becher, *Psychosophia* (1705), p. 316. See also Hassinger, *Becher*, pp. 13–14.

[108] Reußner was apparently in the service of both Jakob and Magnus Gabriel de la Gardie. His correspondence with them and others dated between 1648 and 1654 is extant in the Riksarchivet in Stockholm: Eriksbergarchivet, Autografsamlingen, vol. 53, Jakob de la Gardie; Biographica, Andreas Reußner, vol. 9; Correspondence to M. G. de la Gardie E1534.

[109] Becher, *Närrische Weißheit*, p. 203. Becher also mentions Reußner in the British Library, Sloane Mss. 2867, fol. 259r.

[110] In *Methodus didactica*, p. 45, Becher claims to have been in Danzig when Johannes Buno published his *Neue lateinische Grammatica in Fabeln und Bildern* in 1651.

with him in his travels indicates he may have moved from there to the cosmo-
politan trading city of Breslau, for he had several good correspondents and
"comrades" in Breslau.[111] His mother wrote letters to him from Breslau, and it
is likely that she died there.[112] Perhaps Becher received his introduction to the
manual art of the laboratory in Breslau, possibly with the help of a certain Dr.
Gottfried Stocklöw.[113] He claims to have met learned men on his travels not
only in Sweden, but also in Germany, Holland, and Italy.

Travel and mobility were essential to the alchemist's education as well, and
Becher often quoted Paracelsus's celebrated maxim, "Qui omnia secum portat,
non indiget alieno auxilio" (he who carries all things with him needs not the aid
of others).[114] This adage referred to the philosophers' stone, by which base
metals were transmuted into gold, but it had additional significance in Becher's
thought, derived from another book that accompanied him on his travels, and
probably formed another essential link in his autodidactic education. This
book, *Zodiacus vitae* by Marcellus Palingenius, was a long encyclopedic poem

[111] On Breslau in the seventeenth century, see Hugo Weczerka, "Entwicklungslinien der schlesischen Städte im 17. und in der ersten Hälfte des 18. Jahrhunderts," in *Die Städte Mitteleuropas im
17. und 18. Jahrhundert*, ed. Wilhelm Rausch (Linz and Donau, 1981), pp. 119–42.

[112] I base these conclusions on the list of "der f. Mutters Sachen," Mss. var. 2, fol. 674r–v, and
the list of Becher's effects, Mss. var. 2, fols. 678v–681v, entitled "Sachen die auff die Reise
gehören, d.i. Herrn Joachim Bechers Sachen." This contains a list of clothes and linens in one white
trunk and a list of books, letters, personal papers, and manuscripts that filled two other trunks.
Many of the letters are listed as having been sent by correspondents in Breslau. Among other
correspondence are listed six letters from his mother in Breslau, thirty-three letters from his
"Cammerraten Johann Lorentz" from Breslau and other places, and five letters from Dr. Gottfried
Stocklöw in Breslau. The list of Becher's effects should probably be dated sometime in the early
1660s, as he lists letters from Dr. Jobst in Munich (fol. 681r) and an "Instruction" for the *Kurfürst* of
Mainz.

[113] Becher lists five letters from Stocklöw (also Stocklowe) in Mss. var. 2, fol. 681r, and
Stocklöw appears in Becher's *Natur-Kündigung der Metallen* (Frankfurt: Joh. Wilh. Ammon &
Wilh. Serlin, 1661), *Parnassus Medicinalis Illustratus* (Ulm: Joh. Görlin, 1662–63), and *Institutiones Chimicae Prodromae, i.e. . . . . Oedipus Chimicus. Obscuriorum Terminorum & Princi-
piorum Chimicorum, Mysteria Aperiens & resolvens* (Frankfurt: Herman a Sande, 1664), where
Becher quoted poems of congratulation and praise that Stocklöw sent to him. Zedler, *Grosses
vollständiges Universal-Lexikon*, vol. 40, s.v. "Stocklev, Gottfried," states that Gottfried von
Stocklev was a "Kayserlicher Titular-Leib-Medicus" in Breslau, who had converted to Catholicism, and wrote religious tracts with a natural philosophical content under the name of Leo a
Stipite. Stocklev died a very old man in 1713. I assume that Zedler's Stocklev and Becher's
Stocklöw are the same man.

[114] The source of this maxim was Morienus, although Becher ascribes it to Paracelsus. The
writings of Morienus, first translated from Arabic into Latin in 1182, recounted Morienus's depar-
ture from Rome to lead a hermit's life, and his subsequent call to the court of King Kalid. The king
sought Morienus out because he was reputed to know the secret of the alchemical tincture. When
the king finally succeeded in bringing him to the court, Morienus did indeed produce the tincture
but, having accomplished this, he left the powder standing in a vessel, on the outside of which he
had inscribed the words, "Omnes qui secum omnia habent, alieno auxilio nullatenus indigent," and
departed the court again for his desert retreat. See Ferguson, *Bibliotheca Chemica*, 2:108–9.

encapsulating universal knowledge in a string of commonplaces and was used as a school book for generations of students from its first publication in 1560. Becher used Palingenius's words and authority constantly. Book 10 of the *Zodiacus*, entitled Capricorn, had become a *locus classicus* of sorts for alchemical writers, for it was here that Palingenius discussed the philosophers' stone and mercury. In this section, Palingenius conflated the philosophers' stone with virtue, so that he who carried all things with him could be either an alchemist or a virtuous man.

Palingenius defined a rich man not as one who has real property or a hoard of gold—the popular definition of wealth—but one who is learned in both wisdom and art, and is upstanding and virtuous. This man could carry his wealth with him wherever he went, unlike the man concerned only with his material possessions. The philosophers' stone, made from changeable mercury, was similar to learning and virtue for it brought and sustained happiness, wherever the storms of *fortuna* might toss a man:

> Him truly and in proper kind *A rich man* call we may,
> That flowes with *wit* and *eloquence*, with *wisdom* and with *Art*,
> And wheresoever he becomes, can gaine an honest part,
> To divers places farre from home, his substance with him takes,
> And portion for himself to live. And though he journey makes
> And never wanteth needfull thinges a joyfull life to leade,
> Nor feares the theeves, nor doth the sword, or cruell robbers dread,
> And quickly doth him selfe repaire thoughe he be spoyled quite:
> For *Vertue* true gives neuer place to Fortunes frowning spite.[115]

Wealth of learning and virtue was more valuable than property because it allowed mobility:

> For every dwelling in the worlde doth natiue soile appeare
> Unto the vertuous man, and well he liveth euerie where.
> But he that vertue lackes, althoughe he great possessions hould,
> And purses stuffed full with coine and Coffers full of golde,
> Yet can he not go where he list, nor trauell every place,
> To see the countrie strange abrode, and men of sundry grace,
> And euerie where to live: for house and ground, and Castles strong,
> He can not beare about with him, in all his iorneys long,
> Least that perchance with theeves he meete, or perish on the shore,
> And then for gods sake aske his meate at every other dore.
> At home therefore he alwaies dwels, and in his countrey lives,

---

[115] Marcellus Palingenius, *The Zodiake of Life*, trans. Barnabie Googe (London: Rause Newberie, 1576; facs. repr. New York: Scholars' Facsimiles & Reprints, 1947), pp. 186–88, for this and the following passages. The list of Becher's possessions, Mss. var. 2, fol. 680r, contains Marcellus Palingenius as one of the authors in the two trunks of books.

> Where as his ground a great increase of Corne and wine him gives,
> And as a banisht man he feares beyonde the boundes to go,
> That slouthfulnes of minde, and chaunce to him assigned so:
> Wherby the goodly sightes abroade he can not viewe nor marke,
> While stil at home he hidden lies, as pent in dongeon darke.

Palingenius used the regenerative and mobile qualities of the philosophers' stone to represent the movable forms of wealth:

> Therfore the olde *Philosophers* by fine inuention found,
> *A certaine stone*, that where they went or traueiled any grounde,
> Provided them of needfull thinges, and neuer would decay.
> By aide wherof, full many landes and countries farre away,
> They might behould, and alwaies learne of many sundry arts.

The effective agent of the philosophers' stone was Mercury, the master of movement and artifice:

> And thus of olde the Gods above, besought with humble hearts,
> The sacrifice on altar slaine before he was the trade
> To *Mercurie*, the *Sonne*, and *Moone*, Lo thus their praiers made.
> O *Titan*, beauty of the worlde, O fairest God in sight,
> O thou *Latona* driving hence the shadowes of the night,
> *O swiftly fleeting restlesse Impe of Ioue* and *Maia* borne.
> That able arte to change thy selfe, to shapes of sundry forme.

Because it was a mobile and virtuous form of wealth, the philosophers' stone gave freedom from the tyranny of fortune's wheel:

> Then whiche no art more worthy is, the Heavenly Stone to frame,
> Which wicked people never knowe, nor can obtaine the same.
> And this whosoever doth enjoy may dwell in any land,
> Bothe free from feare of fortunes wheele, and force of robbers hand:
> But unto fewe the Gods vouchesafe so great a gift to give.

In his work, Becher would draw upon the connection that Palingenius made between alchemy and virtue. He would exploit as well the full range of meanings alchemy could evoke; he used it to exemplify practice and theory, as embodying the promise of material productivity, and as a symbol of mobility. He would, in the end, conflate it with commerce.

Becher was himself much tossed about by Fortune, and mobility (perhaps restlessness), as Leibniz noted, was an essential mark of his life. The exigencies of war and the death of his father meant that he was not educated into a traditional profession, and so he fit into no established position in his society. Becher would, however, use his own peculiar education, experience, and mobility to define a place for himself at the centers of power in the Holy Roman

Empire. For like other new men at the noble court in the early modern period, Becher was part of a slow but profound transition in the creation and formation of a sense of self:

> The received sense of personal identity, seen as founded on God-given attributes such as birth, was slowly giving way to the more modern notion that the individual creates himself by his own actions. This new view was enticing to those on the rise, but it threatened those who resisted sharing their positions or who feared they would be displaced. The latter proposed the distinctions . . . the former read the courtesy books. . . . The effect of this . . . was to articulate a sophisticated rhetoric, indeed an epistemology, of personal social identity—a new understanding of *how people tell who they are*. The texts that articulated this struggle combined practical action and creative intellectual exploration. They were both tools and the kinds of activity we now describe as literature, history, and philosophy.[116]

Becher grasped opportunities and ideas as they came to him—from the books of authorities, from newspapers,[117] from the evidence of his own senses, and from the concepts and structures of the world of his mother and father—and created out of them both an identity for himself and a vision of society and reform. That vision, which he carried with him to the noble territorial court and there converted into published works and projects, showed the mark of his wanderings, the contents of his baggage, and the fluctuations of his *fortuna* in the two decades between 1635 and 1655.

[116] Whigham, *Ambition and Privilege*, p. x. Stephen Greenblatt, *Renaissance Self-Fashioning from More to Shakespeare* (Chicago: University of Chicago Press, 1980), also discusses the creation of identity in the early modern period.

[117] Newspapers, developing out of the tidings, printed ships' manifests, and intelligence gathering of the commercial world, were the texts par excellence of Becher's world, and his *Nachlaß* contains several numbers of different newspapers—for example, Mss. var. 1(2), fols. 648ff., and 1(3), fols. 201ff. Jürgen Habermas, *Strukturwandel der Öffentlichkeit. Untersuchungen zu einer Kategorie der bürgerlichen Gesellschaft*, 6th ed. (Ulm: Luchterhand, 1974), pp. 28ff., associates the rise of commerce and newspapers.

TWO

OECONOMIA RERUM ET VERBORUM: CONSTRUCTING A

POLITICAL SPACE IN THE HOLY ROMAN EMPIRE

B ETWEEN 1655 and the late 1660s Becher achieved a status from which, with his particular skills, his inelegant (even incorrect) Latin, and his precociousness in *res chymicas*, he could take part in active public life. During this time he established a place at the noble court—the locus of *praxis* in the Holy Roman Empire after 1648—by becoming a *Hofmedicus und -mathematicus*. He consolidated his position within the republic of letters—the locus of *theoria*—by taking on the title and duties of the profession of medicine. During this time he also developed a network of contacts among artisans and merchants—the locus of the productive knowledge of practice or *ars*.

In securing and making indispensable the position he constructed at court, Becher became an interpreter of social forms existing outside the court, an intermediary between the court and artisans, and an articulator of artisanal knowledge for the state. He developed a new means of discourse to talk to his patrons at court about the subjects of the mechanical arts and trade—subjects that did not fit into the structure and rhetorical conventions of courtly life. He articulated an understanding of the organization of knowledge that allowed him to transfer his own talents (in the practice of mechanical arts) and his knowledge of nature and of natural processes (his medical theory) to the body politic (the ruling of a territory). Becher proposed to draw the productive knowledge of material things into the realm of politics and words. This would not only confirm his own position and livelihood at court and carry wealth and reputation to his patrons, but would also bring power, prosperity, indeed a material restoration to the Holy Roman Empire.

Courting a Patron

geht man zu nah [an grossen Herren]/ so verbrennt man sich/
geht man zu weit darvon/ so erfrört man.

When one goes too near to great nobles, one gets burned, when
one goes too far away, one freezes.
(*Becher*, Methodus didactica)

From at least 1655 Becher was a purveyor of choice secrets, especially of an alchemical sort. In that year, we find him in Vienna, searching for patrons, sending alchemical promises to Emperor Ferdinand III.[1] He was also hard at work on perpetual motion machinery and inventions of a spectacular kind. Becher seems to have been fond of making lists of his inventions, and many survive from these years. They illustrate his interest in mills, long-burning fire, and any sort of perpetual motion machines. One of these lists, entitled "Specification der Inventionen Johanni Joachimi Becheri," lists inventions in statics, mechanics, hydraulics, optics, and pyrotechnics.[2] Becher copied out this list again in German, modeling his vernacular copy on a list of the inventions of a *hofbefreite* artisan from Augsburg in the employ of Ferdinand III, Daniel Neuberger. The title of Becher's "Memorial etlicher Künste und Wissenschafften Johann Joachim Bechers von Speyer" (Report on various arts and sciences of Johann Joachim Becher of Speyer) follows precisely that of Daniel Neuberger's "Memorial etlicher Künste undt Wissenschaften, Daniel Neubergers von Augspurg. Gemelten Kaysl. Sculptoris," except that whereas Neuberger had a court title, Becher could only append his place of birth to his name.[3] Daniel Neuberger, a sculptor of wax objects, would leave Vienna before Becher would be able to claim a title for himself there, but Neuberger would surface again and again in Becher's life.[4] A favorite of princes all over the empire, this *hofbefreite*

---

[1] Mss. var. 1(1), fols. 272r–273r, a draft or a copy of a treatise addressed to the emperor and dated 24 January 1655. This treatise is about the universal menstruum (ripening force) in the animal, vegetable, and mineral kingdoms. The sections on the animal and vegetable kingdoms are not in Becher's hand, but beginning on fol. 272v with the section on the mineral realm, Becher seems to have taken over. The treatise ends in Becher's hand: "hoffe ich daß es werden I.K.M. an meinen underthänigsten offenbahren nicht allein ein gnädiges gefallen tragen, sondern auch gnädige anordnung thun mehrers damit zu erfinden, die praeparation und application sollen I.K.M. nach begehren auch allezeitig allerunterthänigst angedeutet werden." This is a letter typical of the purveyor of secrets to a potential patron. He first sends announcement of a miraculous curiosity, then offers to send the preparation and application if the patron shows any sign of interest (perhaps by taking the inventor into his service or sending a sign of favor). Mss. var. 1(1), fols. 270r–271r is an incomplete draft of a "Definitio Praparationis Menstruindi universalis," which mentions the earlier letter to the emperor and offers the preparation for the universal menstruum.

[2] There are numerous drawings and plans for machinery and waterworks in Mss. var. 1(1). Fol. 521r–v contains the "Specification der Inventionen Johanni Joachimi Becheri Spirensis," which includes the perpetual motion clock, various mills, optical instruments, and a fire that burns in a room for seven years at a stretch.

[3] A fair copy of Becher's list follows his "Specification der Inventionen Johanni Joachimi Becheri," on fol. 534r–v. Daniel Neuberger's "Memorial" is found in Mss. var. 1(1), fols. 504r–506v. The list contains an introduction, which explains the objects listed as Neuberger's "Proben" in the Imperial Schatzkammer, and it is signed by Neuberger as former *"Künstler"* to Ferdinand III.

[4] Daniel Neuberger was born in Augsburg in 1625 and died in Regensburg in 1680. He was resident in Vienna from 1651 to 1663. See Heinrich Klapsia, "Daniel Neuberger: Beiträge zur Kunsttätigkeit am österreichischen Kaiserhofe im 17. Jahrhundert, III," *Jahrbuch der Kunsthistorischen Sammlungen in Wien* 45 (n.s., 9) (1935): 223–48.

Figure 3. Daniel Neuberger, *Allegorical Self-Portrait,* ca. 1651, wax relief.
Neuberger, in artisanal dress of an earlier era, sits in contemplation between Chronos
and a female figure wearing armor and luxurious dress. Chronos holds a skull
crowned with a laurel wreath, and the female figure raises her shield in one hand and
points with the other to a human head, snakes writhing in its hair. The *vanitas* theme
was to be constant in Neuberger's work, and here he seems to be contemplating both
the choice between *fama* and vice as well as the ultimate vanity of reputation (a
putto, blasting the trumpet of fame above the group, holds a flickering torch). With
permission of the Kestner Museum, Hanover.

artisan provided a model for Becher, the mechanical virtuoso on the threshold
of a career at court (figure 3). Although Becher seems to have modeled himself
on Neuberger at the beginning of his career, he would go on to create a new
place at court for himself in which he was neither mechanic nor artisan, but
rather someone who could control artisans and their knowledge. In time Becher
would become an agent for Neuberger's works and, more significantly, would
call himself a natural philosopher.

A letter to his brother from 1656 reveals the beginnings of Becher's strategies, for it is full of negotiations with an *inventor* for a mill works that will

perpetually drive several clocks, various mills, waterworks, and cranes. He reports that the inventor has promised to make a model from wood but had "put off the perpetual capability of the machine until he can make it from steel and iron."[5] In this letter, he tells his brother of the inventor's need for funds to continue the work, and mentions at least two noble patrons who could be convinced of the importance of this work.[6] Here, Becher can be seen acting as intermediary between an artisan-inventor and the nobility. By 1657 Becher styled himself mathematician to the emperor,[7] and had converted to Catholicism.[8]

In 1658 Becher surfaces in Mainz, attracted perhaps by the reputation of the elector Johann Philipp von Schönborn and his *Oberhofmarschall*, Christian von Boineburg, two powerful figures interested in natural knowledge and known for their patronage of the ingenious in mechanics and natural philosophy. Schönborn and Boineburg shared a curiosity about natural things, which sprang from a desire to bring about the religious unification and the material regeneration of the Holy Roman Empire (and indeed of European Christendom) that at times bordered on the millenarian.[9] Becher's reputation as ingenious artisan and purveyor of novelties becomes clear from the regular letters written by Henry Oldenburg, later secretary to the Royal Society of London, to Samuel Hartlib describing the *curiosi* he met traveling through the empire and France. Oldenburg writes in 1658 to Hartlib:

> We met in our passing through Maintz a rare artist, called Becher, a young man, who hath found, he saith, ye perpetual motion, ye possibility wherof hath been hitherto so much disputed by Philosophers. He hath almost finished a work, wherein he doth demonstrate by invention, wch we have seen, and the dessein and

[5] Copy of a letter from Becher to his "Lieber Bruder," dated Vienna May 1656, Mss. var. 2, fol. 673r–v.

[6] Mss. var. 2, fol. 673v.

[7] In the letter from Becher to his brother, dated Vienna May 1656, Becher signed himself as "M.D." and speaks about the court. Mss. var. 2, fol. 673r–v. Becher drafted several works in which he titled himself "Mathematicus" to the emperor. One dated in 1656 is in Mss. var. 2, fols. 657v and 659r. In a draft of a title page for a work on a perpetual motion machine in Mss. 1(1), fol. 433r, Becher refers to himself as "Johannes Joachim Becherus Spirensis Sacra Caesarae Majestatis Ferdinandi III. Mathematicus."

[8] It has always been assumed that Becher converted to Catholicism in Mainz (after 1660), but it is clear from a manuscript draft of a religious tract entitled "Johannis Joachimi Bechers von Speyer der Römisch Kayserl. Mayt. Mathematici, Wohlbedachten und von ihm selbst annoch bey seiner gutten gesundheit auffgesetzes Testament und Letzter Wille," dated 1656 in Mss. var. 2, fols. 657r–660v, that he was already a Catholic by 1656.

[9] Becher may have been in Mainz by 1657. "Sophiae Christianae," Mss. var. 1(1), fol. 104r is dated Mainz 1657. At a Reichstag in Regensburg, Johann Philipp von Schönborn (ruled 1647–73), archbishop-elector of Mainz and bishop of Würzburg and Worms, bought and transported back to Mainz Otto von Guericke's copper spheres and air pump, which von Guericke had demonstrated

way whereof the master told me himself he would within a few a very few weeks put in print here at Frankford wch being, I shall buy severall copies of it to communicate to friends.[10]

Three months later, Oldenburg wrote that he had "more fully informed myselfe about the perpetuum mobile at maintz, and found the engin thereof perfected, being the wthal the way of its motion, wch the author wth much civility shewed us himselfe." At the same time, Becher communicated another of his inventions to Oldenburg, which he called "Nova inventio Argonautica,"

by which individual ships of war may be built at small cost and made ready and repaired in a short time, that are indestructible and can safely survive upon any shore and in any harbor, that can move under and beneath the water, and inflict enormous damage upon the enemy without endangering themselves.[11]

Oldenburg described Becher to Hartlib as

A young man yet, but very ingenious and of much experience, having travelled exceedingly all over Europe, and searched and made acquaintance wth the ablest men, yt he could meet wth every where. When I proposed unto him a far of[f], if upon a call from Holland or England he could resolve to obey and to travell into those parts, he answered, not to be unwilling, if he might be assured to reap advantage by it, as he would assure such a country, as might call him, should doe.[12]

---

before the Reichstag. It is not unlikely that Becher was brought to Johann Philipp's court by Johann Christian von Boineburg (1622–72), the *Oberhofmarschall* and *Ratspräsident* who seven years later would be instrumental in having a young lawyer by the name of Gottfried Wilhelm Leibniz appointed as legal advisor at the court. Von Boineburg entered von Schönborn's service in 1652, converted to Catholicism in 1653, and was arrested and disgraced in August 1664 (shortly after Becher left Mainz). In 1668 he was publicly rehabilitated and returned to Mainz where he and Leibniz collaborated on various projects. Becher became involved in one of these projects in 1668 (see Chapter 3). As an introduction to von Boineburg, see Heinrich Schrohe, *Johann Christian von Boineburg, Kurmainzer Oberhofmarschall* (Mainz: Joh. Falk 3 Söhne, ca. 1926).

[10] Oldenburg to Hartlib, Frankfurt, 18 July 1658, in Henry Oldenburg, *Correspondence*, ed. A. R. Hall and M. B. Hall, 13 vols. (Madison: University of Wisconsin Press, 1965–86), 1:170–71. Mss. var. 2, fols. 371r–431v, contains an explanation of the perpetual motion clock, dated 1657, and some drawings. On the back of one of these pages (fol. 404v) is written, in Becher's hand, "Henry Oldenburg" and "Richard Vice-Comes de Ranelaugh," Oldenburg's noble pupil, with whom he was making the grand tour.

[11] Notes on and drawings of this invention are in Mss. var. 1(1), fols. 433r–442 and fols. 506–514. A copy of a description of the argonautic invention still exists in the Hartlib Papers, Bundle 26, according to Oldenburg, *Correspondence*, 13:395 n. 4.

[12] Oldenburg to Hartlib, 18/28 October 1658, *Correspondence*, 1:186–89.

The interest shown by Oldenburg and Hartlib in the perpetual motion clock and the underwater ship continued through 1659,[13] and Hartlib sent on news of Becher to Robert Boyle.[14]

In early 1659 Oldenburg wrote a very complimentary letter to Becher, trying to draw him out about his inventions. His strategy in the letter is obvious: he sketched for Becher the intense interest aroused in England by news of his mechanical inventions, but tempered this picture by mentioning that some virtuosi were skeptical and all were eagerly awaiting the further explication of his works. Oldenburg notified Becher that Dr. Rupp claimed his perpetual motion scheme to be purely mechanical rather than depending on an unexplained force or spirit. Thus, enthused Oldenburg,

> where he seems to depict your work he omits the heart of it, which is its masterpiece. Indeed, all the virtuosi desire nothing better than that your clock should run down, so that they may be convinced by their own experience that it may be wound up again by your ethereal spirit alone, and not by any other means.[15]

By mixing skepticism with flattery, Oldenburg attempted to draw Becher out about his secrets. He noted to Hartlib that,

> In the interim, such kind of men [as Becher] should be some long time conversed with, and some expences hazarded by liberal entertainments, to get their familiarity and affection; after which they will more easily be induced to discover themselves and the depth of their knowledge.[16]

[13] Hartlib reports to Oldenburg in a letter of 2 December 1658 that he received a description of the perpetual motion clock through a correspondent, Mr. Beet (who had in turn received it from his correspondent, Dr. Rupp): "Moreover, Dr. Rupp from Mainz writes as follows: 'Becher's perpetual motion for a perpetual clock is made of iron. It has been built at the Elector's expense, and erected in the belfry on the market square. It has its own perpetual motion and goes on and on as an everlasting instrument without the touch of a human hand. The device moves a clock-hand, but does not strike the hours. This mechanism is based on a proper knowledge and application of the balance. Everything in it is performed by the weight, together with nine metal balls each weighing two pounds. These balls running in a channel, alternately assist each other's motion and raise the weight, and hence the perpetual motion is established.'" This extract from Beet's letter (dated 7/17 January 1659) is included with Oldenburg's extract of Hartlib's letter of December in Royal Society Mss., *Correspondence*, 1:192–97. Translation of this extract by Hall and Hall. See also letters from Oldenburg to Hartlib, March 1658/59 (*Correspondence*, 1:211); Oldenburg to Hartlib, early April 1659 (ibid., pp. 212–13); Oldenburg to Becher, March 1659/60 (ibid., p. 359).

[14] Hartlib to Boyle, 10 August 1658, in *The Works of the Honourable Robert Boyle*, ed. Thomas Birch, 6 vols. (London: J. & F. Rivington, 1772), 6:112–13; 5 April 1659, 6:116–17; and 12 April 1659, 6:118–19. In each of these letters, Hartlib quotes letters from Oldenburg.

[15] Paris, 22 March 1659 n.s., Oldenburg to Becher, *Correspondence*, 1:208–10. Translation by Hall and Hall.

[16] Oldenburg to Hartlib, March 1658/59, *Correspondence*, 1:211.

Becher probably attempted to draw out his artisan-inventors in the same way that Oldenburg tried to induce Becher to "discover" himself. Becher, however, had no means with which to lavish the liberal entertainments on his artisans, as Oldenburg, who was in noble service, could expend on Becher.

Whom Oldenburg meant by "such kind of men" becomes clear from a letter in which he sets Becher at the head of a list of those whom he has met in his travels. His list continued with other men who "maintain that a rich air impregnated with the celestial spirit which gives life to all things is the true pabulum of all the different forms of life that inhabit the globe," a man at Montpellier who had drawn this spirit from salt of tartar, a gentleman nearby who had found a universal healing oil, and one who had retired to private life in order to refute the *Annals* of Baronius as being harmful to Protestantism. There was also a monk in Toulouse who had developed a water-drawing magnet, an adept at La Rochelle who had a universal medicine, a certain Pascal in Paris who had issued a mathematical contest and given the prize to himself, and a Dutchman who had invented a lantern for illuminating large rooms.[17]

Oldenburg regarded Becher as one of a number of inquisitive and ingenious people who, though in need of some cajoling, might be valuable to the reform of knowledge and society. He told Becher that an "assembly of men learned and ingenious in all sorts of useful sciences" had formed in England. In the same letter of 1659/60 he reported that matters in England seemed to be tending to a "republican settlement."[18] Oldenburg's acquaintances, who may not have had the vision of reform that he shared with Samuel Hartlib, reacted differently to his reports. Hartlib reported to Robert Boyle that William Petty "laughed heartily" on hearing of Becher's perpetual motion clock.[19]

Becher understood Oldenburg's regard, and, as he was searching for a patron, he followed up Oldenburg's overtures. In 1660 Becher reported to Oldenburg that,

> As my naval invention increases in perfection from day to day, so it needs sponsors to bring benefit to its inventor and its patrons; if a Maecenas comes forward, Horace and Virgil will not be wanting, for I draw practice to myself. I have certain hydraulic works in hand, by means of which it is possible to raise a huge quantity of water with little power. My remaining time I devote to medical and chemical avocations where I deal with matters that are rare, new, and useful. And my lips are not sealed, for if God please I will lay certain things before the public. . . . What I learn in your letter of the English design to build up the liberal sciences with wonderful skill, is new and welcome to me: if only they remain of the same mind, and keep faith with us, as we with them. So far as I can, if I may be of service to the

---

[17] Oldenburg to Freiherr von Friesen, 26 April 1659, *Correspondence*, 1:233–38.

[18] Oldenburg's notes on a letter sent to Becher, 2 March 1659/60, *Correspondence*, 1:359.

[19] Hartlib to Boyle, 10 August 1658, in Boyle, *The Works*, 6:112–13. William Petty was himself full of schemes; perhaps he saw a rival in Becher.

English state [Reipublicae Anglicanae], I am ready to do so; and once my salary and position are settled, I shall not hesitate to declare myself publicly.[20]

A few months later Becher wrote again to Oldenburg, asking how he could further his "mathematical affairs" in England, and reporting that he has "discovered some new, and hitherto unknown, things about magnetic sympathy." He added again that "if any Maecenas were about, I would perhaps divulge it."[21]

Although the negotiations between the two men did not in the end bear fruit, they do make clear Becher's concern to find a patron, as well as the form which negotiations for patronage could take.[22] Becher desired to leave the precarious status of mechanic and purveyor of secrets for a position akin to Oldenburg's, in which he could draw out the knowledge of artisan-inventors by hazarding the expenses of his patron. Becher's immediate search came to an end in 1660, when on 28 June the elector and archbishop of Mainz, Johann Philipp von Schönborn, appointed Becher *Hofmedicus und -mathematicus* (court physician and mathematician). Becher's mechanical inventions, which had tantalized Oldenburg both as curiosities and as components of a much larger reform of knowledge, probably attracted the Catholic reformer Johann Philipp in much the same way, and Becher continued his perpetual motion and mechanical projects in Mainz.[23]

Settling at the Noble Court: Finding a Place for Practice in the Sphere of *Praxis*

In the late 1650s Becher not only searched for a patron for his mechanical abilities, but also developed a notion of the wider significance and scope of his alchemical and mechanical projects in order to draw them more firmly into the sphere of politics. Becher had for some time been thinking about the organization of knowledge, and when he came to the court of the elector at Mainz, he began a scheme to marshal all knowledge into tables, one of which he entitled

[20] This is quoted by Oldenburg to Hartlib from a letter (no longer extant) from Becher to Oldenburg, Paris, 3 March 1659/60, *Correspondence*, 13:393–94, trans. from Latin by Hall and Hall.

[21] A copied extract from a letter from Becher to Oldenburg sent to Hartlib by Oldenburg, Mainz, 17 September 1660, *Correspondence*, 1:393–94, trans. from Latin by Hall and Hall.

[22] Becher was in contact with others besides Oldenburg in his search for a patron. For example, a draft of a tract on the *perpetuum mobile* is dedicated to the king of Spain (Mss. var. 2, fols. 449r–451r), and a summary and pictures of the clock are addressed to the Spanish legate (Mss. var. 1(1), fol. 694r–v).

[23] In 1658, Dr. Rupp reports to Samuel Hartlib that the elector has had Becher's perpetual motion clock erected in Mainz. There is ample evidence in the *Nachlaß* for Becher's mechanical projects. Mss. var. 1(3), fols. 188r–189r, contains, for example, a contract between Becher and a Carthusian prior in Mainz for a water system, dated 1 July 1661. In 1660/61, Becher proposed millworks and waterworks (Mss. var. 1(3), fols. 182ff., and 1(3), fols. 188–191).

"Honey of the sciences." Becher announced in 1662 to Elector Johann Philipp that he had found a "new and very useful manner of bringing into methodical tables different sciences that have never before been contained in tables."[24]

Becher sought to consolidate his place at court by making his mechanical projects relevant to the *praxis* that occupied the prince in the governing of his territory. He considered his interests and abilities in alchemy and mechanics to be associated with three larger areas of knowledge: *oeconomia*, medicine, and mathematics.

Before he came to the court, he had considered *oeconomia* as a sphere for his actions. *Oeconomia*, along with politics and ethics, was one of the three parts of Aristotle's practical sphere of "things done," and concerned the provenancing and support of a household, and by extension, a *polis*. In the seventeenth century, *oeconomia* had been incorporated into the genre of the *Hausvaterbuch*, tracts of rural household management for the paterfamilias. In these works, the rural landholder headed a household engaged in a self-sustaining cycle of production and consumption. He was responsible for every aspect of the running of the household, watching over the material, physical, and spiritual welfare of the members of his house; a "kleiner König" in his own house and lands.[25] A manuscript work marked Vienna 1657 and entitled "Tractatus Au-

---

[24] In 1662, Becher requested an imperial privilege for "Mel Scientiarum, omnium fere Doctrinarum Tabulas Methodicas exhibens" and for "Tabulae Juris Puplici [*sic*], seu loci communes Recessuum S. Rom. Imperii." Vienna, Haus-, Hof- und Staatsarchiv, Impressoria, Karton 45. The draft of the letter to the elector: Mss. var. 1(1), fol. 4r. In it Becher asks for a special privilege from the Mainz officials to protect his Compendium of the recesses of the Reichstag. Other tables of knowledge extant in Becher's *Nachlaß*: a system of knowledge about the cosmos in outline form, Mss. var. 1(1), fols. 729r–730r; a "Systema Generale Supra Alveare Juridicum," Mss. var. 1(1), fols. 23r and 682r–683r; and a "Idea Juris Feudalis," Mss. var. 1(1), fols. 24r–25r; an outline for a definition of "cognitio historica," Mss. var. 1(1), fol. 40r; and, the most comprehensive, Mss. var. 1(1), fols. 643v–544r, "Bilanx Aurea," discussed later.

Becher's tables are often arranged "ornamentally," for example, an elaborate chart on the generation, ennoblement, and medicinal preparation of natural bodies in Mss. var. 1(1), fol. 244r; and the tables on grammar, medicine, and the description and cure of gangrene in the form of branching trees in Mss. var. 1(1), fols. 251r–264r. The most elaborate tables are in Mss. var. 1(1), fols. 274r–316r, entitled "Signaturarum Medicinalium," about the nature and virtues of bodies in the three realms of nature. The entire work is an extremely complex effort to correlate (by means of lists of numbers) parts of animals, vegetables, and minerals, medicinal preparations from them, and their applications. Each part, preparation, and application is numbered, then these numbers are arranged in charts; however, without a key to the entire work, they are incomprehensible. These tables may well have been intended as memory schemes; one is particularly reminded of the Lullian memory charts arranged in the form of branching trees. The importance of memory schemes as a means to organize a single subject or all of knowledge continued in significance in court culture, where oral presentation and spoken wit was important (especially to the projector presenting his schemes before the prince).

[25] This phrase is taken from the Vorrede of Becher's *Kluger Hauß-Vater/ verständige Hauß-Mutter/ vollkommner Land-Medicus* (Leipzig: Friedrich Groschuff, 1698). The view of the noble court as primarily a family household continued into the seventeenth century even as the court moved off the land and into the city of residence. This can be clearly discerned in sixteenth- and

reus" or "Bilanx aurea de vera hominis Felicitate seu vade mecum per quod-
quilibet Homo" (The golden balance, concerning the true happiness of man, or
a vade mecum for everyman) displays Becher's view of the place of *oeconomia*
in the organization of knowledge, as well as his own ambitions within the
learned sphere.[26] In one of his ubiquitous tables, Becher divided all knowledge
in terms of the pursuit of four ends: "Requieta conscientia," "Requieta fama,"
"Requieta sanitate," and "Requieta alimentatione." Corresponding to each of
these four theoretical goals was a practice: "Opus theologicum," "Opus poli-
ticum," "Opus medicinae," and "Opus oeconomicum." Becher's desire to comprehend personally all four parts of knowledge is made clear in his placement of
his initials under each of the four columns in the table: J.J.B.S., Johannes
Joachim Becher Spirensis.

Theological practice consisted in meditation on the true theology, the teach-
ings of right theology, the correct prayers, and the means of avoiding sin.[27] The
practice of politics was the acquiring and retaining of "fam[a] & honest[um]
nom[en]."[28] Medicine consisted in understanding the three kingdoms of
nature—animal, vegetable, and mineral—and in knowing how to distill medicines from these three realms. *Oeconomia*, which consisted in "certo victu &
alimentatione," encompassed all theory and practice of the other three areas of
knowledge: it included chronology (the keeping of a "calendario vitae" in
which all things were noted), correct record keeping, proper private and public
contractual arrangements, and the "Speculatio de victu," which encompassed
"res philologicas & theologicas, mathematicas & mechanicas, politicas & mil-
itares, philosophicas, medicinales & alchymias." Finally, "Praxis in victu," the
last part of the practice of *oeconomia*, involved the means of acquiring livelihood and wealth, which, besides maintaining life, would also sustain the pursuit of all the arts listed as part of the speculation about acquiring sustenance.[29]

---

seventeenth-century *Hofordnungen*. See examples in Arthur Kern, ed., *Deutsche Hofordnungen
des 16. und 17. Jahrhunderts*, 2 vols., (Berlin: Weidmannsche Buchhandlung, 1907). The standard
introduction to the *Hausvater* literature is Otto Brunner, *Adeliges Landleben und europäische
Geist. Leben und Werk Wolf Helmhards von Hohberg, 1612–1688* (Salzburg: Otto Müller, 1949).

[26] This draft manuscript takes up fols. 592r–650r of Mss. var. 2. A chart, dated 1658, setting out
the topics which make up the manuscript's chapters is found in Mss. var. 1(1), fols. 643v–644r.

[27] Mss. var. 2, fols. 610r–619r.

[28] The manuscript for this section is Mss. var. 2, fols. 620r–624r, and the topics are set out in
Mss. var. 1(1), fol. 643v. For example, the acquisition of reputation (*fama*) is through nobility of
the blood, nobility of the hand (ennoblement), nobility "extra natura," and "nobilitas civilis."
Conservation of one's honest name is achieved by observation, such as in acquiring privileges and
testimonies, and by demonstration and exhibition. The third important component of acquiring
reputation is "Annotatione Familiae"—recognizing consanguinity, keeping genealogical charts,
and observing the characteristics of the family members. The fourth requisite of *fama* was a
"politica moralis," but this is not developed.

[29] A clear statement of the "Opus oeconomicum" in the chart is on fol. 644r of Mss. var. 1(1).
The binding of Mss. var. 2 makes the manuscript version of this section, located on fols. 641v–
644v, almost illegible, while the end of this section becomes merely a hasty outline.

Thus *oeconomia*—the running of the household—encompassed all theoretical and practical knowledge, and Becher's activities as alchemist, mechanic, mathematician, and medical doctor were relevant to the household of the prince and its provisioning.

In 1662 Becher applied for a privilege of ten years to publish a work entitled *Oeconomia ruralis et domestica viginti libris absoluta*.[30] The topics of this book survive in manuscript, and they too attest to Becher's vision of *oeconomia* as encompassing all knowledge.[31] The practice of the *Hauß* included religious knowledge and duties as well as a mundane command of real and movable possessions. It comprehended knowledge of the three realms of nature and expertise in drawing human sustenance from them. Arithmetic, reading, and writing also played a role in administering the house, as did an ability to maintain correct social relations both in and outside the house. The *Hausvater* must also have familiarity with the lessons of history as well as competency in philosophy and the knowledge of natural things. Finally, the *Hausvater* must be able to construct a calendar in order to reckon the time.[32] Becher, however, did not publish this projected work, for by 1662 he had changed his tack and moved to a more conventional strategy of establishing himself at court, a strategy that he perhaps perceived to be more relevant to the environment of the noble court at which he resided: he became a doctor of medicine.

Medicine had always included an element of practice, but after Paracelsus had elevated the status of the barber-surgeon's practice, all manner of practitioners began to call themselves doctors of medicine, and medicine became more than ever associated with practice. Moreover, doctors of medicine had

[30] Becher made at least two petitions from Mainz to Emperor Leopold in 1662. The privilege was granted in 1663. Vienna, Haus-, Hof-, und Staatsarchiv, Impressoria, Karton 45.

[31] Mss. var. 1(1), fol. 11r–v, entitled *Oeconomia perfecta ruralis & domestica daß ist Bechers Grosses [Maintzisches] Hauß Buch*. In 1685, a work entitled *Volkommene Ross- und Vieh-Apotheck*, ostensibly by Becher appeared, and in 1698 a work was published entitled *Kluger Hauß-Vater/ verständige Hauß-Mutter/ vollkommner Land-Medicus, wie auch wohlerfahrner Roß- und Viehe-Artzt/ nebst einem deutlichen und gewissen Handgriff die Haußhaltungs-Kunst innerhalb 24. Stunden zu erlernen/ also/ daß man mit Ersparhrung grosser Unkosten solche Nahrung glücklich fortsetzen/ sich vor Kranckheiten praeserviren/ auch vermittelst eines geringen Capitals von 364. Thlr. jährlichen mit guten Gewissen und ohne schändlichen Wucher 1000. Thlr. profitiren könne*. The chapters of the published work do not correspond to the twenty topics of the manuscript, and it cannot be determined whether the Leipzig publisher had access to Becher's drafts for the book (if these in fact existed), and, if he did, whether the finished book was faithful to those drafts. The work may be by Sturm. Otto Brunner printed the manuscript version in "Johann Joachim Bechers Entwurf einer 'Oeconomia ruralis et domestica,'" *Sitzungsberichte der österreichischen Akademie der Wissenschaften* 226, pt. 3 (1949): 85–91.

[32] While this work was written with the *cameralia* of the prince or landholder in mind, Becher began to see these as connected with *commercia*. Becher's house is no longer a self-sufficient agrarian whole, but takes account of the market of the city also. This is Brunner's view in "Entwurf," pp. 88–89.

always been a fixture at noble courts.[33] Still hard at work at the organization of knowledge, Becher produced yet another list of topics, in which he placed medicine midway between the spheres of *theoria* and *praxis*: the knowledge of scholars and the knowledge of the active human domain. He gave medicine a place after philology, mathematics, *physica* and *chymica*, but before *oeconomia, commercia, cameralia, politica,* and *moralia*.[34] Medicine became a way in which Becher could join theory and practice and draw them both into the realms of *praxis*.

Settling at the Noble Court: Joining Practice to Theory

When Becher was called to the court in Mainz, he continued his mechanical pursuits and considered how they might fit into the larger sphere of the elector's activities, but he also initiated a broader series of activities that gave him a new status both at court, as a man of theory, and within the republic of letters, as a member of an accepted profession.

Becher believed that theory and practice were inextricably linked; however, because theory was the fundament of practice, it must precede practical activity. In 1661 Becher began to build the theoretical foundations for his practical actions. He considered philology to be the basis for all theoretical learning, and in 1661 he published a system of universal language, which would allow people without a common tongue to converse in hieroglyphics.[35] In the same year, he published an (al)chemical work that he claimed was not simply another book of chemical recipes but rather an integrated work of theory and practice— "rationes" and "experimenta." In this work he established his notion of the precedence of theory over practice.[36] These two works began twenty-one years of polymathic publications in which Becher was always careful to unite theory to practice, as well as to assert the primacy of theory over practice.[37]

The most significant consolidation of Becher's position at court and within

---

[33] See Vivian Nutton, ed., *Medicine at the Courts of Europe, 1500–1837* (London and New York: Routledge, 1990).

[34] Mss. var. 1(1), fol. 731r–v.

[35] *Character pro Notitia Linguarum Universali.*

[36] *Natur-Kündigung*, Vorrede, v recto, and pp. 70, 262.

[37] In his chemical and political works Becher returned again and again to the importance of unifying theory and practice. In the *Politischer Discurs*, the first part of the book makes up the theory of society and political rule, and the second part is composed of the documents, letters, and treatises that he had produced in the practice of commerce. The *Physica Subterranea* was a work of theory in which the principles of subterranean processes (in the laboratory of nature) were explicated, and his three supplements (1671, 1675, 1680) were the practical demonstration of these processes in the chemical laboratory.

the republic of scholars came in 1661 when he was officially inducted into the profession of medicine. After doctoral examinations and a public disputation on epilepsy, he was awarded the title of doctor of medicine from the university in Mainz. His inaugural address upon admittance to the faculty of medicine was on the reality of the philosophers' stone.[38] In the next years he published works on chemistry and medicine, saw patients connected to the elector's court, and participated in the duties of the medical faculty.[39] In 1662, he married Maria Veronika,[40] the daughter of Ludwig von Hörnigk, counselor to the elector and to the emperor, doctor of both laws and senior professor on the faculty of medicine. The important witnesses to the marriage show how Becher, then twenty-seven, had succeeded up to that point.[41] Becher's favored position at the elector's court must have been as important to the university faculty of medicine as the scholarly position on the faculty was important to Becher's consolidation of his own authority. In 1663 Becher took over his father-in-law's position as *Professor publicus et ordinarius* on a temporary basis.[42] Maria Veronika, who provided Becher with his entry into the world of theory, would for the rest of her life be concerned with the practical details of Becher's moves, caring for their

[38] "An Lapis Philosophicus sit arte parabilis" defended the possibility of transmutation. This lecture is mentioned in the protocol of Becher's *Doctorexamen* in the Protokollbuch der Mainzischen medizinischer Fakultät 18/160, 19 September 1661, in the Mainz Stadtarchiv, fol. 83. In Mss. var. 2, fols. 86r–89v, there is a lecture of this title in Becher's hand dated 6 July 1661.

[39] The texts were *Panegyricus Atlanti Medico, seu Magno Lexico Medico D. Ludovici de Hornigk* (Frankfurt: Serlin, 1662); *Parnassus Medicinalis Illustratus* (Ulm: Joh. Görlin, 1662–63); and *Aphorismi ex Institutionibus Medicis Sennerti* (Frankfurt: Balthasar-Christ. Wust, 1663) dedicated to his two superiors on the faculty at the university. A manuscript list of patients he cured in Würzburg, Mss. var. 2, fol. 278v, includes noble members of the court as well as cooks, soldiers, musicians, and court gypsies. There is also a prescription for "Hr. Khrauters frau," dated 20 September 1662, Mss. var. 2, fol. 265r. From 28 November 1661 Becher began participating in the activities of the medical faculty at the university, taking part in regulating the activities of doctors with university degrees, barbers, and other practitioners, and he represented the faculty in petitions to the elector. Becher also presided over qualifying disputations. The text of one of these, "Disputatio Medica de pharmacorum qualitatibus, praeparationibus, Dosibus et usu" by Henricus Diephauß, with Becher listed as presiding professor in 1663, is in Mss. var. 2, fols. 90r–93v. A published version exists in the British Library 1185.c.4. The Protokollbuch der Mainzischen Medizinischer Fakultät, Mainz Stadtarchiv, p. 101, lists two students promoted to the doctoral degree by Becher and von Hohenstatt. For a complete account of his activities, see Heinrich Schrohe, "Johann Joachim Becher in Mainz," *Zeitschrift für die Geschichte des Oberrheins*, n.s., 42 (1929): 444–50.

[40] Maria Veronika, probably born in 1642, was a daughter of Ludwig von Hörnigk's second marriage, and one of his sixteen children who lived to adulthood.

[41] Domscholast Karl Heinrich von Metternich-Beilstein and Winneburg would later become rector of the university and, in 1679, elector of Mainz. Heinrich Freiherr Brömser von Rüdesheim was *Vizedominus*. (See Schrohe, "Becher," p. 448.) The presence of these electoral representatives at the marriage points up well the unification of electoral and university interests in Mainz.

[42] See Schrohe, "Becher," pp. 446–48. After Becher became an ordinary professor he gave lectures on the *Institutiones Medicinae*. The lectures were in the form of explanation and dictation.

children, and fetching his arrears of salary when he became persona non grata with a noble patron.[43]

Becher meanwhile, having established his right to speak both within the realm of theory and of practice, turned back to the problem of his activities' relevance to the sphere of politics. In one of his first lectures as professor of medicine, he took pains to establish that medicine was a necessary part of statecraft.[44] Repeatedly after 1661, Becher called upon his profession of medical doctor to establish his right to speak at court in matters that rightfully belonged to the sphere of politics:

> I look at my profession, and my published writings show that I am a medical doctor. Here the question arises again, what have I to do with political affairs, like Saul among the Prophets? In short, I have not lacked knowledge of the material in these matters so much as a reason to approach this material. But this reason lies in the general rule, "salus populi suprema lex esto" [health or welfare of the people shall be the supreme law].[45]

Becher transferred the commonplace "salus populi suprema lex esto" from politics to his profession as medical doctor and the concern he must have for the health (*salus*) of his patients. He then transferred the adage back to the political sphere and, in this way, justified his political concerns with the welfare of the body politic.[46] This phrase thus provided an entry point from medicine into political *praxis*.

[43] Maria Veronika collected Becher's arrears in Vienna and Güstrow (Christian Philipp to Leibniz, 2/12 July 1679, Gottfried Wilhelm Leibniz, *Sämtliche Schriften und Briefe*, ed. Preussische Akademie der Wissenschaften et al. [Darmstadt: Otto Reichl et al., 1923–], ser. 1, vol. 2, p. 496), but she was left without livelihood after his death. Her fate is made clear in a letter from 1688 that her brother, Philipp Wilhelm von Hörnigk, wrote to Leibniz. This letter tells us that Maria Veronika was in Würzburg, while one of her sons was in the workhouse in Munich, and the youngest was in Vienna. Von Hörnigk seems to have been giving some financial support to Maria Veronika and the youngest son; however, he says that he had promised his sister that if she came to him in Regensburg, he "would send her forth with his feet." In this letter, Hörnigk makes amply evident his feeling that Becher's family had not shown proper gratitude to him for his aid. Leibniz, *Sämtliche Schriften*, ser. 1, vol. 5, p. 110.

[44] A general introductory lecture (undated) in Latin by Becher, Mss. var. 2, fols. 82r–85v, establishes that medicine is essential to the common welfare as part of the necessary defenses of a land. At the conclusion of the lecture, Becher announces that his lectures on the "*Institutiones Medicinae juxta Veteres & Neotericos*" will be given succinctly in aphorisms with commentary "*ad calamum*" (for writing down). He "will dictate and hold forth at 7 o'clock Tuesdays and Fridays."

[45] *Politischer Discurs*, 2d ed. (1688; facs. repr. Glashütten in Taunus: Verlag Detler Auvermann, 1972), p. 300.

[46] The source of this commonplace was Cicero, *De legibus* 3.3.8: "His salus populi suprema lex esto" (i.e., [for the rulers of countries] the welfare of the people shall be the supreme law). The use of this political commonplace by medical doctors was by no means unusual. Before Becher, Christoph Besoldus (1577–1638) and Hermann Conring (1606–81) had justified their writings with just this phrase. On the use of this phrase, see Jutta Brückner, *Staatswissenschaften, Kameralismus*

Becher's medical degree and position within a medical faculty gave him authority in the republic of scholars and improved his position as *Hofmedicus* at court. His connections to the world of *theoria* also gave him status and power in the world of *hofbefreite* artisans, mechanics, and purveyors whence he had lately emerged. Medicine also made possible and justified his entry into the world of *praxis* and the political concerns of his patron, and his ability to enter into this sphere carried him along in his venture to become indispensable to the holders of power.

After 1661, Becher needed this improved status at court in order to carry out a new order of activities, one that was within the sphere of *praxis* but without precedent at the court in Mainz. Sometime after 1661, Becher moved back to the world of *ars*, now no longer attempting to "sell" his machine and his knowledge to patrons, but instead seeking to organize and reorder this world. Becher began to enter into the transactions of commerce, not as a participant, but as a director: two years after his call to the court in Mainz, Becher and the cathedral canon in Mainz, Dietrich Kaspar von Fürstenberg, requested a privilege from the elector of Mainz to found a company that would "set up . . . and introduce trade, manufactures, millworks and other things that pertain to the prosperity and use of our city-state."[47] The purpose and guiding idea of this company was to be "Salus civium suprema lex esto."[48] Becher here used this maxim to provide an entry into commerce. For Becher, commerce would become closely associated both with the oeconomy of the court and the ability of the territorial ruler to retain power. The household of the ruler ordinarily sustained itself from the income of the ruler's lands. This was the domain of *cameralia*, to which *commercia* was external. Becher sought to draw commerce into treasury matters (*cameralia*) and transform it into an ordinary source of revenue.[49] Treasury officials would regard such an attempt with skepticism, and Becher would resort even to alchemy to bring about his plans. That, however, lay in the future. To effect his commercial projects in Mainz, Becher needed access to greater numbers of artisans—the holders of productive knowledge—and so he moved back into contact with the world of *ars*, but by

---

und Naturrecht (Munich: C. H. Beck, 1977), p. 35; Wilhelm Kühlmann, *Gelehrtenrepublik und Fürstenstaat* (Tübingen: Max Niemeyer Verlag, 1982), pp. 69ff.; and Michael Stolleis, ed., *Hermann Conring (1606–1681). Beiträge zu Leben und Werke* (Berlin: Duncker & Humblot, 1983). Becher listed Conring, as well as Julius Caesar Scaliger and Hieronymus Cardanus, as doctors of medicine, who like him had treated politics (*Politischer Discurs*, 2d ed. p. 301).

[47] "auf das auffnehmen undt nutzen unserer Statt sehen, handel Wandel, manufacturen, Mühlwercke und andere sachen . . . anzurichten und . . . einzuführen." A draft of the petition in Mss. var. 1(3), fols. 204r–207 is undated, but Hassinger, *Becher*, p. 22, dates it after 1661.

[48] Mss. var. 1(3), fol. 206r.

[49] In a list of topics—*philologica, mathematica, physica, chymica, medica, oeconomia, commercia, cameralia, politica, moralia*—Becher had at first written "Cameralia" then crossed it out and substituted "Commercia." While this might be no more than a mistake, it may indicate how closely related *commercia* and *cameralia* were in Becher's mind. Mss. var. 1(1), fol. 731r–v.

now he had a new status and a new desire to differentiate himself from the purveyors whom he hoped to induce to "discover themselves."

Settling at the Noble Court: Mediating between Practice and *Praxis*

So ist leichtlich zu erachten dass sich berührtes Salarium auff
solche last nicht proportionire, die Zeit solche hauptsachen zu
verrichten zu kurtz falle, die propositionen auch an sich selbst so
weitt aussehent seyn, dass sie, wo man auch gleich den besten
fleiß anwendete könnten disputirt, und ich, zumahlen zwischen
den Verlegern und Ewer Churfürstl. Durchläucht etwan nicht
allzeit ein Vergleich getroffen werden könnte, gleichwohl in
meinem Vornehmen verhindert, undt also in gefahr undt
ungelegenheit gesetzt würde.

Thus it is easily recognized that the salary mentioned is not in
proportion to the burden, the time is too short to effect such
important projects, the propositions themselves are so broad that,
even if one applied the best industriousness, they could be
disputed, and for myself, especially when an agreement between
the Verlegern and Your Electoral Highness could not be made,
would be hindered in my plans and set in danger and
disadvantage.
(Becher to Elector Karl Ludwig of the Palatinate, ca. 1664)

Becher became an intermediary between the court and artisans—between *praxis* and practice. This position "between the Verlegern and Your Electoral Highness"[50] could often be uncomfortable, even dangerous, but it made him particularly valuable to the court. By following the development of his position as intermediary from the early 1660s until 1671, it is possible to see how he shaped that position in such a way as to distinguish himself from the artisans and purveyors.

Much evidence survives of the manner in which Becher built up these connections. He collected interesting recipes, wrote letters to individuals who might provide him with ideas, and asked for news of curiosities from his

---

[50] While in this passage Becher addresses the elector of the Palatinate, his strategy in Mainz and at the Bavarian court would be the same. Copy of letter from Becher to Elector Karl Ludwig, Mss. var. 1(3), fol. 209v. Just before leaving Mainz, Becher attempted to reach an agreement with Elector Karl Ludwig to assume the position of counselor and director of a *Vorsteheramt* that Becher wanted to establish in order to police civic affairs and implement commercial schemes in the elector's newly created city of Mannheim. An agreement was not reached, but Becher printed two documents concerned with these negotiations in *Politischer Discurs*, 2d ed., pp. 437–41.

correspondents.[51] One activity natural to his position as physician was the collection of alchemical processes. Becher composed at least one contract between the elector and a certain Monsieur Colonel Boon for an augmentation process that was to increase four thousand ducats worth of gold by 5 percent weekly. The elector promised to allow Colonel Boon to coin the four thousand ducats worth of 23.5 karat gold weekly, and the colonel obligated himself to pay the Mint warden "one ducat for each hundred weekly," thus forty ducats weekly, or 20 percent of his gross profit. Boon claimed that he could produce such a profit on the gold through "true alchemical augmentation," and the four thousand ducats worth of gold, although continually recoined, would never decrease. The Mint was to supply the gold and pay Boon's expenses for a year. In the first six months of that time, Colonel Boon was obligated to teach the elector the art of augmentation, both orally and in writing, until the elector could carry out the process in the absence of the colonel with any amount of gold he desired. At the end of the year, if the process had proved to be a genuine alchemical augmentation that increased the gold by the promised amount, and if Boon had successfully taught the process to the elector, he would receive three thousand ducats reward.[52]

Becher's position as intermediary between the worlds of theory, practice, and

[51] A recipe Becher received from a Spanish doctor in Vienna who claimed that it was a prescription used by the empress Margarita (Leopold married his niece Margarita of the Spanish Habsburg line in 1666), called for 100 pounds of cacao and 200 "Baynillas" (presumably vanilla beans). Mss. var. 1(2), fol. 603r. There are several lists of machines and mills in the *Nachlaß* (e.g., Mss. var. 2, fols. 358r–359v). Becher collected a printed pamphlet by Geo. Christoph Werner on waterworks (*Natur- und Kunstgemässe Vereinigung deß Leichten mit dem Schweren/ & Vice Versa*, Augsburg, 1670), and wrote to Werner presumably asking for information. Becher's letter does not survive, but the reply from Wolfgang Schätz, Apothecary, informs Becher that Werner died three years previously and nothing remains of his machine models. Mss. var. 2, fols. 437r–445v, 447r–v. Becher asked an Italian correspondent to send him a pound of Italian sulfur and a pound of English lead, along with the prices. He also desired to know the frequency and prices of iron and other metals in Italy. Mss. var. 1(1), fol. 733r–v. Becher's activity appears to be much closer to industrial espionage than to the gift exchanges of natural philosophers described by Paula Findlen, "The Economy of Scientific Exchange in Early Modern Italy," in *Patronage and Institutions: Science, Technology, and Medicine at the European Court, 1500–1750*, ed. Bruce Moran (Woodbridge, Suffolk: Boydell, 1991), 5–24.

[52] Mss. var. 1(3), fols. 184r–185v, contains drafts for three contracts with Colonel Boon; one a general contract, one a specific contract specifying the characteristics that the augmented gold must have, and one setting out the conditions for teaching the elector the process. Colonel Boon is named as "Herr Obrister" in the third contract, and, in sections of the second contract the amount of augmentation is changed from 5 percent to 4 percent. The draft contracts are couched in straightforward legal language. The text of the first contract (fol. 184r) provides an example of this: "Es will Monsieur Colonell Boon die Müntz wochentlich auff sein kosten mit Vier tausend ducaten capitel avanciren undt auff approbation des Wardeins ducaten 23½ karat fein ad 71 ass Müntzen lassen, auch vor jedes hundert wochentlich ihr Churfürstl. Gnaden einen geben, den soll der Müntzmeister also bald erhalten auch alle unkosten bezahlen, undt solchen ein jahr continuiren, wie gesagt auff sein kosten undt des Wardeins gefahr, durch das vorgesetze augment. de dato aber des anfangs will er sich obligiren, innerhalb sex monath Ihr. Churfürstl. Gnaden die Kunst zu lehren, undt will

praxis is illustrated in the journals that he kept while on trips to Holland in the service of his different patrons. His first trip took place early in 1660 in Elector Johann Philipp von Schönborn's service. Becher made a number of contracts with artisans and produced a list of his activities with notes on the ingenious machines and processes he saw in Holland. He contracted with a Jacob Godfried of Amsterdam to teach the representative of the elector of Mainz (i.e., himself) the art and science of making saltpeter,[53] with a bellmaker to make a "Zymbalwerk" of several different-sized bells,[54] and with a "Plaats-Snyder" to print Becher's description and illustration of his perpetuum mobile.[55] Becher brought word of several artisans who desired to work for the elector. One, a Swede who had made a "mechanical structure of the entire human body with all its nerves, veins and arteries," which Becher saw in the university at Leiden, offered his art to the Elector for the use of the university at Mainz and in order to do away with the necessity of human anatomies in the medical faculty. Another "Mechanicus" offered to produce a clock for the elector similar to the "precious astronomical clock" that he had made for the duke of Holstein. A man from The Hague promised to teach the elector orally a special art of making pearls, and another promised to show Johann Philipp a divining rod for finding ores ("ertzseiger"). Becher also met with Johann Rudolf Glauber, a German chemist and apothecary living in Amsterdam, and obtained the preparation for his *sal mirabile* and a process for separating gold and silver from copper by means of a "spiritus salis Urina." Becher spoke about brandy making and firearms to another contact, and he ended his list of contacts with the coda: "obtained many other wonderful secrets and thoughts from one and another."[56]

Instead of schemes for the organization of knowledge, Becher's papers from this period are filled with lists of contacts and recipes, testimony to his continuing collecting and networking. In 1664, while traveling to Holland and Brabant to find shareholders and artisans for the silk manufactory and to negotiate the

---

solche wieder auff sex Monath prob gewesen, begehrt als dann 3000 ducaten undt will weither, an dis Werck keinen anspruch mehr haben."

[53] A notarized contract between Becher and Jacob Godfried van Gersdorp, dated Amsterdam 30 January 1660, in Mss. var. 1(3), fol. 193r–v.

[54] Notarized contract between Becher and François Hemoni, Glockengiesser, dated 31 January 1660, in Mss. var. 1(3), fol. 195r–v. A notarized statement dated 15 May 1660 from Jacobus van Noort, organist, Salomon Verbeeck, bell ringer, and Michiel Nouts, bell ringer, attested that the *Glockenspiel* was of good quality and sound (Mss. var. 1(3), fol. 199r–v). Hemoni was a famous French bell maker, whose method of tuning bells is described by Philipp von Zesen, *Beschreibung der Stadt Amsterdam* (Amsterdam: Joachim Nosch, 1664), pp. 206–7. Von Zesen wrote that besides his tuning methods, Hemoni had invented a new "plaything," similar to the modern xylophone.

[55] A notarized contract between Becher and Theodorus Matham, dated 3 February 1660, in Mss. var. 1(3), fol. 197r.

[56] In a list entitled "Pro principe Expeditio Hollandica" in Mss. var. 1(3), fol. 201r–v. Glauber also told Becher of his forthcoming book, which, according to Becher's list, was *Ewig wehrendes Bergwerck*.

acquisition of a colony,[57] Becher made a list of several things to do, among them to ask Glauber about his saltpeter process and about when Robert Boyle's "experimenta" might appear. On this trip he was charged with commissions all along his route. He looked up an Italian glassmaker on the way through Mainz, met with his publisher in Frankfurt, bought Virginian tobacco, and visited a gunsmith in Utrecht.[58] He obtained "some white, milky glasses . . . as well as some smooth crystal drinking glasses" for his patron in Munich, the count von Fürstenberg.[59] He collected testimonials and references from various artisans. He brought back to the electoress a letter from a "Haussfrau" who claimed to be able to make lace, artificial flowers, and embroider with gold and silver. She supported her family alone, her husband having left with forty thousand guilders because her daughter had converted to Catholicism. She assured the Catholic elector that her younger daughter was not yet either Catholic or Calvinist.[60] While in Munich, Becher also took written notes on different processes described to him by artisans, one for example, from a master soapmaker.[61]

[57] Becher had prepared his journey in advance by correspondence with a contact person in the Netherlands. In his letter, Becher explained the purpose and structure of the company, which was mainly to do business in woven textiles, and tried to excite interest in it by providing a glowing description of the geography and economic situation of Bavaria (*Politischer Discurs*, 2d ed., pp. 392–402). Evidence of preparation for the trip is found in the *Extra-ordinarii Post-Zeitung* of 14 September 1664, in which a short notice under the byline Brabant announced that a Bavarian electoral minister was staying at Antwerp with orders to transact with merchants in order that trade be improved in Bavaria. (This number of the newspaper is bound into Mss. var. 1(3) and paginated as fol. 222v. In the margin there is a handwritten notation marking this particular announcement.)

[58] A list on Mss. var. 1(3), fol. 237r.

[59] This list directly precedes the notes for the 1660 trip in Mss. var. 1(3), fol. 192r, but I believe it properly belongs with the 1664 journal in Mss. var. 1(3), fols. 223r–249r. The 1664 journal makes fascinating reading, made more gripping by the fact that Becher was very concerned about the plague raging at that time in the provinces of Holland and Brabant. He reports that he had heard no one was being allowed into Brabant, but decided nevertheless to head first for Antwerp. He procured a "Fide de Sanita" for himself in Cologne to carry with him, bought medicaments to use against the plague, and took the expensive step of renting a private room on the ship to Antwerp (fol. 223r). While traveling from Brabant to Holland, his ship had to be inspected before it landed in The Hague, and so Becher hired a private boat to take him the rest of the distance to Rotterdam (fol. 223v). Once there, he found his contacts had retired to the countryside (fol. 224r), and so he hired a private wagon to Utrecht "because it is so dangerous in the ships by reason of the number of people and the worry of infection" (fol. 224r).

[60] Mss. var. 1(3), fol. 244r. In order to receive employment in Bavaria, it was necessary to belong to the Catholic church or at least make a statement to the effect that the possibility of conversion was not precluded. Ludwig Hüttl, *Caspar von Schmid (1622–1693), ein kurbayerischer Staatsmann aus dem Zeitalter Ludwigs XIV* (Munich: Kommissionsbuchhandlung R. Wölfle, 1971), p. 17. According to Merry E. Wiesner, *Working Women in Renaissance Germany* (New Brunswick, N.J.: Rutgers University Press, 1986), p. 20, if a man left his family for religious reasons, city authorities were somewhat more forthcoming with aid for the remaining wife and family.

[61] "Aussage M. Thomae Balts Seiffensieder in der ledergassen beym häring dem Weißgärber," Mss. var. 1(2), fol. 605r–v. This document, partially illegible due to the binding of the *Nachlaß*,

A particularly vivid example of this activity as intermediary appears in the draft of a contract from 1664, instructing Johann Daniel Crafft[62] in the investigation of a "secret" that Becher undertook for the elector. Becher instructed Crafft that he would find the individual with the secret, a lackey, in a particular tavern where he would be waiting under the assumed name of Nicolaus Veit. Crafft was to ask Veit a series of questions, which would better establish his identity. After this, Crafft and Veit were to leave the tavern, and Becher specified that only when they got outside was Crafft to ask three more identifying questions: (1) What was the name of the tavern run by his relatives in Frankfurt where Becher and he had often gone? He was to answer, "Schwartzer Bock." (2) What was the name of his friend, the medical doctor in Frankfurt? He was to answer Gerhard Thilenius or Thilen. (3) What was the name of the secretary in Mainz where he had his mail sent? He was to answer Günther. If Veit answered correctly, Crafft was to have him sign a contract agreeing to use one hundred ducats given him by Crafft to investigate the "secret." If the secret turned out to be useless or false, he was to return the one hundred ducats (in cash!), but if it was successful, Veit was personally to communicate it to the elector, for which he would be rewarded.[63]

Over time, Becher established himself as an indispensable intermediary at court, and during this time he also transformed traditional court posts into positions from which his own program could be carried out. As he had brought his own position as *Hofmedicus* to encompass politics, he also redefined the duties of other established court positions. For example, Becher extended the duties of a weekly correspondent to the court, Joannes Müller of Antorff in Holland, to cover the collection of commercial information, in addition to the traditional political events. Becher helped Müller write a petition to the elector of Bavaria in which Müller asked that his position of weekly correspondent and intelligence gatherer for the elector be made official and titled "Factor" (agent). In this petition, he promises to report to the elector on "ordinary things," "secret things," "and also commerce." Becher then provided a specific list for Müller as to what the reports on commerce should contain: "1. Cameral subjects from Paris, Spain, England, and the Lowlands; 2. Cargo from Holland; 3. Price of goods in Antwerp; 4. All sorts of manufactures and manufacturers; 5. Becher's

---

seems to be a complaint about the lack of a guild in Munich, and also contains a recipe for soap and a calculation of prices for raw materials and the finished soap.

[62] Johann Daniel Crafft is an intriguing and ubiquitous figure in the German Empire in the seventeenth century, most visible now in his correspondence with Leibniz. He is virtually unknown today because he published nothing (a single anonymous work is attributed to him). He seems to have been a constant rival/intermediary for Becher, very useful, but likely to steal the whole project. He was a medical doctor, like Becher, and had traveled extensively in the New World. Biographical information is scarce and to be found only in the article in the *Neue deutsche Biographie*, and Rudolf Forberger, "Johann Daniel Crafft. Notizen zu einer Biographie (1624 bis 1697)," *Jahrbuch für Wirtschaftsgeschichte*, pts. 2–3 (1964): 63–79.

[63] Mss. var. 1(3), fol. 220r–v.

proposition concerning a certain project."[64] The court intelligencer has here been transformed into a commercial agent. By such transformations, Becher drew a net of workers around his own position at court.

By the mid-1660s, when he had moved to the court in Bavaria, Becher called himself a *Commissarius*, modeling his position on that of the independent adjudicator called in to advise the ruler.[65] While Becher continued to collect information from contacts and act as *Commissarius* at the Habsburg court in Vienna, his program to refurbish established court positions becomes even more marked.[66] This emerges clearly in a set of instructions probably written by Becher for a representative of the emperor in England in 1674. The instructions commanded the envoy to report on English flora, fauna, processes, and political customs. He should take note of new or unusual animals such as sheep, goats, birds, and particularly of the Gloucester oysters and the silken, long-haired goats. He is ordered to send samples of New World plants such as winter sugarcane, recipes for the making of white lead (*Bleiweiß*), red mercury sulphide (*Zinnober*), French verdigris, and English glass and mirrors. The instructions commanded him to send information on all interesting manufacturing techniques, instruments, and inventions, as well as the laws by which the English "further their commerce and manufactures." He must report on prices, opportunities for trade with the Habsburg lands, new books, and propositions made to parliament about commerce. Lastly he should send information on the Royal Society, especially any alchemical processes, as well as the Philosophical Transactions (the "ephemerides Anglicanas").[67]

Through an adroit handling of opportunities and a conscious program of

[64] Mss. var. 1(3), fols. 242r–243r.

[65] In this position, Becher claimed to have examined the universal language scheme of Bengt Skytte, a Swede who arrived in Munich (*Politischer Discurs*, 2d ed., p. 1104), and a chemical process from Johann Rudolph Glauber. Such a position, Becher asserted, brought him great ill will. (*Chymisches Laboratorium*, Vorrede, b3v.) The position of *Commissarius* was ideal for such mobile outsiders as Becher at the noble court. For a discussion of the wider significance of this position, see Otto Hintze, "Der Commissarius und seine Bedeutung in der allgemeinen Verwaltungsgeschichte," in *Gesammelte Abhandlungen zur allgemeinen Verfassungsgeschichte*, ed. Fritz Hartung (Leipzig: Koehler & Amelang, 1941), 1:232–64.

[66] Becher collected recipes and processes at the Habsburg court, possibly in preparation for setting up his Kunst- und Werckhauß. Among these is a recipe for pan drying salt sent by an official of the saltworks (Mss. var. 1(2), fols. 615r–616v); a description of a model tanning works established on Count von Pötting's land in Bohemia (fol. 617r–v, dated 1672); a report from a tanner on the making of leather, with marginal notes by Becher (fols. 618r–620v); a recipe for Hungarian ox soup that will keep for three weeks; and calculations for buying and salting five hundred Hungarian oxen (619v–624v).

[67] The instructions were for Wilhelm von Schröder who had been resident in England for several years and a member of the Royal Society of London since 1662. Emperor Leopold sent him back to England in 1673. A copy of these instructions, Mss. var. 1(2), fol. 600r, dated 1674. Heinrich von Srbik reprinted the instructions from a draft in the Hofkammerarchiv, Vienna, dated 1675 in *Wilhelm von Schröder. Ein Beitrag zur Geschichte der Staatswissenschaften* (Vienna: Alfred Hölder, 1910), pp. 157–58. Hassinger, *Becher*, p. 177, discusses the question of Becher's authorship of these instructions.

making himself indispensable to the court from 1660 to the 1670s, Becher moved from a position as a purveyor of secrets and alchemist to become a counselor to his noble patron. The transformation can be discerned in the comparison of two letters from Becher to his patrons. Becher wrote the first in the early 1660s to Elector Johann Philipp of Maïnz, and the second a decade later to Emperor Leopold I in Vienna.

In the letter from the earliest days of his career in Mainz, he uses the language of an ingenious purveyor of secrets. Becher attempts to extricate himself from a quarrel with another purveyor/projector that had come to the attention of the elector. He encloses a written document that he claims will establish his innocence and persuade the elector to remain his patron. He moves quickly past this quarrel to promise the elector new metallic and mechanical wonders: a new process for making steel—for which Becher includes the recipe—a new gun, and an instrument for precision shooting. Becher ends, "I remain, commending myself to the holy refuge and merciful continuing affection of Your Estimable Electoral Grace":

> With the present letter, I have desired abjectly and obediently to pay my respect to your Estimable Grace, and also to excuse myself, after I learned that Dr. Grüber had complained to Your Electoral Grace that I had made common the process that he had communicated to me [when I was] acting in your name. If Your Estimable Grace would graciously deem to read the attached letter to Dr. Grüber, You would recognize his suspicion and my innocence, and You would remain as much as ever my Patron.
>
> Besides this I have received information [*kundschafft*] from Pater Emmerich Stahl [a hermit in the Schwarzwald], and spoken to him about chemical matters. The opportunity has also presented itself to reassess Fürstenberg's art of steelmaking because Father Emmerich said that he knows an easier way to make ingot or cast steel from old iron pieces or cast iron in great quantities for a profit, without cementation. With my encouragement he communicated his process by his own hand, a copy of which I hereby send to Your Estimable Grace. If the furnace will not be too long lacking, this could be tried. The projection powder could also be made anywhere, and the smelterers would know out of what it is to be made.
>
> I have, at your Electoral Grace's command, delivered a firelock musket which is now finished. It can shoot sixteen or twenty shots as accurately as a rifled barrel at 300 to 450 paces. Each shot can be aimed separately, and it can fire four shots in the time that a musketeer shoots only one. It is perfectly simple and safe, not in the manner of Prince Rupert's, for the barrel remains together. If Your Estimable Grace favors it, I desire to bring it to you; Your Estimable Grace will have gracious satisfaction of it. I have also tested my instrument for shooting straight. It performed somewhat better than the quadrat, but I desire the large binocular that Your Electoral Grace possesses, and, because it is of no use anymore, I desire to take it apart and bring it down with me, in order to await Your Estimable Grace's intention.

I remain, commending myself to the holy refuge and merciful continuing affection of Your Estimable Electoral Grace,

Johann Joachim Becher[68]

The letter to Emperor Leopold, from the 1670s, shows how Becher's estimation of himself and his ambitions had changed. Instead of promising processes and secrets in this letter, Becher instead attempts to convince the emperor of the need to create a regular advisory position that would adjudicate the claims of purveyors and alchemists. He contrasts the selfish motives of the common artisan and purveyor of novelties with his own desire only to create a special adjudicatory post for the good of the emperor and his lands. He notes the artisan's desire to withhold information to ensure that he receives recompense. In fact, Becher's portrayal of the selfish and gain-seeking projector resembles remarkably his own situation ten years earlier:

If I had a private interest from this letter, I would have held back the communication of certain important things and demanded a recompense. I passed over this opportunity because, with this letter, I seek nothing but truth, Your Imperial Majesty's reputation and profit, and the preservation of the good name of the noble art of alchemy.[69]

Becher concludes the long letter by recommending that the emperor employ an adjudicator of chemical processes and adepts:

Above all, however, because Your Imperial Majesty has a desire to have some trials made in these things, it would be necessary to take into service a loyal, honest, and knowledgeable subject, whom Your Imperial Majesty could trust with the processes of such worthless vagabonds, and who, privately and secretly, could in silence faithfully work out the processes and report on them to Your Majesty. If this does not happen, Your Imperial Majesty will never get to the bottom of this, nor understand the nature of these things, but instead will always be duped by these scoundrels.[70]

From 1655 until the early 1670s Becher moved from being an ingenious mechanic to the securer position of advisor to nobles.[71] He accomplished this

---

[68] Mss. var. 1(3), fol. 208r. Another example of this type of strategy can be found in Becher's proposition for a mill placed on a ship or ship-bridge across the Rhine in Mainz: he writes "whichever of these two types pleases your Electoral Grace, I will bring it into action, against an agreed-upon recompense, according to my promise." Mss. var. 1(3), fol. 182v (dated before 1661).

[69] Mss. var. 1(1), fol. 146v (entire letter fols. 146r–151r). See Pamela H. Smith, "Alchemy, Credit, and the Commerce of Words and Things: Johann Joachim Becher at the Courts of the Holy Roman Empire, 1635–82" (Ph.D. diss., Johns Hopkins University, 1990), appendix 1, for a transcription of this letter.

[70] Mss. var. 1(1), fol. 150v.

[71] This change in Becher's position can also be seen in the way he comported himself on his journeys to Holland. When he became representative of the emperor, Becher's needs on a trip changed, as his journal from a 1671 trip to Holland attests. On this 138-day trip he spent 1,500

by becoming acceptable to the court as a man of theory with an established position within the republic of letters and at court. He also assiduously worked on his connection with the sphere of *ars*, by building up a network of contacts, clients, and patrons that would both promote his own ambitions and the interests of his patrons by furthering his projects at court. He and others called this activity and its result *Kundtschafft*. Since the nineteenth century, this word has come to apply only to the clientele, custom, and patronage of a merchant, but earlier it had also connoted the goodwill, information, and scouting that must go into building up such a clientele. Its meaning extended as well to taking exact notice, obtaining news, a wide acquaintanceship, recognition at the noble court, the taking of oral testimony from a witness, and oral information as opposed to written documents.[72] For Becher, constructing a network of contacts involved *Kundtschafft* in all its multivalent connotations, not least of which was information about the enemy gained secretly in wartime by espionage.[73]

Becher's use of this word harks back also to his earliest days as a purveyor of alchemy and Paracelsian alchemical medicine. Paracelsus used the word *Kuntschafft* to denote the physician philosopher's comprehension, or *experientia*. In a characteristic reversal of traditional social and intellectual categories, Paracelsus defined *scientia* as the "virtue present in natural objects," which the physician must "overhear" and with which he must achieve union. The physician puts *scientia* to the test in his cure of the sick, and from these tests, he gains *experientia*. *Experientia* constitutes the only true knowledge of objects, and it is gained by testing the *scientia* of the object.[74] Paracelsus turned the traditional relationship between *scientia* and *experientia* on its head, as well as shifting the sphere of *Kundschaft*. Where *Kundschaft* had traditionally referred to the

---

Reichsthaler, where in 1664 he had spent only 335 Reichsthaler for 78 days. As he made clear to the Hofkammer in Vienna, he could hardly be expected to comport himself in a manner less elegant as representative of the emperor than he had previously as servant to the electors of Bavaria and Mainz. Expenses for the 1664 trip: Mss. var. 1(3), fol. 224v; for the 1671 trip: Mss. var. 1(3), fol. 542r. The letter is in Mss. var. 1(3), fols. 528r–530v.

[72] Jacob and Wilhelm Grimm, *Deutsches Wörterbuch* (Leipzig: S. Hirzel, 1854–1960), list these definitions s.v. "Kundschaft."

[73] Johann Heinrich Zedler, *Grosses vollständiges Universal-Lexikon* (Halle and Leipzig: Johann Heinrich Zedler, Verleger, 1732–50), vol. 15, defines *Kundschafft* this way, as well as dwelling on its purely eighteenth-century definition of the documents issued to and carried by an artisan to establish his right to practice his trade. As an advocate of guild regulation, Zedler is most concerned with this definition. Becher notes in a 1669 journal that a Swedish projector, knowing of his *Kundtschafft*, had asked him to gather together artisans for a huge "Sophopolis" project, in which all arts and knowledge would be displayed in a "Theatrum artis et naturae" (*Politischer Discurs*, 2d ed., p. 1104). Becher discusses the *theatrum* in *Methodus didactica*. In 1670 Becher called the network of merchants that can attest to the credit worthiness of a borrower "Kundtschafft" (*Politischer Discurs*, 2d ed., p. 709).

[74] Paracelsus's notion of *experientia* and *scientia* is discussed by Walter Pagel, *Paracelsus: An Introduction to Philosophical Medicine in the Era of the Renaissance*, 2d ed. (Basel: Karger, 1982), p. 60. He quotes Paracelsus: "Scientia ist in dem, in dem sie Gott geben hatt: Experientia ist ein Kuntschafft von dem, in dem Scientia probiert wirt."

(largely oral) activity of artisans, merchants, and artificers, Paracelsus used it to mean the highest form of knowledge that the physician could possess in the pursuit of his sacred duty of healing. Where *scientia* had previously connoted a corpus of knowledge defined by the books of authorities, Paracelsus used it to mean the innate virtue inhering in natural objects. Becher's transit from alchemical purveyor to man of theory was assisted by the new notion of knowledge and action that developed out of Paracelsus's elevation of sense observation and experience in the late sixteenth and early seventeenth centuries. Becher described his own informal education as having been based on just the sort of experience and *Kundschaft* that Paracelsus raised to new significance. Paracelsus had advocated travel, observation of things, experience, and contact with artisans—all those things for which Becher had had ample opportunity as a youth. Becher grasped the opportunity that his fortune had presented to him, purveying it as his own particular brand of knowledge, transmuting it into court positions, and finally building a career around it.

A New Means of Discourse

> ich bin durch ein Land gereiset/ da haben die Leute keine Köpff/
> sondern Scheidel/ keine Ohren/ sondern Lappen/ keine Nasen/
> sondern Schnauzten/ keine Mäuler/ sondern Flappen . . . auch
> seynd etliche keine Menschen/ sondern Pommerinchen/ worauß
> klar zu sehen/ wie leicht auch nur eine Sprach mit eben derselben
> Wörtern kan *confundirt* werden/ wann man sie *metaphoricè* von
> den Dingen gehen wil.

> I've traveled through a country where the people have no heads,
> but rather skulls, no ears, but hounds' ears, no noses, but snouts,
> no mouths, but maws, . . . and some are not humans, but little
> Pomeranian dogs, from which it is clearly to be seen how easily
> just one language that uses the same words can become confused
> when one uses it to speak about things metaphorically.
> (*Becher,* Methodus didactica)

Becher's *Kundtschafft* brought him personal power and social status and, if his projects were successful, also gave his patrons reputation and power, which made his own position at court even securer. To succeed, however, Becher had to mediate effectively between the court and artisans. As intermediary, Becher had to be able to participate in court discourse, as well as to understand the technical vocabulary of artisans. This was not an easy task. Becher's effort to discuss a commercial project with a member of the noble court at Mainz illustrates the difficulties:

I have received both Your Excellency's letters and, as you asked, hereby give my reply to them, for now in German because some terms come up which cannot be rendered so well in Latin and [the use of Latin] would obscure the meaning. If I am not so clear in German and perhaps offend your Excellency in this or that, I very much desire to explain it, which is much better to do in all things orally. Such subjects never allow themselves to be so clearly and thoroughly treated in writing as in speaking.[75]

The commercial subjects Becher desired to treat did not lend themselves easily to rendering in Latin, the language of scholars, and they were subjects not normally set into writing. For this reason, Becher often collected and wrote down artisanal processes that were told to him orally. The artisanal use of the vulgar tongue[76] or the discussion of such common objects might offend the members of the noble court. He desired to find a new way of talking to the court about these raw subjects—subjects in which he commanded authority as a man of theory and practice, and in which he commanded power in the form of *Kundtschafft*.

Becher sought this new means of discourse in a new method of language teaching and learning.[77] Language was the basis of the transmission of knowledge between humans or spheres of activity, for the tongue was the servant and translator of all knowledge. Language was the basis of "Lehren und Lernen," by which all arts and sciences and the human society they support were preserved.[78] Finally, language was the foundation of human society; it caused humans to become civil beings; it was "der erste Grad *ad Societatem civilem*,"

---

[75] Copy of a letter from Becher to Johann Christian von Boineburg, undated but ca. 1668, Mss. var. 1(2), fol. 504r. This letter discusses a scheme to elect a particular German candidate to the Polish throne. Becher proposes a scheme whereby the candidate would undertake certain commercial projects. This scheme is discussed more fully in Chapter 3.

[76] Becher considered the use of Latin to characterize a learned person, whereas the failure to learn Latin indicated a vocation in the mechanical arts: "wer nicht Latein kan/ wird nicht vor Gelehrt gehalten/ dieweil er das Mittel nicht hat gelehrt zu werden/ und ist ein Zeichen/ wann die Eltern ihre Kinder nicht haben Lateinisch lernen lassen/ daß sie solche zu Handwercks-Sachen haben appliciren wollen." *Methodus didactica* (1668), Vorrede, unpaginated.

[77] Becher set out his theory of language and pedagogy in *Methodus didactica, das ist: Gründlicher Beweiß/ daß die Weg und Mittel/ welche die Schulen bißhero ins gemein gebraucht/ die Jugend zu Erlernung der Sprachen/ insonderheit der Lateinischen zuführen/ nicht gewiß/ noch sicher seyen/ sondern den Reguln und Natur der rechten Lehr und Lern-Kunst schnurstracks entgegen lauffen/ derentwegen nicht allein langweilig/ sondern auch gemeinigliche unfruchtbar und vergeblich ablauffen. Sambt Anleitung zu einem besseren* (Munich: Maria Magdalena Schellin, 1668). He provided a work of practice to accompany his theory: *Appendix practica über seinen* Methodum Didacticam (Frankfurt: Johann David Zunner, 1669), and published lists of words to be memorized in *Methodi Becherianae Didacticae Praxis, Ejusdemque Liber seu annus primus, primam Vocabulorum connexionem continens* (Frankfurt: Johann David Zunner, 1669); and *Novum, breve, perfacile, & solidum Organum pro Verborum copia, in quavis materia, expedite acquirenda, omni scriptioni & dictioni perutile* (Munich: Sebastianus Rauch, 1670).

[78] *Methodus didactica*, Vorrede, unpaginated.

causing the formation of society[79] by creating friendship, understanding, and trade ("Handel und Wandel").[80]

For Becher, language determined the understanding of reality and the perception of relations between things in the world. Becher's method would not only teach the words of a language, but also give knowledge of the things to which they referred, as well as indicating the relations between objects.[81] On this basis, his method would enable the youth to exercise judgment—*Judicium*—the only true aim of education.[82] According to Becher, *Judicium* was one of the three essentially human activities of discourse, judgment, and practice: "reden, urtheilen, und thun."[83]

> Language learning, like any art, must follow nature: nature has her course, art does nothing except put together and combine. Although nature goes along very slowly, she proceeds very simply and art has only to look after the combination, for which it needs its instruments, the compass, ruler, plumb, saw, hammer, ax, and others,

[79] Ibid., p. 3.

[80] Ibid., p. 2.

[81] For a discussion of the place of Becher's ideas in the history of pedagogy, see Theodor Ballauff and Klaus Schaller, *Pädagogik. Eine Geschichte der Bildung und Erziehung, Vom 16. bis zum 19. Jahrhundert*, vol. 2, *Orbis Academicus. Problemgeschichten der Wissenschaft in Dokumenten und Darstellungen* (Freiburg and Munich: Verlag Karl Alber, 1970). Klaus Schaller also discusses Becher's pedagogical program in *Die Pädagogik des Johann Amos Comenius und die Anfänge des pädagogischen Realismus im 17. Jahrhundert* (Heidelberg: Quelle & Meyer, 1962), pp. 389–96 and passim; idem, *Studien zur systematischen Pädogogik*, 2d ed. (Heidelberg: Quelle & Meyer, 1969). Other works that discuss Becher's didactic theory with less success are Heinz Kelbert, "Johann Joachim Becher. Ein Beitrag zur Erforschung des berufspädagogischen Erbes," *Studien zur Geschichte der Berufsausbildung*, ser. 23, 1 (1954): 7–55; and Alfred Heubaum, "Johann Joachim Becher. Ein Beitrag zur Geistesgeschichte des 17. Jahrhunderts," *Monatsheft der Comeniusgesellschaft* 9 (1900): 154–74. I am grateful to Klaus Schaller for allowing me a copy of his manuscript of "Die Pädagogik des Johann Joachim Becher. Psychosophia contra Pansophiam," in which he characterizes Becher's pedagogical reform as "bürgerlicher Realismus," and contrasts it with the "pansophischer Realismus" of Comenius. He makes the point that Becher's pedagogy aimed at presenting the things in themselves, which was equivalent for Becher to presenting them in their utility for humankind. See also Gunter E. Grimm, "Muttersprache und Realienunterricht," in *Res Publica Litteraria. Die Institutionen der Gelehrsamkeit in der frühen Neuzeit*, ed. Sebastian Neumeister and Conrad Wiedemann, 2 vols. (Wiesbaden: Otto Harrassowitz, 1987), 1:299–324, who charts the movement in pedagogy by means of "realien" from the encyclopedic, millennial pedagogy of the first half of the seventeenth century to the mercantilist pedagogy of the second half.

[82] *Methodus didactica*, Vorrede, p. c2v and p. 1.

[83] These correspond to the *ars loquendi, judicium*, and *exercitio* of Ramist dialectic. See Walter J. Ong, *Ramus, Method, and the Decay of Dialogue* (Cambridge, Mass.: Harvard University Press, 1983), chap. 8, pp. 171–95. Becher, however, had his own particular definition of each of these activities, which was peculiarly material. For example, "thun" was not exercise of reason through logic, but simply the sum of external human activities, such as taking up a profession, the courtly exercises of fencing, dancing, singing, the exercise of the mechanical arts, and the "*Apparatus Eruditionis, Pansophiae*" of the universities. *Methodus didactica*, p. 168. Becher would develop his thinking more fully in *Psychosophia* (1705), pp. 73–84.

in which art is very modest and simple, so that it will not be other than an ape of nature or her servant.[84]

Becher emphasized that language learning was an art by calling a learned or second language, a "Kunst-Sprache," an artificial language,[85] and, for him, even the formation of a pedagogical program demanded a mechanical, "mathematical" spirit and ingenuity.[86] He believed that language teaching had never been undertaken properly, for previous authors had not set forth a natural order; rather, they had advocated the unnatural means of learning vocabulary by alphabetical order, topics, or the *loci communi*.[87]

Becher claims that his method will pay attention to the "organic and physical speech in a language" ("*Organ*ischen und Physischen Reden in einer Sprach") and will present a "living grammar" ("*Grammatica viva*").[88] In the *Appendix Practica* to his *Methodus Didactica*, Becher explains that to "speak organically" means to name things with their proper names and "speaking physically" means to speak about the common necessities and characteristics of things. This language forms "a universal but simple physics . . . which all those who learn their mother tongue from life, that is the words from the things, learn without noticing. They see by the light of nature that a cow is not a bird."[89]

Language must be learned from things and life, rather than words; even the picture books of Comenius and Johannes Buno cause a multiplication of entities that hinders the memory of the learning child. These entitites "lead the youth from living to dead things, from the original to the copy. These etchings and pictures bring a new and unnecessary third entity into the memory of the child that throws, instead of light, a shadow."[90] The memory is like a magnet

[84] *Methodus didactica*, p. 130.

[85] Becher discussed the differences between a "Mutter-Sprach" and a "Kunst-Sprach" in *Methodus didactica*, p. 38.

[86] Becher said that writing the *Methodus didactica* had required "memori," "iudicium," and "laboriosum & dispositum Mathematicum ingenium." Vorrede, unpaginated.

[87] Becher's call for language learning based on nature was by no means original. (See Ong, *Ramus*, on dialectic as the imitation of nature, esp. p. 177.) However, for Ballauff and Schaller, the particulars of Becher's "natural" pedagogical program distinguish it from those of his contemporaries. The study of the thing in itself, rather than the thing as part of an overarching order, allowed the student to use his *judicio* in manipulating the things into any order that he chose. (See *Pädogogik*, pp. 244–47.) According to these authors, the advantage of using a "Naturalienkabinett" or "Naturaliensammlung" in teaching was that the objects did not have to be presented in any one particular order, but could be displayed in any order desired (p. 224).

[88] *Methodus didactica*, Vorrede. Becher's didactic theory draws from Ramist ideas and method, probably by way of Comenius's *Didactica magna* (1633). Although Becher loudly descries Comenius's pedagogic method, his own ideas are very similar to it. On Ramism and Comenius's use of Ramist developments, see Ong, *Ramus*.

[89] *Appendix practica*, p. 36. Becher called this physics a "Physica Practica" (*Methodus didactica*, p. 128).

[90] *Methodus didactica*, pp. 49–50.

that pulls the things of the world toward it; to place words or pictures between this magnet and its object only dilutes its powers. Characteristically, Becher gives an example of this process observed from life. He recounts his pedagogic efforts with his young son, Philipp Friedrich, to whom he showed a picture of a cat. His son did not make the connection of this picture with a living object until Becher pointed out to him a living cat. Then, Becher claimed, the concept entered his son's mind with such vigor that when he looked again at the picture cat, he "said 'cat,' and wanted to pull the picture cat by the ears."[91] Becher is claiming here that the image or representation of a cat does not bring knowledge of the living cat. Where Comenius had substituted a picture of the object for a description in words, claiming that this brought humans nearer an understanding of the nature of things, Becher insists that only the objects themselves can lead to such an understanding.

The problem of the relation between *res et verba* stretched back to antiquity, when writers on rhetoric claimed that words could move men to understanding and finally to action. Comenius, searching for a new basis of understanding and action, believed humankind could only be moved to right action by things, and so used images that represented things in his pedagogical program. Becher in turn believed that only the objects themselves or three-dimensional copies could move human beings to right understanding and action. Representation of things by images was no longer close enough to life for Becher; only the things themselves could display and make clear their own nature. Becher located understanding completely in the material world and in humankind's sensory perception of it. He understood a long and complex debate in the context of his own experience, education, and place at the noble court, and formed his particularly material contribution to this controversy within the terms of that experience. It was exactly his sort of material vision that informed natural philosophy in the seventeenth century.

Focused as he was on the practical, Becher went on to consider the down-to-earth needs of his program: how could all objects in the world be learned from life? His solution was characteristically material. He proposed a *"Theatrum Naturae & Artis"* in which "alle *Naturalia*, und *Artefacta Instrumenten* und *Manufacturen*" would be arranged. One gallery of this theater would house the animal kingdom. The larger animals could be portrayed by a skillful taxidermist or by a particularly good wood sculptor, and the smaller animals could be made in wax. The second gallery would contain a perpetually green garden, full of wood and wax plants, and the third gallery would display specimens from the mineral realm. The last gallery would contain all kinds of tools and manufactured items. Every specimen would be displayed on a pedestal with its name written in several languages below. Objects would be ordered in natural categories and their relationships displayed on charts on the walls. Becher recalled the

---

[91] "Katz gesagt/ auch solche in der Figur bey den Ohren wollen zopffen" (ibid., p. 50).

anatomical model that he had seen in Leiden on his 1660 trip and suggests this as a model for the objects in such a collection.[92]

Becher's conclusion to his description of the theater shows us how his own experience, especially within the world of the court, helped to form his particularly material vision and accounted for his insistence on using and examining objects rather than representations of the objects. Becher ended his description of the *Theatrum* with a call for its patronage. He desired that the prince not only consider it as a place of learning, but also of diversion, and even of pecuniary profit:

> Briefly, would it not be a recreation worthy of a prince, indeed of the Emperor, that might also have its economic use, for if a person gives a half Batzen to see a bear, an ape, or a fool, what would he not give to see the whole of nature in such admirable richness? Someone might say, "but what will it cost?" The answer: perhaps not more than a single jousting tournament, a ballet, or some other recreation, but this one is perpetual. This single means would be enough to bring prosperity back to a university or gymnasium that has fallen into decline.[93]

The necessity of selling his project to a prince, and of making it a perpetual source of revenue, compelled Becher to envisage and propose ideas to his noble patron as objects of property that could be physically displayed and would bring the prince *fama* and revenue. The spectacle created around the object would redound to the credit of the prince and to his territory.[94]

---

[92] "Ich habe in Holland zu Leiden bey einem *Studioso Medicinae* einem Schweden ein artliches *Sceleton* gesehen/ da die Nerven/ *Arterien*, und der *ductus venae cavae* alle gefärbten Diäten dem Leben nach/ und der Natur/ und Anatomi gemäß gemacht/ und *exprimirt*, auch mit Zetteln bezeichnet waren/ wie wäre ein solches Ding ein herrliches Werck/ auff eine Teutsche *Universität*/ oder ein solches *Theatrum Naturae & Artis*? dardurch einer in einem Tag mehr lernen kan/ als in der blutigen *Anatomia* in vil Wochen/ zu malen/ wo man nicht *Copium* der todten Cörper/ oder *Licentiam* solche zu *Anatomiren* haben kan/ dann die Leut bey uns in Teutschland hierinnen gar seltzam seynd/ ich habe zu Würzburg einsmals *permissu Superiorum* ein *Justificirtes* Weibsbild *anatomirt*, darüber ist mir die gantze Stadt feind worden/ wie sie dann auch nicht nachgelassen/ biß sie mich von dannen getriben/ welches bey einem solchen *Sceleton* nicht zu befahren/ ist auch vor die besser/ welche den Gestanck/ und Blut nicht leiden mögen." Ibid., p. 51.

[93] Ibid., pp. 52–53.

[94] The need for scholars to present their ideas to noble patrons in the form of objects of property to be possessed and displayed was a feature of early modern courtly society. This need was especially acute for natural philosophers. Galileo's telescope is an example of one such object. See Robert S. Westman, "The Astronomer's Role in the Sixteenth Century: A Preliminary Study," *History of Science* 18 (1980): 105–47; Richard S. Westfall, "Scientific Patronage: Galileo and the Telescope," *Isis* 76 (1985): 11–30; and Mario Biagioli, "Galileo's System of Patronage," *History of Science* 28 (1990): 1–62; idem, "Galileo the Emblem Maker," *Isis* 81 (1990): 230–58. Paula Findlen, *Possessing Nature: Museums, Collecting and Scientific Culture in Early Modern Italy* (Berkeley: University of California Press, 1994), also makes clear the uses of natural objects in courtly patronage relationships, while David S. Lux, *Patronage and Royal Science in Seventeenth-Century France* (Ithaca: Cornell University Press, 1989), shows how the demands of patronage brought about two distinct scientific styles and research programs. The use of a natural philosophi-

The child trained in Becher's *Theatrum*, in the process of memorizing words and their relationships to each other, would learn a complete system of nature.[95] This knowledge was to be gained by understanding the physical properties of nouns and the qualities and properties that can be predicated of them. Such a child could "speak and discourse of a thing, not morally, oratorically, rhetorically, or through a few grand figures of speech, but naturally and purely physically." He would spout forth a stream of information on a single word that could last "for a year and a day."[96]

Becher meant his new method of discourse to be natural; it was based on material things, rather than words, and it was stripped of all ornament. The things of the world would be shown in their true and natural relations to other material objects. Such a study of objects led the mind to correct judgment, to divine wisdom, and finally to the practice of that wisdom in the exercise of human virtue in the public sphere (*praxis*).[97]

In the practical section of his *Methodus didactica*, Becher developed this material course of pedagogy into a method of material cognition. His first statement of this new method, which he called a *"Methodus Gnostica (intelligendi, cognoscendi),"* is reminiscent of the Paracelsian empathetic understanding of the observer and his union with the thing observed:

> [If] the understanding and the things one wants to understand are properly compared, then the understanding sees the things as they are in themselves, and it obtains the truth of the things from the things themselves. In this acquisition, the understanding-observer and the things being understood become one, in the same manner that the things that are represented in a mirror appear themselves to stand visibly in the mirror. In such a way the truth and the nature of things present themselves in the understanding itself.[98]

---

cal spectacle as part of the economic strategy of an institution is wonderfully portrayed by Giovanni Ferrari, "Public Anatomy Lessons and the Carnival in Bologna," *Past and Present* 117 (1987): 50–106. Michael Hunter, *Establishing the New Science: The Experience of the Early Royal Society* (Woodbridge, Suffolk: Boydell, 1989), chap. 4, shows how the foundation of the Royal Society's "Repository" was meant to demonstrate the Society's vitality after the plague.

[95] Becher did not however advocate the attempt to indoctrinate the student into an entire philosophy, an attempt he attributed to the "Pansophien" and "Polymathien." He says of them that "when the teacher wants to make talented people quickly, and the parents would like quickly to have highly learned children, then such pansophical trade comes about very quickly" (*Appendix practica*, p. 38). Becher seems here to make a distinction between a philosophy (such as the Pansophism of Comenius) that he claims is superimposed on the things of nature, and the natural order of things that is absorbed in learning a mother tongue. He is in effect claiming that knowledge of things can be unmediated and unordered, and can capture nature directly.

[96] *Methodus didactica*, p. 124. The information began with the word itself, its primitive form, its derivations, whether it was a quality, substance, or a predicate, and continued through a long list of points.

[97] Ibid., Vorrede, unpaginated.

[98] *Appendix practica*, p. 50.

A decade later, he would develop this method more explicitly, and at that time he would construe judgment itself as a material process. In this version, *Judicium* consisted in the understanding of corporeal things first through the senses and then through reason. There were four steps in the process of judgment: First, use of the senses by mathematics, in numbering, measuring, and weighing; second, observation of the active and passive qualities of the objects, as well as of the accidental and substantive qualities (a "physical" observation); third, correlation and comparison with other objects; and fourth, through reason by "ratiocination" or "Vernunfft-Kunst" which led to the forming of definitions, distinctions, *praecisiones*, axioms, and hypotheses. The aim of ratiocination was divine wisdom and, finally, the understanding of how the objects serve civic use ("wie sie *ad usum civilem* dienen").[99]

Becher's new means of discourse and method of judging would be of particular use to the court person, for it would divest objects and relationships of a meaningless overlay of words that had accumulated through improper thinking, learning, and discourse. Nowhere was the meaningless overlay thicker than among the ornaments at court, and nowhere was there more need of judgment, virtue, and prudence.[100]

To understand this, let us study for a moment Becher's account of an interchange at court.[101] A small event that took place after Becher had established himself at court becomes in Becher's telling a parable of his larger project. He tells of a French orator, chiromancer and fortune-teller who made his living from the "artem Lullianam extempore perorandi."[102] This character arrived one day in Munich and was brought to the noble table to exhibit his art.[103] He was given a trivial subject that lay close at hand on the table: salt. While small and trivial at table, salt actually had great importance for the Bavarian nobility, and

---

[99] *Psychosophia* (1678), p. 77.

[100] That courtiers needed practical abilities is reiterated many times in courtiers' manuals, beginning with Baldesar Castiglione, *The Book of the Courtier* (1528). This is noted by Norbert Elias, *The Court Society*, trans. Edmund Jephcott (New York: Pantheon, 1983); idem, *Power and Civility*, trans. Edmund Jephcott (New York, Pantheon, 1982), among others.

[101] *Methodus didactica*, pp. 126–27.

[102] See Frances A. Yates, *The Art of Memory* (Chicago: University of Chicago Press, 1966), for an explanation of the Lullian memory scheme. As Yates explains, the Lullian memory system does not have its origin in the classical rhetorical tradition, but instead comes out of a philosophical tradition that claims to base memory on "philosophic 'reals'" (p. 175). If Becher's early charts and tables in the Rostock *Nachlaß* are visual memory schemes, it is significant that Becher attempted here to distance himself from the French orator by calling him a chiromancer and fortune-teller and making light of his memory scheme and his organization of the subject matter. It is one more example of Becher's attempt to create a permanent space at court for himself that distanced him from the vagaries of fortune to which the wandering orator and the purveyor of alchemical and mechanical secrets were subjected.

[103] Table talk was a well-developed art by the seventeenth century. See Michel Jeanneret, *A Feast of Words: Banquets and Table Talk in the Renaissance*, trans. Jeremy Whiteley and Emma Hughes (Chicago: University of Chicago Press, 1991).

furnished the elector with a great part of his cameral income. Becher tells us that the orator spoke for a quarter of an hour on the moral, physical, theological, and historical significance of salt, embellishing his speech with rhetorical ornaments. When he finished he was applauded, and Becher, jealous of the applause and scornful of the orator's performance, announced that he could better this French orator. The banquet guests agreed and gave to Becher the subject of another trivial item on the table: the silver salt cellar. Becher warned that his speech would not be rhetorically pretty but instead would speak purely and physically from the things themselves. Receiving permission, he began with an explanation of the nature of metals, their relation to each other, their growth and development in the earth, and their mining, smelting, and working techniques. He went on to discuss the manufactures that produce and market silver objects. He discussed silversmiths and silver and gold beating, coinmakers, musical instrument makers, and the tools of these craftsmen, their technical vocabulary, what raw materials they used, and finally he returned to the salt cellar. He reported that he spoke for a good hour and was just about to make a digression about the silversmith when he was given a sign by the restless dinner guests to stop talking. Becher tells us that he won the prize that evening, and that the orator came to him later and suggested to Becher an exchange of skills, in which he offered Becher money or the secret of his own method in return for learning Becher's method. Becher said:

> But I declined, because whoever can speak of the nature of things will easily find a manner in which to speak about them, and a purse is found more easily for money than money for the purse [i.e., the ornamental trappings are more easily found than the substance]. Thus by my method of speaking, it is not necessary to profit by the art of chiromancy, for my method does not need such props.[104]

Becher spoke to the court about their silver ornaments—the salt cellar— seeking to strip these ornaments of their decorative and theatrical qualities and to invest them instead with a material significance that demonstrated to the court their place within a whole network of unfamiliar relations and productive activities. The manufactures of the city were a realm outside the court, and the artisans' unornamented vocabulary and their raw materials not normally spoken of at table. The unproductive overlay of ornamental words that had accumulated in conventional court discourse not only hid the real relations of objects, but could even be dangerous to human society.[105] Only by learning how to talk about the material significance of things through a method of material cognition

---

[104] *Methodus didactica*, p. 127.

[105] Many princes "suchen ihren Kindern ihres gleichen hoffärtige *alamode* Esel zu *Praeceptoren*, davon sie dann in der Jugend das süsse Gifft der Hoffart unter dem *praetext* einer *alamod*ischer Höfflichkeit lernen" (seek for their children schoolmasters who, like themselves, are proud, fashionable asses, so that the children in their youth learn the sweet poison of pride under the guise of a fashionable courtesy). *Moral Discurs*, p. 58.

could the court come to understand the objects Becher believed were capable of producing material increase and reform.

Productive Knowledge

Becher first attracted the attention of the court at Mainz with his perpetual motion machine, and he earned the title of *mathematicus* for his mechanical abilities. In the position of court mathematician, Becher could have been expected to direct fortification building and repair, or to conduct surveying activities, but instead Becher saw the sphere of mathematician as associated with an entirely different set of activities. When he described the development of his vocation, he noted that he had first studied mathematics and mechanical subjects, from which he learned artisanal techniques, their mechanical skills, and technical vocabulary. This led him to speculate how manufactures might more easily be set in place and how their products might be sold. Thus, through mathematics, he came to a *scientz* of commerce.[106] In its relation to the mechanical arts, commerce was part of a much broader scheme, which finds its expression most clearly in the work of Erhard Weigel (1625–99), a friend to Becher and a professor of mathematics at the University of Jena whose students included Gottfried Wilhelm Leibniz and Samuel Pufendorf.[107]

Weigel considered the practice of the mechanical arts capable of yielding a new kind of knowledge that would reform philosophy. His publications and projects indicate the breadth of his interest in the mechanical arts: he attempted to form a "Collegium artis consultorum," he built a "pancosmus" pedagogical machine (like Becher's *Theatrum*) and a machine for instructing children in Latin, and he published many works that attempted to apply mathematical forms to other areas of knowledge, for example, *Arithmetische Beschreibung der Moral Weißheit* (Arithmetical description of moral philosophy).

In a treatise on the mechanical arts, Weigel explained how *ars* came into being. Before the Fall, humans had known the secrets of God and nature, but afterward these things were obscured from sight, and humankind had to rely on its own power of creation to supply its daily needs. This power of creation lay in art; a uniquely human trial-and-error *imitation* of the nature left behind in Paradise. The goal of the liberal arts, which arose naturally out of the movements of the body, such as speech and discourse, was understanding. While understanding was mainly a tool for individual perfection in the knowledge of God, it also used the power of the body and of the body's movement in order to create and produce the necessities that eased human life. Thus the mechanical

[106] *Methodus didactica*, Vorrede, unpaginated, and *Politischer Discurs*, Dedication to Georg Ludwig von Sinzendorff, b recto.

[107] Weigel was called to Jena in 1653 and shortly thereafter became *Hofmathematicus* and *Ober-Baudirektor* to the duke of Saxony-Weimar.

arts originated from an understanding of the creative capacity of the body. In time, the professions developed, and, of these, jurisprudence provided for the common welfare, medicine for health, and philosophy for the bodily comforts. The most important part of philosophy in this respect was practical mathematics, which for Weigel, as for Becher, included trade as well as arithmetic, mechanics, architecture, fortification, astronomy, geometry, geography, music, and optics.

Weigel believed every university student should complete a propaedeutic course in the mechanical arts, and he recommended making practical mathematics, as the most important part of philosophy, a separate professional faculty in the university that would join medicine and jurisprudence. The faculty of the mechanical arts would pursue a new sort of knowledge, which he called "*Real-Weisheit*" (knowledge of things or *realia*).[108] This knowledge was grounded in material things rather than words, and involved active doing and creating rather than talking and writing. The result of such knowledge would be material increase and economic prosperity. Weigel expected this new materially productive knowledge to usher in a reign of peace and prosperity that would stand in contrast to the past of war and confusion, which had resulted from an education grounded in disputation and words.[109] Commerce, as a component of the mechanical arts, formed part of this knowledge of material things.

Becher's statement that he came to the "science" of commerce as the result of interest in the mechanical arts, his effort to ground instruction in things, his belief in a new material discourse, and his construction of a network of

[108] Weigel was not the originator of this pedagogy. Grimm, "Muttersprache und Realienunterricht," pp. 299–324, traces the development of (and opposition to) the view that the inclusion in the curriculum of the mechanical arts, taught in the vernacular, will bring about a reform of society.

[109] Erhard Weigel, *Vorstellung der Kunst- und Handwercke/ nechst einem kurtzen Begriff des Mechanischen Heb- und Rüst-Zeugs. Samt einem Anhang/ Welcher Gestalt so wohl der gemeinen Leibes-Nothdurfft/ als der Gemüths-Wohlfarth und Gelehrsamkeit selbst/ durch die Wissenschafft der Mechanischen Künste geholffen werden möge. Auf veranlassung im Mertzen dieses Jahrs erschienenen Neuen Cometen unmassgeblich entworffen* (Jena: Johann Jacob Bauhofer, 1672). Becher cites this book in *Psychosophia* (1705), p. 348. Weigel made plans for the institutionalization of mathematicians in civic society. He advocated that a director of the mechanical arts be placed in all cities on the model of a *Stadtphysikus*, and that laboratories be opened where those learned in mechanics could make "Proben/ *experimenta* und Erfindungen." He desired to found a "General Collegium Naturae Consultorum Medico-Mechanicum autoritate publica" (p. 111). Another treatise by Weigel that merits lengthier study is entitled *Tertius interveniens mit einem allgemeinen Friedens-Mittel*, 1673(?), reprinted in Erhard Weigel's *Gesammelte pädagogische Schriften*, ed. H. Schüling (Gießen: Universitätsbibliothek, 1970). In this very interesting work Weigel defines the difference between animals and humans as the human ability to "reckon" (rechnen), but reckoning for Weigel does not simply mean measuring and counting, but "erforschen und erkennen/ thun und machen/ können" (investigating and recognizing, doing and making; creative ability/art/power). *Können* means "to be able," and *Kunst* is derived from it, but it also connotes power (as in *pouvoir*). Weigel believed that this power of reckoning must be instilled in young minds in order that they become active seekers and creators of common good. This will bring about an economic and a moral instauration. Again, Weigel makes practical mathematics the basis of a creative, material power that will bring about reform.

Kundtschafft all point to his concern with producing a material knowledge that would bring about moral reform and material prosperity. This is also clear in the preface to his *Methodus didactica*:

> What is the true interest of Germany other than its well-being [*Wolstand*]? Its well-being consists in Germany being considerable—a force to be reckoned with, it will be considerable when it is powerful; it will be powerful when it is populous; it will be populous when it has sufficient sustenance (for the vultures gather where the carcass lies); it will have sustenance if it is rich in money; it will be rich in money when the money that flows out of Germany is retained within it and when yet more money is brought into Germany from foreign countries. This will happen when wares that are paid for in money and brought into the territory are either done without or are reined in and made in the territory, and when the useless foreign wares that draw money out of the country are forbidden. This will happen when princes and lords work together, and they will do this when they are united. They will be united when they trust each other. They will trust one another when their interests do not run counter to each other. This will occur when each is content with his God-given own. He will be content when he is not brought up and accustomed from his youth to superfluity, pride, greed, insatiety, disorder, mistrust, immodesty, and faction. See how all these consequences flow from education [*Kinder-Zucht*]. For the manner in which the education of rulers has been carried out determines their rule, and as their rule is, so will the subjects commonly be.[110]

The proper pedagogical method, grounded in material things, would produce personal virtue, societal harmony, trade, wealth, welfare, and power—in short, a reform founded in material increase. The knowledge that brought about this material reform depended on *ars*, artisanal practice, and the harnessing of the productive knowledge of artisans. In his rise from ingenious mechanic to commercial advisor, Becher sought to capture this practice and knowledge for the court. By his work as intermediary, Becher made the skills and techniques of individual artisans available to the court, and by his *Kundtschafft* of artisanal knowledge, he sought to capture the productive knowledge by which the artisan created objects out of raw materials. He attempted to make this knowledge and its promise clear to the court in his discourse on the salt cellar. In this speech at table, Becher spoke to the court about ornamental objects in the speech of things instead of wordy ornaments, and he tried to make clear that material increase depended on practice and the knowledge of things.

. . . . .

In the 1660s, Becher established a place for himself in the Holy Roman Empire. He found his way to court, settled himself within the republic of scholars, and sought to make his place within the court secure and his person indispensable to

---

[110] *Methodus didactica*, Vorrede, unpaginated.

his patrons. His mechanical abilitites made him *Hofmathematicus* and his chemical abilities brought him the title of *Hofmedicus* and professor of medicine. He became a man of theory who could direct the practice of artisans. Having attained this position, he set about proving his relevance to the concerns of the prince in directing his household. Becher sought to capture the productive knowledge of *ars* for his commercial projects and draw it into the sphere of governing, where it would bring wealth, power, and reputation to the prince and, via the increased prosperity of the prince, to his own meager person. In this position, Becher moved between the court and artisans.

An analogy can be drawn between Becher's function of intermediary at court and his intellectual position. As a man of theory, Becher was best suited to harnessing and directing the productive capacity and propensity for invention of the artisan and art. As a medical doctor and chemical adept, Becher concerned himself with the natural world and the transformation and *physis* of material things. He parlayed this natural knowledge, through the office of physician, into the world of politics, and became an intellectual intermediary between the worlds of theory, practice, and territorial *praxis*. Theory alone was sterile, and practice by itself was confused and self-serving, but the unification of the two areas of knowledge and their incorporation into the human sphere of *praxis* would bring about a new world replete with "bürgerliche Nahrung" and civil harmony.[111]

Becher sought to harness the productive capacity of commerce and pull it within the sphere of the territorial prince, but the direction and ultimate possession of that capacity belonged to the state. Becher attempted to entice the territorial ruler into taking possession of that sphere of his rule, as he had taken control of so many other areas in the previous century. If he did so, Becher believed that all productive knowledge could become a *materia status*, both a material foundation of the state and a matter of state.[112] This would happen, however, only if the members of the court—the prince, above all—took Becher seriously and understood the importance of productive knowledge and, especially, of commerce. Moreover, its introduction into the court had to be accomplished without upsetting the delicate balance of power established by the traditions of court comportment. The way in which Becher attempted to introduce productive knowledge and the activity of commerce into the court of the Bavarian elector without destroying the prince's power is the subject of the next chapter.

---

[111] Becher criticized his predecessors in chemistry for two sins. The first was that of remaining solely in the realm of theory, which was completely sterile and unproductive, for the contemplative knowledge of tradition rested only "on the empty word" ("auf blose Worte," *Physica Subterranea*, p. 9). The second was that of staying solely in the realm of art, which resulted in only random techniques, because it was undirected by the moral imperatives and certainties of theoretical knowledge (ibid., pp. 10–11). In contrast to his predecessors, Becher claimed his chemistry would unite these two in order to form productive knowledge that was directed to the common good.

[112] The clearest statement of this is found in the *Methodus didactica*, Vorrede, unpaginated.

THREE

THE COMMERCE OF WORDS: AN EXCHANGE OF CREDIT AT THE COURT OF THE ELECTOR IN MUNICH

Teutschland hat zu seinem Schaden/
Oder grossen Raserey/
Fremde Kauffleut eingeladen/
Daß es ja bald Geld arm sey/
Fremde Waaren/ welche leyder/
Bringen nichts als fremde Kleyder/
Dadurch wird die Teutsche Welt/
Reich an Hoffart/ arm an Geld.

To its harm or great recklessness,
Germany invited in
foreign merchants
so that it is almost out of cash.
Foreign wares which unfortunately
bring nothing but foreign clothes.
Through them the German world
becomes rich in pride, poor in cash.

(*Becher*, Politischer Discurs, 2d ed.)

Handlen/ wandlen und verkauffen/
In der Welt herumher lauffen/
Bald zu Wasser/ bald zu Lande/
Nutzet trefflich jedem Stande/
Wo die Kauffmanschafft recht blühet/
Und die Nahrung nach sich ziehet/
Da kan mancher noch auff Erden/
Reich und wol begütert werden.

Trade and selling,
traveling around the world
now by land, now by sea
is useful to every Estate.
Where merchants prosper
and draw sustenance to themselves;
in that place many a person, still in this
earthly life,
can become rich and propertied.

(*Becher*, Politischer Discurs, 2d ed.)

Dann ein Bauer wäre gern ein Handwercks-Mann/ und wohnete lieber in der Statt/ als auff dem Landt/ ein Handwercks-Mann wäre viel lieber ein Kauffmann/ und lieffe in der Welt herumb/ als daß er in der Werckstatt säß/ ein Handels-Mann hingegen wohnete lieber in einem Adelichen Schloß/ als in seinem Contor, kurtz/ natura hominum est novitatis avida, aber omnis mutatio periculosa.

A peasant would rather be an artisan and live in the city than on the land; an artisan would rather be a merchant and travel the world, instead of sitting in his workshop; a merchant would rather live in a noble palace than in his counting house. In short, the nature of man is eager for new things, but all change is dangerous.

(*Becher*, Politischer Discurs)

O N 23 June 1664, Ferdinand Maria, elector of Bavaria, called Becher to his court as *Hofmedicus und -mathematicus* (court physician and mathematician), the same position Becher had occupied until then at the court of the elector and archbishop of Mainz. The Bavarian court, however, was larger and Becher's projects took on a broader scope there. The six years that Becher spent in the service of the Bavarian elector were the most productive of his life, and it was here that he wrote his two major works on chemistry and commerce, the *Physica Subterranea* and the *Politischer Discurs*. While in Munich, he also wrote the *Methodus didactica* (1668) and the *Moral Discurs* (1669), as well as organizing many projects aimed at increasing trade and commerce in the territory of the elector.[1] Becher spent much of the first three years in Bavarian service at the emperor's court in Vienna, where he attempted to obtain imperial privileges and cooperation for the Bavarian projects. While in the employ of the elector, and especially while in Vienna, Becher's projects and writings promoted not only the elector's interests but also his own.

All of the projects Becher undertook while in Munich were at one and the same time attempts to increase the income of the Bavarian elector, steps in the careful cultivation of his own career, and elements in a broader political agenda of drawing the noble, landed territorial ruler into a commercial society. This chapter primarily addresses Becher's pursuit of the larger political agenda while in Munich and examines how Becher promoted it within the established court structure that he found on entering the elector's court in Bavaria. Such an examination necessitates the description of the court, the structures of power that existed within it, the conventions to which it adhered, and the way Becher manipulated these established structures and conventions to achieve his aims.

The Territorial Prince and His Court

When Becher came to Bavaria in 1664, he encountered a particular structure of power within which he formulated and articulated his political ideas. In expressing these ideas he had to appeal to a certain constellation of power holders within an established hierarchy who acted within a particular form of comportment and understood a certain idiom.[2] The structure and expression of power

[1] Herbert Hassinger, *Johann Joachim Becher, 1635–1682. Ein Beitrag zur Geschichte des Merkantilismus* (Vienna: Adolf Holzhausens, 1951), provides useful information about Becher's stay in Bavaria and the projects he carried out there.

[2] A burgeoning literature on the culture of the noble courts of Europe differs significantly (except in the fact that much of it continues to focus on the French kingdom) from the studies of absolutism that shaped the field in the past. Recent scholars have gained direction from sociologists such as Norbert Elias and Max Weber, as well as the work of anthropologists such as Marcel Mauss and Clifford Geertz. Work on the French noble court by literary historians and critics such as Louis Marin and Jean-Marie Apostolidès, and the study of Spanish and German baroque literature have also helped set the new orientation. For a general overview, see August Buck et al., eds., *Euro-

particular to Bavaria in the 1660s had formed largely as a result of the Thirty Years' War, but was also a consequence of longer-term changes, and differed significantly from that which had existed at the beginning of the century.

In the year Becher arrived at court, the territory of Bavaria was ruled by Elector Ferdinand Maria of the Wilhelminian line of the Wittelsbach house and his consort Henriette Adelheid, daughter of the duke of Savoy. Ferdinand Maria's father, Duke Maximilian, had received the electoral dignity of the Palatinate in 1623 when Frederick V, Elector Palatine and "Winter King" of Bohemia, was dispossessed of his patrimony. The Peace of Westphalia upheld Maximilian's new status (and created an eighth elector in the empire by returning the Lower Palatinate to Frederick's son, Karl Ludwig), as well as making final the transfer of the Upper Palatinate and the Dukedom of Cham to electoral Bavaria. In his long reign (1597–1651) as duke and then elector, Maximilian I had secured a great leap in rank for himself and his heirs within the German Empire, and as territorial ruler had brought order into the finances of his territory, enforced religious homogeneity, and greatly reduced the legal and economic powers and privileges of his nobility, thereby increasing his own power.[3] By the time Maximilian died, he had raised his house and territory to a power in the Holy Roman Empire inferior only to the House of Habsburg. Under his leadership, the territory became strong enough to pose a serious threat to the House of Habsburg in the imperial election of 1657/58, when French interests supported Maximilian's son, Ferdinand Maria, as candidate for emperor.

Maximilian's rule set an example that was difficult for his heir, Ferdinand Maria (reigned in minority 1651–54, in majority 1654–79), to match. Ferdinand Maria was not the warrior-prince that Maximilian had been during the Thirty Years' War; his advisers regarded him as somewhat dim and his wife considered him physically deficient.[4] But the office of ruler in the German territory of the seventeenth century was maintained more by the manipulation of symbols than by the physical prowess of its occupant, and Ferdinand's father had made certain that his position as elector would endure no matter what the mental or physical strength of his son. He reanimated the legend that Charlemagne was the *Stammvater* of the Wittelsbach house and kept alive the memory of the single Wittelsbach emperor, Ludwig IV. He had cultivated the princely office during his rule by introducing Spanish court etiquette and by building an imposing residence in the city, which expressed in its every detail

---

päische Hofkultur im 16. und 17. Jahrhundert, 3 vols. (Hamburg: Dr. Ernst Hausmedell, 1981), and John Larner, "Europe of the Courts," *Journal of Modern History* 55 (1983): 669–81.

[3] F. L. Carsten, *Princes and Parliaments in Germany from the Fifteenth to the Eighteenth Century* (Oxford: Clarendon Press, 1959), documents these developments. The Jesuits were firmly established in Bavaria by 1570 (p. 383).

[4] Eberhard Straub, *Representatio Maiestatis oder churbayerische Freudenfeste* (Munich: Kommissionsbuchhandlung R. Wölfle, 1969), develops this picture of Ferdinand.

the position of the prince.[5] Thus, despite his personal liabilities, Ferdinand Maria stepped into an already established persona. Moreover, Maximilian had directed his education and his reading of *Fürstenspiegel*, operas, panegyrics and sermons. The picture of ruler as conservator of order, embodiment of virtue, and servant of his people was firmly embedded in Ferdinand Maria's psyche by the time he reached majority in 1654.[6] Throughout his life, Ferdinand Maria was particularly scrupulous about the observation of his dignity and could become enraged when he felt he had been slighted.[7] Moreover, he and his consort continued to manipulate the symbols of power in their decoration of the residence and the planning of their festivities.[8]

In order to maintain his power as ruler of his lands as well as the power of the Wittelsbach house within the empire, it was important that Ferdinand Maria sustain and enhance the rank and majesty that his father had so carefully cultivated.[9] He attempted to increase the number of titles and amount of wealth of the house, and was always conscious of his hereditary prerogatives and claims and defended them vigorously.[10] He sued for *Wildfangrecht* in the Palatinate (the right to make serfs of all children born out of wedlock) and for the Palatinate's traditional right to the position of *Reichsvikar* (who assumed power upon an emperor's death in the absence of an elected Roman king). In order to increase the wealth of his house, Ferdinand Maria continued Maximilian's policy of wresting power over the finances of his territory from the hands of the Estates. He treated the direct taxes (*Contribution*) traditionally collected and administered by the Landstände (composed in Bavaria of prelates, knights, nobles, and the representatives of towns and market towns) as his own income by right, as were the *landesherrliche Kammergüter* (territorial revenues) such as regalian rights, tolls, fines, coining of money, and other revenues. Before Maximilian's long occupation of the electoral throne, the *jus*

---

[5] Ibid., pp. 12, 50, 146.

[6] Ibid., p. 17, on the ideal characterization of the ruler. Maximilian's concern for his son's education can be seen in the many directives printed by Friedrich Schmidt, *Geschichte der Erziehung der Bayerischen Wittelsbacher von den frühesten Zeiten bis 1750* (Berlin: A. Hofmann, 1892). The longest and most revealing of these directives was Maximilian's "Monita paterna," written in the 1640s for Ferdinand Maria, printed by Christ. von Aretin in a facing Latin and German edition as *Des großen Kurfürsten Maximilian I. von Baiern Anleitung zur Regierungskunst* (Bamberg and Würzburg: Goebhardtische Buchhandlung, 1822).

[7] Straub, *Representatio*, p. 180.

[8] The literary basis of the symbols used in the residence and the festivities are found in Straub, *Representatio*, and Denise Arico, *Il Tesauro in Europa* (Bologna: Collana del Dipartimento di Italianistica, Università degli Studi di Bologna, 1987), pp. 161–63. I am grateful to Jay Tribby for calling my attention to this latter work.

[9] In Maximilian's "Monita Paterna," he counseled "pietas in parentes et sanguineos" (Aretin, p. 33). With this, he directed Ferdinand Maria to cleave to family ties and to increase the family's status by dignities, rights, and wealth.

[10] Ludwig Hüttl, *Caspar von Schmid (1622–1693), ein kurbayerischer Staatsmann aus dem Zeitalter Ludwigs XIV* (Munich: Kommissionsbuchhandlung R. Wölfle, 1971), p. 51.

collectandi and the administration of the taxes collected were rights belonging to the Bavarian Landstände. As in other territories, the Bavarian Estates' right to collect taxes in the territory had been established at a time when the territorial ruler needed the Estates' local knowledge and connections to develop a machinery of tax collection and government at the local level. The Estates also provided the ruler with a larger pool for the supply of money as well as playing the part of guarantor for loans to the often insolvent and always credit-unworthy ruler.[11] The money that the Estates collected in taxes had been treated as part of the Estates' (not the prince's) treasury and was *granted* to the prince in return for certain privileges (one of which was the collection of taxes itself). In the early sixteenth century the Bavarian dukes began to levy excise (indirect) taxes on wine and beer and, later, on other goods such as iron, wool, horses, oxen, and pigs.[12] These taxes were collected and administered directly by the duke and his court, thus circumventing an important source of the nobility's negotiating power with the duke, as well as its tax-collecting administration. When Maximilian came to the throne in 1597, he established a state monopoly on salt and *Weizenbier* (a Bavarian beer brewed from wheat),[13] and these monopolies, combined with the excise taxes and the traditional regalian revenues, came to account for more income than the Landstände collected.[14] Maximilian had begun his reign in 1597 with a debt of almost 1,500,000 gulden; he ended it in 1651 with a surplus of over 2,000,000 gulden.[15] Ferdinand too ended his reign in 1679 with a surplus for his heir, Maximilian II Emanuel (ruled 1679–1726), due in large part to the subsidies paid by the French after 1670 to secure his neutrality.[16]

---

[11] The Estates could obtain loans of money where the prince could not, because a prince's credit was notoriously bad. Carsten, *Princes*, pp. 404, 428–29. Charles P. Kindleberger, *A Financial History of Western Europe* (London: George Allen & Unwin, 1984), p. 43, notes that loans to sovereigns were secured by pledges of jewels, plate, or the assignment of revenues, or were guaranteed by a city because a city could be sued for repayment where a sovereign could not.

[12] Carsten, *Princes*, pp. 368, 384.

[13] Ibid., p. 392.

[14] A good summary of the structure of taxes and government in Bavaria at the end of the Thirty Years' War is provided in Hüttl, *von Schmid*.

[15] When Maximilian came to power the ducal debts amounted to 1,450,000 gulden. By 1608 the debts had been repaid, and by 1629 Maximilian had built up a surplus of 2,070,000 gulden. This surplus assisted Maximilian in financing the Catholic League and its army during the Thirty Years' War (Carsten, *Princes*, p. 392).

[16] Ferdinand Maria adhered to Maximilian's admonition, "fuga luxus," as well as his warning, "fuga aeris alieni" (Aretin, "Monita," pp. 49, 115). For more information on the Wittelsbach house, see Max von Freyberg, *Pragmatische Geschichte der bayerischen Gesetzgebung und Staatsverwaltung*, 4 vols. (Leipzig: Friedrich Fleischer, 1836–39); Michael Doeberl, "Innere Regierung Bayerns nach dem dreissigjährigen Krieg," *Forschungen zur Geschichte Bayerns* 12 (1904); Michael Strich, *Das Kurhaus Bayern im Zeitalter Ludwigs XIV und die europäischen Mächte*, 2 vols. (Munich: Verlag der Kommission, 1933); Heinz Dollinger, *Studien zur Finanzreform Maximilians I. von Bayern in den Jahren 1598–1618* (Göttingen: Vandenhoeck & Ruprecht, 1968).

Wealth and power went together, and both Maximilian and Ferdinand Maria were not only concerned with the wealth of the Wittelsbach house, but also their own political authority within the territory. By the early sixteenth century, the Estates were already complaining that the duke was appointing "doctores" and foreigners in advisory positions at court, thereby usurping their traditional positions as counselors. Maximilian continued both the bureaucratization and the policy of drawing power away from the local nobility.[17] He had formed his court counselors into more or less permanent advisory and administrative bodies. A Hofkammer (treasury) had been formed in the 1560s, itself a sign of the lessening control of the Landstände over the administration of the finances of the ruler and the territory,[18] and other governing organs—a Hofrat and a Kriegsrat—were also formed in the sixteenth century. Ferdinand Maria continued this practice by forming a Geheime Konferenz out of a select group of counselors from the existing Hofrat.[19] This new advisory body soon became an active governing body to which the Hofrat, Hofkammer, Kriegsrat, and geistlicher Rat were subordinate. The president of each of these bodies was a member of the Geheime Konferenz. Thus the head of the Geheime Konferenz, the *Kanzler*, directly supervised all branches of the administration. This very powerful and unusually central position was filled during Becher's tenure at court by Caspar von Schmid, a doctor of both laws, and a native of the Upper Palatinate.[20] The degree of centralization in the Bavarian government in 1664 was unusual among the territories of the German Empire at this time. Indeed, in other territories, councils were usually collegiate arrangements in which all members had the same power, although they usually chose one member as nominal head.[21]

The growth of the Bavarian sovereign's power in the sixteenth and seven-

---

[17] Carsten, *Princes*, pp. 355–56.

[18] Ibid., p. 390.

[19] In the "Monita paterna" (Aretin, p. 119), Maximilian wrote under the heading "*Prudentia*," that the wisest of all rulers is he who can decide and execute all things himself. The second wisest is he who follows good advice and makes it his own. For the most part Ferdinand Maria followed this latter practice.

[20] The position of *Kanzler* was filled from 1662 to 1664 by Johann Georg Oexl, but, according to Hüttl, *von Schmid*, from 1662 von Schmid (at that time *Vice-Kanzler*) was primarily in charge. The formal organization of these governing and advisory bodies should not be overestimated, for, although they were regularized to a certain extent under Maximilian and Ferdinand Maria, they continued to reflect their history as bodies that had evolved rather than been created by governmental fiat.

[21] The dynamics of power, however, meant that this was not a static state of affairs. See, for example, Otto Hintze, "Der österreichische und der preußische Beamtenstaat im 17. und 18. Jahrhundert," in *Gesammelte Abhandlungen zur allgemeinen Verfassungsgeschichte*, ed. Fritz Hartung (Leipzig: Koebler & Amelang, 1941): 1:324, in which he discusses (with a note of regret) how die Hofkanzlei in Vienna, in which the position of *Hofkanzler* had developed into a very powerful and central one, was rearranged in 1654 on a collegiate basis in order to limit the power of the *Hofkanzler*.

teenth centuries was reinforced by the establishment of a single territorial law by Maximilian in 1616, the Codex Maximilianeus, and by the parallel development of a local network of territorial representatives to enforce the law. In Bavaria, the office of *Rentmeister* was reinstituted and given power to oversee electoral financial interests in the territory and to enforce the *Polizei* ordinances decreed by the elector and meant to replace local ordinances. In a flourish of paternalism and self-interest, the elector declared that this new office had as its purpose the protection of the inhabitants of the territory from exploitation by city officials and the local nobility.[22] While this was no doubt sincerely intended, the move effectively put the subjects of the territory under his direct control, eliminating the previously existing layers of authority and undermining their power. This development in Bavaria was similar to the implementation of the better-known offices of *intendant* in France and the military *Commissar* in Brandenburg. While the Bavarian *Rentmeister* did not have the same judicial power as the corresponding French and Brandenburg-Prussian officials, the institution of this position clearly marked the same tendency to increase and regularize the central authority of the territorial prince.

As territories were centralized under the jurisdiction of their princes, law making itself increasingly came to be seen as the sole prerogative of the territorial rulers.[23] European sovereigns actively promoted the articulation of natural law because its theories brought a new authority to the territorial prince. Natural law was considered the basis of government (practical philosophy), and brought together the functions of law giving and government in the sphere of the sovereign.[24] Moreover, because this law was conceived to be universal and fundamental to all humankind, the government's intervention in any and all of the human activities—political/social, moral, and economic—included in the traditional sphere of *philosophia practica* was justified. Thus, the foremost theorist of natural law in the seventeenth century, Samuel Pufendorf (1632–94), declared that the legitimate powers of the sovereign cut across all military, legislative, punitive, judicial, and economic areas.[25] In the Bavarian territory of the seventeenth century, Becher's activities at the Munich court would assist the realization of this conception of law and of the ruler's sphere.

---

[22] In 1669, von Schmid rewrote the Rentmeisterinstruktion of 1613. This is discussed by Hüttl, *von Schmid*, pp. 180–84.

[23] For examples in Bavaria, see Hüttl, *von Schmid*, p. 32.

[24] See the excellent article by Horst Denzer, "Samuel Pufendorfs Naturrecht im Wissenschaftssystem seiner Zeit," in *Samuel von Pufendorf. 1632–1982. Ett rättshistoriskt symposium i Lund 15–16 Januari 1982* (Lund: Bloms Boktryckeri, 1986), pp. 17–30. Pufendorf: Natural law is "die Architectur und die Baukunst im großen Gewölbe des Corpus Politicus," quoted on p. 22. Also see Jutta Brückner, *Staatswissenschaften, Kameralismus und Naturrecht. Ein Beitrag zur Geschichte der Politischen Wissenschaft im Deutschland des späten 17. und frühen 18. Jahrhunderts* (Munich: C. H. Beck, 1977), esp. pp. 168–75.

[25] Leonard Krieger, *The Politics of Discretion: Pufendorf and the Acceptance of Natural Law* (Chicago: University of Chicago Press, 1965), esp. pp. 135–41.

While princes drew political power away from the Estates throughout the German Empire in the seventeenth century, this was especially marked in Bavaria. There the Estates' loss of power can be gauged by the number of Landtage called: for the seventy years before Maximilian's reign, there was a Landtag almost every other year, while Maximilian called only two Landtage in his entire reign (1597–1651),[26] and Ferdinand Maria (1651–79) called only one, in 1669, the last in its traditional form.

In spite of this decrease in constitutional power and effectiveness, the Bavarian nobility did not by any means disappear from the scene of this increasingly centralized, "absolutist" territory. On the contrary, the elector needed his "old" nobility in order to justify his own central and noble place in the ancient scheme of things and his "new" nobility to provide him with money and credit. The value of the old nobility's estates had declined after the war and the cost of maintaining at least the appearance of nobility (especially as this appearance was of a costly French fashion) had increased, leaving the established nobility little wealth. The nobility continued, however, to function as a known and visible hierarchy at the head of which the territorial ruler could preside. The new nobility, on the other hand, made up of rich townspeople, military officers, and courtiers had money (often having profited from the war) but lesser status. This class did not have, nor did it ever attain the *Edelmansfreiheit*, which gave jurisdiction in certain court cases, rights to demand statute labor, and hunting rights. In Bavaria these privileges were accorded only to those families who had been in possession of their land before 1557.[27] The new nobility sought to buy up the old nobility's land and reestablish its cultivation—something that the elector encouraged on the one hand, as it meant revenues for his Hofkammer, but something, on the other hand, that he monitored closely, for if nobility and status came to depend on the power of money alone, the position of the ruler himself would be undermined.

The plight of the nobility can be read in the demands its members made to the elector in the last Landtag of 1669. They requested that the elector give Bavarians preference over "foreigners" in positions at the court, for the court had become the stage and center of power, and if they were to share in power they had to become actors there. They also requested that French, Italian, dance, and fencing be taught at the Jesuit university at Ingolstadt.[28] The old

---

[26] Carsten, *Princes*, pp. 386–87.

[27] Hüttl, *von Schmid*, p. 21.

[28] Felix Joseph Lipowsky, *Des Ferdinand Maria . . . Churfuerstens . . . Lebens- und Regierungs-Geschichte* (Munich: Jakob Giel, 1831), p. 195, mentions Landtag demands, and Hüttl, *von Schmid*, summarizes the state of the *Landadel* after the war, pp. 19–20. Lipowsky's book is a hagiographic account of Ferdinand's rule, but it inadvertently provides some important details. On the rivalry between the old and new nobility and the university-trained court officials, see Bernd Wunder, "Hof und Verwaltung im 17. Jahrhundert," in *Europäische Hofkultur im 16. und 17. Jahrhundert*, ed. August Buck et al. (Hamburg: Dr. Ernst Hausmedell, 1981), 2:199–204. Rudolf Schlögl, "Der Bayerische Landtag von 1669," *Zeitschrift für bayerischer Landesgeschichte* 52 (1989): 221–54, gives a detailed account of the 1669 Landtag.

landed nobility needed places for their sons, and such an education could prepare them for a future in an office at court, in the military, or in the church. Naturally this education had to be *standesgemäß* (corresponding to their rank), hence the call for a different and courtly course of education.[29] The new nobles also benefited from such a course; through it they acquired the overlay of courtly manners they needed to smooth their transition to a higher social station.[30]

The other privileged members of Bavarian society represented in the Landtag were the towns and the religious foundations. The towns of Bavaria had little economic power and could not compete commercially with the free imperial cities of Augsburg, Nuremberg, Regensburg, and Frankfurt. The artisanal guilds in the towns complained that even the peasants bought foreign goods and that artisans in Munich could obtain no foundlings as apprentices, as too many of them were becoming court servants or joining religious orders.[31] The religious foundations, on the contrary, were the largest holders of capital in Bavaria, presiding over large tracts of land (about 50 percent of the total cultivated land in Bavaria), much of it granted by the ruler, and administering many charitable endowments.[32]

In the rivalry between the old and new nobility that composed the court economy, different forms of "credit" bought favor and alliance with the prince. Within the established hierarchy and the commerce of symbols that sustained it, the old nobility possessed (and regulated access to) social credit, and the new nobility attempted to gain access to social credit by mimicking the traditional manipulation of symbols. In the new commerce of material wealth, however, the new nobility possessed access to (money) credit, and the old nobles could do nothing but shore up their hierarchy, display the symbols of their power, and keep a vigilant watch that this sort of credit did not undermine their own. The policies of Elector Ferdinand Maria and of his *Kanzler*, Caspar von Schmid, were directed toward balancing the power of these competing groups of the nobility (and keeping them less powerful than the central prince) while harvest-

[29] The course of learning demanded by the nobles was similar to that offered by the Ritterakademien. See Norbert Conrads, *Ritterakademien der frühen Neuzeit. Bildung als Standesprivileg im 16. und 17. Jahrhundert* (Göttingen: Vandenhoeck & Ruprecht, 1982).

[30] Courtiers' manuals had a similar function. See Norbert Elias, *The Development of Manners* (New York: Urizen Books, 1978), *Power and Civility* (New York: Pantheon Books, 1982), and *The Court Society* (New York: Pantheon Books, 1983), all translated by Edmund Jephcott; Marvin Becker, *Civility and Society in Western Europe, 1300–1600* (Bloomington: Indiana University Press, 1988); Jacques Revel, "The Uses of Civility," in *A History of Private Life*, vol. 3, ed. Roger Chartier (Cambridge, Mass.: Harvard University Press, 1989), 167–205; Frank Whigham, *Ambition and Privilege*. C. Stephen Jaeger, *The Origins of Courtliness: Civilizing Trends and the Formation of Courtly Ideals 939–1210* (Philadelphia: University of Pennsylvania Press, 1985), proposes a very different starting point and source for "the civilizing process."

[31] Leonhard Memmert, "Die öffentliche Förderung der gewerblichen Produktionsmethoden zur Zeit des Merkantilismus in Bayern," *Abhandlungen aus dem Staatswissenschaftlichen Seminar an der Universität Erlangen* 7 (Leipzig, 1930): 24, 22.

[32] Hüttl, *von Schmid*, pp. 18, 22.

ing both the social and financial credit that they could provide to the elector.[33] Becher's promotion of commerce can only be understood within the context of these tensions, for he would attempt to reconcile the conflicting values that lay behind the rivalry between the old and new nobility and between social and financial credit.

Land and Money

> heutiges tags viel Landt und Unterthanen erfordert werden, biß
> man so viel par gelt zusammen brächte.
>
> nowadays much land and many subjects are needed to be able to
> bring together so much cash.
> (*Becher to Emperor Leopold, after 1674*)

The gain of power by the territorial ruler over the course of the sixteenth and seventeenth centuries was accelerated in Germany by the abrupt decrease in agricultural incomes and in the value of land occasioned by the loss of population in the Thirty Years' War. The territory of Bavaria, like most of the German Empire after 1648, continued for several decades to suffer from the war's effects, which had been especially severe in Bavaria after the Swedish entry into southern Germany in 1635. The population in some areas was reduced by more than a third; this led to a surplus of agricultural products, a decrease in their price, and a depression in land values. In addition, Bavaria's most important export—woolen textiles—lost its markets to other suppliers during the war and never recaptured them.[34] Trade bypassed the territory, for even the residence of the court, Munich, could not compete with the imperial trading cities within and around the Bavarian lands. What large-scale commerce did exist in Bavaria was mostly carried on by foreign merchants.

Although this economic development weakened the standing of the old nobility and the town governments, enabling the prince to take over many of their functions in the territory, it also decreased the income the prince himself received. Although "ordinary" revenues (*Contribution* and the income of the *landesherrliche Kammergüter*) were increasingly under the sole control of the territorial ruler, these taxes decreased with the drop in population and the lower prices for agricultural products. Similarly, although the "extraordinary" taxes traditionally imposed only in times of emergency (such as Maximilian's excise

---

[33] Hüttl, *von Schmid*, provides an excellent summary of these developments, and I follow his interpretation of Schmid's activities in the service of the elector.

[34] On the economic situation in Bavaria, see the summaries in Hüttl, *von Schmid*; Hassinger, *Becher*, chap. 2, sec. 1; and Wilhelm Störmer, "Wirtschaft und Bürgertum in den altbayerischen Städten unter dem zunehmenden absolutistischen Einfluss des Landesfürsten," in *Die Städte Mitteleuropas im 17. und 18. Jahrhundert*, ed. Wilhelm Rausch (Linz and Donau: Der Arbeitskreis, 1991), pp. 237–66.

taxes) had become permanent and under the direct control of the elector, the revenue from these levies also declined as a result of the effects of the war. In the last half of the seventeenth century the Bavarian territory provided few sources of revenue for the elector.

Many of these taxes were collected in kind, increasingly unsatisfactory for the prince because of his need for specie. Money had become the very basis of a prince's material welfare and power by the middle of the seventeenth century. During the Thirty Years' War money was central in order to pay the *solde* of the *soldatesca*, the troops of mercenary soldiers. After the war, large standing armies of mercenaries were formed, which necessitated a steady flow of cash.[35] In Bavaria, Ferdinand Maria needed a regular supply to support his standing army of twenty thousand men and his improvements to the fortifications at Ingolstadt and Braunau.[36]

Money was necessary not only to secure the borders of the territory from the neighboring powers, but also to display and secure the power of the prince within his own territory and among his Estates. Public actions at court were ceremonies for displaying the outward signs of majesty, power, and rank. The elaborate rituals, festivals, pageants, and public appearances involving the prince and his court presented a picture of the place and power of the ruler (a *representatio* of real power) and the hierarchy of society that descended from it.[37] As one writer stated:

> If the subjects are to recognize the majesty of the king, they must comprehend that the highest power and authority lies with him. . . . The common man who depends solely on the external senses and uses reason seldom, cannot of his own accord imagine what the majesty of the king is. Through material things which appear to the eye and which touch the other senses, however, he receives a clear concept of the king's majesty, power, and authority.[38]

---

[35] For a brief summary of this development, see Peter Claus Hartmann, *Geld als Instrument europäischer Machtpolitik im Zeitalter des Merkantilismus* (Munich: Kommission für bayerische Landesgeschichte, 1978), introduction.

[36] Lipowsky, *Ferdinand Maria*, pp. 52–54, 106, 130, 147.

[37] Studies on the representation of power include Jean-Marie Apostolidès, *Le Roi-Machine. Spectacle et politique au temps de Louis XIV* (Paris: Minuit, 1981); Peter Burke, *The Fabrication of Louis XIV* (New Haven: Yale University Press, 1992); Hubert C. Ehalt, *Ausdrucksformen absolutistischer Herrschaft. Der Wiener Hof im 17. und 18. Jahrhundert* (Munich: R. Oldenbourg Verlag, 1980); Clifford Geertz, "Centers, Kings, and Charisma: Reflections on the Symbolics of Power," in *Local Knowledge* (New York: Basic Books, 1983), pp. 121–46; David I. Kertzer, *Ritual, Politics, and Power* (New Haven: Yale University Press, 1988); Jürgen Freiherr von Kruedener, *Die Rolle des Hofes im Absolutismus* (Stuttgart: Gustav Fischer Verlag, 1973); Louis Marin, *Portrait of the King*, trans. Martha M. Houle (Minneapolis: University of Minnesota Press, 1988); Roy Strong, *Art and Power* (Woodbridge, Suffolk: Boydell, 1984); idem, *Splendor at Court* (Boston: Houghton Mifflin, 1973); Sean Wilentz, ed., *Rites of Power: Symbols, Rituals, and Politics since the Middle Ages* (Philadelphia: University of Pennsylvania Press, 1985).

[38] Julius Bernhard von Rohr, *Einleitung zur Ceremoniel-Wissenschaft der großen Herren*, 2d ed. (Berlin: Johann Andreas Rüdiger, 1733), p. 2.

In the seventeenth century the "public" or audience for these costly ceremonies was not restricted to a ruler's subjects but included the prince's own court household, the foreign resident ministers, and any visiting persons of rank. Thus in 1658, as the newly elected Emperor Leopold I passed through Munich on his return journey to Vienna from Frankfurt, Ferdinand Maria spent more than 300,000 gulden to entertain him. The ceremony, banquets, and plays given for the emperor by the elector were laden with the heraldry of the houses of Habsburg and Wittelsbach and representations of their relative power.[39]

While he reigned, Ferdinand Maria sought to endow his house, his court, and the city of his residence with a reputation equal to the rank of elector and second power of the empire. He was stimulated in these plans by his consort, Henriette Adelheid, whom he had married *pro procuram* in Turin in 1650 and in person in Munich in 1652. Henriette Adelheid had first been groomed to become the wife of Louis XIV. When this match did not eventuate, she consoled herself in the infinitely lesser position of electoress of Bavaria by bringing French court ritual and dress and large numbers of Italian artists, musicians, workmen, and architects to Munich in her entourage.[40] The electoral couple built a theater and an opera house early in their reign and they called many religious orders, among them the Carmelites, the Theatines, and the Ursulines, to Munich and Landshut where the elector provided churches, quarters, and support.[41] These projects significantly increased the size and style of the court, and Ferdinand Maria, like other princes in Europe, came to find that the symbolic representation of power was very costly.

Unlike many other territorial rulers, Ferdinand Maria could rely upon his monopoly on salt and *Weizenbier* to provide him with revenue, but he was able to leave a surplus to his heir only by drawing on two time-honored methods for a prince to obtain extraordinary income: subsidies and loans from foreign powers. Ferdinand Maria received subsidies from the French for his guarantee to remain neutral in case of war between France and the Habsburgs, and he received loans guaranteed by his Estates. Neither of these sources was permanent or self-sustaining, or involved the territorial ruler in a cycle of production that would insure a continued flow of cash.

While specie was quite obviously central to the sovereign's exercise of power, it was excluded as a determinant of social rank. The possession of money and the ability to obtain financial credit were by themselves no measure of social credit, as is clear from the social gap that separated the new and old nobility in Bavaria.[42] While integrated into the commercial economy as con-

---

[39] For a description of the emperor's visit, see Straub, *Representatio*, pp. 210–17.

[40] Michael Strich, "Kurfürstin Adelheid von Bayern," *Historisches Jahrbuch* 47 (1927): 63–96.

[41] For details of the festivals and operas, see Straub, *Representatio*.

[42] This was a general phenomenon at European courts, as Sharon Kettering shows in *Patrons, Brokers, and Clients in Seventeenth-Century France* (Oxford: Oxford University Press, 1986). She gives examples of this at the French court in the rivalry between the new noble Régusse and the old

sumers, noble courts still operated within a social economy determined by gift and patronage.[43] Money within a landed court had less an intrinsic value than the value it gave to display rank and status and to create reputation. Prince Karl Eusebius von Liechtenstein (1611–84) could say: "Das Geldt ist nur schene Monumenten zu hinterlassen zue ebiger und unsterblicher Gedechtnuß" (Money is only for leaving behind beautiful monuments to one's eternal and undying memory).[44] The spendthrift conduct of the old nobility in building palaces that broke them and entertaining guests on borrowed funds was thus "rational" behavior within the court context. For money was to be consumed, not saved and counted as it was by the urban merchant.[45] The disjunction between the values of the court world and the market economy—of which the court had become an inextricable part—became especially acute in the late seventeenth century as the need for money at court became absolute, but its production and acceptance lay outside the noble sphere.

When Becher arrived in Munich in 1664, he entered a court poised in the long moment of transition from an agricultural and feudal society to a commercial society. For despite the economic changes that had occurred around the court, the structure of the court hierarchy, the scale of values on which rank at court was measured, and the symbols of noble power remained agricultural and feudal. The composition of the Bavarian court, divided between old and new nobility, and the uneasy balancing act of the elector reflected these values. Becher offered his commercial projects to the beleaguered prince as a new source of revenue. He was, however, politic enough to respect the court hierarchy and its symbolic needs, and he formulated his projects in a way that enabled the prince to transmute monetary gain into the acquisition of rank and

---

noble Oppedé (pp. 50ff.), and in the Valbelles' claim to be descended from a tenth-century vicomte of Marseille when in fact they were a family of merchants, recently ennobled (p. 76).

[43] Marcel Mauss's 1950 essay, *The Gift*, trans. W. D. Halls (New York: W. W. Norton, 1990), has provided a general theoretical framework for works on the gift economy and systems of patronage, such as Sharon Kettering, "Gift-giving and Patronage in Early Modern France," *French History* 2 (1988): 131–51, and her *Patrons, Brokers, and Clients*.

[44] Quoted by Otto Brunner, *Adeliges Landleben und europäischer Geist. Leben und Werk Wolf Helmhards von Hohberg, 1612–1688* (Salzburg: Otto Müller, 1949), p. 59.

[45] The contrast between noble and bourgeois attitudes to money comes through in classic form, for example, in Molière's *Le bourgeois gentilhomme*, and was first treated extensively by Norbert Elias, whose views are finally beginning to receive the critical examination they have long deserved. Otto Brunner, another scholar of ancien régime culture whose works are similarly receiving new attention, also drew the contrast between noble and commercial values in *Adeliges Landleben* and "Das 'ganze Haus' und die alteuropäische Ökonomik," in *Neue Wege der Sozialgeschichte* (Göttingen: Vandenhoeck & Ruprecht, 1956). On Brunner, see the excellent introduction to Brunner's *Land and Lordship: Structures of Governance in Medieval Austria* by the translators Howard Kaminsky and James Van Horn Melton (Philadelphia: University of Pennsylvania Press, 1992), and H. C. Erik Midelfort, "Curious Georgics: The German Nobility and Their Crisis of Legitimacy in the Late Sixteenth Century," in *Germania Illustrata*, ed. Andrew C. Fix and Susan C. Karant-Nunn (Kirksville, Mo.: Sixteenth Century Journal Publishers, 1992), pp. 217–42.

status, not so much by means of an exchange of coin but rather by an exchange of "credit."

At Court

> durch gnädigste Annehmung meiner wenigen Person in dero Dienste.
>
> Through gracious acceptance of my humble person into the service of Your Highness.
> (*Proposal, Becher to Elector Ferdinand Maria, 1664*)

> In this dangerous Land-Navigation none shou'd dare to sail but in broad day-light, or carrying the Lanthorn of his Prudence lighted; and morning and evening on his Knees, beseeching Heaven to send him a good Voyage: For in a Court, to bring the Ship of ones hopes into a safe Harbor, is a Happiness which depends more on Divine Assistance, than on any human Prudence.
> (*Boccalini*, Advices from Parnassus)[46]

In the framework of rank and power that prevailed at the Bavarian court, Becher was a *homo novus*, armed only with his title as *Hofmedicus und -mathematicus*, his *Kundtschafft*, and his commercial projects. In implementing his plans and taking part as an effective actor on the court stage, Becher was constrained by the particular structure of power and the rules of comportment resulting from the dynamics of power at work within this structure. The elector was the source of a fluid current of power in the territory. He was surrounded by an emergent bureaucracy—the court officials within the advisory bodies, each representing his own lesser eddy of power. In addition, other groups and individuals were not fully integrated into the court power structure, such as the nobles who were not members of the court, large merchants, and town representatives. These people constituted smaller vortices of external power, sometimes creating disturbances in the flow of power down the court hierarchy and sometimes joining into it. At the wide and muddy mouth of this stream of power were those, like Becher, who had very little official power and who depended upon the patronage of an official or upon acts of favor from the prince.

The hierarchical structure—determined by rank, friendship, family tie, enmity, and rivalry—gave relative position, status, and reputation paramount

---

[46] Advice 23 is a brief satirical comment on the perils of the courtier, in which Apollo commissions Euclid, Ptolemy, Aristotle, Guido Bonatti, Balthazar Castiglione, Columbus, Vespucci and others to draw up a chart for the "land navigation" of courtiers. The forces operating in the court, however, prove too uncertain to be charted on the principles of sea navigation, and the project has to be given up.

importance and bred an intense struggle over place. Because personal power depended on rank and its observance by others, all in the court society were compelled to abide by a complex set of rules and rituals by which the whole hierarchy of power (and their own individual place in it) could be upheld.[47] As *Hofmedicus*, Becher was part of the established hierarchy of the court; he was one of seven *Hofmedici*, and received the salary of a middle-level member of court: six hundred gulden a year in salary, forty gulden a year for house rent, and one and a half measures of wine, two measures of beer, and two loaves of bread daily.[48] Becher had been appointed *Hofmedicus*, but he had been called to court on the strength of his treatise, which he had expounded in the presence of the elector, entitled "Impartial considerations about the increase of commerce and the interest of the Elector that rests upon this increase."[49] The nature of this treatise[50] clearly indicated that Becher was also de facto to be considered

[47] This is the structure, based on the French court, set out by Norbert Elias in *The Court Society*, who summarizes this necessity to maintain the rituals in order to uphold one's own power: "Like boxers in a clinch, none of the various privileged groups dares alter its basic position in the slightest because each fears that it might thereby lose advantages and others gain them" (p. 274). Orest Ranum, in "Courtesy, Absolutism, and the Rise of the French State, 1630–60," *Journal of Modern History* 52 (1980): 428, notes that the rules of courtesy and rank were codified and rigidly enforced in the seventeenth century.

[48] This was a raise of 250 gulden over his salary in Mainz, but was still only about a quarter of the salary of the most senior court physician (Munich, Bayerisches Hauptstaatsarchiv [BHA], HR II f. 248 Besoldungsbücher 1664, fol. 30r–v). An advisor to the elector received slightly more, and the *Obrist-Cämerer* (highest councillors) received 5,000 gulden a year, so Becher can be placed as a middle-level member of court. Heinrich Volberg, *Deutsche Kolonialbestrebungen in Südamerika nach dem Dreißigjährigen Kriege* (Cologne and Vienna: Böhlau-Verlag, 1977), p. 52, provides information about salaries. Becher never received an actual increase of salary in his six years, but one year he did receive an extra 150 gulden for a scribe (BHA, Hofzahlamt Kurbayern, Hofzahlamtsrechnung no. 116, 1667) and in 1667 he petitioned for and received the yearly addition of 40 gulden a year for house rent and, daily, the wine, beer, and bread mentioned earlier. (BHA, HR I 291/27/1). The elector also gave him 100 Reichsthaler in 1667 to develop his system of teaching Latin (*Methodus didactica*), and other costs were taken over for him, for example, his laboratory was completely financed by court expenditures, and the publishing costs of one of his books were paid by the court. (See BHA, Hofzahlamt Kurbayern, Hofzahlamtsrechnungen nos. 113–119, 1664–1671.) Becher once complained however that for every 1,000 gulden he received from the elector, he spent 1,000 more on the elector's business, and in addition to that had to do much waiting with bared head at the elector's convenience (BHA, HR I 219/27/1). In 1666, Becher was appointed *Commerzien-Rath* (commercial advisor) to the emperor with a yearly salary of 1,000 Reichsthaler, a position he held concurrently with the position in Bavaria.

[49] "Dr. Bechers unvorgreiffliches Bedencken/ wegen Auffnehmung der Commercien-Sachen/ und des darauff beruhenden Chur-Fürstlichen *Interesse*, in München" was presented to the elector on 18 June 1664. Five days later, Becher was called to the court as *Hofmedicus und -mathematicus*. Becher printed this tract in *Politischer Discurs*, 2d ed., pp. 260–96. An undated manuscript copy is in BHA, GR 272/1.

[50] This treatise listed fifteen "Mercantilische Reguln und axiomata" (mercantile rules and axioms), which advocated that money be kept and drawn into the territory of the elector, tariffs be placed on imports not exports, raw materials be imported, refined, and then exported, the territory be as self-sufficient as possible, and trade within it be free of tariffs and tolls. He also was concerned

commercial advisor to the elector. He was not simply named commercial advisor because, as he himself noted, this position had not existed previously in Munich, and so would require the establishment of an entirely new center of power.[51] The establishment of any new power at court aroused fierce opposition as it upset existing balances of power and threatened those already holding power. However, because this de facto position involved Becher in activities that fell outside the normal compass of a court physician, he needed a protector at court to introduce him, to intercede for him with the elector, and to arrange audiences with the elector. Becher found such a protector in Herman Egon von Fürstenberg, *Obersthofmeister* at the Bavarian court.

A measure of status and rank at court was favor, or *Credit*, as it was called by Becher and his contemporaries. There was continual discussion about who was "in credit" and an omnipresent concern to maintain one's own. Documents in the Bayerisches Hauptstaatsarchiv in Munich relating to Becher's employ at court give ample evidence—despite their fragmentary nature—of this overarching concern with credit. A report sent from Vienna to Ferdinand Maria in 1666, entitled "Gründliche Information über daß Doctor Bechers Verübte Insolentien" (Thorough report about the insolence practiced by Dr. Becher), described an incident that began when Becher wanted to leave Vienna, where he had been negotiating for an imperial privilege for the Bavarian silk manufactory, to go to Munich. He requested a letter from the emperor testifying that he was in "credit" at the imperial court (i.e., that he was not leaving Vienna in disgrace), and that he had worked in the elector's interest (not against it or solely in the emperor's interest) while in Vienna. According to the report, the emperor wrote this "letter of credit" and gave it to the imperial treasurer, Georg Ludwig von Sinzendorf, to deliver to Becher (Sinzendorf being at that time Becher's protector at the Habsburg court), but at precisely that moment, Sinzendorf claimed to have been warned that Becher and his wife were out of credit at the Bavarian court and should not be trusted. Thus instead of giving Becher the emperor's testimonial, Sinzendorf supplied him with a letter to the elector inquiring into the truth of the rumor that Becher was out of credit in Munich. Contrary to all decorum, Becher broke the seals on Sinzendorf's letter, read it,

---

to attract artisans and peasants to the territory and so discussed problems of food supply and guild problems of monopoly and polypoly (a surplus of master guildsmen). In short, these axioms advanced the commonweal. The signs of a territory concerned with the common good were expensive land and housing, many and wealthy artisans, a sound currency, a warehouse and market open to all producers in the territory, a workhouse for the poor, and a rich bank (*Politischer Discurs*, 2d ed., p. 260).

[51] Becher writes that the elector should have a commercial advisory board: "akin to that which is well known in the Hansa cities and has now been organized in the Electorate of Saxony and by the Duke of Würtemberg. In order that the salary of this advisor not constitute a burden on Your Highness, in the beginning, a few knowledgeable men, who concern themselves with the common good, and drawn from among the court, and the treasury advisors, and several from the most highly ranked merchants, artisans and citizens of the city, could be appointed" (ibid., p. 267).

and promptly appeared at Sinzendorf's estate where he insulted the treasurer, then thought better of his words and escaped, the report notes, through the garden and over the wall.[52]

Rivalry and scheming, set in motion by the court structure and the concern with credit, were an essential dynamic of court society. The overweening concern with the most minute insults to personal reputation so typical of any baroque court devolved from the absolute necessity for the court person to develop a fine sensibility to alliance, status, and the observance of rank. The preservation of rank, and the preservation of real and apparent power that went along with it, could only be accomplished by a carefully constructed strategy. Becher charted his course at court between three main rivals and sources of enmity. These were the court officials near the source of power, the merchants and townspeople of Munich on the fringes of power, and the projectors at the mouth of the stream. All of these groups vied with Becher for a place close to or in direct contact with the source of power, the prince's favor. Each of the following incidents involving these three groups illustrates the nature of their rivalry with Becher.

Becher appealed directly to the elector to gain power for himself and a favorable hearing for his commercial plans. This made him a rival to the members of the established hierarchy of the court bureaucracy, who believed he sought to circumvent them and to decrease their power and influence with the prince. A scuffle between Becher and the courtiers occurred only months after his call to Munich, when he submitted a project to the elector to create a fund that he claimed would supply the revenue for the salaries of all court officials. The proposal foundered when it became known to the courtiers that this fund would necessitate a 5 percent reduction of their salaries. Becher planned to use the savings from their salaries for a fund that could be invested and yield (according to Becher's ever optimistic projections of material increase) an annual return of 100 percent.[53] The project was never implemented, but Becher continued to skirmish with court officials.

The most important of the court officials with whom Becher clashed was Caspar von Schmid, *Vize-Kanzler*, then *Kanzler* to the elector.[54] Becher re-

---

[52] BHA, Kasten Schwartz, 3 July 1666. That this quarrel was apparently patched over is shown by the letter that Sinzendorf wrote to the *Obrist-Hofmeister*, von Fürstenberg, in Munich assuring him that the "differences" between himself and Becher were resolved because Becher had given him "all satisfaction" (Sinzendorf to *Obrist-Hofmeister*, 25 July 1666, *Politischer Discurs*, 2d ed., pp. 581–82). When Becher finally returned to the Habsburg court four years later in 1670, however, he felt it necessary to write beforehand to Sinzendorf to ascertain whether he could expect favor there (Sinzendorf to Becher, 14 August 1670, ibid., p. 583).

[53] Ibid., pp. 322ff.

[54] Becher published many of the documents—letters, reports, commissions—in the second edition of the *Politischer Discurs* in order to reply to his "detractors [*Widersacher*]." He claimed that these documents proved his actions had been directed by his concern for the common interest (i.e., the interest of his prince), while the actions of his detractors were driven only by self-interest.

counted their rivalry to the elector's resident minister in Vienna. This minister's report provides a vivid picture of the atmosphere of the court:

> The Vice-Kanzler knows very well that Becher never speaks well of him and therefore has tried very hard to cause that your Highness the Elector should give [Becher] no audience, but he was despite this admitted to an audience, and in fact received with such good favor that Your Highness the Elector came half way toward him in the room, offered him Your hand and showed that You were pleased by his presence. His enemy standing in the antechamber perceived this as he saw Becher coming from the inner chamber and had to recognize that Becher had broken through all the obstacles that had been put before him.[55]

Becher accused Caspar von Schmid of self-interest, calling him "der Schwäbische Frantzose" (the Swabian Frenchman), thereby doubly impugning von Schmid's ability to devote himself to Bavarian interests: once for his place of birth and again for his friendly policy to the French. Becher asserted that von Schmid acted as a pawn of the Munich merchants, hindering him from completing many useful and ingenious projects.[56] It may have been von Schmid who in turn questioned Becher's capacity for loyalty to Bavaria, asking why he did not stay in his own fatherland (Speyer) and make his proposals there.[57]

Von Schmid's opposition to Becher originated not only in a fear of losing power but also from an opposition to commercial activities in general. Where Becher saw the elector's income to be founded upon artificial sources of wealth, such as commerce, von Schmid considered it to rest upon the natural wealth of the elector's agricultural lands and the traditional sources of princely income. Von Schmid once argued in a meeting of the Geheime Konferenz that the prince should not become a merchant, for where this happens, the subjects will be ruined. There are other ways, von Schmid claimed, for a prince to increase the income of his land without lowering himself to the place of a merchant.[58] Von Schmid, a member of the new nobility, courtier, and dedicated to increasing the status and power of his prince, the elector of Bavaria, was perhaps particularly sensitive to this point.[59] Becher, on the other hand, criticized courtier-

He emphasized that these private documents were "not unknown to *Vice-Cantzler* Schmid"(ibid., p. 428).

[55] The Bavarian resident minister in Vienna, Stoiberer, was here reporting a conversation with Becher and, in this instance, was quoting Becher's own description of his quarrels with von Schmid. Stoiberer to Elector Ferdinand Maria, 25 September 1670, BHA, HR I 291/27/1.

[56] Becher, *Närrische Weiszheit*, bk. 1, no. 27, and bk. 2, no. 13.

[57] *Politischer Discurs*, 2d ed., pp. 300–301. In a draft of this treatise, dated 20 October 1664, in Mss. var. 1(1), fols. 549r–559r, Becher wrote: "warum ich nicht zu Hauß bleibe/ und meine Anschläge meinem Vatterlandt mitheile (*wie mir einstens einer von Euer Churf. Durchl. primis ministris unbesonnen vorgeworfen*)" (fol. 550r; the italicized portion was expunged when the treatise was included in the *Politischer Discurs*).

[58] Lipowsky, *Ferdinand Maria*, pp. 173–74, bases his work on archival documents, which he unfortunately does not cite.

[59] Hüttl, *von Schmid*, makes the point that von Schmid was of the new nobility, yet limited that group's power to buy up the land of the old nobility with the Amortisation Law of 1669 (pp. 173–

statesmen like von Schmid for not seeing the importance of commerce to the state. In the *Politischer Discurs*, Becher sought to make clear to the treasury officials that the court must be involved in production if it was to continue its massive consumption:

> Treasury matters do not consist only in revenue and expenditure and the correct reckoning of these, but are founded also on the furthering of the interests of the entire land, and assisting the common man to means. That is, one must instruct the common man where he should take from, when one commands him to give. The former demands more artfulness and is of more necessity than the latter.[60]

Becher would later maintain that the artfulness required of the treasury official was that of understanding and capturing the creative and regenerative principles of nature.

Besides criticizing the treasury officials for their reliance on income from traditional sources in the face of increasing expenditure on consumption, Becher accused them of furthering their private interests instead of the common good.[61] Becher admonished the officials of German territories to follow the example of Holland, a country that made of commerce a duty of state (a *materia status*) rather than making a matter of commerce of their duties—that is, lining their own pockets in an act of supreme self-interest.[62]

The second group with whom Becher interacted at court was not directly connected with the court, and its members formed smaller eddies of power around and outside the court. This group was made up of merchants engaged in large-scale import and export, and townsmen organized in guilds. Not without reason, the merchants feared that Becher's commercial projects would result in their luxury imports being banned, their monopolies being taken over by companies chartered by the elector, and their activities being regulated by new ordinances concerning trade.[63] Becher claimed that for the sake of their own private interests, the merchants sabotaged every effort he made to further the common good. The merchants for their part claimed that Becher as a medical doctor knew nothing about commerce. Becher responded that a doctor needed only money to become a merchant, whereas the merchant may ornament him-

---

80). The new nobility had a vested interest in maintaining the hierarchy that the old nobility and the prince represented because they sought to rise within the established structure of power.

[60] *Politischer Discurs*, Dedication, sig. bij recto.

[61] Becher claimed that officials often received direction from their prince: In the *Moral Discurs*, p. 52, he claimed that certain princes say to their *Cameralisten*, "not, if you love me, watch over my sheep, but more often, if you love me, shear my sheep" (nicht: *Si amas me, pasce oves meas*; sondern sie sagen vielmehr: *Si amas me, tonde oves meas*).

[62] "Etliche unserer Teutschen Staatisten meynen nicht/ dass an den Commercien/ und derer Auffnehmen soviel gelegen/ sondern machen vielmehr auss ihrer *Statistica* eine *materiam commerciorum*, aber die Holländer machen *e contrario* auss den *commerciis* eine *materiam Status*." *Politischer Discurs*, p. 108.

[63] Störmer, "Wirtschaft und Bürgertum," chronicles the loss of power by the old governing stratum in Munich and other Bavarian cities under Ferdinand Maria.

self with velvet and money but will remain a blockhead. The man who knows theory can put it into practice, but the man of practice, who knows no theory, can never rise to another station.[64] A merchant in Antwerp countered Becher's claim when, in a letter to the elector's privy secretary, Dr. Jobst, he warned that even if a thousand doctors like Becher came to Antwerp carrying documents and testimonials, they would not be trusted on the strength of their status at the noble court alone, for it was credit and contacts that made a successful merchant.[65]

The baroque courtier never missed an opportunity to publicly condemn his enemies, and Becher was no exception. While Becher's descriptions of his rivals must be read with a grain of salt, it is possible to extract the tenor of the opposition to his plans from them. Such an opportunity is afforded by his description of an incident in 1664 when it appears that the Bavarian merchants successfully hindered one of his projects. Becher had a questionnaire sent to cities and villages in Bavaria that would, he claimed, yield information about the productive capability of the territory: the number of artisans, masters, the cost of raw materials and of finished goods, and the amount of tolls and taxes levied on goods. But the merchants, Becher reported, thought "Your Highness the Elector wanted to pull all trade to himself and make a monopoly, exactly like that with the *Weissbier*, so from this false assumption, they brought together a faction of merchants." These merchants convinced the elector's counselors to take their side, and through public rumor stirred up the "Poefel" (common people) against the elector. In the end the merchants made a "Collecte" among themselves and brought together a sum of money with which they "stopped the mouths" of those who approved of the plan. In the end, only Becher, the elector, and Becher's protector at court, Graf von Fürstenberg, stood by the plan, and although they finally sent out the questionnaire, Becher concluded that the results could not be considered reliable.[66]

The townspeople of Bavaria clashed with Becher because his commercial plans called for the importation of foreign skilled workers to initiate the proposed manufactures. Becher acted as intermediary between artisans and the court, and used artisans in his projects, but these workers were outside the

---

[64] "Ihre Rede ist/ *Doctores* verstehen nichts von den *Commerci*en . . . aber ein *Doctor*, wann er Geld hat/ kan eher ein Kaufmann/ als ein Kaufmann ein *Doctor* werden/ dann ob man gleich manchem Kaufmann Sammet und Geld anhencken thäte/ ist und bleibt er doch ein Stockfisch." *Politischer Discurs*, Dedication, aV recto.

[65] "kämen gleich 1000 doctorn und brechte noch vill schein, und beweiß mitel, wie er haben kan, und mag, so gibt mann selbigen khein glauben, oder er muß alhir bekhandt sein, und sich so gewisse lauth zu referiren wissen, sonst ist er nichts" Extract of letter, Johann Miller to Jobst, 9 April 1666, BHA, GL 2646/179.

[66] *Politischer Discurs*, 2d ed., pp. 387–91, "Frag an die Kauffleut in Bayern," undated. A copy of the original in BHA, GR 272/1 is dated 22 November 1664. Two returned questionnaires are extant in the BHA and they have been transcribed and printed by Freyberg, in *Pragmatische Geschichte*, 2:390–91.

guilds and typically foreign. Becher recounted the sentiment voiced by the Munich townspeople that nonguild workers would ruin the native town inhabitants by taking their business and leaving with their money. This was a characteristic claim of guildsmen who saw their closed world threatened. Becher called their accusation closed-minded, self-interested, and typical of Munich: "I answer them that it is a typical Munich accusation, which is jealous of and hostile to all foreigners" ("dem gebe ich zur Antwort/ daß solches ein Münchner Einwurff seye/ die allen Frembden neidisch und feind seyn"). Resentment against foreigners was so great, Becher continued, that the townspeople attacked the foreigners' reputation, persecuted them, charged them higher prices, and even beat them to death, as had been demonstrated in a recent case involving a French hatmaker. Like merchants, the townspeople had economic and social interests separate from those of the common good, for, as guild members, they owed loyalty to a corporate body outside the court and the territory. Becher attempted to convince the elector that these groups needed to be regulated and controlled, and, in his political writings, he would argue that the groups owing loyalty to corporate bodies independent of the court be reorganized under the direct authority of the prince.

The last group at court who schemed to bring about Becher's ruin were men similar to himself, projectors, who were his direct rivals in appealing to the central power of the prince and who sought a direct line to the elector's favor.[67] They not only competed with one another for this favor but also came into conflict with the established bureaucracy because they bypassed normal routes to the elector's favor. This figure was a typical phenomenon at the courts of the seventeenth century, an outgrowth of the development of the central power of the prince and his court. One example was Martin Elers, a merchant whom Becher had found in Antwerp and brought to Bavaria to organize a silk company. Becher had once described Elers as "a very clever man of commerce, who professes to know the arcana in this subject," but within a year, Elers and Becher were vying fiercely for the elector's favor, and Becher was calling him an "insolent fool."[68] The correspondence among members of this group, which is preserved in the Bavarian archives, is particularly complex, and illustrates the intense rivalry among them as well as the intricate nature of their projects. In one incident—according to a letter from Elers to his protector at court—Elers had asked Becher to deliver letters to the elector (Becher being at this time an

---

[67] For an account of such projectors in England, see Alex Keller, "The Age of the Projectors," *History Today* 16 (1966): 467–74.

[68] "sehr kluge[r] Mann in *Negotien*/ der *profession* macht/ die *Arcana* in solchen Sachen zu wissen" (*Politischer Discurs*, 2d ed., p. 404). For more details of their rivalry, see Hassinger, *Becher*, chap. 2, secs. 2 and 3, esp. p. 41. Mss. var. 1(3), fol. 373r, contains a pencil note in Becher's hand entitled "The pretentions of that insolent fool Martin Elers to the Bavarians," which lists Elers demands to the elector. They included a salary of 4,000 gulden plus the title of a *Kammerrat*.

intermediary for Elers). Elers received a reply from Becher saying that he had delivered the letters, but that the elector had responded so unfavorably that Elers must understand that he no longer had any credit at court.[69] Elers then received a letter from Johann Daniel Crafft,[70] who had ostensibly been assisting Becher in certain business. Crafft told Elers that he had received a letter from Becher who complained that Elers never wrote and reiterated that Elers was out of credit with the elector. Crafft, knowing that Elers had been writing faithfully, sent to Elers a copied extract of Becher's letter. Elers, now enraged, sent this extract to his protector at court, along with a letter laying bare Becher's scheming. He alleged that Becher had never delivered his letters to the elector[71] and demanded that his protector at court force Becher to deliver the letters. He then wrote a letter to the elector (not to be delivered by Becher this time) in which he related the entire alleged deception on Becher's part.[72] The struggle between Becher and Elers onto which this correspondence opens a window continued until Elers became involved in other projects and Becher left permanently for Vienna.[73]

Becher clashed with the courtiers, merchants, guildsmen, and projectors at the Munich court because he competed with them for credit and favor, power and position. Court officials disliked him because he attempted to circumvent the hierarchy of the court, while merchants and townspeople feared his attempts to integrate them into the court world by breaking down their corporate power and drawing them into the sphere of the prince. He skirmished with his fellow projectors because a projector could only succeed at court by establishing his project as better or more spectacular than that of the next man.

As a member of the Bavarian court, Becher had the court person's sensitivity to rank and was quite clearly aware of the necessity for a defined status and credit in order to chart a successful career around the schemes of his rivals and

[69] Copy of letter, Elers to Begnudelli, 5 August 1665, BHA, GR 273/10. See also Elers to Begnudelli, 10 January 1666, BHA, GR 273/10.

[70] Typically, Crafft played a pivotal role in this intrigue; seemingly working both for and against Becher. Perhaps Crafft had deep schemes to foment rivalry between Elers and Becher in order to lessen their power relative to his own. Like Becher, Crafft acted as an intermediary for the Bavarian court. In April 1665 Crafft wrote to von Fürstenberg to report on the progress of the attempt to obtain a colony in the West Indies and to regret that the process for *Rothstein* that he had previously reported on through Becher unfortunately could not be ready before his arrival (BHA, GL 2646/179).

[71] Extract from Becher's letter to Crafft, 2 December 1665, included in a letter from Elers to Begnudelli, Mainz, 10 January 1666, BHA, GR 273/10.

[72] Elers to Begnudelli, 17 August 1665, BHA, GR 273/10.

[73] Their rivalry seems to have abated when they met again in 1677, for Johann Daniel Crafft reported from Amsterdam that "Herr Martin Ehlers . . . lebt mit Herrn Becher in vertrauter Freundschaft anjetzo" (Martin Ehlers now lives with Becher in close friendship), Crafft to Leibniz, 20 November 1677, quoted in Hermann Peters, "Leibniz als Chemiker," *Archiv für die Geschichte der Naturwissenschaften und der Technik* 7 (1916): 224, n. 39.

opponents. He was anxious to define his position at court precisely. Officially he was court physician and mathematician, and he justified the diversity of his activities to his detractors and opponents by referring both to his status as *medicus* and as *mathematicus*. Becher claimed that commerce and mathematics were related, for it was through the study of mathematics that one came to knowledge of commerce.[74] Moreover, the mechanical arts to which commerce was related were the source of productive knowledge.

Becher also appealed to the similarities between the duties of a doctor and the duties of a political advisor. In a tract entitled "Beweiß/ was einem Fürsten an seinem Land gelegen" (Consideration of the interest a prince has in his land),[75] Becher defended his own treatment of an area of knowledge—cameral matters—that lay outside the professional competence of a medical doctor:

> When I consider that these affairs [of the treasury] relate neither to my profession nor to my situation (because I do not belong to the advisors who are dedicated to these matters), I can do nothing other than judge that I, like a scythe in another's crop, meddle and interfere in their affairs. When I remember my Fatherland [of Speyer], I cannot deny that I am a foreigner [here], and if I would form my own judgment, namely, what concern are foreigners to me, what moves me to serve them? Why don't I stay at home and make my proposals to my Fatherland, which probably needs them most? Then I look at my profession, and my published writings show that I am a medical doctor. Here the question arises again, what have I to do with political affairs, like Saul among the Prophets? In short, I have not lacked knowledge of the material in these matters so much as a reason to approach this material. But this reason lies in the general rule, *salus populi suprema lex esto* (health or welfare of the people shall be the supreme law). This rule can also be translated into German, namely, that Your Highness and the welfare of Your lands comes before all other considerations, determines everything, and everything flows into a center in that consideration. It is not a counselor's title, rank nor pay that make a councillor, rather it is loyal service. The person who understands a subject belongs in it. I say that the subject is proper by natural law to this person. He who does not understand it, does not belong in it, whether or not he was forcibly installed. Further, wherever a person is paid and wherever he eats his bread, that is his home. Indeed, where one simply stays the night, even there he should serve the common good as much as possible. There is no profession that is exempted from this. . . . In addition to all this comes Your Highness's gracious will and command in demanding my meager thoughts in these matters. This was the principal reason that gave me simultaneously heart and courage not only to produce this writing, but also, through the gracious acceptance of my humble person into your service, gave me reason, besides the help of God, to put it into practice.

[74] *Politischer Discurs*, p. b recto, and *Methodus didactica*, Vorrede, unpaginated.
[75] *Politischer Discurs*, 2d ed., pp. 297–322.

No one except an enemy of the Fatherland would claim that I could have spent this time of hard labor better if I had saved a few old wives in the hospital from death for a few months or if I had read the urine of a few peasants or had done some other such work. Rather, the lovers of truth and the common good will admit that I have loyally served their Fatherland and primarily Your Highness much more than I have sought my own advantage, which I hold to be the highest that can be said of an upright man.[76]

In this important passage, Becher addressed the entire constellation of power at court. He established his own place within the court hierarchy when he used a commonplace in political discourse, "salus populi suprema lex esto," and transferred it to the relationship that the medical doctor must have for the health (*salus*) of his patient, and back again to the political sphere. He addressed the central power of the prince when he "translated" this principle into "German," for in the Bavarian court world, the elector was the center of all power. On the other hand, Becher reinforced his own position by associating himself with the power of the elector and emphasizing that the elector had asked for his suggestions and had called him into service. Becher also responded to the opposition of the court officials in claiming that he was as qualified as they (if not more so) in advising the prince, and called on natural law to support his qualifications. To the insults of the self-interested merchants and townspeople, he responded that someone interested in the common welfare of a land could call himself a native of that land, whereas only an enemy of the Fatherland (even though a native) would claim that self-interested actions would be better. Becher here asserted the ethics of his own mobility against those of the closed world of the townspeople. A *homo honestus* ("ehrlicher Mann"), even though a *homo novus*, who concerned himself with the common interest was better qualified to advise the prince than the most powerful but self-interested advisor. With this statement of his own abilities and qualifications, Becher sought to establish authority for himself in the schemes and rivalry of the court, which would legitimate his commercial projects and, through them, his program to draw productive knowledge into the court.

Commerce and the Republic

Et si Galliae vel Angliae Exemplo non contenti simus, unica
Hollandia nos convincet, quae Mercaturis Commerciis adeo dives
facta est, et populosa, ut omnes in admirationem, plurimos in
invidiam et formidinem, omnes in certitudinem trahat [*sic*],
Commercia ad materiam status principaliter pertinere.

[76] Ibid., pp. 300–301.

And if we should not be content by the example of France or of
England, we are convinced by the singular [example of] Holland
which has been made rich and populous by the commerce of
merchants. For [Holland] compels all people to admiration, many
to jealousy and to fear, [but] all to the certainty that Commerce
principally pertains to the material of the state.
(*Becher to the Spanish legate in Vienna, ca. 1670*)

A list in which Becher described his accomplishments at the end of his first year
at the Bavarian court portrays the diversity of his proposals and projects for
establishing commerce.[77] In it Becher mentions a trip to the Netherlands, where
he made inquiries for the elector about obtaining a colony in America from the
Dutch West India Company in order to establish *Negotien*—commerce—in
Bavaria.[78] To initiate trade, Becher planned to establish a workhouse in which
manufacturing could be carried out, a warehouse where finished goods could be
stored and sold, and a trade company with investors from Bavaria and other
states. On the trip to the Netherlands Becher was to seek investors for this
company and make contact with anyone interested in setting up manufactures in
Bavaria.[79] Becher collected advice from officials and merchants in the Netherlands and hired Martin Elers to set up a silk company and manufactory and to
bring artisans to Bavaria.[80] By 1664, Becher claimed to have already constructed a model of the silk manufactory, as well as models of the spinning
wheel to be employed in it, and to have established a small workshop.

In his initial year in Munich, Becher also became active in chemistry
("Chymische sachen"), primarily of a utilitarian sort, proposing a laboratory for
the making of potash, saltpeter, soap, and the improvement of wine.[81] He also
suggested two places in which to begin mining exploration,[82] and called for the

---

[77] Mss. var. 1(3), fols. 216r–217v, and Hassinger, *Becher*, p. 36.

[78] This project seems to have been especially promoted by the electoress. It was from her that
Becher received instructions, authority, and a privilege to negotiate with the West India Company.
Becher's journal and accounts of the trip show that he was underway for seventy-eight days, from
16 August to 2 November 1664. He spent 305 Reichsthaler and received 300 in recompense.

[79] Becher's letter of authority is in *Politischer Discurs*, 2d ed., pp. 392–93, undated. According
to Hassinger, this is dated 8 August 1664 in the Patentarchiv. On this trip, Becher attempted to find
persons interested in investing in a Bavarian company that would manufacture woven textiles.
(Documents relating to this company and the trip are in ibid., pp. 392–402.)

[80] Becher himself also tried to find artisans and others who might prove useful to his projects or
to the elector on this trip. He made memoranda to himself and collected testimonials of people who
might in future be able to serve him. See Chapter 2 for details of this activity.

[81] Becher noted that he was waiting on the elector's permission to purchase materials and
instruments for the laboratory in order to make a start on his experiments, as well as awaiting the
return of the ubiquitous Johann Daniel Crafft to help him in this work.

[82] Court expenditures on mining exploration do in fact rise in 1665 and 1666. After years of less
than 100 gulden spent annually on "Pergwerk," BHA, Hofzahlamt Kurbayern, Hofzahlamtsrech-

building of canals to join the Isar, the Amper, and the Ilm. Not all these projects had long lives, and some, such as the canal project, had no life at all. Becher's proposed canals were not completed until the nineteenth century. The only canals begun in Bavaria in the seventeenth century connected the residence in Munich with the hunting palace of Nymphenberg and the summer palace of Schleißheim outside the city. Bavarian nobles navigated these canals in the gondolas they had constructed according to Venetian models.[83]

The hurried pace of Becher's proposals and projects continued in his second year in Munich, when he traveled again to the Netherlands in the employ of the elector, and, in the last month of 1665, when he went to Vienna to obtain an imperial privilege for the Bavarian silk company and to conduct negotiations about the salt treaties between Bavaria and Austria.[84] Becher was busy on this trip in his own interest, with the result that on 4 February 1666 the emperor appointed Becher imperial commercial advisor (*Commercien-Rath*) with a salary of one thousand Reichsthaler.[85] Later in the same month the emperor granted an imperial privilege, not for the Bavarian silk company, but for a new *Austrian* silk company. Two months after obtaining his imperial appointment, Becher returned to Munich to find that the shareholders in the company there had petitioned the elector for his exclusion from the company because he had worked to their disadvantage in Vienna.[86]

Nevertheless, a few weeks later, Becher returned to Vienna to negotiate a joint East India Company for Bavaria and the Habsburg Austrian territory, and to set up a spinnery on the lands of the president of the Hofkammer with workers from the Munich silk company.[87] In July 1666 Becher left Vienna, not to return until 1670. In these years, Becher wrote and published all his major works, worked intensively in the laboratory, and attempted to put his projects on a firmer footing. In 1669 he spent another three months in Holland, and, on this trip, although he was still in the service of Bavaria, he obtained a colony from the Dutch West India Company for Friedrich Casimir, count of Hanau. In 1670, before he left Munich permanently for Vienna,[88] he perfected a method

---

nungen, nos. 114 (1665), fol. 449 shows 577.41 gulden spent on "Berg Probierer," "Bergs Befahrung," "eröffnung der Grunden zu Haylbren," and trips to Reichenhall. In 1666 (no. 115, fol. 447) a similar amount was spent. After this they drop again.

[83] One project Becher does not mention in this list is his plan to form a company to mine peat in the bogs outside Munich, from which he claimed an oil could be extracted (Hassinger, *Becher*, p. 36).

[84] Documents pertaining to these negotiations in BHA, Kasten Schwarz, 6/3–5 in a file entitled "Negotiation in Wien, 1666–1667."

[85] Documents pertaining to this appointment printed in *Politischer Discurs*, 2d ed., pp. 490–94.

[86] BHA, GL 2646/179.

[87] Hassinger, *Becher*, pp. 40–41.

[88] His salary in Munich was cut off after the third quarterly payment in September 1670 (BHA, HR II f. 249).

for extracting iron from nonmetallic substances[89] and took steps to set up a sugar refinery in Munich.[90]

These commercial projects advanced a larger political agenda by which the prince's territory would become productive of money wealth. Becher formulated his political agenda within the structure of court and territorial power established in Bavaria by the policies of Maximilian and Ferdinand Maria. In his commercial theory and practice, Becher addressed the prince as the center of power in the territory and attempted to strengthen this central place by extending the elector's authority over groups such as the merchants and the guildsmen. At the same time, Becher attempted to impose a new set of values on the courtiers and the prince himself. Becher's political theory, which informed all of his projects, was contained in the *Politischer Discurs von den eigentlichen Ursachen deß Auf- und Abnehmens/ der Städt/ Länder und Republicken* (Political discourse about the true causes of the rise and fall of cities, territories and republics), published in 1668 on his return to Munich from Vienna.[91]

"The true cause of the rise and fall of cities, lands, and republics," was commerce. According to Becher, "*die Commercien*, negotien/ Handel und Wandel" could make a society flourish or could ruin it.[92] Becher claimed to have written a book of use to the officials of the Hofkammer, containing "*Materia Cameralis*" sure to be familiar to them, but he expected that its single focus on commerce would surprise them. His apology for the single-minded emphasis was rendered in language clearly meant for court ears: "they [in this case, the Habsburg court] would become so powerful from this alone, that no lord on earth would be their equal in riches, money, and population."[93]

---

[89] Becher described this process in *Experimentum Chymicum novum, quo Artificialis & instantanea metallorum* Generatio & Transmutatio *ad oculum demonstratur* (Frankfurt: Johann David Zunner, 1671). This process occasioned great excitement in the scholarly world. Gottfried Wilhelm Leibniz saw the experiment performed by Becher before the elector of Mainz (on Becher's journey to the Netherlands in 1669). He wrote to Henry Oldenburg who had the experiment repeated before the Royal Society.

[90] On 12 February 1670 Becher received a privilege from Ferdinand Maria to found a sugar refinery in Munich (*Politischer Discurs*, 2d ed., p. 1260). In BHA, HR I 291/27/1, there is a patent for Becher to travel in Italy, dated 10 April 1670, although the purpose of travel is not specified. However, Mss. var. 1(2), fol. 625r, is a contract dated Venice 1670 between Becher and a certain Carlo Astore in which Astore promises to come to Munich to set up a sugar refinery in return for payment for the trip to Munich, free lodging, and firewood once he is there and twenty Venetian ducats per month.

[91] Although back in Munich by this time, Becher's sights were still oriented toward the emperor and the Viennese court, as is clear from the fact that he addressed the dedication to Count Georg Ludwig von Sinzendorf, the president of the Habsburg Hofkammer.

[92] *Politischer Discurs*, Dedication.

[93] "daß sie allein darauß so mächtig würden werden/ daß ihnen kein Potentat auf der Welt an Vermögen/ baaren Mitteln und Volck würde gleich seyn" (ibid., Dedication, sig. biij recto).

The book opened with an account of civil society. The human being is the *"materia"* of society and a sociable animal (*"animal sociabile"*).[94] The desire for society and sociability distinguishes humans from the beasts, therefore the preservation of human society ("menschliche Gesellschaft") must be the "single and sole founding cause, the beginning, middle, and end of all laws and ordinances" ("einig und allein die Grund-Uhrsach/ Anfang/ Mitl/ und End aller Gesätze/ und Ordnungen"). The form of civil society is a "Volckreiche Nahrhaffte Gemeind" (populous, sustaining community), which Becher identified with the city republic. This community forms a model for any true society, whether it is a village, free city, territory, or empire.[95] In this model city, which resembled the guild town of the Holy Roman Empire, the cycle of production and consumption of everyday life ordered and shaped the human material into its societal form.[96] There were two levels of members in the community: the servants of the *Gemeind* (community), and the actual members, or citizens, of the *Gemeind*. The servants of the community were composed from the *Obrigkeit, Geistliche, Gelehrte*, and *Soldaten*. Becher divided the members of the community, who were the true citizens of the community, into three *Stände* (estates): the *Bauern-Stand*, peasants, who worked the earth; the *Handwercks-Stand*, artisans, who refined the raw materials produced by the peasants; and the *Kauffmanns-Stand*, who bought up and sold (both inside and outside the city)

[94] Ibid., p. 1. Becher's use of Aristotle's oft-repeated phrase that man was a political or sociable animal (*Politics*, 1.1.9–11) contrasted sharply with his use of Paracelsus's radical statement, "Qui omnia secum portat, non indiget alieno auxilio" (he who carries all things with him needs not the aid of others). This is brought out more distinctly by Aristotle's text: "even when men have no need of assistance from each other, they nonetheless desire to live together" (*Politics*, 3.4.2–3). Basing himself on Aristotle, Hieronymus Cardanus (whom Becher frequently cited), in *Arcana politica sive de Prudentia civili*, stated explicitly that the individual needed the other members of society: "Solus enim . . . alieno auxilio indiget, quia sibi non sufficit" (Leiden: Elzevir, 1656, p. 1). Human society thus formed a system of interlocking needs and services that bound its members together, as, for example, in the free imperial town. Becher developed the view of society as a tightly bound whole in his *Politischer Discurs*, but in his alchemical works he stressed the mobility that alchemy made possible. His adoption of these two incompatible views of the individual's place in society reflects the conflicting legacy of his mother's and father's worlds in his thought. Only once did he confront this contradiction, in his 1678 *Psychosophia*, pp. 130–31, where he stated that although alchemical transmutation was possible, it should not be pursued by all members of society, for alchemy could disrupt the fabric of society by making individuals independent of one another, thus breaking the system of interlocking links. If everyone could make gold, no one would make shoes or bread.

[95] *Politischer Discurs*, p. 2.

[96] "also entspringet die Nahrung auß der Gemeind; nemlich/ daß die Leut eines Orts einander unter die Arme greiffen/ und einer dem andern durch gemeinen Handel und Wandel zu seinem Stück Brod verhelffe: dann es bestehet die Gemein nicht darin/ daß die Leut eines Orts nichts gemein/ als die Unglückseligkeit/ sage Armuth/ Arbeit/ Steur/ Aufflagen/ und Contribution haben/ sondern diß ist die rechte Gemein/ wann die Glieder der Gemein ihre Sachen also anstellen/ daß einer von dem andern leben/ einer von dem andern sein Stück Brod verdienen kan/ ja einer dem anderen die Nahrung in die Hand spielet/ daß ist die rechte Gemeind." *Politischer Discurs*, 2d ed., p. 3.

the goods produced by the artisans.[97] Becher called the peasants, the largest of the three *Stände*, the fundament of the community, for without them society would not exist. The merchants, the smallest *Stand*, were the animating principle of the community, for they facilitated the transactions—commerce—within the society, and brought money into the cycle.[98] Among these three groups of the civil society, true commerce—the ceaseless and regenerative cycle of production and *consumption* of goods—took place:

> Consumption sustains these three estates. Consumption is their soul. Consumption is the sole bond that binds and fastens the estates to one another and makes them sustain each other. Indeed it is because of consumption that the estate of the merchants is so necessary in a community and that the estate of the peasants is so large, for the latter increases the number of people, and the former nourishes them.[99]

The view that consumption held an importance equal to that of production, and that the activity of merchants was "nourishing," was antithetical to the values of the town world of the German Empire. By such a reversal, however, Becher sought to portray commerce as natural and productive rather than unnatural and parasitical. If accepted as part of a natural cycle, commerce could register on the scale of noble values.

The servants of the community (i.e., the government) lived off the surplus generated by this cycle. For this reason, the governmental officials must be carefully proportioned to the numbers of true members in a city, for "nothing destroys and more easily ruins the lords, their lands and people so much as these large unnecessary courts."[100]

According to Becher, the industrious productivity of the three *Stände* kept them from aspiring above their station in society, and locked them into a fixed and stable order. The *Obrigkeit* (rulers) of the community watched over them so that they would fulfill the greater end of human society: redemption and salvation. The division of humankind into rulers and subjects was instituted by God after the Fall, and its function was to restrain humankind within the "Stand der Menschheit" (estate of humanity) and within the "Gesetze der Natur" (laws of nature).[101] By the phrase "estate of humanity," Becher expressed man's place in the cosmic order of Creation, Fall, and Salvation. Man was a being created in the image of God, cursed by the Fall to strive for, but never attain, divine

---

[97] *Politischer Discurs*, pp. 4–8.

[98] Ibid., p. 22: "sie [i.e., the *Verläger*] allein vor Grundsäulen dieser dreyer Ständen zu halten seynd/ dann von ihnen lebt der Handwercksmann/ von diesen der Bauer/ von diesen der Edelmann/ von diesen der Lands-Fürst/ und von diesen allen wieder der Kauffmann/ das seynd die jenige Hände/ welche einander vereinigen müssen."

[99] *Politischer Discurs*, 2d ed., p. 102.

[100] "kein Ding seye/ welches die Potentaten sambt Land und Leuten mehr verderbe/ und ehender *ruinire*, als eben diese gar grosse unnöthige Hoffhaltung." *Politischer Discurs*, p. 5.

[101] *Politischer Discurs*, 2d ed., pp. 42, 40.

perfection on earth. Only through a life of labor in society could humankind redeem itself. Becher saw man as the imperfect imitator of the five essential characteristics of God, which were existence, perfection, omniscience, omnipotence, and eternity. Humankind's imitation of these characteristics led to a search for knowledge of the divine, of perfection, of the natural world, of power, and how to extend life. Thus in human society, the "laws of nature" dictated that all men had a right to follow a religion, to practice virtue, to educate themselves, to own property and maintain themselves honestly, and to live a long life in good health.[102] If the society of the three *Stände* observed these laws, private and societal *Glückseligkeit* would result. The governors of human society were responsible for enforcing these natural laws and, in certain cases, could be held accountable to their subjects for respecting the laws.[103] Becher's theory of human society charged the *Obrigkeit* with overseeing all possible areas of human activity. The territorial lord thus became the representative and guardian of the common good of society.[104] This control of subjects' lives was to be accomplished by the establishment of five typical administrative bodies or "Collegia": a religious college (*Collegium spirituale*), a moral college (*Collegium morale*), an educational council (*Collegium doctrinale*), a financial and commercial body (which he significantly titled the *Collegium civile*), and a council for health (*Collegium vitale*).[105] The five pursuits characteristic to human society and these five *Collegia* coincided precisely with the areas of Becher's published writings: ethics, moral discourse, didactic theory, commerce, and chemistry.

Becher believed the government that administered the laws of human society should be a mixed rule, composed of elements of each of Aristotle's three sorts of government, monarchy, aristocracy, and democracy. Mixed government reflected the structure of the Holy Roman Empire; with the emperor representing the monarch; the eight electors the aristocracy of the *patres conscripti*; and the Estates (nobility and cities) the democracy.[106] Mixed rule was a means to avoid the excesses of any single form of government and was, according to Becher, best exemplified by what he called a republic:

> Now the republics have their Duke which gives a monarchical authority and in different places is more or less restrained. After him follow the city councillors, *patres conscripti* and *primates*, and these are a part of the aristocratic rule. Last

[102] Ibid., p. 40.

[103] A government could be held accountable to its subjects only as the result of an orderly, impartial judgment of the case (ibid., pp. 44–47).

[104] Walther Merk, *Der Gedanke des gemeinen Besten in der deutschen Staats- und Rechtsentwicklung* (1934; rpt. Darmstadt: Wissenschaftliche Buchgesellschaft, 1968), shows how the notion of common good was taken over as one of the most important tenets of natural law and used by territorial rulers to justify any number of their actions.

[105] *Politischer Discurs*, 2d ed., p. 48.

[106] Ibid., p. 18.

comes the Great or Common Council, in which the most important citizens are found, and that represents an appearance of democratic government.[107]

Becher considered the organization of society in a republic to be the most productive of material and social well-being. His view of society organized as a city republic strongly echoed Jean Bodin and Johannes Althusius, especially in the importance of a bond based on mutual exchange. In *The Six Books of the Republic* (1576), Bodin elaborated a theory of society based upon corporate groups held together by friendship (*amicitia*) like that which held together artisanal guilds.[108] Johannes Althusius, in *Politica Methodice Digesta* (1603), based his explanation of society on the city republic,[109] and considered the exchange of goods, or commerce, to form the bond that held society together. In his view, the inhabitants of society (or the city) depended on each other in a self-renewing act of mutual, interlocking aid. Thus the exchange of goods and services involved not simply an economic transaction, but a moral and political one as well.[110] While Becher's cycle of sustenance resembled that of Althusius, he nowhere drew explicitly from Bodin or Althusius.[111] In fact he cited very few political writers, but among those to whom he did allude, the Dutch de la Court brothers stand out,[112] for their notion of "commerce" was that of large-

---

[107] Ibid., p. 16. "Nun haben die *Republiquen* ihren Hertzog welcher eine *authoritatem Monarchalem* gibt/ und ein und anderen Orten mehr oder weniger *restringi*rt ist/ hernach folgen die Rathsherrn/ *Patres conscripti*, und *Primates*, diese seind ein stück von der *Aristocrati*schen Regierung/ letzlich folget der grosse/ oder gemeine-Rath/ worinnen die vornembsten Bürger seynd/ und das ist ein Schein von der *Democrati*schen Regirung."

[108] Antony Black, *Guilds and Civil Society in European Political Thought from the Twelfth Century to the Present* (Ithaca: Cornell University Press, 1984), pp. 129–31.

[109] Ibid., p. 132.

[110] Ibid., pp. 131–36.

[111] In the Rostock *Nachlaß*, there is a long book list that contains many political writers, some checked off with a different type of ink. One of those noted is "Bodin, *Methodus Histor.*"

[112] *Politischer Discurs*, 2d ed., pp. 12–13. Becher's only citation of Pieter and Jan de la Court is in reference to the disadvantages of a state governed by a pope or other religious leader, an odd choice of citation on Becher's part because the de la Courts also discuss fully other types of government in *Politike discoursen handelende in Ses onderscheide Boeken van Steeden, Landen, Oorlogen, Kerken, Regeeringen, en Zeeden* (Amsterdam: van der Gracht, 1662), bk. v, chap. 9, pp. 95–166. Because the Calvinist de la Courts advocated popular rule, Becher was perhaps citing them on the one point he was sure would lead to no unpleasant consequences at the Catholic Bavarian and Habsburg courts. Apparently Becher's book had at first been banned for religious reasons. In the second edition of the *Politischer Discurs*, Becher claimed that the first edition of his book was banned in some places because he quoted "Calvin" on the title page. This was taken to be "der *Theologus Calvinus*," where in reality it was the (Catholic) "*Juris-Consultus Calvinus*" in the *Lexicon Juridicum* (*Politischer Discurs*, 2d ed., Vorrede, Xiij recto). The quotation from Calvin was "Publicè interesse ducitur, quod in commune expedit, & ad totius reipublicae utilitatem spectat, licet quae ad omnes pertinent, plerumq; à singulis negligantur" (*Politischer Discurs*, title page). In fact, Calvin's lexicon only *defines* public and private interest, but does not add the "à singulis negligantur." Ioannis Calvinus, *Lexicon Iuridicum*, 3d ed. (Hanover: Wechelian, Impensis Daniel & David Aubriorum & Clemens Schleichius, 1619), p. 449. Becher stated he expected the

scale movement of goods, rather than a town cycle of interlocking sustenance and exchange.

The brothers Jan and Pieter de la Court wrote in support of the *Ratspensionar*, Jan de Witt, in his struggle against the House of Orange. They drew on the republican tradition, but their concept of the republic was not one based on free, landowning citizens, but instead on the unhindered practice of commerce. Because a civil society in Holland simply could not be physically achieved by means of landownership and agriculture, they maintained that the Dutch had been compelled to find other sources of revenue. In the *Politike discoursen handelende in Ses onderscheide Boeken van Steeden, Landen, Oorlogen, Kerken, Regeeringen, en Zeeden* (1662) and the *Interest van Holland ofte gronden van Hollands welvaren* (1662), the de la Courts explained these sources to be fishery, manufacture, merchants, and the work of artisans, and wondered (in the German translation) at the way these industries could keep the inhabitants "wunderlich aneinander geknüpffet" (marvelously interlocked with one another).[113] For the de la Courts, it was commerce, not agriculture, that made possible the large population of Holland, and as a consequence, the great majority of the people of Holland were not bound to the land. The nobility, however, was bound to the land because its traditional seat of power was a specific piece of land and this connection to land sustained its office. For this reason members of the nobility fought tenaciously to control their subjects and keep them in a state of servitude, bound to the land.[114]

In their books published after 1660, the de la Courts vigorously advocated popular rule over aristocratic, monarchical, or mixed government in a republic, and their works were openly hostile to monarchy. Becher, employed in the

---

Politischer Discurs would satisfy no one, for to non-Catholics it would seem too Spanish or imperial, whereas to the Catholic party it would seem too "Holländisch": "werde ich wohl keiner Parthey recht thun können/ den Uncatholischen werde ich zu sehr Käyserlich oder Spanisch/ uns Catholischen aber selbst etwan zu sehr Holländisch vorkommen." Becher assured his readers that he did not necessarily agree with all the opinions presented in his book, but he had set them there in order that the reader could cull out the best of them (*Politischer Discurs*, 2d ed., Vorrede, unpaginated).

[113] The *Interest van Holland* was translated as *Interesse von Holland oder Fondamenten von Hollands-Wohlfahrt* (N.p., 1665), this phrase, chap. 8. Eco O. G. Haitsma Mulier, in *The Myth of Venice and Dutch Republican Thought in the Seventeenth Century*, trans. Gerard T. Moran (Assen: Van Gorcum, 1980), contrasts the English political writers of the seventeenth century, for whom commerce was a problem in the republic, to the brothers de la Court, for whom commerce was a means of preventing a democracy's debasement into aristocracy (p. 164). J.G.A. Pocock discusses these ideas in an English context: *The Machiavellian Moment: Florentine Political Thought and the Atlantic Republican Tradition* (Princeton: Princeton University Press, 1975); and *Virtue, Commerce, and History* (Cambridge: Cambridge University Press, 1985).

[114] *Interest van Holland*, 1662, in Etienne Laspeyres, "Mitteilungen aus Pieter De La Courts Schriften, ein Beitrag zur Geschichte der niederländischen Nationaloeconomik des 17ten Jahrhunderts," *Zeitschrift für die gesammte Staatswissenschaft* 18 (1862): 358. See also Wilhelm Roscher, *Geschichte der National-Oekonomik in Deutschland* (Munich: R. Oldenbourg, 1874), pp. 223–26.

service of territorial rulers, did not take over their arguments for popular rule, but instead drew from their work the idea that a civil society could be achieved by commercial sources of income. In the de la Courts' work, the landowning citizens of the republican tradition became trading citizens, while in Becher's political theory, the guild town citizens became part of a commercial cycle, and the landed prince (necessary to hold society in the estate of humanity) presided over a commercial cycle of production.

Becher's attempt to graft the de la Courts' antimonarchical arguments for a commercial republic onto a discussion of princely territorial rule was fraught with tension. Nowhere is this more evident than when he employed the de la Courts' statement that popular rule was more desirable than aristocratic or monarchic rule because when a democracy follows the maxim, "Salus suprema lex populi," it acts in accordance with its own welfare.[115] Becher repeated this sentiment when he asked "why the republics and imperial cities always flourish better than the provincial cities that are subject to a monarchical government," and gave the surprising answer that "a republic has only one interest, but a territory has two, namely its own and its lord's."[116] An echo of the perspective of the town world of Becher's mother can be heard in Becher's opposition of the community interest to the self-interest of the lord. But in the same work, Becher translated "salus populi suprema lex esto" into German as "the welfare of Your Highness and of your lands precedes everything, determines everything and everything flows into a center there."[117] In this "translation" (not of words, but of cultures), Becher equated the *salus populi* of the community republic with the *salus principis* of the territory, and strove to fuse "public" and "private" interest in the territorial sovereign's domains.[118] While this might be viewed as the moral equivalent of "L'état c'est moi," Becher saw his "translation" not

---

[115] Jan de la Court, *Consideratien van Staat ofte Polityke weegschaal* (Amsterdam, 1661), trans. Christophorus Kormarten as *Consideratien van Staat oder politische Wag Schale mit welcher die allgemeine Staas [sic]-Angelegenheiten Haupt-Gründe und Mängel aller Republicken* (Leipzig und Halle: Fickischer Buchladen, 1669), pt. 3, bk. 3, p. 651. In the *Polityke Weegschaal*, de la Court wrote, "Popular governments of themselves [have] always . . . occasioned very large, and as a rule trading, cities, overflowing in riches lawfully acquired" (p. 280, quoted in Mulier, *Myth*, p. 139).

[116] "Es ist eine fürnehme politische Frage/ warumb die Republicken und Reichs-Städt allzeit besser floriren/ als die Provincial/ oder solche Städte/ welche Monarchischer Regierung unterworffen/ und einem Herren zugehören? Hierauff gib ich zur Antwort/ daß die aufflösung gar leicht seye. Dann eine Republick hat nur ein *Interesse*, aber ein Land hat zwey/ nemlich ihr eigenes/ und ihres Herren." *Politischer Discurs*, 2d ed., pp. 256–57.

[117] "Ew. Churf. Durchl. und der Landen Wolfahrt gehet alles vor/ *determinir*t alles/ alles laufft in einem *centro* darinnen zusammen." Ibid., pp. 300–301.

[118] What Becher called mixed government, Hobbes called monarchy: "where the publique and private interest are most closely united, there is the publique most advanced. Now in Monarchy, the private interest is the same with the publique. The riches, power, and honour of a Monarch arise onely from the riches, strength and reputation of his Subjects." *Leviathan* (London, 1651), chap. 20.

primarily as an expression of absolute power, but rather a means by which the notion of common good from the town community could be welded to the landed society of the noble court. Becher was compelled to make this translation explicit because the de la Courts and the Bavarian nobility considered the values of the land-bound nobility to be opposed to the interests of the commercial republic.

The Court, the Town, and Money

Becher's political theory sought to impose the common goal of a town community on the territorial prince's court, and simultaneously to convince the prince that his traditional governing duties in society could be maintained by commercial revenues. Becher drew from various models in formulating his theory: from the guild town, the Dutch Republic, and the large free Imperial cities of the Holy Roman Empire, such as Augsburg, Nuremberg, and Regensburg.[119] The free imperial cities were a model easily understood by the German nobility, for these large centers combined artisanal and commercial activity to generate enough surplus to finance the Habsburg dynasty's rise to vast imperial power in the sixteenth century under Charles V.[120] Within the territory of Bavaria there

[119] There are many examples of proposals for improving "bürgerliche Nahrung" by reliance on commerce similar to Becher's, but they are usually regarded as applying only within a city. In the Vienna Hofkammerarchiv, for example, there is a 1663 proposal for a set of *Polizei-ordnungen* for the city of Brünn, the language of which is striking in its similarity to Becher's: ("Waß macht eben die Reichs und viel andere Städt in Frembden Ländern so reich und populos alß die Manufacturen"). "Gemaßgebige Politische Puncta wie die Stadt Brünn, in einem bessern Standt, und Ordnung zue bringen, welche von mire Paul Ignatio Morgenthaler, wohlmeinend dem Gemeinen Weeßen zum Besten zusammen getragen worden im 1663sten Jahr," Hofkammerarchiv, Verschiedene Vorschläge, Fasz. 6, fols. 16–41. While earlier political writers, such as Georg Obrecht and Veit Ludwig von Seckendorff, had also seen the possibilities of commerce for the state, Becher does not cite them. See Hans Maier, *Die ältere deutsche Staats- und Verwaltungslehre*, 2d ed. (Munich: C. H. Beck, 1980). If Becher drew his model of society and the city expounded in the *Politischer Discurs* (and perhaps even the title of his work) from a single source, then it is Book 1 of Jan de la Court's *Politike discoursen* about "Stads-saaken." In this book, de la Court describes the city as a "Civile societeit" (p. 1), similar to Becher's *"Civil soci*etät" (*Politischer Discurs*, p. 1). De la Court also divides the members of a civil society into the "Boeren," who live around the cities, the "koopen handwerks-luiden," and the political, financial, military, and judicial officials who live in the cities. It is the "koopmanschap" that make a city large and wealthy (pp. 3–5). While de la Court is among the very few authors Becher cites by name (as "la Courte" and "la Curte"), I do not believe that Becher drew from only one source, or that he used only published works. His *Nachlaß* contains ephemeral literature such as pamphlets, newspapers, and proclamations of ordinances, with ideas for sources of income circled and marked out by hand (e.g., Mss. var. 1(2), fols. 327r–662r).

[120] Otto Brunner makes this point in *Adeliges Landleben*. The Fugger loans to the Habsburgs largely financed the campaigns and reign of Charles V as both emperor of the Holy Roman Empire and king of Spain. As security on the loans, the Fugger received the silver mines of the Habsburg

existed the imperial cities of Augsburg, Nuremberg, and Regensburg, less important since trade had moved to the maritime nations, but still wealthy and powerful enough to maintain their independence while surrounded by an increasingly centralized territory. These cities, like Becher's primary model, Holland, had made their fortunes and gained their independence and political power through commerce, but they were also centers of artisanal productivity.

Commerce, the merchants associated with it, and the exchange economy which it fostered were part of a different world from that of the court at which Becher was employed, and from that of the town he had left as a child. The money economy of a city might finance a territorial ruler (as the free imperial cities had financed the Habsburgs), but the prince did not produce this wealth himself. The prince's domain was landed property that was outside both the community cycle and the commercial transactions of the large city. The prince needed money to maintain his power, but in seventeenth-century society he did not usually engage in the activities of the commercial society himself.

Commerce, money, and merchants did not enjoy a high reputation either at court or within the town world. To these worlds, trade was a risky, dangerous, and uncertain business, and the merchant occupied a *status corruptus* in society, for his movable money wealth destroyed established moral and social structures. In the Bavarian court world, rank and status depended on land, a natural, regenerating, safe, and immovable wealth. Moreover, possession of money led easily to vanity, striving above one's station, and endangerment of personal salvation. To suggest that the prince should take up the activities of a merchant, not to say take on the character of a merchant, as Becher did, brought objections from Caspar von Schmid, who argued that society would be destroyed when a prince became a merchant.

Becher's program of commerce, which began at the Bavarian electoral court and culminated at the imperial court, thus had a threefold aim: it sought to integrate the prince into the community cycle by identifying the prince's interest with that of the productive community, and attempted to place the prince in the position of overseer and governor of the community cycle. Finally, it sought to convince the prince and his advisors that commerce was an honest activity, appropriate to noble blood.

Becher portrayed commercial activity as part of the productive town cycle, thus capable of providing a "natural," regenerative source of territorial revenues. Von Schmid considered the natural wealth of the elector's agricultural lands the basis of state income. Becher, on the other hand, proposed that commerce take its place, and he criticized "Kameralisten" and "Statisten" for being the real parasites on the community cycle because they did nothing but

---

territory. The large infusions of capital needed to develop these mines could be supplied by the Fugger and the shareholding companies they formed. See Eli F. Hecksher, *Mercantilism*, trans. Mendel Shapiro, 2 vols. (London: George Allen & Unwin, 1935), p. 337.

weigh down the community members with ever greater tax burdens.[121] Becher presented commerce as an entirely new source of income that would not constitute a tax on anyone but, instead, would be part of a natural, productive cycle that resulted in material increase in the form of money. It would, moreover, strengthen the traditional relationship between prince and peasant, while increasing the material welfare of both.

The goal of commerce, according to Becher, was to enable the peasant to change his natural agricultural products into money; to "versilbern" them. This transmutation was achieved by the cycle of "Consumption," which took place in the transactions among the three *Stände* of Becher's model society. It began in the peasant's harvest of the natural fruits of the earth. The artisan then bought these natural fruits and refined them into products that he sold to the merchant. The merchant either exported the artisan's products, which brought money into the territory, or he sold them within the territory, which provided sustenance for the society.[122] This cycle of interlocking support was self-generating and always productive of money surplus. Because this cycle, which involved a process of the refinement of raw materials, was achieved by the labor of the true society (the three *Stände*), it could be placed in the context of a familiar cosmic order. Because the cycle began in natural products of the land, which were refined into the noble product of specie, it could be seen as analogous to the processes of nature, which were imitated by humans in the labor of earthly life. Becher thus portrayed the cycle of commerce not only as a natural source of material increase and profit, but also as the means of cohesion in a Christian society.

At the center of this cycle stood the territorial ruler. The cycle enabled the peasant to pay his rents in money, rather than in natural goods, which brought specie to the ruler at the center. The cycle of consumption brought about by commerce, while providing a new source of money income, did not take place outside the traditional landed social structure and the traditional "ordinary" income due to the prince. Commerce would thereby bring the landed territorial ruler into the commercial society without upsetting his established place, power, or means of governing.

Becher also portrayed commerce as fitting to the social status of the prince. In a *"Remonstration, daß die Proposition wegen der Münchnerischen Negotien gut seye"* (Remonstration that the proposition for the Munich commerce is good), Becher assured the elector and his advisors that commerce was a way to make a territory stronger and richer. Becher claimed to be able to bring to bear

---

[121] The rhetorical tradition that used "Kameralisten" and "Statisten" as derogatory labels and portrayed them as parasitical on the community was already old by 1668. See Wolf-Hagen Krauth, *Wirtschaftsstruktur und Semantik. Wissenssoziologische Studien zum wirtschaftlichen Denken in Deutschland zwischen dem 13. und 17. Jahrhundert* (Berlin: Duncker & Humblot, 1984).

[122] Becher divides these two sorts of consumption into the categories of domestic and foreign. *Politischer Discurs*, pp. 23–24.

on his arguments the examples of kings and princes, all of whose "reputation has not been diminished by commerce but has, besides increasing land and population, become more considerable and larger."[123]

Becher defended money wealth by connecting the representation of power with the sustenance (*Nahrung*) and money wealth (*Gelt-reich*) possessed by a territory:

> What is the true interest of Germany other than its well-being [*Wolstand*]? Its well-being consists in Germany being considerable—a force to be reckoned with, it will be considerable when it is powerful; it will be powerful when it is populous; it will be populous when it has sufficient sustenance . . . it will have sustenance if it is rich in money; it will be rich in money when the money that flows out of Germany is retained within it and when yet more money is brought into Germany from foreign countries.[124]

Thus, power and the show of power were deeply implicated in the concept of *Wohlstand*—of material welfare, which Becher directly connected with money and commerce.

Money gave authority:

> When a prince is set in place by God in order to hold his subjects to their religion and preserve them in justice and peace, he must have authority to do this. Such authority, however, arises from hard cash, for today, he who has no money, has no authority, and each of his neighbors seeks to overrun him. He who has money, however, is taken seriously, is powerful and is distinguished by everyone. Now, perhaps this should not be the case, and virtue and respectability should be more highly regarded than money and affluence, but the *mores saeculi* are so corrupted and the habits so firmly entrenched, that he who wants to live in this world and exist in peace must act accordingly and must, for the sake of his lands and subjects, put himself in a position of defensiveness and power. This cannot happen without money wealth.[125]

Money was the source of a prince's authority and thus the source of his ability to keep his central place in the court hierarchy. Consequently the government of his finances, like the scrupulous bookkeeping practices of a merchant, was of the utmost importance. Becher advised that the prince's hereditary lands—the source of ordinary income—be well looked after and that he not make extraordinary taxes into ordinary income.[126] Furthermore, the prince should build up a

---

[123] *"Reputation* durch die Commercien nicht geschmählert/ sondern neben Auffnehmen Land und Leuten *considerabler* und grösser worden." September 1665, *Politischer Discurs*, 2d ed., pp. 358–81 (quotation from p. 374).

[124] *Methodus didactica*, Vorrede, unpaginated.

[125] "Dr. Bechers Gutachten wegen rechter Bestellung einer Hoff oder *Finanz*-Cammer," pp. 889–908, in *Politischer Discurs*, 2d ed., p. 889.

[126] Ibid., pp. 890–91.

treasure of "baares Geld" and of "Kleinodien." Becher maintained that the cash was more useful than the jewels, however, for jewels and trinkets could only be used "mehr zum *luxu & ostentatione*," while gold and silver could be minted as cash and then recast into ornaments when the need for money was past.[127] Becher thus recast and confused the realms of movable and immovable wealth. He hoped to convince the prince that specie could meet the needs of court display and ritual as well as it could meet those of the money economy.

At the same time that Becher sought to enhance the reputation of commerce at court, he attempted to improve the status of the merchant within society and at court. He argued that the merchant was the soul of the cycle of production, the most valuable *Stand* within the productive city community.[128] The society Becher set out in the *Politischer Discurs* was modeled on the town society, but it was to be held together by the transactions of commerce, and thus would produce a money surplus. Becher called the merchant who carried out commerce in his model society the "Verläger" (the putting-out merchant). For Becher, this merchant was the "Grundsäul[e] der Gemeinde" (foundation stone of the community).[129] In the world outside Becher's model community, the putting-out merchants were destroying the structure of the guilds and the fabric of the guild towns, but Becher believed that if properly controlled these merchants would become part of a productive community:

> The merchants are the only ones who can secretly ruin a land or bring it to a flourishing state. The body of merchants [in a society] is, however, the only way by which the state can increase its money and means of sustenance. After nature, trade is the sole wet nurse that can bring the new growth of the most barren land to germination, to bloom, and finally to wonderful fruition.[130]

If overseen properly, commercial activity could thus become a natural means of bringing a land to fruition, and merchants could truly be viewed as the only

---

[127] Ibid., p. 892.

[128] Becher was not the first. From the beginning of the seventeenth century, there were attempts to rehabilitate the merchant. Georg Obrecht in 1610 wrote: "For merchants are in the body of the republic, as it were, attendant, carriers, feet," and "consequently, I hold it as more honorable than despicable when noble and high persons carry on trade for the sake of lightening the burdens of their subjects and of discharging public obligations with the least difficulty." Translated by and quoted in Albion W. Small, *The Cameralists: The Pioneers of German Social Polity* (New York: Burt Franklin, 1909), p. 53. The secondary literature on seventeenth-century economic thought and the status of the merchant is very broad, but one of the best analyses of economic thought in the seventeenth century is contained in Wolf-Hagen Krauth, *Wirtschaftsstruktur und Semantik*, who attempts to identify the debates in which the authors were taking part, and is able to group seventeenth-century economic writings on this basis, rather than by imposing a positivist framework on them. Wilhelm Roscher, *Geschichte der National-Oekonomik in Deutschland*, approaches the economic and commercial literature from a very different standpoint than Krauth, but his book remains a useful and exhaustive summary of the literature.

[129] *Politischer Discurs*, 2d ed., p. 102.

[130] Ibid., p. 107.

group in society that could bring money—the sustenance of authority—into a territory.

Merchants remained, however, self-interested individuals, and their self-interest would always conflict with the common interest of the society; therefore, they could not be left to themselves. Becher advocated that they be formed into shareholding companies, "Kauffmanns Compagnien und Gesellschafften," and that these companies be privileged and watched over by the prince.[131] Similarly, Becher advocated that the guilds and townsmen—corporations that conflicted with the common interest of Becher's society—be organized into new guilds over which the prince had complete authority.[132] By these means, Becher attempted to make the prince governor of the entire productive cycle of society. He argued that the prince himself become a "Verläger," buying up raw materials, employing artisans to work them, and selling the finished goods through special houses. These activities would take place in the "Proviant-Hauß," "Werck-Hauß," and "Kauffhaus" that Becher proposed the prince establish in his lands to control the merchants' activities and markets.[133] When the prince reigned personally over the cycle of sustenance, his need for money would not only be fulfilled, but the corrupted state of commerce and merchants would be improved as well.

Credit and *Credit*

In the midst of the extraordinary intrigues among France, Austria, and Russia that preceded the election of a Polish king in 1668/69, Becher was commissioned by Johann Christian von Boineburg, formerly the *Oberhofmarschall* at the court in Mainz, to promote the election to the throne of the compromise candidate, Count Palatine, Philipp Wilhelm von Neuburg.[134] Becher produced a typical plan combining commerce and kingship that was supposed not only to bring von Neuburg to the throne but to endow Poland with new prosperity as well. Von Boineburg also enlisted Gottfried Wilhelm Leibniz, who produced a pseudonymous pamphlet, *Specimen demonstrationum politicarum pro eligendo Rege Polonorum novo scribendi genera ad claram certitudinem exactum*, which deduced in strict logical—or as Leibniz called it, "geometrical"—

---

[131] *Politischer Discurs*, pp. 34–39. There would be as many companies as types of wares to be traded. Becher also advocated the formation of artisans into guilds (where they were not already so formed), and the governing of these guilds by "Policey-Reguln" dictated by the prince. Ibid., pp. 30–33.

[132] *Politischer Discurs*, 2d ed., pp. 113–16. This is an example of the concept of common good being used against corporate groups as discussed by Merk, *Der Gedanke des gemeinen Besten*, p. 62.

[133] *Politischer Discurs*, 2d ed., pp. 236–59.

[134] Oswald Redlich, *Weltmacht des Barock. Österreich in der Zeit Kaiser Leopolds I.*, 4th ed. (Vienna: Rudolf M. Rohrer Verlag, 1961), pp. 72–74, provides a brief account of the election.

sequence that von Neuburg was the only candidate worthy of election.[135] The differences between Leibniz's publication and Becher's project tell us much about Becher's thinking and strategy while in Munich. Leibniz, the scholar and jurist, invoked the certain demonstration of geometry to give his text authority, while Becher, the autodidact and mechanical *mathematicus*, proposed a scheme based on the productive sphere of commerce and the mechanical arts. Becher's commercial project typically positioned himself as intermediary between Polish "partisanen" with money, who desired a safe investment for their wealth, and Count Neuburg, who had credit, connections, and a reputation among merchants, but not enough money to single-handedly resuscitate the crown of Poland, which Becher maintained had been "mächtig depauperirt" (severely impoverished).[136] The "partisanen" desired a safe investment and a secret agreement because their interests had been damaged when Johann Kasimir, a king who had *not* understood commerce, had confiscated their money before he abdicated.[137]

Becher proposed that the count establish a shareholding company for the *Verlag* of wool, silk, wine, and sugar. Then, when von Neuburg had been elected "ein teutscher könig" in Poland, and "seine parol giebet" (gave his word of honor) that he would privilege the company in different locations in Poland, Becher would set his "partisanen" into motion. They would open a bank in Poland, bringing millions into the country, from which the manufactures could be financed. In this way, Poland could regain its credit lost both with financiers and among other crowned heads of Europe.[138] No previous king had brought the honor, credit, and advantage to Poland that von Neuburg, if elected, eventually would, for only von Neuburg had the proper noble *and* commercial credit. Of the other candidates for the crown, Becher claimed that both Florence and France "have no credit with merchants . . . and would never advise the establishment of manufactures in Poland because their own lands would lose by this." The candidate from Moscow would also damage Poland, for he could not even establish manufactures in his own land. Becher concluded: "This is the

---

[135] Leibniz's work was published in mid-June 1669 under the pseudonym Georgius Ulicovios Lithuanus, after the election had already taken place. Reprinted in Leibniz, *Sämtliche Schriften und Briefe*, ed. Preussische Akademie der Wissenschaften et al. (Darmstadt: Otto Reichl et al., 1923–), ser. 4, vol. 1, pp. 1–98, with information on pp. xvii–xx. In this work Leibniz sought to establish his argument as certain and irrefutable by writing the entire work as a series of syllogisms. In the preface, he stated that in the present century, the certitude of mathematics had begun to flow out into other sciences for the good of humankind. ("Etiam nunc nostro saeculo certitudo earum artium bono generis humani, exundare in caeteras scientias coepit"). He wished to transfer the certainty of mathematical demonstration to civil affairs.

[136] Becher and von Boineburg were in correspondence about this scheme, but only a copy of one letter survives, from Becher to von Boineburg, in Mss. var. 1(2), fols. 504r–505v. Quotation comes from fol. 504v.

[137] "Ihr Herr gar *despotice* handelt," Mss. var. 1(2), fol. 504r.

[138] "Also die kron dardurch den verlornen Credit wieder erlangen" (Mss. var. 1(2), fol. 505r).

only impartial and legitimate means to help Poland and to bring it credit, renown, prosperity, recognition, and reputation, for where sustenance is, the restless spirits of all sorts of factions and war are pacified and they assume a single interest."[139]

In this unsuccessful attempt to elect a merchant-king in 1668, Becher came close to obliterating the space dividing noble and merchant. He finally joined them together completely while in the service of the emperor at the Habsburg court. In a set of instructions written for Leopold I in 1671 about the acquisition of credit—in this case, the ability to borrow money from the Dutch—Becher sought to convince the emperor that he should aspire to the status and reputation of the merchant.

"*Credit*," Becher explained in this tract, derives from "credere" (to believe or trust) as in "*credere in foro civili*"; thus true financial credit means (as it is understood in Holland) that one can borrow money simply by promising to pay it back. This "true credit" depended not on collateral but simply on "die ehrliche parole" (the word of honor).[140] Equating financial credit with the noble world of honor brought the merchants' social world and that of the noble—whose existence depended on his word of honor—much nearer.

Becher continued his explanation: a person can have very little money and much credit—this is called merchants' credit ("Kauffmanns-*Credit*")—or much money and no credit, which the Dutch call "*Civil-Credit*."[141] Merchants' credit can bring together large amounts of money in a few hours and it does not have as high an interest rate as common credit. The possession of merchants' credit allows the borrower to register at the bank in Amsterdam so that he need never deal with the actual money, for the account of credit allows him to write letters of credit. This gives the merchant even greater mobility, as he can obtain money in other cities, and never need worry about "Kisten und Kasten" (baggage).[142] Becher celebrates the very mobility of this wealth by exclaiming that in Holland, "credit, banknotes and hard cash are transmuted into each other every hour."[143]

Becher claimed that most nobles did not recognize the importance of monetary credit for their reputations, and so an inverted situation had arisen in which

[139] Mss. var. 1(2), fol. 505r. The connection Becher makes here between sustenance and peace, and his view that commerce could bring about this pacification forms an interesting connecting link for Albert O. Hirschman's argument in *The Passions and the Interests: Political Arguments for Capitalism before Its Triumph* (Princeton: Princeton University Press, 1977). He claims that a positive rhetoric about commerce existed in the seventeenth century, which was elaborated upon in the eighteenth, in which commerce was regarded as capable of pacifying the passions.

[140] "Dr. Bechers *Special-Relationen*, wegen *Anticipation* einer Million Reichsthaler vor Ihro Käyserl. Majest.," 1671, *Politischer Discurs*, 2d ed., pp. 697–725; this phrase is on pp. 698–99.

[141] Ibid., p. 700.

[142] Ibid., p. 702.

[143] "*Credit*, Banck/ und baar Geld/ lassen sich in Holland alle Stund ineinander verwandlen." Ibid., p. 703.

merchants could claim to possess a greater sense of honor than nobles, or, as Becher exclaimed in boldface, double-size type, "EIN GROSSER HERR KÖNTE NICHT SO VIEL TREU UND GLAUBEN HALTEN ALS EIN KAUFFMAN" (a great lord cannot keep his word of honor as well as a merchant).[144] Nobles did not realize "how much depends on having credit, and how damaging it is, indeed what a number of consequences it has, when credit is not held to or is lost."[145] Even if a prince has enough money from domestic sources, he should acquire merchants' credit, not only for the extra money (there can never be enough),[146] but because merchants' credit

> makes a noble lord respected when he has credit with foreigners, for the inhabitants [of his own lands] as well as neighboring countries will be that much more animated to assist him when they see that foreigners go before them with a good example. It is hardly necessary to show that credit is useful to a noble lord, for where credit is, there also is reputation and respect, and where these are, there also is power. From this springs love and fear, which are as necessary in a government as their efficient cause, namely authority. Authority is maintained by power and credit. Otherwise there exists a case of empty passion without potence, which can be seen daily in different kingdoms that are not well regarded by the Dutch, because the Dutch know these kingdoms have no particular money or credit. Credit is also very useful because it is a sign that loyalty and trust are kept, and where such things are demonstrated, it indicates constancy, with the result that such places are sought out as allies and friends. In short, if loyalty, trust, reputation, and power are necessary in a government, then credit is also necessary, for it is the cause of all these effects. When subjects trust their lord, they owe it to him and must do it partly out of fear. When foreigners, however, who are not dependent on the lord, freely trust him, that is a sign of true credit, which stems from love and affection, not from indebtedness and pressure from the creditors. A ruler should hold this true credit as dear as his honor.[147]

In this passage, Becher transferred the value represented by money credit to a value in terms of the traditional social "credit" at court. He made equivalent the commercial value of credit and the landed, court value of honor, and thus inextricably linked social and personal reputation (court *Credit*) with the ability to borrow money (merchants' credit).[148]

Becher also advocated that the prince take on the activities and values of the

---

[144] Ibid., p. 704.

[145] "Wie viel daran gelegen/ daß man Credit habe/ und wie schädlich es sey/ ja eine lange *consequenz* es mache/ wann man denselben nicht halte/ oder verliere." Ibid.

[146] Ibid., p. 723.

[147] Ibid., pp. 705–6.

[148] Here is evidence of the transition from a social and moral system based on real property to one founded on mobile property that Pocock locates in eighteenth-century English debates about credit and land. See Pocock, *Machiavellian Moment*, chap. 13.

merchant, but hastened to assure the emperor that this would not damage his honor. He explained that the ability to obtain financial credit depended upon presenting oneself as having a project that would yield a good return on the money borrowed. Only one activity generated cash, said Becher, and that was manufacture.[149] The prince who wants to fight wars (the outcome of which is uncertain) or build palaces (the maintenance of which brings debts instead of money to pay the interest) will receive no credit.[150] The prince must take up the occupation of a merchant by founding manufactories, rather than simply follow the traditional pursuits of the nobility; he must embrace merchants by chartering them in organizations similar to guilds. Finally, he must ascribe to the merchant's view that money has intrinsic value.

The prince who cannot immediately acquire merchants' credit can still get something equal to it if he consorts with the merchants himself—that is, if he builds a network of contacts with them, by which they guarantee him. In effect, these merchants become his collateral or, as Becher called it, "die *Materia* des *Credits*" (the material of credit) and "Kundtschafft."[151] But consorting with merchants will not damage the reputation of the emperor, for the credit, Becher declares (again in double-size type), is of such a quality that "DERGLEICHEN KEIN POTENTAT IN DER CHRISTENHEIT HABEN SOLLE" (the like of which no potentate in Christendom will have).[152] Not even the king of France could borrow from Holland for less than 8 percent interest with collateral. The duke of Lothringen could do no better than obtain a loan from Switzerland against "Hypothec" and stiff interest.[153] Thus "it will especially create respect for Your Imperial Majesty when you are the first among so many noble Christian rulers and kings to have such good credit at the public bank in Amsterdam."[154] And if the emperor decides not to take on this extraordinary credit now, there are other lands that are waiting and eager to increase their power by as much as the Habsburg lands would be diminished through loss of this credit.[155] Thus, Becher assured the prince that although he might take up the occupations and assume the social values of the merchant, he would not lose his reputation among the noble houses of Europe. Indeed, by becoming an actor in the exchange economy, he would in fact gain respect and power in the court world.

Becher concluded his instructions to the emperor with a complete conflation of commercial credit and court credit: "through the system of credit, a person

---

[149] An essential part of credit was to create the appearance of planning a project: "daß man nemblich vorwende/ man habe etwas vor/ worduch man könt Nutzen schaffen/ und darüber noch ein ehrliches Interesse geben" (*Politischer Discurs*, 2d ed., pp. 706–7). The verb *vorwenden* usually means simply to make the appearance of doing something.

[150] Ibid., p. 707.

[151] Ibid., p. 709.

[152] Ibid., p. 720.

[153] Ibid., pp. 705–6.

[154] Ibid., p. 723.

[155] Ibid., p. 725.

can see how he stands in the affections of other people."[156] In this final argument, Becher made the ability to obtain financial credit a measure of social credit. Thus, when one was able to borrow money, it indicated that one also possessed a fund of social credit. Court and city values were thereby made identical. The prince would become a merchant, and the values of the merchant and the exchange economy would provide the standards of social value and credit at court.

A very interesting subplot unfolded around Becher's own social and financial credit during the four months of 1671 he spent in Holland attempting to obtain credit for the emperor. This story moves us ahead chronologically in Becher's life, but brings us back to the rivalry and scheming of the court world with which this chapter began. In Becher's account of the trip and subsequent attempt to save his own credit at the Viennese court, the boundaries between his social and financial credit blur, and we find again that the sources from which he drew what we would call today his "economic ideas" could be informal and experiential.

Becher began a trip to Amsterdam in 1671 as an opportunistic response to the trade war between France and the United Provinces. In early 1671, the Dutch had banned French brandy, wine, and other products. Hoping to establish trade with Dutch merchants, Becher set off to Holland in early May with a load of Austrian wine and brandy and carrying various other commissions, among them the negotiation of a million Reichsthaler loan from the Dutch.[157] He kept notes of his business, his visitors, and his trips to the Stock Exchange in a journal that is still extant. This journal would serve him later as a statement of accounts, an explanation of business to the emperor, and as aid to his memory. It tells us that he spent most of his days in conference with the merchant who was to sell the wine and with the group of Dutch "capitalists" who claimed to be ready to lend the emperor a million Reichsthaler. His business concluded on 16 August, and he started back up the Rhine to Germany, noting along the way that he received news his son had died but "otherwise had good tidings."[158]

He arrived back in Vienna on 20 September but his business was only half-

---

[156] "Durch das *Credit*-Wesen kan man sehen/ wie man bey denen Leuten in der *affection* stehet." Ibid., p. 724.

[157] He left Vienna on 6 May 1671 with 47 Eimer of Wine and 4 Eimer of brandy (1 Eimer = 56.589 liters) and returned on 20 September. Hassinger, *Becher*, gives the fullest account of this trip, while the journal Becher kept (drafted in a scribe's hand and edited by Becher), drafts of letters to the president of the Hofkammer, as well as his statement of expenditures is in Mss. var. 1(3), 438–543. The 1671 journal shows a much busier schedule than the 1660 and 1664 trips, with many more trips to the Bourse and *Comparitien* (business meetings) held with merchants. However, Becher met almost daily with a chemist friend in Amsterdam, Dr. Galenus, with whom he carried out various "Proben," and he spoke once with Glauber's widow. He viewed ships, collected rarities, visited Elzevier's printshop, and met various artisans. He proudly notes that he met an Englishman at the Bourse in Amsterdam, "welcher mich complementirt *nomine curiosorum*."

[158] 31 August, Mss. var. 1(3), fol. 537v.

finished. He had succeeded in getting the wine to Amsterdam but some had turned because of the rough trip and a few barrels had been commandeered by the emperor's resident ministers in The Hague. Although various merchants showed interest in taking on the wine, Becher had ended up having to leave it with his merchant contact in Amsterdam, Isaac Telgens, as collateral for the loans he had found necessary to take out to cover his own living expenses. The Imperial Treasury had expected Becher to live off the proceeds of the wine sales while in Amsterdam.[159] In his other commissions, Becher had engaged a silk weaver for the Hofkammer president, and he had obtained the million Reichsthaler loan, but a guarantor still had to be found for it. Becher clearly had a case to make to the emperor not only to save his deals in Amsterdam, but also to save his own *Credit* at court. As soon as he returned home, he began to write furiously to the Hofkammer president.

His most urgent order of business was to rescue his own *Credit*, for from this flowed the completion of all else, not to mention, of course, the continuation of his livelihood at court. He sent the Hofkammer president a record of expenditures, which not only set out the money he had spent in Amsterdam but also made clear his loyal service to his patron and his patron's reputation and honor. He informed the president (and, through him, the emperor) that he had suffered recurring dizziness and when he had purged to remedy it. He noted when he went to Mass but struck out the account of his evening at the "Comedy" and his purchase of a diamond and some silver utensils. He defended his renting of a coach (because of his dizziness, the press of people, the heat, and the large size of the city) and crossed out every instance in his journal where he had recorded walking from place to place. He justified his ordering of breakfast every morning (because of the lateness of the hour of eating in Amsterdam and the necessity not to go to the Exchange and conduct business on an empty stomach). He maintained that he needed two masses (almost three liters) of Rhine wine in Amsterdam rather than water or beer to strengthen himself because of the notoriously bad air of the Lowlands.[160]

Becher recorded his conversations with several artisans whom he believed might prove useful to the Austrian lands or at the emperor's court, and he noted the samples of glass he bought, as well as the tin making, the camphor and borax refining, and other processes he had observed, which, with the continued favor of the emperor, he might introduce into the Habsburg lands. He reported that, as he had been commanded by the emperor, he employed a go-between to notify him of jewels and curiosities, the possession of which might increase the reputation of the emperor. He also made sure that his patrons knew that he had boxed the ears of his tavern keeper for speaking disparagingly of the emperor.

---

[159] Hassinger, *Becher*, p. 170.

[160] Mss. var. 1(3), fols. 528–534. The journal is written in a scribe's hand and edited by Becher who struck out and corrected certain passages.

This had almost caused a serious incident, he said, because "it was not the custom" in Amsterdam to lay hands on anyone, not even on a tavern keeper.[161] He noted but struck out his meetings with other nobles of the empire, as such meetings might perhaps have compromised his single-minded loyalty to the emperor. He sometimes made a record of the cash with which they awarded him, but never reported that he exchanged code with them for future correspondence. He noted his visit to the Amsterdam Town Hall but not his drinking party within it.

Becher complained bitterly that the Hofkammer had advanced him only one hundred Reichsthaler for a trip in which his total expenses had totaled fifteen hundred Reichsthaler. He wrote an impassioned letter to von Sinzendorff about the cost of living in Holland and the social and financial cost to the emperor's *Credit* and reputation when his representatives were perceived as being in straitened circumstances.[162] He stated that the merchants and rentiers in Holland are elegant people ("vornehme Leute") who cannot be treated in a miserly way; besides, "they made the first beginning in favors" and afterward he had to equal their entertainments. He continued:

> It would be seen as a contradiction to negotiate a million and at the same time to carry oneself as a pauper. Hr. Baron Lisola and Hr. Gramprich [the emperor's resident ministers in The Hague] can satisfactorily demonstrate how important . . . the manner one treats a Dutchman is. Not to mention how much it costs in Holland if one maintains oneself only in middling circumstances and wants to eat himself only half-full. . . . Besides I could not maintain myself in worse circumstances than I did previously in the service of the Count [of Hanau] and the Electors [of Mainz and of Bavaria]. . . . Besides the Dutch are so insolent in demanding money and even unchristian and I have had not the least satisfaction in their treatment of me.[163]

Becher made clear what damage it did to his own *Credit* (and ultimately to the emperor's *Credit*) that Telgens, his merchant contact, did not at first want to take the wine as collateral for his loans, and so "left [Becher] sitting in the highest shame and scorn, to the 'disreputation' of His Imperial Majesty, unable to carry out any business." The emperor must be made to understand that sufficient money (or the appearance of such) is necessary to carry out such a commission, "so that one can pass for liquid . . . unless of course one wants to abandon the reputation of His Imperial Majesty."[164]

Becher ends the letter, noting that he was forced to spend his own money, even having to sell a magnet for sixty gulders, and recommends that the Hofkammer send Isaac Telgens the balance of the payment due "so that Your

---

161 13 July, Mss. var. 1(3), fol. 534v.

162 A draft of this letter is in Mss. var. 1(3), fols. 528r–530v.

163 Mss. var. 1(3), fol. 528v.

164 Mss. var. 1(3), fol. 530v.

Imperial Majesty's reputation and *Credit* will in some manner be held together." In addition, Telgens should be given a special recompense for his time because "His Majesty's *Credit* . . . depends upon [how other Dutch merchants] see Telgens being treated by His Majesty."[165] Becher was trying to make clear that the emperor's *Credit* rested on how he treated a merchant. Perhaps this idea was as remarkable as the fact that in Holland a nobleman's representative could not box the ears of a tavern keeper for insulting the honor of the emperor.

After the attempt to secure his own credit, Becher sought to rescue the deal for the one million Reichsthaler loan to the emperor. To this end, he provided the Hofkammer president with a translation (from the Dutch) of the contracts setting out the conditions of the loan. The Dutch merchants agreed to lend the million if a free imperial city stood surety for a period of forty years. Another alternative was to mortgage the estates of the nobility of the Archduchy of Upper and Lower Austria.[166] Ironically, when the Dutch moneylenders drew up a draft of this contract, they appealed to the feudal honor of the Austrian nobility in their position as vassals. They urged the Austrian nobles to sign because the million Reichsthaler would maintain the "reputation and *Credit*" of their feudal lord, His Imperial Majesty as archduke of Austria, to whom, as their liege lord, they had sworn fealty. This is especially interesting language in light of the fact that Becher feared the documents might offend the emperor. On sending the contracts to the Hofkammer president, he wrote across his translation a warning instruction:

> Here follow some points translated from the Dutch into German, in which it must be noticed that because the Dutch are ignorant of the German courts and their style, the points may come across as somewhat unmannerly and hard. Because of this, Your Dukely Excellence will graciously know how much and how broadly to read from it [the contract] to His Imperial Majesty.[167]

This passage points to a difference in the standards of civility in the Viennese court and the Amsterdam Stock Exchange. In translating the documents from Dutch into German, Becher worried that the manner of the Dutch merchants was incapable of translation into the court sphere, and we see again that his project involved a translation not only of language but of cultures.

. . . . .

Credit, in both commercial and noble societies, was a measure of status. The court world measured personal value by social *Credit*, which depended on land, rank, and status. In the commercial world, on the other hand, personal value

---

[165] Ibid.
[166] Mss. var. 1(3), fol. 495r–v.
[167] Ibid.

depended on access to money and financial credit. The exchange economy took place around the court but was not part of it. Becher sought to extend the financial base of the court from land to encompass commerce without upsetting traditional hierarchies of noble power. This attempt to integrate the court world into the commercial society culminated in Vienna in the instructions to the emperor on obtaining credit. Becher appropriated the most important value in the court world, relative personal rank, or *Credit*, and conflated it with financial credit—the ability to borrow money. In doing this, Becher translated the values of the trading city into a language and structure comprehensible to the court. Ritual, the symbols of power, and the display of ornaments upheld the court hierarchy and scale of value. Becher undertook to convert these symbols into material things and to recast the ornaments into coin and specie.

Becher formulated his political agenda in response to the German court world's need for material solutions to a real crisis of economic power and its simultaneous desire to uphold the traditional symbols of political power. At the Habsburg court, Becher would use a new strategy in pursuing this program, one tailored to the *representatio* of the Habsburg house and based on alchemy. Before Becher left Munich permanently for Vienna, however, he made a trip to Amsterdam, the center of the commercial world, to seek a colony for the count of Hanau. This curious project involved him further in the transactions of words and things between the noble court and the commercial world.

WEST INDIAN INTERLUDE

I N THE THREE summer months of 1669 Becher traveled down the Rhine to Amsterdam to acquire from the Dutch West India Company a New World colony for Friedrich Casimir, count of Hanau. Neither Becher nor the count ever saw this strip of coastal land thirty Dutch miles broad and one hundred miles long in what is now French Guiana, but it proved fertile ground for their projections.[1] Becher's trip to Amsterdam and the colony project constitute an epitome of his political and economic goals and his mode of pursuing them. For in his dealings Becher moved between the noble, courtly society of Germany and the commercial society of the Dutch Republic. The colony and its products—sugar, coffee, curiosities—were both courtly luxuries and commercial commodities, and for Becher they operated as a winged Mercury opening up lines of communication between the values of the world of commerce and the world of the court. In a painting commissioned by the Count in 1669 to commemorate the successful acquisition of the colony (figure 4), Count Friedrich Casimir and Becher[2] are portrayed beside the allegorical figures of Mercury, Ceres (the daughter of Saturn and goddess of agriculture and the harvest), and an African slave. Mercury gestures toward a table overflowing with the riches and curious objects to be acquired in the New World: coral, gold, and pearls. In myth, Mercury shuttled between the human world and the realm of the gods, and in material form, mercury formed the essential component in the philosophers' stone, by which base metals could be transmuted into gold. In this painting, Mercury personified commerce and the activity of merchants, and, as messenger of the gods, he also symbolized eloquence. Mercury functioned as a perfect emblem for Becher because he evoked words and texts, as well as natural and "artificial" wealth, but this painting worked as an emblem for the count in a wholly different way. With his left hand, Mercury indicates a

---

[1] A detailed discussion of the 1669 colony project is provided by Heinrich Volberg, *Deutsche Kolonialbestrebungen in Südamerika nach dem Dreißigjährigen Kriege insbesondere die Bemühungen von Johann Joachim Becher* (Cologne and Vienna: Böhlau-Verlag, 1977). Other shorter discussions are by Ferdinand Hahnzog, "Einige unbekannte Figuren im Spiel um Hanauisch-Indien," *Neues Magazin für hanauische Geschichte* 3 (1958): 69–84, and "Das Hanauer 'tolle Jahr' 1669," *Hanauer Geschichtsblätter* 20 (1965): 147–71. Also containing valuable details about the Dutch participants in the project are F. M. Jaeger, "Over Johan Joachim Becher en zijne Relatie's met de Nederlanden," *Economisch-Historisch Jaarboek* 5 (1919): 60–135; and Abraham Hulshof, "Een duitsch econom in een over ons land omstreeks 1670," *Onze eeuw 10* 4 (1910): 65–96.

[2] This figure of advisor to the count may either be Becher or Georg Christian of Hessen-Homburg.

Figure 4. Double portrait of Count Friedrich Casimir of Hanau and Adviser (Johann Joachim Becher?), oil on canvas, 1669, by J. D. Welcker, entitled *Allegory of the Acquisition of Surinam by Count Friedrich Casimir of Hanau*. Depicted (left to right) are Adviser, Count Friedrich Casimir, Mercury pointing to *"Vanitas Vanitatum et omnia Vanitas,"* African slave, Ceres. With permission of the Staatliche Kunsthalle, Karlsruhe.

scroll, on which is written "Vanitas Vanitatum et omnia Vanitas" (vanity of vanities; all is vanity). The choice of the *vanitas* theme for this portrait would, by the end of 1669, turn out to be a particularly apt one.

Becher's strategy was to entice the noble count to enter the monetary transactions of the commercial world. But as the preceding chapter showed, this maneuver involved Becher in fundamental difficulties because the court and commercial worlds had different languages and different sets of social and personal values. In order to reconcile these, Becher had to translate the movable values of the money economy into the stable, immovable values of the landed nobility. Becher attempted such a translation in the colony project of 1669. In his effort, he drew on his knowledge of natural philosophy as a court physician as well as his ideas about political economy.

Dramatis Personae

The story of the colony project begins and ends at a territorial court of the Holy Roman Empire, namely, at the residential seat of the House of Hanau. At the center of this extraordinarily complex court and family was Count Friedrich Casimir (1623–85, ruled from 1647), who had his residence in Hanau, near Frankfurt. For more than a century the House of Hanau had been divided into two family lines, each possessing separate lands. Friedrich Casimir descended from the Hanau-Lichtenberg line with lands around Strasbourg. The Hanau-Münzenberg line, whose lands were situated around Frankfurt, had died out shortly before Friedrich Casimir had come into his inheritance, so that he became ruler over the lands of both family lines. The lands, widely scattered and noncontiguous, lay both to the right and left of the Rhine. The population of the lands of Hanau-Lichtenberg were Lutheran, those of Hanau-Münzenberg Calvinist.[3]

In order to pacify Calvinist fears in his new territories, Friedrich Casimir had married the widow (twenty years older than himself) of his predecessor in the Calvinist line of the family, Sybille Christine of Anhalt-Dessau. But the marriage remained childless. To further complicate matters, he had two brothers with whom it had been politic to divide the lands. One brother had married the sister of the countess, also a Calvinist (who had also previously been engaged to a now-deceased member of the Hanau-Münzenberg line). Their marriage also remained without issue, although this brother had three natural children. The second brother had married a Calvinist daughter of the House of Pfalz-Zweibrücken-Birkenfeld, and, before he died in 1666, the marriage had pro-

---

[3] The House of Hanau on the Calvinist side was distantly related to the Dutch House of Orange, and as a youth Friedrich Casimir had traveled and studied in Holland. Information on the House of Hanau is drawn from Hahnzog, "Hanauer 'tolle Jahr,'" and Volberg, *Deutsche Kolonialbestrebungen*.

duced two sons. These two boys, still very young in 1669, would on majority inherit the entire territory of Hanau. Because of the youth of the boys, their mother and her brother from Pfalz-Zweibrücken-Birkenfeld became their guardians. The rulers of Hessen-Kassel also had an interest in Hanau because the Landgravine Amalie Elisabeth of Hessen-Kassel (1602–51), née Hanau-Münzenberg, had assisted Count Friedrich Casimir in retaining and pacifying his Calvinist territories. In return, he had ensured that the territory of Hanau would fall to Hessen-Kassel in the event that the Hanau-Lichtenberg line died out.

Quite clearly there were several competing interests in the territory of Hanau; small parcels of land and towns lay distant from one another, with differences in geography, agriculture, and commerce. The religious situation in Hanau was particularly complex, and the many minor territories that had a stake in the fortunes of Hanau made political and dynastic relations especially tense. The larger territories surrounding Hanau also looked with predatory interest at this small territory that interrupted the continuity of their lands.

The territorial lands of Hanau had been at the center of the fighting in the Thirty Years' War, and, in 1669, two decades after the Peace of Westphalia, they continued to suffer from the effects of the war. The territory and family were deeply in debt. Impoverished as he was, however, Count Friedrich Casimir had little regard for the finances of his territory. Feeling that the reputation of his person and rule were more important than mere cash, he indulged in lavish displays of pageantry and festivity. For example, when Charles II of England ascended the throne in 1660, Friedrich Casimir threw a very costly, spontaneous party to celebrate this reassertion of noble rule. When he acquired a new piece for his Kunstkammer, the count fired a one hundred gun salute. This sort of thing seriously alarmed his wife, who desired to keep her Calvinist lands intact, and his brother and the guardians of his nephews, who worried that he would squander their sons' inheritance. The first character in the story of the colony project is thus a landed but cash-poor count, who had dreams of glory and reputation far beyond his means, a perfect lure for the projector.

The second character in this drama is the Landgrave Georg Christian (1626–77), younger son of the House of Hessen-Homburg, a small and, if possible, more contested territory than Hanau. Hessen-Homburg had formed the inheritance portion of a younger son of the House of Hessen-Darmstadt (itself a result of the divisions of Hessen). Rule of the territory of Hessen-Darmstadt had been left to three sons, but the eldest forced his brothers to abdicate their rights in exchange for cash sums. In 1622, however, he was hopelessly behind on the payments, so he gave his brothers small territories, although without noble rights. As the younger son of a younger son of the House of Hessen-Homburg, Georg Christian was thus a landgrave and prince of the empire with no territory and no noble rights, a situation he set about changing in 1667. In that year his older brother came into his inheritance, and Georg Christian, who had made a fortune in the Spanish, French, and imperial armies during the war and had recently married a rich widow, convinced his older brother to sell him the Landgrafschaft of Hessen-Homburg. On finally obtaining the territory in 1669, he immediately sought one of the noble rights to which he felt himself entitled as a prince of the realm: minting privileges.[4]

In 1669, the landgrave was also busy in Hanau, where, despite being a Catholic convert, he had become so friendly with the Lutheran count Friedrich Casimir that the count had virtually made him a joint ruler of Hanau.[5] This alarmed the already nervous relatives in the court at Hanau who feared that the count would make the landgrave his heir.[6] Needless to say, it also dismayed the count's Lutheran and Calvinist subjects, who feared the count would convert to Catholicism and begin the struggles of the Thirty Years' War all over again.[7] For his part, the landgrave of Hessen-Homburg had an overarching strategy by which he sought to use the count to improve his own position as prince without rights.

The court of Hanau also housed some lesser figures, who eventually played roles as important as their noble betters in the story of the colony project. One was an artisan from the free imperial city of Augsburg whom we have met before. Daniel Neuberger, whom Becher had once seen as a model for his own activities, had previously been a *hofbefreite* artisan at the court of Ferdinand III, and was now intent on ingratiating himself in Hanau. Neuberger had a protector and go-between at the court of Hanau: a wandering Swedish projector, Bengt Skytte, filled with Wanderlust and enthused in his projects. Like Becher, his guiding star appears to have been the conjuncture of natural philosophy, polymathy, and commerce.[8] At the court of Hanau, he acted as agent and patron of

---

[4] In 1671, Georg Christian had to mortgage Hessen-Homburg to his creditors (among whom Christian von Boineburg counted himself), and in 1673, Georg Christian sold his lands to the landgrave of Hessen-Darmstadt in return for a yearly pension. Margarete Hintereicher, *Georg Christian von Hessen-Homburg (1626–1677)* (Darmstadt and Marburg: Selbstverlag der Hessischen Historischen Kommission Darmstadt und der Historischen Kommission für Hessen, 1985).

[5] The murkiness of their relationship, however, is indicated by the fact that Friedrich Casimir had begun to call the three-years-younger Georg Christian "father," and Georg Christian called the count "son." Hintereicher, *Georg Christian*, pp. 188–89.

[6] Plans were made for the landgrave to take over as interim ruler of the territory when the count made a trip to his new colony. Hahnzog, "Hanauer 'tolle Jahr,'" p. 150.

[7] The Count, urged on by Becher and Landgrave Georg Christian, seriously considered converting to Catholicism, and allowed the landgrave the use of the *Schloßkapelle* for Catholic services. Hahnzog, "Hanauer 'tolle Jahr,'" pp. 148, 160.

[8] Becher calls him "Bent Skylte." He was Bengt (or Benedikt) Skytte (1614–83), baron and senator at the Swedish court. The lives and projects of Becher and Skytte overlap at many points, and they appear to have been rivals at court more than once. Despite Becher's ruthless portrayal of him as a thief and atheist, Skytte was extremely learned and had been a favorite of Queen Christina. Educated by his father in the works of Comenius and the ideals of pansophism, Skytte became a diplomat and advisor to the Crown of Sweden. From 1651, Skytte spent long periods of time at other courts in Europe. He negotiated in London for a Protestant confederation led by Sweden, in

Neuberger, trying to persuade Count Friedrich Casimir to buy the sculptor's wax figures for his Kunstkammer (figures 5 and 6). Then there was Becher himself, the Swede's rival, with a project of his own, the colony. The Swede and Becher competed for the count's favor and money.[9]

Thus members of the court of Hanau in 1669 who are the actors in this story formed two levels. At the higher level are the noble figures of the court: the profligate count, the cunning landgrave, and the alarmed family; and at a lower level are the go-betweens and projectors, Becher and Skytte, and the artisans such as Neuberger, the wax-sculptor.

In the end, the most important entity on this stage was what seemed at first to be just a bit of the scenery: the Kunstkammer itself. Perhaps filling a cabinet or an entire room, this collection of rare objects turned out to be the locus of activity for the whole drama. It determined the fate of Becher's reputation at court, the outcome of the colony project itself, and even the fortunes of the count's power in his own territory.

Scaena

Amsterdam had now, after the age of iron and of copper, also
lived through the age of silver, and she saw the breaking of the
clear morning of a golden age. She now raised her splendidly
crowned head out of the swampy reeds and the damp valleys like
an oppressed but never extinguished palm tree. . . . The sugared
steel yoke that the power of the Burgundians threw around her
and that the rage of the Spaniards tightened; the gruesome storm
of the Anabaptists that threatened to strangle her in this yoke;
indeed all the earlier adversities and misfortunes through which
she had struggled were now fully out of her thoughts. She had

---

Paris for an appointment to the Académie française, and in Berlin for a "*Universitas universitatum, hominum et scientiarum.*" Shortly before the 1669 episode, Skytte had met with Johann Christian von Boineburg (whom he knew as Hessian envoy to the Swedish court) and Gottfried Wilhelm Leibniz (whom he met for the first time). After 1669, several German cities apparently drove him from their walls for advocating atheism and freedom of religious practice. He spent the rest of his life traveling between Sweden, Holland, and England, working on a never-completed universal etymological lexicon. For a fuller description of his life, see Fritz Arnheim, "Freiherr Benedikt Skytte (1614–1683), der Urheber des Planes einer brandenburgischen 'Universal-Universität der Völker, Wissenschaften und Künste,'" in *Festschrift zu Gustav Schmollers 70. Geburtstag. Beiträge zur brandenburgischen und preußischen Geschichte*, ed. Verein für Geschichte der Mark Brandenburg (Leipzig: Duncker & Humblot, 1908), pp. 65–99. See also Susanna Åkerman, *Queen Christina of Sweden and Her Circle* (Leiden: E. J. Brill, 1991).

[9] This threesome had been associated before. At the elector's court in Bavaria, Becher claimed to have adjudicated a scheme of Skytte's, and also to have promoted Neuberger in the plan for the *Theatrum naturae et artis*, for which Neuberger was to provide the wax figures. This is discussed by Becher, *Methodus didactica*.

already seated herself on the golden throne of fortune. Luxury,
wealth, voluptuous pleasure, and honor hovered all around her.
All the merchants of the European world, indeed from Africa,
Asia, and America, vied for her favor and desired to carry on
their trade with her. The Muscovite, the Pole, the Turk, the
Persian, the Greek, the Indian, indeed the grandest people from
east and west, south and north came by land and by sea to wait
upon her.

(*Zesen*, Beschreibung der Stadt Amsterdam)

Against this backdrop of tense court rivalries and politicoreligious tensions,
Becher set out from Frankfurt in 1669 for the very different world of the Dutch
Republic. When the fighting between the Habsburgs and the Dutch had ended
in the Treaty of Münster in 1648, an ongoing internal struggle between the
House of Orange and the powerful city governments of the Province of Holland
continued unabated. The cities had grown rich through commerce, and the
large merchants' companies (such as the East and West India Companies)
sought self-government and free trade. After 1648, city government was overseen by a noble *Stadhouder* from the House of Orange. While the large trading
cities sought freedom from noble rule, other provinces had different interests,
and the House of Orange enjoyed support from the standing army, the few
landed nobles, the rural subjects, as well as the citizens of cities closest to the
southern border with the Spanish Netherlands. When Becher left for Amsterdam in 1669, the commercial cities had the upper hand in this struggle, for in
1653 the noble Stadtholder from the House of Orange had died and the Pensionary of Holland, who represented the interests of the cities, Jan de Witt, was able
to prevent the appointment of a new Stadtholder, thereby becoming ruler of the
United Provinces. The Grand Pensionary de Witt was not to be in power for
long, however, for in 1672, Louis XIV declared war on Holland and de Witt
was assassinated, thus allowing William III of Orange to become Stadtholder-
General for life.

On 22 June 1669, however, Becher set off for the commercial republic to
seek a colony from a merchant company for his noble patron. The fact that the
court of Hanau sought favors from a merchant company in the Dutch Republic
appeared to many people of the seventeenth century to be an inversion of
natural order. Becher for one was both fascinated and alarmed by a country that,
in spite of possessing very little land, was richer and more powerful than many
landowning German princes. This unnatural situation was encapsulated in the
seventeenth-century perception of the two great mysteries of Spain and Holland. Spain, a rich land, ruled by the Habsburg dynasty—the most powerful
family in Europe—had declined despite the fact that it possessed silver and
gold mines in the New World. Holland, on the other hand, a country with no
mines and very little agricultural land had become powerful enough to throw off

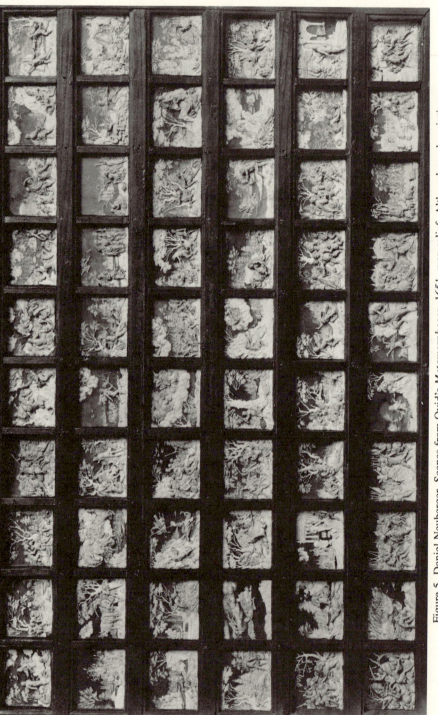

Figure 5. Daniel Neuberger, Scenes from Ovid's *Metamorphoses*, 1651, wax relief. Although no description exists of the wax figures in which Neuberger tried to interest the count, this illustration and the next provide examples of this baroque art form. With permission of the Kunsthistorisches Museum, Vienna.

Figure 6. Daniel Neuberger, *Allegory of the death of Ferdinand III*, 1657, wax relief. The crowned emperor lies in state, while around him skeletons perform a dance of death; one plays a horn, another blows soap bubbles, while in front one extinguishes a torch. At the emperor's head stands an hourglass. With permission of the Kunsthistorisches Museum, Vienna.

the yoke of noble government.[10] Becher summed up this inverted order in his remark that "Holland has its powerful merchants' companies that can defy kings and lords." As a reason for this, he tendered the opinion that, "the Dutch make a matter of state out of commerce and wage costly wars for it because they well know that commerce makes their land populous, prosperous, and into a true community in which each member lives from the other[11] (figures 7 and 8).

Becher's 1669 trip to Holland to obtain a colony brought these two worlds face to face. The court of the count of Hanau epitomized the problems of the small, impoverished German court, and the merchant company with which Becher dealt in Holland represented the wealth and power of the commercial republic. Through the colony project, Becher attempted to graft the commercial world onto the world of the noble court, but to accomplish this, he had to depict for the count his negotiations with the merchants' company in a way that conveyed no hint of base commercial dealings.

Ludus Scaenicus

Becher constructed such a depiction of his trip for the count in the journal he kept while in Holland in 1669. In this journal, Becher shaped the story of his trip to appeal to the noble count.[12] His journey to Holland was the outcome of a

[10] Eli F. Hecksher, *Mercantilism*, 2 vols., trans. Mendel Shapiro (London: George Allen & Unwin, 1935), 2:315, discusses these two "mysteries," and J. H. Elliott, "Self-Perception and Decline in Early Seventeenth-Century Spain," *Past and Present* 74 (1977): 41–61, discusses the perception of Spanish decline. A belief that the money gained by Dutch commerce was tainted went along with the perception of an inversion of natural order. The ambiguous mixture of admiration and moral doubt that the Dutch engendered is clear, for example, in Philipp von Zesen, *Beschreibung der Stadt Amsterdam*. In his discussion of a statue of Mercury in the new Town Hall of Amsterdam (pp. 264–65), of the disregard of the liberal arts in Amsterdam (p. 333), and of the bad air and resulting scarcity of learned men in Amsterdam (p. 389), von Zesen expressed his belief that the concern with commerce in Amsterdam led the Dutch to look more to earthly than to intellectual or spiritual pleasures. See also Simon Schama, *The Embarrassment of Riches: An Interpretation of Dutch Culture in the Golden Age* (Berkeley: University of California Press, 1988).

[11] Becher stressed the agricultural advantages that the German territories had over Holland: great amounts of land, domestic trade and markets, trade generated by the nobility who can produce finished goods within their lands, and cheap fuel and food. Despite this, German princes remained poor. *Politischer Discurs*, p. 108.

[12] In the Becher *Nachlaß* there are journals from trips in 1660, 1664, and 1671 in Mss. var. 1(3). Becher used these journals and the notations of expenses as the basis of the accounts that he presented to his patrons. The journal from the 1669 trip is not in Rostock: rather Becher published it in 1673 in the second edition of the *Politischer Discurs*, pp. 1082–1112. No doubt Becher edited it to prepare it for publication (as he edited the journals extant in Rostock before presentation to his patron), but its faithfulness to his actual trip is not at issue here; rather, I am interested in his construction of an account of the trip, and I will pay attention to the language that he uses and the sort of information that he chooses to emphasize. We must take into account the layers of meaning and intention that went into the different stages of construction of the journal. It developed from a

long series of negotiations for an overseas colony with different seagoing powers of Europe—the Spanish, English, French, and Dutch. Becher had at first negotiated for a colony on behalf of the Bavarian elector and electoress, but he became impatient with the ponderous course of these negotiations and used the information and contacts he had gathered for a hurried deal with the count of Hanau.[13] No archival documents show how Becher first came into contact with Count Friedrich Casimir, but he seems to have had little difficulty in convincing the count that the colony project would yield *fama*, much-needed cash, as well as rare objects for his collection. In Becher's mind, the colony represented a new source of income for a territorial lord. This income would flow from cash crops—such as tobacco, sugar, and coffee—grown in the new lands and sold to other powers in Europe. The colony would also save the court the large sum it spent each year to import these goods, and the settlers in the colony would provide a market for manufactured wares made in the count's territory. Over the course of the summer, however, it became apparent that the count's vision of the colony differed from Becher's.

Before leaving for Holland, Becher met Count Friedrich Casimir in Frankfurt (not at his residence in Hanau) and obtained the necessary letters of authority and of credit, as well as money and gifts. The count granted Becher a retinue of four people: a chamberlain of the count's court, a lackey, a secretary (Becher's brother-in-law), and a servant. In the diary of his trip, Becher noted all the stages of the journey.[14] On the first day, 22 June, he escorted his pregnant wife to the gates of Frankfurt, where she made her way to Munich; then he met the rest of his party and started down the Rhine with them. On the nine-day journey from Frankfurt to Amsterdam, Becher noted that they feared shipwreck twice because of bad weather and a drunken ship's captain. The lodgings ("Logiament") were almost without exception uncomfortable. At Arnhem, they paid off the shipper and hired a wagon, needed for their copious baggage and the precious gifts, to transport them to Utrecht. From there they took a canal boat to Amsterdam, where on 1 July they arrived, as Becher noted, "safe and sound" ("glücklich und gesund").

After a day's rest, Becher met first with the most important of his contacts in Amsterdam, a Portuguese Jewish merchant, Abraham Cain [Coin], who, after fifteen years in Brazil, had amassed a large fortune and was held in high regard

---

diary recording his activities and perceptions on the trip to Amsterdam into a journal aimed at his patron, and finally into a published piece justifying his actions in Amsterdam to a wider audience of potential patrons and shareholders for the company he attempted to found to provide capital for the the colony after the count had failed in this. I believe that in the published version, the account of the journey itself and the stay in Amsterdam remained much as he constructed it for the count, while the story of his return to Frankfurt and the discovery of the count's actions in his absence was directed at a wider audience and sought, to some extent, to disassociate himself from Count Friedrich Casimir.

[13] For details of the Bavarian negotiations, in which Johann Daniel Crafft and Martin Elers had a hand, see Volberg, *Deutsche Kolonialbestrebungen.*

[14] The following is drawn from *Politischer Discurs*, 2d ed., pp. 1082–1112.

Figure 7. The frontispiece of Becher's *Politischer Discurs*, 1673, provides a visual expression of his view of commerce. At the top is the Exchange in Amsterdam (see figure 8), below are merchant ships. To Becher, these two images symbolized commerce. Ships commonly stood for long-distance trade, but for Becher, ships also evoked travel, experience, the progress of human art, and the exchange of things.

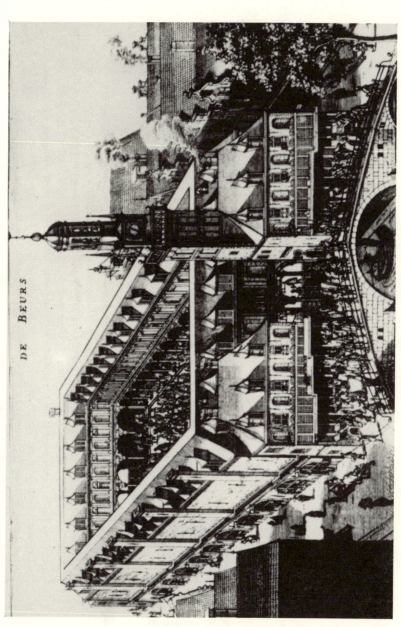

DE BEURS

Figure 8. The Exchange, Amsterdam, 1663. Engraving by Jacob van Meurs(?), in
Philipp von Zesen, *Beschreibung der Stadt Amsterdam*, 1664.

KLEVENIERS DOELEN.

Figure 9. The Kleveniers Doelen, Amsterdam, 1663. The scene of Becher's first meeting with representatives of the West India Company and of the banquet hosted by Becher. This building functioned both as the headquarters for the Amsterdam civic guards' companies and as the most splendid of all the guesthouses in Amsterdam. It was constructed in the remains of a fortified castle (a location thus weighty with significance for the city-state of Amsterdam). Rembrandt van Rijn was commissioned to paint *The Company of Captain Cocq* (better known as *The Night Watch*) for the Assembly Hall of the Kleveniers Doelen. Engraving by Jacob van Meurs(?), in Philipp von Zesen, *Beschreibung der Stadt Amsterdam*, 1664.

by the *Bewindheber*, or directors, of the West India Company. Becher promised him a good recompense if he would work in the count's interest and use his influence and connections with the West India Company. Besides making first contacts, Becher attended to the important business of getting new clothes for his entire party, noting that "everything depends on external splendor" in Amsterdam. Becher had to reassure the count that he would be dealing with "grand gentlemen" ("vornehm[e] Herren"), worth the expense of fine clothes. Becher hinted here at the contrast between the external moneyed splendor of the commercial society and the splendor of the court world based upon innate nobility.

The next day, perhaps in his new clothes, he was ready to meet with lower representatives of the West India Company in a *Wirtshaus*, the "Claveniers Dohle" (figure 9), where he presented his accreditations, mentioned that he had brought gifts with him, and promised his counterparts a recompense if they would ensure that the negotiations were successful. The West India Company welcomed the prospect of a German lord ready to colonize their land. At its founding in 1621, the Dutch government granted the West India Company the privilege to all profits made in the New World. From the beginning, an important function of the company was to contain and harass the Spanish as part of the ongoing war. For two decades, the company brought large portions of the Spanish and Portuguese lands in the New World under Dutch rule and returned huge profits by confiscating Spanish ships, mines, and silver fleets. By 1669, however, the West India Company had lost most of its recently conquered land to Portugal and Spain, retaining only Guiana and a few of the Carribean islands, and was very badly in debt.[15] By their presence and industry, German colonists would help the Dutch retain the small amount of land remaining. The West India Company would also profit from trade generated by the colonists, for after a certain amount of time had elapsed, the West India Company would receive a percentage of all profits made in the colony. Moreover, all goods going to and from the colony were to be transported by the company's ships and transshipped through Dutch ports, thus profiting both the company and Holland.[16]

The day after Becher's meeting with West India Company representatives was a Sunday, and there being, as Becher noted, "nothing to do except for the Church service," he went to view the ships in the harbor with his banker in Amsterdam (Isaac Telgens).[17] The viewing of ships became a regular pastime on Saturdays and Sundays and Becher recorded many visits to the harbor in his journal. The ships of overseas trade anchored in the harbor of Amsterdam were a potent symbol of commerce for Becher.[18]

[15] For details of the West India Company, see Cornelis Ch. Goslinga, *The Dutch in the Caribbean and on the Wild Coast, 1580–1680* (Gainesville: University of Florida Press, 1971).

[16] Volberg, *Deutsche Kolonialbestrebungen*, pp. 121–22.

[17] *Politischer Discurs*, 2d ed., p. 1087.

[18] Ships, representing commercial prosperity, were common in paintings in the seventeenth century, but Becher seems to have been personally fascinated by the potential for import, export,

In the evening of that first Sunday, Abraham Cain's son brought word that an audience had been arranged for nine o'clock the next morning at the West India House (figure 10). Becher recorded for his patron his visit to the seat of one of the most powerful merchant companies in Holland with particular care. The chamberlain, the secretary, and Becher rented a coach so they could arrive in style at the West India House.[19] They were escorted into an antechamber, where pictures hung on the walls. Becher described one of the pictures, that of the city of El Dorado, "with her streets and buildings of gold."[20] Becher rightly thought that the image of the golden city would convey the possibilities of the New World most effectively to the count. Indeed the count would later inform a representative of Hessen-Kassel that he had obtained a kingdom in the New World "where the houses are roofed with pure gold."[21] After a short time meditating on the city of gold, Becher and his retinue were escorted into a large room, where the directors of the company were in session. Around this room, Becher noted, stood "spoils" from the New World: stuffed exotic Indian birds, maps, and two large globes. The *Bewindheber* all rose when Becher entered, honoring the power he represented. He presented his proposal orally, the directors requested a written copy and a draft of the contract, then two lesser members of the house escorted Becher and his company to the door.

Becher promptly wrote out his proposition, hired a copyist to make a clean copy, then a translator to translate it into Dutch, and gave it to a representative of the house. The next two weeks were spent in negotiating the contract, and, during this time, Becher unpacked the gifts and set them out for viewers to look over. These gifts had been selected from the count's Kunstkammer and reflected the noble world from which they came. They included banquet tableware: a marble basin with a silver pitcher, a cut-crystal basin with matching pitcher, and a hartshorn basin and pitcher; objects from the noble hunt: a rifle (*Bürstbüchs*) with ivory inlay, a pair of ivory pistols with powder flask, an ivory dagger and sheath, a drinking cup made of deerhorn and lined with silver, an inlaid and jewel-incrusted hunting knife, a silver-plated Indian pipe, and, last,

---

cosmopolitanism, movement, and trade that real ships represented. One of Becher's longer poems is entitled "Epilogus," and recounts coming into land after a storm at sea (Mss. var. 1(1), fols. 320v–321r). Becher also tells us in the preface to the *Närrische Weiszheit* (1682) that he wrote that work and the *Lumen trinum* while crossing the Channel in a storm that kept them at sea for twenty-eight days. Ships were also effective religious symbolism. Becher's *Nachlaß* contains a poem celebrating the ship's captain "Emmanuel à Salvatore" of the ship *Adam*, which begins "dein ist das schiffe des Menschlichen Leibs" (Mss. var. 1(1), fol. 320r).

[19] Becher said they rented a "coach-sledge (because no coaches may be driven)." Wheeled vehicles were not allowed in Amsterdam.

[20] *Politischer Discurs*, 2d ed., p. 1088.

[21] This occurred in January 1670. Hessen-Kassel had sent the representative to investigate rumors that the Countdom was in rebellion and to ensure that Hessen-Kassel's interests were still intact. Hahnzog, "Hanauer 'tolle Jahr,'" p. 166.

HET WEST INDISCH HUYS

Figure 10. The West India House, Amsterdam, 1663. Engraving by Jacob van Meurs(?), in Philipp von Zesen, *Beschreibung der Stadt Amsterdam*, 1664.

'T HEEREN LOGEMENT

Figure 11. Heeren-Logement, Amsterdam, 1663. The setting for the banquet hosted by the West India Company. Engraving by Jacob van Meurs(?), in Philipp von Zesen, *Beschreibung der Stadt Amsterdam*, 1664.

an object representing the success and continuance of noble rule, a miniature of King Charles II of England.[22]

At the next audience in the West India House, Becher presented the count's gifts, which, as *Praesenden*, substituted for the presence of the count himself. The merchants added these rarities to the exotica on their shelves, promising to display them in memory of the count's dealings with them. To demonstrate their gratitude they gave a tip of twenty-five Reichsthaler to the servants who had carried in the gifts. The custom of tipping another's servants was common, for if the money had been given directly to the gift giver, it would have had the appearance of a base commercial transaction.

When Becher had been in Amsterdam for almost three weeks, the articles of the contract were finally settled on 18 July, and an advocate took it to the Hague to be ratified by the States General. This represented an important stage in the negotiations, and to celebrate, the *Bewindheber* invited Becher and company to a "small Diversion," beginning at one o'clock the next afternoon in the "Herrn-Logiament" (figure 11).[23] Becher recounted this feast for the count with particular care, knowing that the banquet had particular significance in the court world. On that Friday afternoon, they were served exclusively with fish, no doubt, Becher records, out of sensitivity to the fact that he and part of his company were Catholic (although, it should be noted, in the service of a Lutheran prince with crypto-Catholic tendencies and married to a Calvinist). The first course lasted two hours, during which much wine was consumed and toasts were drunk. While the table was being cleared and reset for the second course, the men drank tea and smoked tobacco. Becher thought it worthy of note that new napkins and tablecloths were used at each course. The second course lasted another two hours, and during it, the health of the emperor, of the count and countess, and of the States General was drunk. Becher remarked dryly that "they [the *Bewindheber*] drank the health of Your Excellency bareheaded and kneeling; indeed they showed more affection toward Your Excellency than toward their own Princes [of the House of Orange]."[24] Becher continued, "the glasses were large and it was a powerful, good Rhine wine."[25]

As the banquet continued, the city musicians began to play, and the third course was brought in, consisting of sugar delicacies of every kind ("welche in

[22] Hulshof, "Een duitsch econoom," p. 74, cites a document from 18 July 1669 from the Resolutiën der kamer van Amsterdam, which lists the gifts in more detail and states that, in recompense and recognition of the presentation, Becher and his company were given twenty silver ducats and invited to a meal in the lodgings of the company directors. This list contains gifts that Becher does not mention: a drinking horn, an ivory snuffbox, a pair of ivory scissors, and a knife.

[23] The "Heeren Logiment" was a guesthouse for which the city had donated space in part of a hospital and adjoining brewery. The guesthouse was used by the city to entertain official visitors, visiting noblemen, and foreign envoys. See Zesen, *Beschreibung*, pp. 324–25.

[24] Becher had understandably not emphasized the familial connections of the houses of Hanau and Orange in the negotiations.

[25] *Politischer Discurs*, 2d ed., p. 1092.

allerhand köstlichem Confect bestanden").[26] The party became very jolly; the men began to dance with each other and to speak confidentially with Becher. Twelve hours after it had begun, the banquet ran down, leaving only Becher and the president of the directors alone in the rooms. The president (who was also president of the Great Council of the city of Amsterdam) insisted, against all Becher's pleading, on escorting him to his lodgings. When they arrived, Becher had to rouse one of his own men from bed to escort the president back to his home.

Becher does not fail to tell the count that he demonstrated the largesse and wealth of his patron by tipping the waiters and servants of the company handsomely. In the morning, Becher recounts, he sent blanket thanks to his hosts as well as apologies in case anything unfortunate had been said while he was in his cups. In reply, his hosts sent a tea drink to counteract the richness and pleasure of the night before, which, as Becher attested, resulted in head and stomach aches. By the following day, however, Becher had recovered sufficiently to view a slave ship.

In the next few days, the negotiations for the colony faltered, but Becher made various promises of "gute *Recompens*" to the negotiators and sent his own representatives to The Hague to meet with the States General. Gradually, the difficulties were smoothed over and the negotiations continued. During this time, Becher was visited by two rich merchants who had earlier settled in the area in Guiana for which Becher was negotiating. One was coincidentally a native of Hanau, and this especially trustworthy subject assured Becher of the land's fertility and even showed him specimens of fruits and minerals that grew in the territory. Becher promised them the count's cooperation and enlisted one of them to return with him to Hanau to give the count a firsthand report of the land and to show him the rare objects, which, once in the count's hands, would no doubt become part of his Kunstkammer.

When the contract[27] between the West India Company and Becher was finally signed on 18 July and the Ratification by the States General made ready, it was Becher's turn to invite the directors of the company to a banquet at his expense in the Claveniers Dohle. Naturally, Count Friedrich Casimir received a detailed account of this banquet also. First in Becher's report was the order of seating at the rectangular table, for rank and status were of paramount importance in the court world. By interesting contrast, the table had been round at the

[26] Ibid.

[27] In this contract, the company ceded the land under the terms of feudal tenure to the count, but with the condition that every time the colony changed hands, the company would be paid five thousand pounds of sugar, in return for one hundred ducats. It specified that the company would provision and protect the colony, but all journeys to and from the colony must begin and end in the Netherlands, and all food and wares to and from the colony must be transshipped in the Netherlands. Slaves destined for the colony could only be bought from the company. Becher translated and reprinted the contract in ibid., pp. 1139–48. Jaeger, "Over Johan Joachim Becher," pp. 121–27, reprints the original document in Dutch. The States General ratified the contract on 24 July.

party given by the merchants' company and so a description of seating order had not been necessary. Three courses of fish were served, although it was a Thursday; perhaps Becher desired not to appear to outdo his hosts by serving other meats. Each course lasted two hours and the table was set anew between each of them. Becher had ordered musicians, and after they played he feasted them, as well as the scribes and servants of the West India Company, in a separate room. During the first course, Becher read a welcoming speech; during the second course, the health of the States General, the provinces of Holland and West Friesland, and of the West India Company was drunk. During the third course, toasts were made to the emperor and the count. Everyone stayed until four o'clock in the morning, and Becher assured his patron that all had been thoroughly contented with the evening. Becher reported that the president of the West India Company, who had insisted upon escorting him home before, became so merry at this banquet that he had begun the dancing among the men.

On 3 August the ratification from the States General arrived in Amsterdam and Becher had a last audience at the West India House, at which the directors wished the count good fortune, hoped that he would return his ratification speedily, and promised more presents on their receipt of the signed document. As Becher took his leave from the house, the president of the company paid him and the count he represented the honor of escorting him to the door. A month before, at the end of his first audience, it was only lesser members who had escorted him out.

Becher attended to various other tasks before leaving Amsterdam, including buying a stocking loom and hiring its attendant weaver (no doubt for his next project), taking leave of a chemist friend (Dr. Galenus), and bestowing presents, money, and promises on all the contacts who had brought about the success of the undertaking.[28] The journey back up the Rhine to Germany lasted ten days and Becher sent two of his company ahead as heralds to announce his arrival and the success of the project to the count. Gottfried Wilhelm Leibniz, who happened to be in Frankfurt at the time, scornfully described Becher's project and his return to Hanau:

Becher . . . persuaded the Count of Hanau that there are certain felicitous regions on the other continent. . . . In such a way, he extorted a little money from the

---

[28] This chemist friend would appear to be Galenus Abrahamsz., Mennonite preacher and powerful leader of the Amsterdam Collegiant community. Becher only indicates that Galenus has a religious dimension in *Närrische Weiszheit* (1682). Otherwise he calls him a chemist and seems not to mind that his patrons know about his dealings with Galenus. In fact, in editing his 1671 journal, he crosses out a visit to the duke of Mecklenburg and inserts instead Galenus's name (Mss. var. 1(3), fol. 534v). See Andrew Fix, "Radical Religion and the Age of Reason," in *Germania Illustrata*, ed. Andrew Fix and Susan C. Karant-Nunn (Kirksville, Mo.: Sixteenth Century Journal Publishers, 1992), pp. 35–55. Fix argues that the emphasis placed by the Collegiants in the seventeenth century on the long twilight leading up to the millennium during which God deserts the world led paradoxically to secularism and a rational religion. These connections between radical religion and

inebriated Count, with which he set out for Holland and obtained a fiefdom for his lord from the West India Society. . . . On his return, he ordered that the contractual documents, enclosed in an ivory capsule, go before him, and with this ridiculous pomp, as if celebrating a triumph, he entered Hanau.[29]

Becher returned to Hanau to find the situation at court no longer simply one of tense alarm but one of outright uproar. Apparently Becher and the count had made preparations for his journey in deepest secrecy (hence the meeting in Frankfurt rather than in the residence), and the gifts Becher had presented to the West India Company had infelicitously been removed from the Kunstkammer covertly. While Becher was in Amsterdam, the absence of these objects had been noticed and the rumor spread that Becher had stolen the pieces from the collection and made off with them for West India. This rumor even reached as far as Bavaria and Vienna. Becher attempted to defend himself: he explained that the secrecy of his trip had been necessary to foil the unscrupulous schemes of the Swedish projector; the count had become infatuated with the wax sculptures that the Swede was trying to sell to him, and Becher claimed only to be trying to save the count from this frivolous curiosity by interesting him instead in the colony project. But the count had given in to temptation and, while Becher was in Amsterdam, had paid nine thousand Reichsthaler for the wax figures. In order to raise this extraordinarily large amount of cash, he had borrowed money from the landgrave of Hessen-Homburg, giving him in return title to the territory of Rodheim.[30] It appears that the landgrave hoped to put the count deeply enough into his debt that the count's next step would be to make him an official joint ruler or even his heir. By this exchange, the landgrave would gain some of the rights of a "real" prince. The Swede, Becher's rival, had prudently left town on receiving the cash, and took with him the money that Becher had hoped would go to equipping the colonists. The members of the count's family were in open revolt against the count for mortgaging Rodheim.

Despite this vortex of tensions and schemes whirling about the Kunstkam-

---

the birth of the Age of Reason are particularly pertinent in the case of Becher, who used chemical ideas associated with religious radicals but divested them of their spiritual meaning.

[29] The complete passage reads: "His locis mirifica somnia invalescunt. Becherus Medicus, homo ingeniosus, sed polypragmon Comiti Hanoviae persuasit, esse in alio terrarum Orbe felices quasdam regiones, atque omnia velut divina quadam virgula fundentes, illuc duci Colonias fundarique grande imperium posse, et inde paulatim in omnem Americanam regionem. Ita inebriato Comiti pecuniolam extorsit, qua profectus ad Batavos a West-Indica societate totam Guianam, qua mari alluitur, triginta milliarium latitudine, longitudine centum, feudi iure suo Comiti obtinuit. Reversus literas contractus eburneae capsulae inclusas praeferri sibi iussit, et hac ridicula pompa velut ovans Hanoviam ingressus est. Iam parantur omnia itineri Americano." September 1669, Gottfried Wilhelm Leibniz, *Sämtliche Schriften und Briefe*, ed. Preussische Akademie der Wissenschaften et al. (Darmstadt: Otto Reichl et al., 1923–), ser. 2, vol. 1, p. 26.

[30] Becher claimed that the count paid nine thousand Reichsthaler. The count himself stated that he paid fourteen thousand. Hahnzog, "Hanauer 'tolle Jahr,'" p. 165.

mer, Becher claims to have been received in triumph by the count on his return: he was paraded through the streets, the contract was read publicly and signed by the count, fireworks were set off over the city, and one hundred cannon shots were fired, just as when Friedrich Casimir had acquired a new curiosity. The celebratory banquet was marred only by a French guest who grounded the party momentarily in Realpolitik by noisily trying to win the count to the French faction at court, but he was shown the door in disfavor, and the airy celebrations continued. Becher was given the gold chain of noble service and a medallion stamped with the count's portrait worth two hundred ducats, as well as an offer of a private house in the Countdom.

In the end, however, the colony project was lost in the serious consequences of the count's mortgaging his land to the landgrave of Hessen-Homburg in return for wax curiosities. The count's wife, his brother, his heirs' guardians, and the citizens of Hanau staged a coup, which, after intercession by the Reichskammergericht and the troops of Hessen-Kassel, led to Count Friedrich Casimir being placed in a position of joint dominion with his heirs' guardians.[31] The land in America remained in possession of the House of Hanau, although it was never colonized, and at various times the nobility of Hanau tried to interest the emperor and the English in buying title to it. The Napoleonic Wars finally resolved the fate of this tiny piece of land and it became part of French Guiana.

The Kunstkammer had become the stage for these events and played a part in each act of the drama. The count's expensive taste for rarities made him a target for projectors, and Becher approached him from this angle. The colony project was presented as an alternative to the wax objects that the Swedish projector offered to the count for his cabinet. Becher's appeal to the count was probably much like that of the Swede's, and the count doubtlessly perceived the projects to be of the same type. The colony in the New World would provide rarities for his cabinet, perhaps more impressive ones than the wax figures, and the colony itself was just one of the noble diversions by which boredom at court could be kept at bay and reputation could be gained among other crowned heads.

In Amsterdam, the gifts presented to the West India Company had been selected from the count's cabinet. Becher, in turn, created an image in his journal for the count of the riches of the New World as the exotic spoils and curiosities on the walls and shelves of the West India Company House. In returning to Hanau, Becher brought with him the specimens of minerals and fruits given him by earlier colonists that were probably destined for the cabinet.

Finally, the rumor about the absence of the cabinet objects that met Becher in

[31] The revolution occurred when the countess and the count's brother took over the residence for three days and closed the gates of the city. The citizens of Hanau revolted against the closing of the gates because they had won the right to control the city gates in a Capitulation of 1597. The settlement of the conflict was the result of extraordinary dynastic maneuvering. Representatives from several different territories converged on the territory of Hanau when it was discovered that the count was losing control. See Hahnzog, "Hanauer 'tolle Jahr,' " and Hintereicher, *Georg Christian*.

Hanau portended the failure of the colony project, and Becher found himself inextricably entrapped on the stage where he had chosen to act. He had given life to the colony project by appealing to the count's infatuation with curiosities and his concern with his reputation, but this infatuation ended in directing the project. The count succumbed to the nearest curiosities rather than waiting on the outcome of Becher's more marvelous object, and in doing so brought about the palace coup and his own loss of power. In the end the colony project became nothing more than a curiosity.[32]

Thaumaturgia

But the story of the colony project of 1669 does not end there, for when Becher returned to Germany, he speedily published a pamphlet in his defense. The purpose of this pamphlet was to save his reputation. When he returned to Hanau, a rumor was spreading that portrayed him as nothing more than a charlatan, an unscrupulous projector who had made off with the count's curiosities. To counter this rumor and to attract other patrons through whom he could finance a shareholding company to keep the project alive, Becher made an appeal in the pamphlet to the princes of Germany. Here he translated what he saw as the advantages of the commercial world into a language and a set of symbolic gestures the court world could understand.

Becher begins the pamphlet with a description of the problems of the court of Hanau, which could apply to almost any other German territorial court at the time:

> The long German war is known throughout the world, as is how the Countdom of
> Hanau was drawn into it. Indeed most of the Countdom's debts arose from it. It is

---

[32] Becher did not find himself long entrapped. A characteristic epilogue to the colony project unfolded in 1670 when Becher took up with the Landgrave Georg Christian von Hessen-Homburg, who, after the rebellion in Hanau, became persona non grata there. A report from the elector of Bavaria's resident minister in Vienna from September 1670 tells of Becher spending all his time in the landgrave's *Logiament* and being seen in the landgrave's coach, although the minister could never discover what Becher's business with the landgrave was. The minister believed Becher had traveled with the landgrave to Styria (Stoiberer to Ferdinand Maria, BHA, HR I 291/27/1, 25 September 1670). Some of Becher's business with Landgrave Georg Christian is revealed in an incomplete draft by Becher of a proposal to Emperor Leopold in the landgrave's name about organizing a "Collegium Inquisitionis Status"—an inquisitory and spying organization—on the model of that in Venice. The purpose of this college was not only to uncover political plots, but also to look into religious heresy, and military, judicial, and cameral problems. It would also investigate financial wrongdoing in the Hofkammer. (Mss. var. 1(2), fols. 479r–489r.) By December 1670 Becher had quarreled with the landgrave, who then instituted a formal inquiry into the slander that he had undergone at the hands of Becher and Wilhelm von Schröder. The testimony of the witnesses stated that Becher first injured the landgrave's honor and then began to wave loaded pistols about.

further known that all *Cameralisten* [treasury officials] do not know of any other means to repay their lord's debts and to increase his revenues than through *ordinary* means, namely through *Contribution* [head tax] and excise tax on the subjects. Because of this, others seeking extraordinary means of income have to rely upon dangerous and disreputable ways out when the ordinary means in the end fail and various other kinds of revenues have to be sought. It is also known that in all these things no one other than the Creditors or the subjects must suffer. The subjects' condition is such that they cannot help themselves, and in peace they are almost more ruined than in war. I do not want to say here that no Lord can increase his hereditary revenues separately without increasing the burden of the subjects. Who will think badly of it if His Countly Excellence seeks a means to pull himself out of these embarrassing difficulties. . . . Is that foolishly done by a lord? Is it impossible? Is it dishonorable? The *Cameralisten* accuse the lord of foolishness. Jealous people who begrudge others what they do not have the courage to do themselves say that it is impossible. Those who are not ashamed to practice the commonest trades, say it is dishonorable, and forbid others to carry on commercial business, which even kings practice. . . . No one will deny that extraordinary illnesses require extraordinary remedies, which must above all be decorous [*honesta*].[33]

While the treasury officials had no new ideas for noble income and forbade trade to the prince as dishonorable, Becher, as commercial advisor and chemist—a new man at court—promised that he could provide by commerce what the *Cameralisten* could not. This was a "*Lapis politicorum*" (a politicians' stone), as he called it, that for the prince would match the wonder-working and wealth-giving powers of the alchemists' *Lapis philosophorum*, by which base metals were transmuted into gold.[34] Once again, he called on his status as

---

All witnesses agreed that Becher and the rest were quite drunk, and apparently no action against Becher and Schröder was taken. (Vienna, Haus-, Hof- und Staatsarchiv, General geheime Staatsregistratur, Rep. N., Karton 27, 24 December 1670.)

[33] *Gründlicher Bericht von Beschaffenheit und Eigenschafft/ Cultivirung und Bewohnung/ Privilegien und Beneficien deß in America zwischen dem Rio Orinoque und Rio de las Amazones an den vesten Küst in der Landschafft Guiana gelegenen/ sich dreißig Meil wegs breit an der See und hundert Meil wegs an die Tieffe erstreckenden Strich Landes. Welchen die Edle privilegirte West-Indische Compagnie der vereinigten Niederlanden/ mit Authentischer Schrifftlicher* ratificatton *und* permission *der Hochmögenden Herren Staaten General und den hochgebohrnen/ gegenwertig regirenden Herrn/ Herrn Friedrich Casimir/ Grafen zu Hanaw . . . wie auch an das gesämptliche Hochgräfliche Hawß von Hanaw mit allen* regalien *und* jurisdictionen, *ewig und erblich/ unter gewissen in dieser Deduction* publicirten Articuln *den 18. Julii 1669* credirt und überlassen hat (Frankfurt: Wilhelm Serlin, 1669), p. 5. Also published in *Politischer Discurs*, 2d ed., pp. 1112–1255.

[34] Becher entitled his conclusion to the last section of the *Politischer Discurs*, composed of documents and proposals relating to the attempts to obtain a colony in the West Indies, "Dr. Bechers Politischer Philosophischer Stein in der Indischen *Colonie* beruhend" (pp. 1271–72). By 1678

physician and healer of ills to establish his authority to treat the body politic. The extraordinary debts of the territory must be treated by extraordinary means, unknown to the regular officers of the treasury.

The preceding chapter showed how Becher conflated noble and commercial credit in order to convince Emperor Leopold of the nobility of commerce. In Becher's 1669 pamphlet, he attempted to convince his audience by interweaving traditional natural (court) values, such as land, with the artificial or unnatural values of money and commerce so that they became indistinguishable. In accomplishing this, his knowledge of natural philosophy was indispensable. In his journal, Becher sought to convince Count Friedrich Casimir of the nobility of commerce by dwelling in detail on the golden city, on the tokens of honor accorded to the count, and on the richness of the banquets. But in the pamphlet Becher used a rather subtler means that focused on what was to be the most important product of the colony, namely, sugar.

The history of sugar consumption and the sugar trade has provided some contemporary historians with a means to chart the development of the social and economic forms of the modern world.[35] But sugar was already a curious object of great significance when Becher obtained the colony in 1669, and he manipulated its natural, economic, and political importance to integrate the values of the commercial society into the traditional world view of the court.

In the sixteenth and seventeenth centuries, sugar was found mainly in the apothecary's shop and was an expensive medicine. By Becher's day, it had also become a food of display and representation for the nobility. Sugar sculptures (sometimes life-size) were presented as gifts from one noble potentate to another, and banquets were punctuated with elaborate sugar "subtleties" or confections, such as those that the directors of the West India Company served to Becher and his men as a last course.[36] Sugar was an important exotic delicacy at court, firmly associated with the riches of the New World, and so it was to be one of the most important products of Becher's colony.[37]

Becher had concluded that the philosophers' stone was easier to make than the politicians' stone (*Psychosophia* [1705], p. 171).

[35] Sugar is discussed by Fernand Braudel, *The Wheels of Commerce*, vol. 2 of *Civilization and Capitalism: The 15th to 18th Century*, trans. Sian Reynolds (New York: Harper & Row, 1982), pp. 192–94; Werner Sombart, *Luxus und Kapitalismus*, 2d ed. (Munich: Duncker & Humblot, 1922); and Sidney W. Mintz, *Sweetness and Power: The Place of Sugar in Modern History* (New York: Viking Penguin, 1985).

[36] See Mintz, *Sweetness*, pp. 88ff.

[37] One of his assistants in the colony project in Bavaria promised the Bavarian elector Ferdinand Maria that he would soon be the monarch of a kingdom in the New World, which could supply the whole court with sugar (Elers to Begnudelli, 17 August 1665, BHA GR 273/10). In the 1669 pamphlet, Becher says: "wächst auch der Zucker das gantze Jahr durch über/ und weil der öfftere

As a medical doctor, natural philosopher, and chemical adept, Becher discussed the natural significance of sugar. For Becher, all of nature was envitalized by a universal spirit that derived its power for generation and growth ultimately from God. Omnipresent in the air, this spirit gave mineral springs their healing powers, moved and colored the blood, and ripened and transmuted the metals. The air of the tropics and the New World hung heavy with this essence. Sugar grew in this tropical air, so was of a gentle balsamic quality, as opposed to salt, which was sharp and corrosive.[38] Like all vegetation, the sugar plant grew by drawing up a liquid mixture—a "juice of the earth"—which was composed of the three principles of all matter, salt, sulfur, and mercury.[39] The sulfurous component of this juice went to the nourishment of the plant, just as in human nourishment this component (derived from foods) was "transmuted" (Becher's word) into blood. This principle was also responsible for the fermentation of wine, or, as he called it, the "transmutation" of rainwater into wine.[40] Sugar, when refined ("distilled"), consisted almost entirely of this sulfurous principle, and thus became a powerful fermenting agent and medicament. "Sugar," Becher stated, "is the noblest and sweetest juice of the earth, digested and cooked through by the heat of sunbeams, and thus a noble balsamic substance that is most closely related to the human blood, [because] the inspirited blood burns away in the fire just like sugar."[41] Becher advocated the making of a sugar wine, which was powerful as a healing and nourishing agent because it combined the sulfurous principles of both sugar and wine.[42] It drove out the urine, cleansed the bladder, and healed internal wounds. He considered sugar a

---

Regen die Erd stets befeuchtet/ und von der Sonnen allzeit wieder das Erdreich getrucknet wird/ so kan nicht fehlen die Erde wird gewaltsam fett und fruchtbar/ welches auch die Ursach ist/ daß der Zucker allhier besser als an einem Ort wächset." *Politischer Discurs*, 2d ed., p. 1124.

[38] Becher, *Chymisches Laboratorium*, p. 368.

[39] Ibid., p. 423.

[40] The transmutation of water into wine came about by the action of the sulfurous component (the seeds) of the wine. Becher, *Chymischer Glücks-Hafen*, pp. 71–72.

[41] Here Becher discusses the properties of sugar that make it a suitable ingredient for a medicinal wine: "Referat, oder gründliche Beschreibung was in dem Kunst- Undt Werckhauß sambt beyliegenden Schmeltz- undt Glaßhütten, gethan und operirt wirdt, auch wie selbige angeordnet seye." Vienna, Österreichische Nationalbibliothek, Ms. 8046, fol. 10v. Presented to the Emperor on 19 March 1676.

[42] *Chymisches Laboratorium*, pp. 439–42. It seems that in 1658 Becher had already printed an anonymous treatise on a universal medicine composed of *aurum potabile*, sugar and alcohol ("*spiritus vini*"): The *Nachlaß* contains a manuscript title page and preface in German for a "Wahrhafftiger und Gründlicher Beweißt von dehm Philosophischen Auro Potabili, oder Medicinalischen Trinck Goldt," signed J.J.B. von Speier, Mathematicus & Chymicus, and dated 1657 (Mss. var. 2, fols. 283r–284r). Mss. var. 2, fols. 285r–288v, is an anonymous printed pamphlet in Latin, entitled *Olitor Opportunus, hoc est, Simplex narratio, de nobilissima quadam Medicina tribus sui natura optimis principiis, Auro, Zacharo & spiritu vini philosophice junctis* (Frankfurt: Schönwetter's Heirs, 1658).

powerful preservative, stronger even than salt, and proposed that sugar be used to preserve meat.[43] Sugar was thus a natural agricultural product, closely related to one of nature's most basic and life-giving components, and this merited its place as noble food and medicament.

The economic significance of sugar, as explained by Becher, was also great. It was an agricultural product that was not difficult to "versilbern" (to turn into silver, or money), as opposed to the agricultural products grown by the peasants of the German territories, for they fetched only low prices if they could be traded for money at all. In this regard, sugar was more similar to the artificial manufactured goods that Becher promoted in his other commercial projects than to traditional agricultural products. But the money gained by the "cash crop" of sugar would go directly into the noble ruler's treasury as ordinary agricultural income, similar to the revenues gained from his hereditary lands and his regalian incomes. Thus this money wealth would not only work within the established power structure in a territory but would even reinforce it.

Becher stressed the traditional agricultural advantages of the colony and sugar growth. He praised the West Indian land, which he claimed needed neither to be fertilized nor plowed, and the slavery system, which made it inexpensive to work. It would, moreover, draw on skills with which the German landed lord and peasant were particularly endowed. He believed that "each Nation and Rule has its own characteristics": the Republic of Venice only waged war and supported the nobility, while Holland was good at commerce and shipping (but not agriculture), and Spain sought only gold and silver. Germany, of all nations, was best at "Erdbau" (cultivation of the earth), even better than the English, and so Germans should become colonists.[44] These agricultural skills could be put to use in growing sugar in a colony. It was a natural product of the land that would produce the same artificial wealth that made Holland so prosperous.

The political importance of sugar for a territorial ruler was as a source of money and power. Sugar would bring money wealth into a territory, but within a traditional noble framework. It gave the prince more land and additional titles; it depended on traditional landed power structures and on agricultural methods and skills; and it provided a source of income that mimicked the established ordinary income that flowed from a prince's hereditary lands. In Becher's writings it was a self-regenerative product of nature, indeed one of the noblest, but one that also multiplied the artificial wealth of money. Becher's New World colony, like his other commercial projects, inserted the New World products and economy into an Old World frame.[45]

---

[43] *Chymisches Laboratorium*, pp. 367–71.

[44] Becher, *Grundlicher Bericht*, pp. 30–31.

[45] Michael T. Ryan, "Assimilating New Worlds in the Sixteenth and Seventeenth Centuries," *Studies in Society and History* 23 (1981): 519–38, discusses this phenomenon in other contexts.

Locus Finis

The colony project was just one of Becher's many schemes that sought to harness the wealth of the money economy to the traditional structures of the landed court. Its history at the court of the count of Hanau was interwoven with the story of the count's Kunstkammer. The cabinet itself functioned at three levels: on the level of *theoria* (the contemplative knowledge of scholars), where it represented a polymathic encyclopedia of knowledge, all natural and artificial things collected within it. The second level was that of *praxis* (the active knowledge of human politics, the level at which power and historical events were played out). At this level, the Kunstkammer was part of the symbolic representation of the power of the noble ruler, and it was within the language of this second level that Becher made his propostion about the colony to the count of Hanau. The last level was of *ars* or *technē* (the productive knowledge of unlettered artisans). The cabinet was full of *artificialia*, things made by human art, products of the artifice of artisans from rich trading cities.[46] These objects embodied the unlettered, but productive knowledge of *technē*. This was the level at which Becher perceived the cabinet and the colony project to be congruous with his political agenda, for it was by the knowledge and imitation of nature, especially as exemplified by artisanal production in the city, that material wealth and state welfare were to be found. The colony would be materially productive, yielding goods midway between artificial commercial commodities and natural, agricultural produce that would make the count's coffers and Germany in general rich with artificial money wealth.

Becher placed the colony project within the locus of the Kunstkammer at the court of Hanau for two reasons. By proposing it as a curiosity, he addressed the count's concern with the representation of power (or, if one prefers, he played on the count's infatuation with curiosities), and he attempted to translate his commercial project into tangible objects that would fit within the count's comprehension and cabinet. By drawing on his own knowledge of nature and generation, Becher hoped that the colony's productive aspects would also become clear to the count. Becher called the colony a *Lapis politicorum*, and, as the philosophers' stone of alchemy transmuted base metals into gold, he

[46] The essays in Oliver Impey and Arthur Macgregor, eds., *The Origins of Museums: The Cabinet of Curiosities in Sixteenth- and Seventeenth-century Europe* (Oxford: Clarendon Press, 1985), make clear the variety of goals collectors had in assembling their cabinets. See also Julius Schlosser, *Kunst- und Wunderkammern der Spätrenaissance*, 2d ed. (Braunschweig: Klinkhardt & Bierman, 1978); Thomas D. Kaufmann, *The School of Prague* (Chicago: University of Chicago Press, 1988); *Prag um 1600: Kunst und Kultur am Hofe Rudolfs II*, 2 vols. (Freren/Emsland: Luca Verlag, 1988); and Paula Findlen, *Possessing Nature: Museums, Collecting and Scientific Culture in Early Modern Italy* (Berkeley: University of California Press, 1994). Antoine Schnapper, "The King of France as Collector in the Seventeenth Century," in *Art and History: Images and Their*

Figure 12. Jan van Kessel, *Allegory of America*, 1666, oil on copper. With permission of Alte Pinakothek, Munich.

Figure 13. Jan van Kessel, *Kunstkammer with Venus at Her Toilette, 1659,* oil on copper. Other attempts to place the New World into the traditional forms of the old, similar to Becher's presentation of the colony within the confines of the count's Kunstkammer, can be seen in two paintings by Jan van Kessel reproduced here. These paintings show exotica similar to that which Becher reported seeing in the West India Company House. Rare objects and peoples of the New World are jumbled together in these chambers. The *Allegory of America* depicts a Kunstkammer come alive, yet still framed by the familiar confines of the cabinet. Through the collection of curious New World exotica, the Old World formed an image of the unknown, but this image was constructed within the already established forms of the Old World. Becher depicted his commercial ideas in this way. With permission of the Staatliche Kunsthalle, Karlsruhe.

believed that his politicians' stone would enoble commerce and make it regenerative (figures 12 and 13). But Count Friedrich Casimir refused to be drawn into Becher's ploy to merge curiosity and commerce, and the colony project of 1669 came to be remembered merely as a curious episode.

Becher the court physician and natural philosopher used the metaphor of

Meaning, ed. Robert I. Rotberg and Theodore K. Rabb (Cambridge: Cambridge University Press, 1986), pp. 185–202, points out that in some cases the collectors simply had aesthetic goals.

alchemy in relation to the colony project, and, by means of the politicians' stone, he attempted to transmute the count's interest in curiosities into an understanding of the goods and transactions of commerce as the sources of political power. At the court of the emperor in Vienna, Becher would use alchemy itself to effect this transmutation.

FOUR

THE PRODUCTION OF THINGS: A TRANSMUTATION

AT THE HABSBURG COURT

Und er ist der Hermes gewesen/ der nach der Sündflut aller
Künsten und Disciplinen/ beydes der freyen und so die
Handwerks Leut treiben/ der erst Erfinder und Beschreiber
gewesen.

And it was Hermes, who, after the Flood, was the first inventor
and articulator of all the arts and disciplines, both of the liberal
arts, as well as of those which the artisans practice.
(Turba Philosophorum, *1613*)

The Alchemical Medal

IN 1675, after almost five years as commercial advisor at the Impérial court in Vienna, and a little more than a year before leaving Vienna permanently, Becher transmuted lead into silver. From the transmuted silver he made a commemorative medallion bearing the inscription, "In the year 1675, the month of July, I, J. J. Becher, Doctor, transmuted this piece of the finest silver from lead by the art of alchemy."[1] On the reverse side was portrayed a one-legged, bare-footed Saturn dressed in the clothes of a German peasant, carrying a scythe over one shoulder and his bare, struggling child slung over the other (figure 14). This depiction of Saturn referred to the process of assaying gold and silver by adding them to molten lead in a crucible. Saturn symbolized the base metal, lead, and the act of eating his children was analogous to the behavior of all metals (except gold and silver), which, on being added to molten lead in a crucible merged with the lead. The two noble metals were not absorbed by lead, but instead were left as a "button" at the bottom of the vessel, separated from all impurities. Saturn could not digest these, the noblest of his children, and so he vomited them up again, purified (figure 15).

---

[1] This medallion is housed in the coin collection of the Vienna Kunsthistorisches Museum. See Wolf-Dieter Müller-Jahncke and Joachim Telle, "Numismatik und Alchemie. Mitteilungen zu Münzen und Medaillen des 17. und 18. Jahrhunderts," in *Die Alchemie in der europäischen Kultur- und Wissenschaftsgeschichte*, ed. Christoph Meinel (Wiesbaden: Otto Harrassowitz, 1986), pp. 251–52, 269.

Figure 14. Alchemical medallion produced by Becher, 1675. With permission of the Kunsthistorisches Museum, Vienna.

The appearance of metallic transmutation could be engineered in a number of ways, either through processes that produced the color of the noble metals, or by separation of noble metals already present in the base metal. These techniques, as well as various alchemists' tricks (such as stirring the hot base metal with a hollow wand that had been filled with gold and plugged with a metal of low melting point) were familiar to chemists and were distinguished from genuine transmutation.[2] "True" transmutation was considered to be the instantaneous change of base metals into gold by the projection of the philosophers' stone, or "tincture" (usually a powder) over the base metal. Alchemists explained transmutation as an acceleration of the natural ripening of base metals to their perfected noble state. Such an explanation gave flexibility as to what constituted an authentic transformation. Becher, for example, argued that all transmutation was caused by a ripening of the metals that took place by means of a "ripening force" ("zeitigmachende Krafft"),[3] and that this force, the "universal philosophical substance" was the tool of the chemist in his metallic operations.

Becher thus distinguished between "weaker" transmutations ("*particular-*Zeitigungen") and immediate transmutation by projection of the tincture ("*universal-*Zeitigungen"). These two levels of transformation occurred in accordance with the purity and concentration of the ripening force.[4] The

---

[2] Hermann Kopp, *Die Alchemie in älterer und neuerer Zeit* (Heidelberg: Carl Winter Universitätsbuchhandlung, 1886), pt. 1. Athanasius Kircher, *Mundus Subterraneus in XII Libros* (Amsterdam: Joannes Janslonius a Waesberge & Elzaeus Weyerstraet, 1665), vol. 2, bk. 2, "Chymiotechnicus" contains a detailed and standard list of alchemists' tricks.

[3] "Alle Verbesserung der Metallen beruhe in derer Zeitigung/ und . . . die Zeitigung transmutire[t]" (all improvement of the metals rests in their ripening . . . [and] ripening transmutes). Becher, *Chymischer Glücks-Hafen*, p. 93.

[4] Ibid., pp. 88–96, "zeitigen," p. 93.

Figure 15. Frontispiece to Becher's *Natur-Kündigung der Metallen*, 1661. The scythe identified Saturn with Chronos. Saturn was also a god of agriculture, having taught men to cultivate the earth. Saturn can be seen watering the roots of a tree, the trunk of which is labeled "concipio" (conception). In the leaves hang the six signs of the metals, and above them shine the sun's rays, labeled "gigno" (generation). By cultivation of the metals (represented by the spade labeled "Laboro") through the art of alchemy and with the aid of heat, the metals are conceived and brought forth.

"weaker" transmutations were themselves divided into three sorts. The first was an "Ausbringen":

> For example, a mark of silver which gives nothing by the ordinary process, but which gives a certain amount of gold when treated with fiery sulfurous agents (which in the ordinary process also gives no gold). This is properly a ripening which is a type of transmutation. In this extraction, however, the silver decreases in weight by the amount of gold which is extracted from it.[5]

The second weak transmutation was called an "Einbringen":

> One can make an extract out of the golden earths, such as magnesia, emery, gold quartz, and sulfur, agent of mars and antimony and other golden species, which draws out the tender, volatile embryonic gold. This gold can then be fixed by mercury, oil of sulfur or borax, which gives it entrance into the lead or silver, so that it takes on a metallic form. The amount of gold that is made will be equal to that of the extract that was used. The silver will not decrease in weight, but rather, can be used again and again.[6]

Becher called the third type of weak transmutation "Scheidung," or separation. He claimed that this differed from the common processes of extracting gold from iron and copper, or silver from lead and tin, because his separation process worked by capturing the ripening power and using it to ripen the "raw" gold or silver latent in the sulfurous and mercurous principles of the base metals. This process resulted in a much larger amount of gold or silver than the common processes of extraction.[7] Becher did not include himself in a list of his contemporaries who possessed the philosophical tincture, so he must have considered his own transmutation of lead into silver as one of these weaker "*particular*-Zeitigungen."[8]

Aside from the artifact of his medallion, no reference to Becher's transmutation exists in his works or those of his contemporaries. The significance of his transmutation must be reconstructed from other alchemical activity at the Viennese court, and its timing—July 1675—must be found in the circumstances of Becher's position at the Habsburg court.

---

[5] Ibid., pp. 90, 95.

[6] Ibid.

[7] Ibid., pp. 95–96.

[8] The list is in *Chymischer Glücks-Hafen*, pp. 72–73. Becher disclaimed having ever actually successfully produced and projected the tincture himself in *Psychosophia* (1705), p. 143, and the second supplement to the *Physica Subterranea*, although this is not to say that he did not believe that transmutation by the tincture was not perfectly possible. According to Müller-Jahncke and Joachim Telle, "Numismatik," p. 269, the medallion that resulted from Becher's transmutation is pure silver.

At the Court of the Emperor

Wien ist das Haupt der Welt, Wien ist der Erden Thron.

Vienna is the head of the world; Vienna is the throne of the earth.
(Paul Winkler, poet, on the festivities of Leopold I)

der Kayl. Hoff köndte nicht aigendtlicher definirt werden, dann
daß man sage, ubi nullus ordo, et lux nulla.

The Imperial Court could not be better defined than to say that
where there is no order, there is no light.
*(Bavarian resident minister in Vienna to Elector Ferdinand
Maria, reporting Becher's words, 1670)*

As a second son, Leopold I had been trained by his Jesuit tutors for a contemplative existence. But after his brother died unexpectedly in 1657, Leopold went on to be if not an active warrior prince then at least a very long-lived sovereign. His future hung in the balance for almost a year after 1657, for Louis XIV claimed as much right to the throne of the Holy Roman Empire as Leopold. But after enormous sums of money exchanged hands on all sides, the eight electors at last named Leopold emperor on 18 July 1658.[9] A papal nuncio once accused Leopold of effeminate piety, and his love of learning was sometimes seen as incompatible with the demands of a public life.[10] Indeed, when he came to the throne he seemed hardly capable of holding together the Habsburg lands in the face of the renewed dynamism of the Ottoman Küprülü dynasty, the turmoil to the north in Poland, and the expansionist tendencies of Louis XIV. Leopold's contemporaries (not to mention more recent historians) have viewed the defense of Vienna from the Turks in 1683 and the subsequent stability of Leopold's forty-seven year reign as little short of miraculous. Given Leopold's prodigious veneration of the Virgin, miracle was no doubt a perfectly likely explanation to his fellow travelers in Counter-Reform.[11]

Like other territorial rulers in the last half of the seventeenth century, Leopold ruled with the aid of administrative bodies that had developed in the sixteenth and early seventeenth centuries. By 1658 the territorial government was directed by a number of Privy Councillors (*geheime Räte*), narrowed

---

[9] See John P. Spielman, *Leopold I of Austria* (New Brunswick, N.J.: Rutgers University Press, 1977); Erwin Sicher, "Leopold I of Austria: A Reappraisal" (Ph.D. diss., University of Southern California, 1970); Oswald Redlich, *Weltmacht des Barock. Österreich in der Zeit Kaiser Leopolds I.*, 4th ed. (Vienna: Rudolf M. Rohrer Verlag, 1961).

[10] Redlich, *Weltmacht*, p. 90.

[11] R. J. W. Evans, *The Making of the Habsburg Monarchy* (Oxford: Clarendon Press, 1984), chap. 4.

further by their inclusion in the Hofkanzlei. Ferdinand II established the office of *Hofkanzler* as the overseer of the other two administrative and advisory bodies—the Hofkammer (treasury) and the Hofkriegsrat (war council).[12] When the *Hofkanzler* died in 1665, however, Leopold eliminated this position and appointed himself as central authority.[13] Leopold generally did not consolidate offices; in fact he continued policies which had begun the topsy like growth of the bureaucracy in the reign of his father.[14]

Leopold inherited a situation of complete disarray in the Hofkammer. It is fair to say that from Ferdinand II's time, the Habsburgs lived in a state of constant debt, exacerbated by a situation of near continual warfare and by the increase in size and luxury of the court. Leopold's money worries were complicated by the extreme complexity of the administration and assignment of revenues.[15] For many years, the emperor had lived on loans guaranteed by the revenues of parts of his domains. Thus when Leopold urgently needed a large sum of money in 1665, he discovered that most of his domainal revenues were already tied up. The president of the Hofkammer remarked at that time that the income remaining to the emperor was less than the income of Paris alone.[16] Leopold matched the ingenuity of other princes of the empire in his search for cash. He imposed extraordinary taxes on the free imperial cities to help in the Turkish wars, he sold control of the Jewish quarter in Vienna to the City Council for 100,000 gulden,[17] and he trafficked in offices of state. The troubles of the Hofkammer culminated in the trial and dismissal in 1680 of Georg Ludwig, Count Sinzendorf, its *Präsident* since 1656, for the embezzling of public moneys.[18] Von Sinzendorf had risen high and his fall was spectacular, but the conflation of public and private funds was completely normal at this time. In fact the Sinzendorf family fortune had been a precondition to his appointment as president, for the emperor needed a treasurer who could lend him money if all other sources failed.[19] An official of the court who had paid good money for

[12] Otto Hintze, "Der österreichische und der preußische Beamtenstaat im 17. und 18. Jahrhundert," in *Gesammelte Abhandlungen zur allgemeinen Verfassungsgeschichte*, ed. Fritz Hartung (Leipzig: Koebler & Amelang, 1941): 1:315, 322–28. Leopold established the *Geheime Konferenz* in 1669.

[13] Erwin Sicher, "Leopold I of Austria," p. 102.

[14] See Thomas Fellner and Heinrich Kretschmeyer, *Die österreichische Zentralverwaltung. Von Maximilian I. bis zur Vereinigung der österreichischen und böhmischen Hofkanzlei (1749)*, vol. 1, pt. 1 (Vienna: Adolf Holzhausen, 1907).

[15] Ibid., pp. 81–88.

[16] Jean Bérenger, "Public Loans and Austrian Policy in the Second Half of the Seventeenth Century," *Journal of European Economic History* 2 (1973): 661.

[17] John Gagliardo, *Germany under the Old Regime, 1600–1790* (London: Longman, 1991), p. 277.

[18] Sinzendorf was accused many times of corruption but only fell from power in 1680. Adam Wolf, "Die Hofkammer unter Kaiser Leopold I," *Sitzungsberichte der kaiserlichen Akademie der Wissenschaften* 11 (1853): 475–80.

[19] Bérenger, "Public Loans and Austrian Policy," p. 662.

his office expected that much of his salary would come from the income of the office itself,[20] so that the sale of offices actually amounted to nothing more than a long-term loan for the prince at highly variable rates of interest.[21] The function of such officials was so commonly acknowledged that Shakespeare has Hamlet call the courtier Rosencrantz a "sponge" who "soaks up the king's countenance, his rewards, his authorities." Hamlet goes on to describe to the uncomprehending Rosencrantz how "such officers do the king best service in the end: he keeps them, like an ape, in the corner of his jaw; first mouthed, to be last swallowed: when he needs what you have gleaned, it is but squeezing you, and, sponge, you shall be dry again" (*Hamlet*, act 4, sc. 2).

The expenditures of the Viennese court only grew under Leopold. He loved music, theater, and spectacle, composing scripts and musical scores himself. In his long rule, he mounted four hundred festivals, most a mixture of opera, tournament, horse ballet, parade, and revue.[22] He completed a new wing on the Hofburg in 1666 only to see it go up in flames in 1668, the same year he built a new theater for the court. Only four years later, he began again on the rebuilding.[23]

It was probably this combination of financial woe and love of spectacle that caused Leopold to gain a reputation as a patron of alchemists, although the Habsburg court had long been known as a refuge for alchemists.[24] Most lately, Leopold's predecessor Ferdinand III had patronized alchemy, and their common forebear, Rudolf II, had made the Habsburg court in Prague synonymous with the golden art.[25] While Leopold probably showed more interest in opera than alchemy, Becher maintained that Leopold still gave too much encourage-

---

[20] Fellner and Kretschmeyer, *Zentralverwaltung*, p. 84.

[21] Wolfgang Reinhard, "Staatsmacht als Kreditproblem. Zur Struktur und Funktion des frühneuzeitlichen Ämterhandels," in *Absolutismus*, ed. Ernst Hinrichs (Frankfurt: Suhrkamp, 1986), p. 226. Hubert C. Ehalt, *Ausdrucksformen absolutistischer Herrschaft* (Munich: R. Oldenbourg Verlag, 1980), p. 64, cites the example of Prince Schwarzenberg who bought the office of Oberststallmeister in 1711 for 100,000 gulden in gifts and 500,000 gulden in loans. The yearly salary of this office was 2,000 gulden.

[22] Ehalt, *Ausdrucksformen*, pp. 149–52. Franz Hadamowsky, *Barocktheater am Wiener Kaiserhof 1625–1740* (Vienna: Verlag A. Sexl, 1955), pp. 71–98, contains a list of all the performances given during Leopold's reign.

[23] Ehalt, *Ausdrucksformen*, pp. 88, 108. See also Robert Arthur Griffin, *High Baroque Culture and Theatre in Vienna* (New York: Humanities Press, 1972); and Josef Nadler, "Das bayerisch-österreichische Barocktheater," in *Deutsche Barockforschung. Dokumentation einer Epoche*, 2d ed., ed. Richard Alewyn (Cologne and Berlin: Kiepenheuer & Witsch, 1966), pp. 94–106.

[24] E. G. Rink, *Leopolds des Grossen Röm. Kaysers wunderwürdiges Leben und Thaten* (Cologne, 1713), p. 119, recounted that "es liebete unser Kayser absonderlich die Alchemie."

[25] Alexander Bauer, *Chemie und Alchymie in Oesterreich bis zum beginnenden 19. Jahrhundert* (Vienna: R. Lechner, 1883); Kopp, *Die Alchemie in älterer und neuerer Zeit*; Heinrich von Srbik, "Abenteuer am Hofe Kaiser Leopold I.," *Archiv für Kulturgeschichte* 8 (1910): 52–72; more recently, R. J. W. Evans, *Rudolf II and His World* (Oxford: Clarendon Press, 1973), and *The Making of the Habsburg Monarchy*.

Figure 16. Alchemical medallion produced by Wenceslas Seiler, 1677. With permission of the Kunsthistorisches Museum, Vienna.

ment to fraudulent alchemists, and observed "how in the matter of favor almost too much has occurred."[26]

Becher's transmutation and subsequent production of a medallion commemorating the event was thus by no means unprecedented at the Habsburg court, nor at other courts in Europe. Becher himself claimed knowledge of at least two transmutations in which the metal was afterward cast to commemorate the event.[27] The most famous of these transmutations during Leopold I's reign (1658–1705) was that of the alchemist and Augustinian monk, Wenceslas Seiler (or Seyler), who, after transmuting copper and tin into gold in 1675, was ennobled as Ritter von Reinberg and sent to Bohemia as an officer of the mint.[28] The most spectacular of his transmutations, the changing of a large medallion more than a foot in diameter, from silver into gold, was made on the feast day of Saint Leopold in 1677. Seiler cast the busts of each of the forty-one emperors of the Holy Roman Empire on the face of the medallion, beginning with Pharamend, king of the Franks, and ending with Leopold I in the center (figure 16). In its form, as well as in the fact of its creation on Saint Leopold's Day, this medallion celebrated the genealogy of the Habsburg dynasty and Leopold's place in it.[29]

[26] *Philosophischer Beweisthum* (Becher's translation of 1675 supplement to *Physica Subterranea* [Frankfurt: Johann Haaß, 1680]), p. 28. Becher, *Chymischer Glücks-Hafen*, p. 106, stated that the emperor was inclined "to alchemical, as to other mathematical, and philosophical sciences, inventions, rarities, curiosities, and wants to favor and protect those who cultivate such things. There is no doubt that this has led to many rare and important subjects seeing the light of day and being discovered. Out of which, besides the use of Your Imperial Majesty, not a little pleasure and contentment has been drawn; all the more so as it is praiseworthy when prominent arts and artists are supported and published by high potentates."

[27] Becher listed a man who produced gold in the presence of Emperor Ferdinand III and then in 1658 in Mainz before Elector Johann Philipp von Schönborn. *Oedipus Chymicus, oder Chymischer Rätseldeuter/ worinnen derer verdunckelten Chymischen Wortsätze Urhebungen und Geheimnissen offenbahret und aufgelöset werden* (Becher's translation of *Institutiones Chimicae Prodromae* [N.p., 1680]). This work contains an illustration of the medallion cast in Prague in the presence of Ferdinand III. In *Chymisches Laboratorium*, p. 730, Becher quoted the inscription that Ferdinand III had inscribed on its face: "Gott sey Lob in Ewigkeit/ der ein Theil seiner unendlichen Krafft uns untüchtigen Creaturen hat mittheilen wollen" (God be praised in eternity, who desired to give us undeserving creatures a part of his endless power). In *Chymischer Glücks-Hafen*, pp. 72–73, Becher listed his contemporaries who had performed transmutations before the emperor as Wenceslas Seiler (tin to gold) and Daniel Marsaly (tin to silver). Becher claimed to possess two small medallions made from the gold and silver resulting from these transmutations.

[28] This too was not without precedent. Conrad von Richthausen, Baron von Chaos (died 1663), an alchemist and financier, served as general treasurer of the Hungarian mines.

[29] Held by the Kunsthistorisches Museum, Vienna. See Müller-Jahncke and Telle, "Numismatik," pp. 269–70; reproduction, p. 252. A chemical analysis of Seiler's medallion in the 1930s revealed that it is not in fact pure gold, but an alloy of silver, gold, and copper. According to this analysis, it was probably dipped into cold nitric acid to produce a color change. V. Karpenko, "Coins and Medals Made of Alchemical Metal," *Ambix* 35 (1988): 74. (I am grateful to William R. Newman for making known this reference to me.) *Magnalia Naturae* (London: Tomas Dawks, 1680), ostensibly by Becher but considered by Hassinger to be spurious, gave an account of Seiler's

Leopold's love of theater and display no doubt played a part in his appreciation of Seiler's artifice, but success in alchemical transmutation could be interpreted as confirming princely power and fitness to rule, for alchemical knowledge was revealed only to the most pious, and success in transmutation was granted only to individuals of exceptional moral probity. It was proof of the humility and piety of the Catholic emperor that God granted a transmutation at his court.[30] It was, moreover, evidence of the emperor's attention to his eternal reputation through his patronage of the scholarly and fine arts. Not only did a prince seek *"Divertissement"* and evidence of God's wonders in the alchemical laboratory,[31] but also his own *fama*.[32] Patronage of alchemy as much as patronage of music, letters, or natural philosophy was a way to direct and sustain the representation of the prince. Both Seiler's and Becher's alchemical medallions eventually joined the curious objects collected by the emperors in their Kunstkammer, and they are still displayed in its successor, the Kunsthistorisches Museum, demonstrating to all posterity the accomplishment of a transmutation at the Habsburg court. The reputation conferred today by this feat, however, evokes the deceptions of wax museums and charlatanry rather than the glory gained by Leopold in his own day.

What brought honor to the prince also brought favor to the alchemist. The relationship between alchemy and general metallurgical techniques meant that the successful performer of a transmutation was often regarded as having a particular knowledge of minerals and metals which could be useful in the imperial mines in Hungary and Bohemia, in the mint, or in some other part of the government dealing with regalian income. After performing a transmutation before the court, many alchemists were in fact sent off to prove their processes in the mines.[33] Thus alchemical transmutation could function as a display of chemical and metallurgical knowledge and techniques worthy of patronage in themselves. In fact, the Hofkammer filed the alchemical propositions it received under Hungarian Minting and Mining Affairs (Ungarische Münz- und Bergwesen).[34]

---

discovery of the tincturing powder in a monastery in Moravia, the transmutation of tin into gold, and Seiler's ennoblement and subsequent decline into debauchery. Becher is named as a "Commissarius" for the adjudication of Seiler's art, and although he could not have witnessed the transmutation in 1677 (having already left Vienna), he may well have made an examination of Seiler's other transmutations.

[30] This point is made several times by Becher; see, for example, Letter Becher to Leopold I, Mss. var. 1(1), fols. 146v–147r.

[31] Becher, *Chymischer Glücks-Hafen*, p. 81.

[32] Ibid., p. 106.

[33] Becher stated that princes should have laboratories for three reasons, one of which was in order to examine the mines and minerals within their hereditary property (*Chymischer Glücks-Hafen*, p. 81). Srbik, "Abenteuer am Hofe Kaiser Leopold I." David C. Goodman, *Power and Penury: Government, Technology and Science in Philip II's Spain* (Cambridge: Cambridge University Press, 1988), emphasizes Philip II's interest in alchemy for the production of precious metals, but also notes that Philip II had little expectation of profit from alchemy (pp. 11–15).

[34] Hoffinanz Repertoria, Vienna, Hofkammerarchiv.

Becher recounted the exemplary history of an alchemist who attempted to deceive the court in Vienna, a story that illustrates well the potential for patronage in alchemy, as well as the intrigues in which an alchemist could become enmeshed.[35] Alchemist "N.," a ruined colonel, came to Vienna with a method of extracting gold from silver by means of a powder of "Auripigment." He claimed to desire nothing more than to teach the art in return for a written assurance that he would receive a part of the profit from any transmutation. *Hofkammerpräsident* Sinzendorf responded immediately to such a straightforward request: "How can the man deceive? If his process gives no profit, he gains nothing, the trial costs nothing, the silver that we give him we retain, the powder is ready in a quarter of an hour and costs barely half a gulden, the process can be carried out any day, therefore let it be done." Reassured by his reasoning, Sinzendorf gave "N." the written assurance he desired. The next morning Becher and the imperial *Wardein* (mint warden) performed the process according to the alchemist's verbal instructions, with the *Hofkammerpräsident* looking on. The alchemist himself gave only the instructions and touched nothing in order to avoid the accusation that he had added gold or practiced some other deception. The trial resulted in a "schöne, grosse Gold-Prob." That same evening, Becher and the *Wardein* made a trial by themselves and could produce nothing. This upset the *Hofkammerpräsident*, who was already counting out how many gulden he would spend on this process, and he ordered another round of trials. This went on for some days, with trials made in the presence of "N." producing gold, and trials made in his absence coming to naught. Finally the alchemist said he was tired of playing *Praeceptor* to such dull students and sent the contract back to the *Hofkammerpräsident* before leaving town.

Becher and the *Wardein* wondered what the episode portended until they learned that "N." had shown the *Hofkammerpräsident*'s written assurance to a Count Bucquoy whom he knew to be a *Liebhaber* of alchemy. With this letter, attesting to his high standing at the imperial court, "N." convinced the count that he had only demonstrated to the *Hofkammerpräsident* the smallest portion of his art and desired now only to work out the greater part of it in an atmosphere of solitude and peace not possible at court. The count believed the *Präsident* to be a very circumspect man and therefore gave "N." his full confidence, meals at his table, horse and carriage, and, because the alchemist could not immediately obtain a letter of credit from the merchants, a cash advance of two hundred gulden. He offered "N." as well a "retreat" at his estate in Bohemia, where, Becher claimed, the count provided "N." with a glass furnace, in which "N." began making a type of "Crystallin-Glaß." This type of glass happened to be the same as that which Becher had produced in Vienna, but because "N." could get wood more cheaply in the Bohemian forests, he was able to sell the glass more

<hr />

[35] Becher, *Chymischer Glücks-Hafen*, pp. 96–98. The following information and quotations come from these pages.

cheaply than Becher, and so, to add injury to insult, in addition to deceiving Becher and the Hofkammer, "N." had ruined Becher's business.[36] Becher drew the moral of the tale in the following way: the few hundred ducats and the time that "N." had lost in the confidence game with the *Hofkammerpräsident* were returned a hundredfold by Count Bucquoy, and Becher predicted that the count would now pay the piper: "Time will tell what return N. will give to the Count and how he will lead him on (no doubt not a little). We have already heard that Count Bucquoy wanted very much to borrow 40,000 gulden or more, no doubt in order to effect the transmutation process of N."

Becher's history brings to mind the importance of credit in the court world, and illustrates the part that alchemical claims could play in a bid for credit and patronage.[37] The episode also shows the ease with which claims to alchemical knowledge could lead to employment in some related activity (in this case, glassmaking). Although N.'s alchemical process was tested before reliable witnesses who considered his process to be in some way a deception, this was irrelevant to N.'s goal, for by means of his alchemical artifice he had found a place of employment and a livelihood. Becher, whose plans were on a grander scale than those of N., described him as a fraud and a meddler (and someone who might ruin Becher's own reputation), but N. had actually made a bid for employment that was legitimate within the court structure and its understanding of alchemical transmutation.

Becher's own 1675 transmutation can be seen in the context of the intrigue that enveloped any routes to favor and that swirled particularly around chemical and alchemical processes at the Habsburg court, as illustrated in the story of N. We first hear in December 1672 of Becher's involvement in alchemical intrigue, when Johann Daniel Crafft informed Gottfried Wilhelm Leibniz that in the previous summer a defrocked monk had made various projections with a tincture before the emperor, but no one could repeat his success. Crafft reported that Becher had provided him with information about this transmutation, which Becher considered authentic, and that Becher had promised to send some of the tincturing powder. In the same letter Crafft mentioned that Becher himself had been cheated out of one hundred Reichsthaler by yet another unfrocked Augustinian monk, who styled himself Marsignus.[38] Becher does in fact seem to

---

[36] Becher apparently undertook this glassmaking process at the latest in 1672 in the *Glasshütte* on Georg Ludwig von Sinzendorf's property. He describes this glassworks in the *Referat* on the Kunst- und Werckhaus as prior to and separate from the Kunsthauß itself. See Herbert Hassinger, *Johann Joachim Becher 1635–82. Ein Beitrag zur Geschichte des Merkantilismus* (Vienna: Adolf Holzhausen, 1951), and the "Referat über Marinettis Gesuch" in the Hofkammerarchiv that he cites (p. 201).

[37] The importance of alchemical knowledge (although in a different context) is amply illustrated in Bruce T. Moran, *The Alchemical World of the German Court: Occult Philosophy and Chemical Medicine in the Circle of Moritz of Hessen (1572–1632)* (Stuttgart: Franz Steiner Verlag, 1991).

[38] Leibniz, *Sämtliche Schriften und Briefe*, ed. Preussische Akademie der Wissenschaften et al. (Darmstadt: Otto Reichl et al., 1923–), ser. 1, vol. 1, Crafft to Leibniz, 20 December 1672, pp. 406–9, here p. 409.

have contracted with "Dom. Marsini" (known also as Carolus de Repas) to obtain instruction in a process of making "white tin" in return for one hundred ducats.[39] At approximately the same time he contracted with Marsini, Becher wrote a long letter to the emperor in which he declared "without any passion or interest" ("ohne alle *passion* und *interesse*") that, while he was sure God desired to grace the emperor by demonstrating the truth of transmutation at his court, he was not sure that the two monks the emperor had employed to try this art were suitable instruments of that grace, for they had neither the moral probity, the honesty, the experience, nor the theoretical understanding to carry out the great work.[40] Becher claimed that Marsini's experience was mostly with white copper and tin hardened by an arsenic process, rather than with transmutation. Naturally, Becher knew the particulars of Marsini's process through his own espionage and *Kundschaft*. Furthermore, Becher warned, unless the emperor wanted to make his court into "a receptacle and a den for defrocked, unchaste, deceiving monks and sophists" that would eventually frighten away all honest philosophers, he should appoint a regular chemical advisor who would oversee the alchemists who petitioned the court and would adjudicate their processes.[41] Although Becher did not directly suggest himself as the best candidate for this position, he clearly expected the emperor to draw that conclusion.[42]

---

[39] A draft of a contract between Dom. Marsinus and Becher, Mss. var. 1(2), fol. 607r–v. Becher says that a trial of the process had been made by Marsini "in the presence of Father Felicianus, Capuchin monk, in Vienna." No doubt Becher had heard of the trial through his *Kundtschafft*.

[40] "Es zweiffelt mir nit, Gott werde und wolle Ewer Kayl. Mtt. mit diesem *Philosophi*schen Kleinod seegnen, förchte aber nur, daß die jenige Personen nicht die rechte werckzeug seind welche sich zu dieser Sach angeben. . . . Ob nuhn Gott solchen Leuthen, so große *magnalia* anzuvertrauen pflege, kann ich schwerlich glauben," fols. 148v–149r, copy of a letter, Becher to the emperor, Mss. var. 1(1), fols. 146r–151r.

[41] "Einem *receptaculo et latibulo* von außgesprungenen, untzüchtigen betrüegerischen münchen und *Sophisten*." Mss. var. 1(1), fols. 149v–150v.

[42] There were other alchemical intrigues at court. In 1674, Becher reported to the emperor on the transmutation of tin to silver by Daniel Marsaly, again attesting to the theoretical soundness of the process, but complaining that Marsaly did not have the correct moral qualities to ensure success in the transmutation ("Gutachten über Herrn Daniels Marsaly Process zur Tinctur," 11 May 1674, Ms. 11472, Handschriften-Abteilung, Österreichische Nationalbibliothek [hereafter ÖNB], fol. 7r–v). In 1675 Becher wrote to an acquaintance describing Marsaly as "homo omnium Mortalium impudentissimus, sed etiam fortunatissimus" (the most impudent of mortals, but also the most fortunate). Becher claimed that Marsaly had turned out a trickster, but despite his moral failings had made his fortune by finding favor with the *Hofkammerpräsident*, Sinzendorf, and the prince of Lichtenstein (Mss. var. 1(1), fols. 692–693v, a copy or draft of a letter from Becher to "Doctissime Langi" in which Becher is answering Langus's inquiries about a certain chemist, Pantaleon, who came to the Imperial court during Becher's tenure there). Hassinger, *Becher*, equates Marsaly and Marsini (p. 173), but this is incorrect. In 1676 Becher was also involved in the intrigue surrounding the testing of the Schellenberg process. Becher was one of a group commissioned to advise on the furnace and process for extracting metals from the sludge left by the refining of ores of Wolfgang Ferdinand Freiherr von Schellenberg. Becher concurred in the opinion of the advising body that Schellenberg himself, his furnace, and his process were untrustworthy and deceptive, but at the

Becher's alchemical medallion seems to make sense within a number of complex alchemical intrigues occurring at the Viennese court in the early 1670s, yet his transmutation can also be placed within his ongoing commercial projects of that time. Emperor Leopold I had appointed Becher commercial advisor—"kaiserlicher Commerzien-rath"—in 1666, while Becher was still in the employ of the Bavarian elector. As commercial advisor, Becher had the duties of overseeing meetings of the *Commercien-Colleg* (Commercial Council), and of reporting to the emperor.[43] After his troubles with *Hofkammerpräsident* Georg Ludwig von Sinzendorf in late 1666, Becher returned for four years to Munich, apparently having little contact with the Viennese court during this time.[44] In 1670, he prepared his return to Vienna by writing to Sinzendorf to ascertain his standing and credit at the imperial court,[45] and he reentered the city in the summer of 1670.

Back in Vienna, Becher attempted first to reinvigorate the Commercial Council, a new body he had conceived and established in 1666, but which had fallen into inactivity in the four years of his absence. This advisory council was to study commerce, develop trade and manufacture, and oversee trading companies and guilds in the Habsburg patrimonial lands and in the empire in general. The various commercial projects that filled Becher's six years in Vienna have been carefully reconstructed from archival documents and fully described by Hassinger. As in Munich, Becher established a silk manufactory, but he went far beyond the Munich projects to found two companies, one to trade with the Ottoman Empire, and the other to export goods to Holland. We have already heard about his project to obtain a million Reichsthaler from Dutch financiers. He proposed new taxes on manufactured goods, and endeavored to estimate the return from such a tax by collecting statistics on numbers of artisans in the Habsburg hereditary lands. Finally, he planned and began to build a "Kunst- und Werckhaus" (a workhouse cum manufactory), and he continually urged a ban on French imports.[46] In addition to his projects and his

same time he explained privately to the *Hofkammerpräsident* that the process was possible and needed testing by a true adept, namely himself. This episode is described by Srbik, "Abenteuer," pp. 63–69.

[43] See Hassinger, *Becher*, pp. 146ff.

[44] Hassinger, *Becher*, p. 174, cites a document from 3 January 1673 in which Becher petitioned successfully for a retroactive payment of his salary for the time he was absent from Vienna. In this petition, Becher described the services he performed for the emperor while in Munich. (Hassinger cites HF exp. 27.II.1673 in the Hofkammerarchiv, Vienna.) There is evidence, which Hassinger does not mention, that Becher planned a permanent return to Vienna in 1667. An entry in the Hoffinanz-Protokoll 1667R in Vienna, Hofkammerarchiv, fol. 307v, reads: "Passbrief für Herrn Johann Joachim Becher mit Weib, Khindern und unmauttbaren Mobilien von München hierher nach Wien abzuraisen Frey. 21. Juli."

[45] Sinzendorf to Becher, 14 August 1670, *Politischer Discurs*, 2d ed., p. 583. Sinzendorf welcomes Becher with an invitation to put his projects before the emperor, for which he will derive fine recompense.

[46] Hassinger, *Becher*, chap. 4, gives an overview, and Hassinger's other articles fill in some details: "Johann Joachim Bechers Kampf gegen Frankreich und die Gründung einer Wollmanufak-

duties as commercial advisor, Becher was called upon by the emperor to judge the authenticity and value of alchemical and metallurgical processes.[47]

From the very beginning of his tenure at the Viennese court, Becher struggled fiercely to hold his own with the court officials and with rival projectors. Whereas in Munich Becher had had an established position—*Hofmedicus*—within the court hierarchy, in Vienna he had no such established position. The position of commercial advisor at the Habsburg court was a completely new one, and one that had no clear protocol or authority attached to it. The Commercial Council was also new. In the form first conceived by Becher, the Commercial Council would have been immediately responsible to the emperor, and Becher, as "director" of the council, would have dealt directly with the emperor. This plan ran into such opposition on the part of the established court officials, especially the Hofkammer and its president, Count Sinzendorf, that Becher had to revise it substantially. In the form in which it was finally implemented, the council was in fact subordinate to the Hofkammer, and Becher, as "commercial advisor," had to work through the president of the Hofkammer, who, in the revised council, had become president of the Commercial Council as well.[48]

Because he had no clear authority of his own, Becher depended on the Hofkammer for the implementation of his projects. This body was notoriously unwieldy and its president had garnered many enemies and much power in his many years of controversial government. This man had begun as Becher's protector and promoter at the imperial court but ended as his most bitter enemy.[49] As a result Becher sought other protectors at court. The most powerful protector one could have at the Habsburg court was, of course, the emperor himself, and Becher's proposals received great favor from Leopold; the position of "favorite," however, was a precarious one, for it made one liable to attacks on one's credit by others seeking the emperor's protection, and frequently resulted in spectacular falls from favor.

tur in Salzburg im Jahre 1677," *Mitteilungen der Gesellschaft für Salzburger Landeskunde* 78 (1938): 168–82; "Wien im Zeitalter des Merkantilismus," *Nachrichtenblatt des Vereines für Geschichte der Stadt Wien*, n.s., 3 (1941): 1–17; "Die erste Wiener orientalische Handelskompagnie, 1667–1683," *Vierteljahrschrift für Sozial- und Wirtschaftsgeschichte* 35, no. 1 (1942): 1–53; and "Johann Joachim Bechers Bedeutung für die Entwicklung der Seidenindustrie in Deutschland," *Vierteljahrschrift für Sozial- und Wirtschaftsgeschichte* 38, no. 3 (1951): 209–46. While Hassinger's work does not participate to my knowledge in Nazi rhetoric, he follows the policy of the journal refounded after the Nazi seizure of power in his article, "Wien im Zeitalter des Merkantilismus," by placing an asterisk by the names of Jewish authors.

[47] In 1674, Becher submitted a report on the Marsaly process, in 1676 on the Schellenberg process (Hassinger, *Becher*, p. 202). He also claimed to have judged the Seiler process.

[48] Hassinger, *Becher*, pp. 147–49, on whom I rely here, has carefully reconstructed the development and implementation of Becher's plans from the drafts of the proposal in the Rostock *Nachlaß*.

[49] See among other comments on the *Hofkammerpräsident* by Becher, *Närrische Weisheit*, p. 169.

Ample evidence reveals the struggle for favor and power throughout Becher's employ at the the court of Leopold I, but a particular battle came to a head in the months leading up to the summer of 1675, when Becher transmuted lead into silver. The particular cluster of events that made up this struggle began to form in 1673 with Becher's *anonymous* presentation of a project to the emperor that proposed a particularly profitable new sort of taxation. This was a levy on artisanal goods, which had not traditionally been taxed in the Habsburg patrimonial domain. Taxes on agricultural products, livestock, and staple goods—bread, beer, and wine—were common enough, although strictly defined as extraordinary taxes, but a tax such as the one Becher proposed was not. Moreover, the tax was also novel in the Habsburg lands because it was indirect; the producers were required to pass on the tax to the buyer by increasing the price of the manufactured items. Becher had made this proposal directly to Leopold in order to circumvent the Hofkammer, and he had made it anonymously in order to escape the wrath of the Hofkammer when this body discovered his subversion of its authority. The emperor's extremely favorable reception of this project led to an extraordinary collection of statistics on the artisans of the Habsburg lands in late 1673 by Philipp Wilhelm von Hörnigk, Becher's brother-in-law.[50]

Becher used these statistics on artisans to compile a long *Referat* (report) on commerce, which he presented to the emperor at Leopold's summer palace of Laxenburg in May 1674. This commercial report was entitled

> Referat of Doctor Johann Joachim Becher, His Roman Imperial Majesty's Commercial Advisor, describing how the commerce and common trade presently in Your Majesty's patrimonial lands are constituted, and, by means of a Commercial Council, could be helped along, so that to the honor and use of Your Majesty's hereditary lands, they might flourish better.[51]

The goal of the report was to interest the emperor in the development of trade in his lands and to blow life into the Commercial Council. This petition also found favor with the emperor, and he ordered both its close consideration by the Hofkammer and the Commercial Council and the implementation of the new indirect taxation project.

In July 1674 Becher submitted another proposal to the emperor for increasing revenues in the patrimonial lands, this time by the manufacture of mineral

---

[50] These statistics and von Hörnigk's reports are in the Mss. var. 1(2), fols. 244r–318v and fols. 321r–362v, and are discussed by Hassinger, *Becher*, pp. 177ff.

[51] "Doctor Johann Joachim Bechers Römischer Kayserl. Mayt. Commercien Raths Referat wie die Commercien, auch gemeiner Handel und Wandel gegenwärtig in Ihro Kayl. Mayt. Erblanden, verschaffen seye, auch wie solchem, durch restabilirung eines Commercien Collegii könnte geholffen werden, daß sie den Kayl. Erblanden, zur Ehr und nutzen besser florirten." He presented it on the 11 May 1674, together with an elaborate *Gutachten* (adjudication) on alchemy. ÖNB, Ms. 11472 and Ms. 12467, respectively. As will be developed subsequently, it is significant that Becher presented the two reports together.

dyes.[52] Throughout 1674 and into 1675, the members of the Hofkammer and Commercial Council met in conference on all these proposals; as the meetings dragged on, however, it became clear that the projects would never be implemented.[53] In addition, the attempt to reinvigorate the Commercial Council failed and the continuance of Becher's salaried position as commercial advisor became impossible to maintain. On 14 June 1675, the emperor named Becher *Hofkammerrat* (treasury official) with the same salary that he had received as commercial advisor. Becher however apparently regarded his position at the court during this time as uncertain, for he sought patrons elsewhere for his taxation project. Working through intermediaries, he tried to interest the elector of Brandenburg, the elector of Saxony, and the States General of the Netherlands in the same manufacturing taxes he had proposed to the emperor.[54] And in the month following his new appointment as *Hofkammerrat*, Becher apparently transmuted lead into silver. He had begun the series of proposals in 1673 in anonymity, seeking to circumvent the Hofkammer. With the transmutation of 1675, he tried again to find direct favor with the emperor, this time by means of a potentially more effective way to obtain access to Leopold I, who was known to extend special, lasting, and direct favor to alchemists.[55]

Becher and other projectors always operated on the margins of the court administration. Because they were outside the established court hierarchy (although they sometimes held a court title) and had no status of their own, they relied upon the favor they had with the prince (or even the *reputation* of that favor) to exercise their authority and to effect their projects.[56] Alchemy could help these outsiders in their pursuit of the emperor's favor and the power it conveyed.[57]

[52] Printed by Becher in the *Chymischer Glücks-Hafen*, pp. 103–7. Becher claimed to have had this project submitted to the emperor by Herr P. Donellanus. Also discussed by Hassinger, *Becher*.

[53] This is covered in Hassinger, *Becher*, pp. 177–94.

[54] Ibid., pp. 194–95.

[55] Later during Leopold's reign, in a similar attempt to combat the disinterest and outright hindrances by the Hofkammer to his proposals, Wilhelm von Schröder would also try his hand at alchemy in order to win back the favor of the emperor. See Miriam Haskett, "Wilhelm Freiherr von Schröder: Economic Thought and Projects for Fiscal Reform in Austria in the Reign of Leopold I" (Ph.D. diss., University of California at Los Angeles, 1960), p. 116, in regard to the publication of Schröder's *Unterricht vom Goldmachen*.

[56] These marginal figures could just as easily be natural philosophers or musicians. The problems they encountered and their intense concern with their place in the court and their proximity to the prince's favor is revealed in a story related by the anonymous author of *The Life of Leopold, Late Emperor of Germany* . . . (London, 1706), p. 386: in illustrating the behavior of the musicians, he says, "The Impertinence of these Eunuchs is very notorious in one of them a little before the Emperor's Death [in 1705]: This Person crouding into the Chappel, where he had at that time no Part in the Musick, and pressing upon a Foreign Knight to make way for him, which the other was not forward to do, the Eunuch angrily said to him, *Ego sum Antonius M. Musicus Sacrae Caesarae Majestatis*, as if the Title of Emperor's Fiddler was enough to make every Knee bow to him."

[57] This may account for the hostility often exhibited by the court bureaucracy toward projectors and alchemists, and the abrupt falls from favor and the punishments (sometimes capital) meted out

Alchemy in the Kunst- und Werckhaus

Becher's struggle to obtain a channel to the emperor's eyes, ears, and purse continued through 1676 until he left Vienna in early 1677. His use of alchemy as a direct means to the prince's favor is most overt in the "Referat, oder gründliche Beschreibung was in dem Kunst- undt Werckhauß sambt beyliegenden Schmeltz- undt Glaßhütten, gethan und operirt wirdt, auch wie selbige angeordnet seye" (Report, or thorough description of the processes and operations, as well as the arrangement, of the Art- and Workhouse, including the nearby smelting and glassworks).[58] Economic historians have charted the development of Becher's concept of a workhouse from a jail or poorhouse, which he had attempted to implement in Munich, to a manufacturing center, which he partially completed in 1675/76 outside of Vienna.[59] Although the center never completely functioned before he left Vienna in 1677, Becher's 1676 report was designed to inform the emperor about progress on the construction of the buildings, as well as to seek funds for its completion and for hiring workers.

Becher's report, referred to here as the Kunsthaus Referat, sets out the planned scope of this center, which in its finished form would include several different sorts of manufactures: porcelain making, silk and wool weaving, chemical manufactures, wine making, medicament production, and glassmaking. He envisaged it as a place to shelter and train the vagrant population of the Habsburg lands, where, on mastering a trade, individuals could earn a certificate and an imperial privilege which would allow them to set up independent workshops.[60] The Kunsthaus (as Becher referred to it) would also function as a center of deposit for recipes, for descriptions of artisanal processes and tech-

---

to them. According to Günter Scheel, "Leibniz, die Alchimie und der absolute Staat," *Studia Leibnitiana Supplementa* 19 (1980): 267–83, Leibniz also used alchemy in a similar way. Scheel maintains that alchemy gave Leibniz a hearing among patrons not otherwise interested in his ideas. According to this account, Leibniz did not really "believe" in alchemy himself, but simply used it to further his broader plans. Scheel attributes Leibniz's avid interest in alchemy (which continued throughout his life) to his being forced by the patrons who were "caught" by alchemy to continue alchemical activities. To prove this thesis, Scheel makes much of Leibniz's stated disbelief in transmutation, but many of the sentiments expressed by Leibniz about the reliability of alchemists are standard rhetoric of any seventeenth-century natural philosopher distancing himself from the trickery of dishonest alchemists.

[58] ÖNB Ms. 8046. Presented on 19 March 1676. Hereafter cited as Kunsthaus Referat.

[59] Hassinger, *Becher*, pp. 196–204, and Hans J. Hatschek, *Das Manufakturhaus auf dem Tabor in Wien. Ein Beitrag zur österreichischen Wirthschaftsgeschichte des 17. Jahrhunderts* (Leipzig: Duncker & Humblot, 1886).

[60] This center has much in common with Théophraste Renaudot's Bureau d'Adresse and with Samuel Hartlib's projected Office of Addresse. See Howard M. Solomon, *Public Welfare, Science, and Propaganda in Seventeenth Century France* (Princeton: Princeton University Press, 1972), and G. H. Turnbull, *Hartlib, Dury and Comenius: Gleanings from Hartlib's Papers* (London: Hodder & Stoughton, 1947).

niques, and for privileges and patents. Inventors and projectors seeking a hearing could bring their projects to this house where they would be tested. From this house, artisans trained in the new manufactures would spread new processes, new manufactures, and new arts throughout the patrimonial lands of the emperor.[61] The house would serve in addition as a Kunstkammer and a center for correspondence with the societies of *Curiosi* in Florence, London, Amsterdam, and Paris. Machines and instruments were to be displayed and perpetual motion to be demonstrated—both "practicé" as well as "theoricé"—by a perpetually running clock.[62]

Becher proposed that extensive chemical laboratories form the core of this house of manufacture, where goods with value for court use and for export were to be produced. Salts and acids would be manufactured for use in the production of mineral dyes. The manufacture and export of these dyes would maintain all the other operations of the Kunsthaus, so that it would be self-sustaining, requiring no financial outlay (and no control) on the part of the Hofkammer.[63] Further products of the chemical furnaces were to be majolica ware, a white alloy of copper invented by Becher for use in making household utensils, and nonmineral medicaments for sale in the apothecary attached to the complex.[64]

The ennoblement of metals was also to be undertaken in these laboratories. Indeed, those sections of the report that treat alchemy most clearly reveal the purpose and nature of Becher's appeal to the emperor. It is clear from the contracts and other documents recording the building and financing of the Kunsthaus that Becher once again attempted to circumvent the Hofkammer in this project.[65] In the beginning of the project, Becher had approached the emperor for funds through Albrecht von Zinzendorf, *Obersthofmeister* of the empress dowager's court.[66] This attempt to circumvent the Hofkammer proved impossible, however, because the Hofkammer had to approve the large sums necessary for construction. Although the emperor had endorsed large sums for the project, they had never been paid out by the Hofkammer, and construction

---

[61] Kunsthaus Referat, fol. 17r.

[62] Ibid., fol. 14r–v. The perpetual motion clock was one of the most constant projects of Becher's life; plans for it appear in his earliest papers, construction of the clock was one of his first projects in Mainz, and a plan for the clock was submitted to the Royal Society and published in 1680.

[63] Becher claimed that the importation of these dyes cost the hereditary lands 100,000 gulden yearly. The imported dyes were often made from minerals mined within the hereditary lands that had been exported out of the Habsburg lands in their raw form and then reimported as finished dyes. Accord between Becher and Graf Albrecht von Zinzendorf, 21 May 1675, included in the copies of documents appended to the Kunsthaus Referat, fols. 17v–20v.

[64] Ibid., fols. 5r–6v.

[65] Becher appended annotated copies of these documents to the Kunsthaus Referat. These record its origin in 1675, the agreements made between Becher and his intermediaries with the emperor and the Hofkammer, and between Becher and the Hofkammer, as well as the costs incurred in the building and the amount still owing for the construction. Kunsthaus Referat, fols. 17v–34r.

[66] Hatschek, *Das Manufakturhaus*, p. 31, esp. n. 1.

only began in 1675 when the Hofkammer president finally rented his own land (at one hundred Reichsthaler per year) to Becher for the project. This site made it wholly impossible to maneuver around the *Hofkammerpräsident*, and the terms of finance for the project became less and less favorable to Becher, until in November 1676, a contract was drawn up which burdened Becher with the entire financial responsibility for the project.[67]

In this context, the March 1676 Kunsthaus Referat can be seen as Becher's last-ditch effort to interest the emperor directly in this project and to open up a direct line for funds that would save it. The report's form, its language, and the place of alchemy in it attest to this purpose.[68] The Kunsthaus Referat opens with an elevation drawing and floor plans for the entire compound (figures 17, 18, 19). In the opening letter to the emperor, Becher assured Leopold that an eternal reputation was to be gained by patronizing and supporting this project. In fact, Becher said, that reputation was already under construction, for many men of rank and foreign ambassadors had already seen and admired the few completed buildings of the Kunsthaus.[69] In the body of the Kunsthaus Referat, Becher led the emperor room by room through the buildings, and explained the manufactures carried on within each room. He described many of the manufactures to the emperor as "secrets," and he promised the revelation of many more such secrets if this house of invention and manufacture was generously supported.[70] He made much of the wonder-working medicaments and "Dr. Bechers universal pills," which were to be sold in the apothecary.[71] Moreover, Becher promised that the Kunsthaus would produce a steady stream of curiosities for the emperor's diversion, which would be enhanced through the correspondence to be opened up with learned academies all over Europe.[72]

This appeal to the emperor's love of curiosities and his concern with reputation was made most strongly in the sections that dealt with alchemy. After dwelling on the 100,000 gulden that were to be earned through the manufacture of mineral dyes, Becher revealed that the laboratories would also be used to demonstrate the truth and usefulness of "*Alchimy*":

> Thus in this laboratory the truth and use of alchemy will also be demonstrated by means of various processes, such as the ripening of lead into silver, with the result that a centner [50 kilograms] of lead will deliver up 25 to 50 lots [250–500 grams]

---

[67] Ibid., pp. 30–34, and Hassinger, *Becher*, pp. 199–203, reconstruct this sequence of events, drawing upon the documents attached to the Kunsthaus Referat and, in Hassinger's case, additional archival material in the Hofkammerarchiv.

[68] Hassinger, *Becher*, p. 200, notes in passing that this was a goal of the Kunsthaus Referat.

[69] Kunsthaus Referat, fol. 4r–v.

[70] For example, ibid., fol. 10r, in regard to the medicaments, and fol. 11r in regard to the copper alloy.

[71] The description of the apothecary and of the medicaments to be produced in it compose the longest section of the Kunsthaus Referat, fols. 6v–10r.

[72] Ibid., fol. 14r.

of a silver that is rich in gold; by a process that extracts 100 lots of silver from a centner of copper, by a gold extraction which is very rich; and by a chemical process that will bring a 1 percent profit weekly that could well reach 2 percent. This last process operates week after week, so that great amounts of capital could be employed in it. Thus this laboratory is securer and richer than mines or exchange banks, and it alone will return the costs of the project.[73]

Becher apparently did not consider a simple statement of these rich alchemical processes as sufficient to catch the emperor's eye, for he twice added "nota bene" in his own handwriting in the margin beside this section (figure 20). At the end of this paragraph he pointed out, again in an addition in his own hand, that for the development of these processes alone, he requested 4,000 gulden, a substantial sum for this part of the Kunsthaus alone, given that the entire project had so far cost 11,123 gulden.[74]

Becher resorted again to overt exploitation of the emperor's interest in alchemy when describing the small laboratory that was to form a part of the Kunsthaus director's (i.e., Becher's) quarters. This laboratory—to be used only for the preparation of the philosophical tincture—could quickly and easily be completed for only 700 gulden (again a significant proportion of the total cost of construction).[75] Becher complained that true transmutation in this laboratory was being held up by the interference of other members of the court and the difficulty in finding funds for construction of the director's building.

In instructions to the chemical advisors of princes, Becher held them responsible for faithfully considering their "lord and patron's final intention." If his patron desired only medicaments, the advisor must seek and test processes with medicinal ends. If the patron's goal consisted in gold and silver making, the advisor must not waste time on other processes, but pursue this goal.[76] In the report on the Kunst- und Werckhaus, Becher subverted his own advice, for he knew of the emperor's predilection for alchemy, but instead of pursuing only alchemical processes, he tried to use this interest to further all the commercial and chemical projects to be included in the house. In fact, it appears Becher had to tread a careful path of catching the eye of the emperor with alchemy and then transmuting this interest in alchemy into one for commercial projects. When Becher compiled a list of circumstances that would cause Count Albrecht Zinzendorf to become unfit as inspector of the Kunsthaus, he made "a sole

---

[73] Ibid., fols. 5v–6r.

[74] The text of the Kunsthaus Referat was written by a secretary, and Becher made corrections and insertions. Thus it is quite clear that this was an insertion by Becher before presentation of the Referat. Costs of the project were included in the documents appended to the end of the Referat. The costs of the projects are from Hassinger, *Becher*, p. 200, who also notes the significance of Becher's request for 4,000 gulden.

[75] Kunsthaus Referat, fol. 15r.

[76] Becher, *Chymischer Glücks-Hafen*, p. 88.

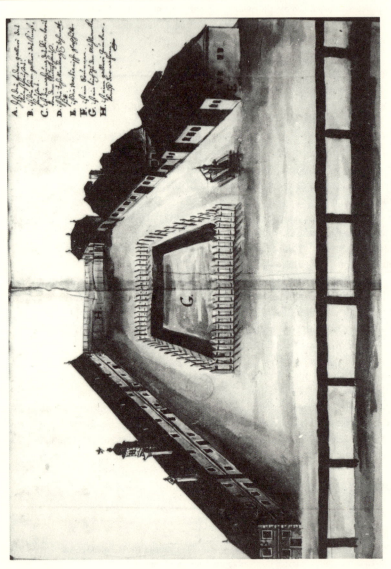

Figure 17. Elevation view of the Kunst- und Werckhaus, 1676. *Key*: A. Lower gallery—first floor. B. Upper gallery—second floor. C. House of the director. D. Schellenberg smelting works. E. Venetian glassworks. F. Fountain. G. Pond for the millworks. H. Gallery for sale of wares. Österreichische Nationalbibliothek, Handschriften-Abteilung, Vienna, Ms. 8046.

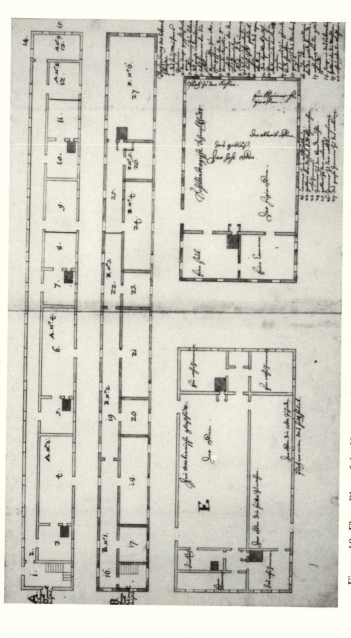

Figure 18. Floor Plan of the Kunst- und Werckhaus, 1676. *First floor:* 1. Housemaster's room. 2. Long, paved corridor. 3. Living room attached to laboratory. 4. The large laboratory. 5. Living room for the potters. 6. Kiln for majolica pottery. 7. Room for the fired majolica. 8. Living room for the master weaver. 9. Kitchen and entry to the weavers' room. 10. Apothecary kitchen. 11. Living room for the apothecary. 12. The apothecary. 13. Room where the medicaments are sold. 14. Fire for smithing and smelting. 15. Corridor to the director's house. *Second floor:* 16. First upper gallery for the goldsmith. 17. Living room for the goldsmith. 18. Stairs down into laboratory. 19. Gallery for the painters. 20. Living room for the painters. 21. Storage room. 22. Gallery for joiners and clockmakers. 23. Living room. 24. Room for the ribbon looms. 25. Gallery for weaving. 26. Room for carding wool. 27. The large weaving room. Österreichische Nationalbibliothek, Handschriften-Abteilung, Vienna, Ms. 8046.

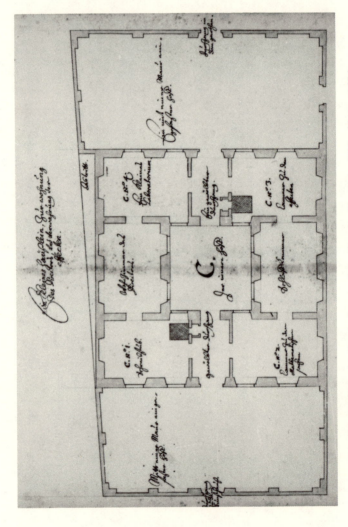

Figure 19. Floor plan for the house of the director, Kunst- und Werckhaus, 1676.
Österreichische Nationalbibliothek, Handschriften-Abteilung, Vienna, Ms. 8046.

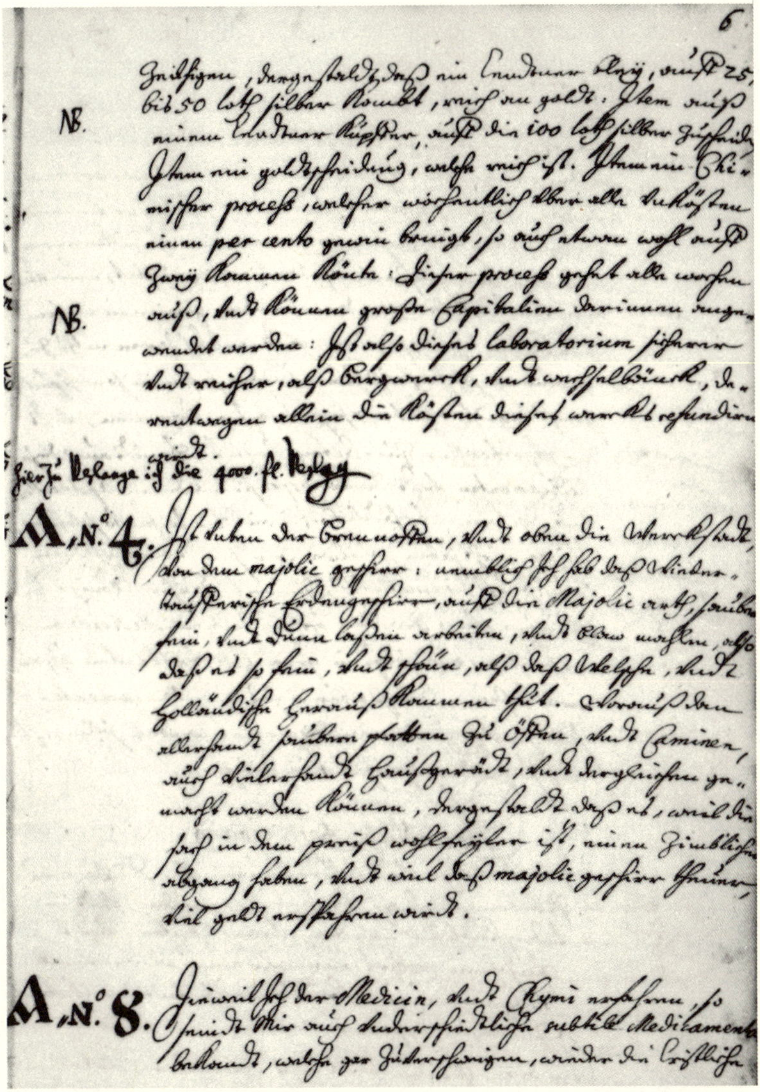

NB.

NB.

A. N° 4.

A. N° 8.

Figure 20. Becher's Marginalia to the Emperor, "NB" in left margin.
Kunsthaus Referat, 1676, fol. 6r. Österreichische Nationalbibliothek,
Handschriften-Abteilung, Vienna, Ms. 8046.

concern with 'goldmachen'" one of the entries.[77] Although an interest in alchemy on the part of the patron was useful for Becher's ends, the sole concern
with gold making could in fact harm them, for Becher had a larger political
agenda by which he hoped to draw the prince into the commercial world. As
was discussed in Chapter 3, he sought to change the values and actions of
the prince while retaining the language and symbols of the landed court world.
Becher sought to make alchemy serve as a means to this end, without allowing
it to become an end in itself.

Alchemy at the Habsburg Court

Alchemy had a long history of patronage at the Habsburg court by the time
Leopold took up the regalia of the emperor in 1658, and Becher's transmutation
can be located within this tradition. Rudolf II's interest in alchemy connected
the Habsburg name forever with occult practices, which later historians have
treated with more or less subtlety, ranging from near apoplectic outrage[78] to
sensitive nuance. R.J.W. Evans, in *Rudolf II and His World*, exemplifies the
latter. He locates the interest in alchemy at the Rudolfine court (1576–1612)
within an educated world view that sought an intellectual reconciliation between the contraries of the Catholic and Protestant confessions and among the
growing divisions in the territories of the Holy Roman Empire. This reconciliation was to be achieved through a metaphysical rendering of the multitude of
particulars in the temporal world into a unified and meaningful whole. Alchemy, in particular, provided a material demonstration of a superior power[79]
and made intelligible the generation and decay of the visible world by showing
these processes to be part of the divine plan. Moreover, it harnessed the power
that gave humankind the potential to change the world and, in the process, to
redeem itself. Humankind achieved its redemption by laboring within the natural world to sustain itself and to separate God's vital traces in the world from the
material dross that resulted from the Fall. Alchemy, as the imitator of nature,
demonstrated the processes by which the dross of matter could be separated
from pure essence and the redemption of humankind could come about. This
chiliastic component of alchemical activity fit into the irenical and unificatory
strivings of the Rudolfine imperial court.

The Thirty Years' War showed these contraries to be incapable of resolution
at this level. Thus in the Leopoldine court in the seventeenth century, the
educated occultism, of which alchemy was a part, took on a mainly "preserva-

---

[77] Other conditions were death, and a desire to monopolize the "scientz" for his own profit.
Kunsthaus Referat, annotations on fol. 19r.

[78] The classic statement of this approach was Henry C. Bolton, *The Follies of Science at the
Court of Rudolf II* (Milwaukee: Pharmaceutical Review Publishing, 1904).

[79] Evans, *Rudolf II*, pp. 212, 225.

tive" function in legitimating the imperial power of the Habsburg emperor. Instead of seeking to resolve the contraries into a unified whole, it simply sought to reinforce the symbols of power that preserved the emperor's place as center of the Counter-Reformation church and of the territories of the Holy Roman Empire.[80] Evans's framework encompasses Becher's transmutation of lead into silver in 1675, for the spectacle of alchemical transmutation was clearly a part of the culture of theater and representation at the Viennese court through which the symbols of Habsburg power were displayed. Alchemical transmutation confirmed the power and fitness of the Habsburg emperor's rule and proved the depth of his piety.

This assessment of alchemy at Emperor Leopold I's court overlooks, however, an essential aspect of the change that took place between the Rudolfine and the Leopoldine courts, which Becher's alchemy clearly illustrates. For on the surface, Becher's alchemy is indeed the chiliastic—and fundamentally Paracelsian—endeavor that absorbed the alchemical writers of the sixteenth and early seventeenth centuries. He draws from the Paracelsian sources and tradition, but his enterprise is no longer, or not immediately, the religious redemption of the world, but rather the maintenance of the symbols of power and, the point which Evans overlooks, the *manipulation* of these symbols in order to make comprehensible to the emperor the actual material sources of power that had become so necessary after the Thirty Years' War. These sources of power in late seventeenth-century Europe were manufactured wealth and money. While Becher's alchemical medallion fits into the court intrigues and the pursuit of patronage at the Viennese court, it can also be seen as the expression of a far deeper strategy through which he sought to equate the manufactured thing with the thing of nature; the productive potential of nature with that of art; the alchemist with the commercial advisor; and, finally, alchemy with commerce. To comprehend how Becher proposed to carry through this whole series of transmutations requires an analysis of his theory of chemical processes.

The Chemical World

The chemical laboratory was the locus of practice, the site where the meaning of "solve mihi hunc syllogismum" was played out. One of Becher's oldest projects for the laboratory was the production of chemicals for export as part of his commercial program to bring specie into the empire. This practical use of the chemical laboratory is readily apparent in the proposal for the Kunst- und Werckhaus, but Becher had had this in mind for more than a decade by 1676. He had built up a laboratory while in the service of the elector of Bavaria, the

---

[80] Evans, *The Making of the Habsburg Monarchy*, chap. 10.

fortunes of which can be followed in the record of court expenditures.[81] "Dr. Pecher's Laboratorium" first appears in the records in 1665,[82] and expenditures reached a high point in 1667 (after his return from Vienna).[83] In that same year Becher even hired a *Laborant* for the laboratory, and the contract between Becher and the worker, Michael Moser, specified that the *Laborant* would do his chemical and metallic "labores" industriously, loyally, honestly and silently, that he would not use the materials or the instruments for his own work or that of another, and that he would hold the knowledge and processes learned in the laboratory secret "bis in seine grüeben" (into his grave).[84] The nature of the processes to be carried out in this laboratory is indicated by one of Becher's first proprosals to the elector in which he considered the success of soapmaking, winemaking, potash, and saltpeter production to rest on the completion and outfitting of this chemical laboratory.[85] A commonplace about alchemy in the seventeenth century stated that even if gold did not result, many fine and useful things were nevertheless discovered while pursuing gold: "If they have found no gold, they have meanwhile discovered good medicaments and other admirable arts, not to mention gunpowder, glassmaking, enamel, dyes, medicines, and now the rediscovered eternally burning material [i.e., phosphorus]."[86] Becher's chemical laboratory had, however, more potential than simply a practical place in which useful and valuable goods were produced. It was a place where theory and practice were unified to yield material things.

According to Becher's testimony, the *Physica Subterranea* (1669) was the result of four years of work in the Munich laboratory.[87] When Becher dedicated the *Physica Subterranea* to his then patron, Ferdinand Maria, elector of

[81] BHA, Hofzahlamt Kurbayern, Hofzahlamtsrechnungen, nos. 113 (1664) to 119 (1671) (no. 118, 1670 is lost). These expenditures are listed s.v. "Allerlay aintzige Außgaben."

[82] When 173 gulden 60 pfennig was spent for various work done in the laboratory, glassware, and supplies from the *Materialisten*.

[83] When 685 gulden 60 pfennig were recorded, which was more than Becher's salary at the time (BHA, Hofzahlamt Kurbayern, Hofzahlamtsrechnungen, no. 114, 1665, fols. 484r, 488v, 489r, and no. 116, 1667, fols. 495r–502r). In 1667 Becher also received an extra 150 gulden a year for a scribe for the dictation of the *Physica Subterranea*. (BHA, HR II f. 247 [Besoldungsbücher], 1667, fol. 34v). In the preface, Becher says he dictated this book: "excuso latinitatem in hoc opere, quam barbaram esse fateor, ob materiam & ob scriptionem, in specie scriptionis modum, ex ore enim dictantis totum opus conceptum est, hinc rebus attentus verba neglexi" (Preface, 1669, C recto).

[84] This contract is inexplicably included in BHA GL F2646/179, a file of correspondence entitled, "Die Correspondenz unterschiedener Handlsleute mit dem Hr. Geheim Sekretario Begnudelli wegen . . . Seidenfabriquen . . . 1668–1671." The contract ends: "abgefast den 29. Marty 1667. In meiner Hr. Dr. Bechers anwesenheyth."

[85] Mss. var. 1(3), fols. 216r–217v.

[86] Becher, *Psychosophia*, (1705), pp. 140–41. See also Becher, *Philosophischer Beweisthum*, p. 14.

[87] Translated as "Acts of the chemical laboratory in Munich, or two books of subterranean physics." On the last day of 1667 Becher finished the first draft of this book, his largest chemical work. The 1667 draft, "Laboratorium Naturae Subterraneum, daß ist Werckstatt der Natur under der Erden," eventually became the *Physica Subterranea*. The draft is in Mss. var. 1(1), fols. 155r–192r. The draft (in some places a mere outline) and the published work differ substantially, not only

Bavaria, he made clear to the prince that in supporting the study of natural things he could make radiant the glory of his reign and court. Becher promised Ferdinand Maria that he would, like his father the previous elector, go down in history with the reputation of "Aller-Weisesten" and the name of German Solomon[88] for giving patronage to scholars in all areas of learning, but especially in chemistry. In the *Physica Subterranea*, Becher promised not the manufacture of gold but rather knowledge about the nature of "made" gold ("verspricht nicht des Goldes Factur/ sondern des gemachten Goldes Natur"). The support of the investigation of the nature of things was "truly like Solomon, truly royal, and truly altruistic."[89] But the study of natural objects in the laboratory should also be patronized because it yielded knowledge "highly necessary not only for science, but also for civic industry."[90]

For Becher, as for most of his contemporaries, chemistry was both an art, learned by work with the hands, and a discipline, learned by the study of books ("die *Chymie* ist zugleich ein Handwerck/ und zugleich ein *Studium*").[91] It was an eminently practical art, involving all the senses—skilled hands, sharp eyes, smell, taste, and touch—and it resulted in useful inventions.[92] Chemistry was a mechanical art, but it was simultaneously part of the realm of the liberal arts as a part of physics. It yielded *theoria*, natural knowledge of the most profound sort, for it dealt with the creation, generation, and the passing away of the things of nature, and brought understanding of divine Creation. Hermes, the legendary discoverer of chemistry was considered the inventor and articulator of both the liberal and mechanical arts, for chemistry unified theory and practice in a universal knowledge that incorporated all the arts and knowledge necessary for the survival and salvation of humankind after the Fall.[93]

---

in purpose (the draft seems to have had a much more practical orientation) but also in content—the famous theory of three earths, although present in the draft, was differently conceived, with the "terra lapidea" (Kalck-erden), "terra pinguis" (sulfuric), and "terra fluida" (mercurial earth) of the book appearing as the "Saltz-Erde" (substance), the "Schwefel-Erde," and a "Kalck-Erde" (which contributes fluidity) in the draft.

[88] Becher translated the *Physica Subterranea* with its three supplements into German in 1680, under the title *Chymisches Laboratorium, oder Unter-erdische Naturkündigung* (Frankfurt: Johann Haaß, 1680). I will cite this translation of the work, unless otherwise noted, although I continue to call it *Physica Subterranea* in the text. *Physica Subterranea*, Dedication, A2v.

[89] "welches Tuns (nemlich der Dinge Natur untersuchen) Beförderung recht Salomonisch, recht königlich/ recht leutselig ist." *Physica subterranea*, Dedication, A7v.

[90] *Physica Subterranea*, p. 9: "wann man fleissiger überlegte/ so würde dieser Lehr entweder Nutz/ oder Nothwendigkeit niemand verborgen seyn/ der nicht festiglich daher schliesse/ dieses sey nicht nur zur Wissenschafft/ sondern auch zum bürgerlichen Gewerck hochnothwendig."

[91] Becher, *Chymischer Glücks-Hafen*, p. 791, and *Natur-Kündingung*, pp. 159–61ff.

[92] The chemist tasted and smelled the chemicals to test their qualities. In *Oedipus Chymicus*, p. 86, Becher noted that mercurial sulfur colors and flecks the teeth. Becher complained several times about the physical danger of chemical work.

[93] Not all practitioners agreed on the cosmic significance of alchemy and chemistry in the seventeenth century. A university scholar and teacher such as Guerner Rolfinck saw chemistry as not moving outside its use in medicine. He stated categorically that chemistry "Non tamen est ars peculiarus, sed medicinae pars" (is not a separate art, but a part of medicine); Guerner Rolfinck,

Becher had investigated the *theoria* of chemistry for almost two decades before publishing the *Physica Subterranea* in 1669. He considered work in the laboratory to be primarily a search for knowledge about the generation, growth, and change that minerals and metals undergo. He called it a "natural history of the metals, how to mature, improve, and transmute them; this is called Studium Mineralogia, Spagyrica or alchemy."[94] For Becher, however, this was just one element of the work in a laboratory, for chemistry and alchemy could extend to all three realms of nature. He followed other Paracelsian chemists in viewing laboratory work as a search for the principle of creation, generation, and growth in its broadest sense.[95] Such a search is evident in Becher's earliest published work of 1654. *Solini Saltzthals Regiomontani Discurs von der Großmächtigen Philosophischen Universal-Artzney/ von den Philosophis genannt Lapis Philosophorum Trismegistus* dealt with the preparation and effects of the philosophers' stone—the principle of generation—in the three realms of nature.[96] In many ways, this work was a typical alchemical pamphlet, promising much, but leaving out crucial details, for, Becher claimed, "the curse of the philosophers,

Chimia in artis formam redacta, sex libris comprehensa (Jena: Samuel Krebs, 1661), p. 28. Rolfinck was vehemently opposed to the alchemical world view (see, for example, his view on the correspondence between the microcosm and macrocosm, p. 7, and his opinion on the authenticity of the Hermetic texts, p. 7). Becher publicly called into question the chemistry of Rolfinck.

Allen Debus, *The Chemical Philosophy*, 2 vols. (New York: Science History Publications, 1977); Hélène Metzger, *Les doctrines chimiques en France du début du XVIIe à la fin du XVIIIe siècle* (Paris: Albert Blanchard, 1923); and Betty J. T. Dobbs, *The Foundations of Newton's Alchemy or, "The Hunting of the Greene Lyon"* (Cambridge: Cambridge University Press, 1975), provide general overviews of chemical activity in the seventeenth century. More recently, in a discussion of the textual tradition upon which Robert Boyle drew, Jan Victor Golinski, "Language, Method and Theory in British Chemical Discourse, c. 1660–1770" (Ph.D. diss., University of Leeds, 1984), summarizes the different chemical traditions existing in the seventeenth century. Jost Weyer, *Chemiegeschichtsschreibung von Weigleb (1790) bis Partington (1970)* (Hildesheim: Verlag Dr. H. A. Gerstenberg, 1974), provides a good summary of different trends in the historiography of chemistry and alchemy.

[94] "Naturkündigung der Metallen/ dieselbige zu zeitigen/ zu verbessern/ und zu verwandeln/ welches *Studium Mineralogia, Spagyrica* oder Alchymie genennet wird." *Psychosophia* (1705), p. 135.

[95] For Paracelsus, generation was the "universal process dominating nature, inorganic as well as organic." Pagel, *Paracelsus*, p. 115. For background to this view, see William R. Newman, *The Summa Perfectionis of Pseudo-Geber* (Leiden: E. J. Brill, 1991). Becher drew on traditional alchemical texts and sources that were published in numerous editions and found in the great alchemical collections, such as the five volumes of the *Theatrum Chemicum* (Strasbourg, 1602–61). Becher noted the *Theatrum Chemicum* in a list of chemical works, presumably for his own consultation, written ca. 1659 (Mss. var. 2, fol. 262r–v). Other such collections included the *Bibliotheca Chemica* (1653) of Nathan Albineus, the *Turba Philosophorum* (1613) edited by Philipp Morgenstern, and the *Verae Alchemiae Artisque Metallicae, citra Aenigmata, Doctrina* (1561) of Guglielmo Gratarolo.

[96] This work is separated into three books, and each discusses the different philosophers' stone that belongs to each of the realms of nature. Each of these stones is associated in some way with heat, while disease and corruption are caused by an excess or lack of heat. Becher supported this view by citing Hippocrates' dictum that death is the absence of heat.

[the common man's] misuse and the obvious simplicity of this science ha[d] sealed [his] mouth, and prevented a practical explanation." In place of explanation, therefore, he could provide only hints and veiled language about the principle of generation in each of the three realms. He maintained that all bodies contained their own seeds, which are made from a "flüchtig und fixen materia," a mix of the mercuric and sulfuric principles.[97]

In concluding his theoretical discussion, Becher set down an allegorical dream that he assured his readers made clear to initiates of chemistry the process for the preparation of the philosophers' stone. The dream began with Becher setting out from the city "Ignorantia" in a boat called "Ratio" with oars named "Oratione" and "Labore." He arrived at a mountain, from which flowed a mineral spring called "mercurius duplicatus universalis & Microcosmicus," which watered a kingdom, "Terra," surrounding it. The water from this spring caused the growth of animals, plants, and minerals, and every year a few hundred centner of gold could be harvested from the earth of the kingdom.[98] Becher's dream illustrates a theory of generation that posited a generative principle common to all the realms of nature that ripened metals and caused growth. This generative principle was most effectively and strikingly captured by the chemist in the transmutation of base metals into gold—the art of the alchemist thus imitating generation and growth in nature.

The search for generative principles and substances is evident in the various alchemical tracts and projects of Becher's early years but is especially prominent in Becher's first chemical work published under his own name, *Natur-Kündigung der Metallen* (Natural philosophy of metals), in 1661. In this work he promised to set out both the theory and practice of chemistry rather than to provide simply another "recipe book" ("*Process*-Buch").[99] Drawing on various alchemical authorities, Becher set out the principles of the "conception" and "birth" of minerals by impregnation of the earth with the mineral vapors of mineral springs. A subtile, sulfurous, salty substance formed the nutriment that caused growth in the animal, vegetable, and mineral realms. By capturing this principle by art, the chemist assisted and impelled nature to complete the process of growth in metals.[100] In this, as in other works, Becher drew on analogies between generation and growth in the animal and vegetable realms in order to explain these processes in the mineral kingdom. Becher concluded this

---

[97] "Der Philosophorum Fluch/ euer Mißbrauch/ und offenbahre simplicitet dieser scientz aber/ haben mir ein Siegel auf meinen Mund gedruckt/ nicht mehrers practicè davon zuschreiben," *Solini Saltzthals . . . Discurs*, bk. 2, unpaginated.

[98] Ibid., bk. 3.

[99] *Natur-Kündigung*, Vorrede, iii verso. Becher claimed that he had been inspired by Bernhardus to read first and "solchen *Process-Clamanten* zu widerstehen/ und dieses mein Buch mit *Rationibus* und *Experimentis* so viel von nöthen/ zu bewahren" (Vorrede, v recto).

[100] In this work Becher also explained that metals are homogeneous in material and made up of pores and "atomos." These pores close when cooled and dilate when heated. The entrance of air into the opened pores accounts for the melting of metals when heated.

book, too, with the account of an allegorical dream, which records the progress of his thought between 1654 and 1661. In this dream, a *Liebhaber* of alchemy resolves to give up alchemy for beer brewing (fermentation of beer was analogous to metallic transmutation), but he falls asleep and Saturn appears to him in a dream. Saturn begins to explain the preparation for the philosophers' stone, but before he can finish, the alchemist is suddenly awakened by his wife. The would-be beer brewer returns to the laboratory where he spends the rest of his days, albeit without success.[101]

In this early work, Becher continued to draw parallels between the mineral and vegetable realms, but, more significantly, he appears in this dream of beer brewer turned alchemist to be on the verge of making a connection between alchemy and civic life. He had not yet settled on the view he eventually took at the Habsburg court that alchemy and chemistry were part of the civic sphere, for in this 1661 dream, the alchemist hovers between the contemplative life of theory and the most typical of civic activities, beer brewing. In the end, he does not give up private and contemplative activity in the laboratory for civic life. However, the presence of his wife—perhaps personifying civic life—who had woken him before Saturn could reveal the process for the tincture, caused the lack of success that attended his subsequent alchemical labors. This allegory reveals the tension in Becher's thought at this time between alchemy as a project of cosmic redemption and one of civic industry. To the end of his life, he would claim that the chemist was called to his work by God,[102] but his chemical work (and his alchemical allegories) would become increasingly concerned with material production.

Throughout the 1660s, Becher's works continued to emphasize the concern of chemistry with the generative principles in all three realms of nature. In 1664, he published the *Institutiones Chimicae Prodromae i.e. . . . . Oedipus Chimicus. Obscuriorum Terminorum & Principiorum Chimicorum, Mysteria Aperiens & resolvens*, in which he expounded the three parts of the Hermetic philosophy: "Scheidekunst" consisted in the knowledge of breaking things down into their ingredients and recombining them in order to use them for the other two parts, namely, "Chymia" and "Alchymia." Chymia taught about the vital fluids, their composition and the method of their analysis, purification, and perfection; all knowledge necessary for medicine and for the generation of things. Thus Chymia dealt with all three realms: animal, vegetable, and mineral, while Alchymia dealt only with the mineral realm, and within that, only with the metals.[103]

A fuller depiction of the knowledge of natural things that could be gained through work in the laboratory came in the *Physica Subterranea* (1669), the most comprehensive of Becher's chemical works (figure 21). In this book,

[101] Becher, *Natur-Kündigung*, pp. 294ff.
[102] Becher, *Chymischer Glücks-Hafen*, p. 28.
[103] Becher, *Oedipus Chymicus*, p. 152.

Figure 21. Frontispiece to Becher's *Physica Subterranea*, 1669. Mother Nature with the sun as her head holds the terraqueous globe in her lap. The globe contains the "three workshops of nature"—animal, vegetable, and mineral—in which generation occurs.

Becher set out a theory of subterranean physics that established the principles of coming to be and passing away in the mineral kingdom. In doing so, he followed Paracelsus and Joan Baptista van Helmont in attempting to supplant the philosophy of Aristotle with a chemical cosmology.[104] Becher began the work with a "natural philosophical" explanation of the words of Genesis, in which he claims that the chemical principles of generation and corruption originated at God's creation of the cosmos.[105] The elements of Genesis— water, earth, air and spirit—are posited as the basis for all *physis* (change) on the terrestrial globe. Water and earth form the basic materials of all things in the three great dominions of nature, and different mixtures of these two elements account for the external forms and qualities of material things.[106] Becher moved from the processes of the Creation to the form of the terrestrial globe by which these processes had been continued through history. The processes of the terrestrial world were explained as generation, mixture, and corruption.[107]

The *Physica subterranea* and Becher's other works provide an understanding of the nature of Becher's chemical investigations, and the animistic conception of nature that underlay them. Fundamental to this conception was the unity of nature (both between and within the three great realms). The constant circulation of a universal spirit, deriving ultimately from God, unified nature: there was "in Nature an omnipresent, conserving essence . . . whence comes the spirit, force, and life of all bodies."[108] This humid essence, spread throughout the air, caused fermentation in the vegetable realm, was inhaled and mixed with

---

[104] For a general description of this chemical cosmology, see, for example, Metzger, *Les doctrines chimiques*; Debus, *The Chemical Philosophy*; and Kathleen Winnifred Fowler Ahonen, "Johann Rudolph Glauber: A Study of Animism in Seventeenth-Century Chemistry" (Ph.D. diss., University of Michigan, Ann Arbor, 1972), esp. pp. 275–76.

[105] This was neither a unique use of Genesis nor a unique view of chemical processes—for example, one of Becher's frequent sources, Josephus Quercetanus (Joseph du Chesne), *Ad veritatem Hermeticae medicinae ex Hippocratis veterumque decretis ac Therpeusi* . . . (Paris: Abrahamus Savgrain, 1604), chap. 15, pp. 184ff., explained how the account of Creation in Genesis provided information about the three principles. Another of Becher's frequently cited sources was Gerhard Dorn, who in his "De medio Spagirico Dispositionis . . . Hermetis Trismegisti. Cum expositionibus Gerardi Dorn," p. 362, in *Theatrum Chemicum*, vol. 1, 1602, ed. Lazarus Zetzner, claims that "Spagiricum artificium docetur meditatione creationis mundi" (Spagirical artifice is taught by meditation on the creation of the world). Another source for Becher was the "Rosarium der Philosophorum" in *Turba Philosophorum*, pt. 2, p. 191, where the following verse is found: "Wer unsern künstlichen Stein will bawen/ Der soll auff den anfang der Natur schawen."

[106] *Physica Subterranea*, pp. 52–53. Becher's elaboration of three earths—*terra pinguis, terra lapidea, terra fluida*—comes out of this theory.

[107] These subjects—creation, the form of the world, generation, mixture, and corruption— form the five main sections of the book. In the remaining two sections Becher attempted a classification of all subterranean things.

[108] There is "in der Natur ein durchgehendes erhaltenes Wesen . . . daher aller Leiber Geist/ Krafft und Leben kommet"; *Experimentum Chymicum Novum: Oder Neue Chymische Prob, Worinnen die künstliche gleich-darstellige Transmutation, oder Verwandelung/ derer Metallen/ augenscheinlich dargethan* (Becher's translation of his 1671 supplement to *Physica Subterranea* [Frankfurt: Johann Haaß, 1680]), p. 75.

the blood to sustain life in the animal realm, and brought about alchemical transmutation.[109] The universal spirit was more copiously present in the air of the tropics and the New World (hence the more verdant growth of these climes), existed in mineral springs and the vapors of the mines (*Bergwitterung*), and could be obtained and used by the chemist through his art.[110] The belief in the existence of such an essence was the basis for the analogy that Becher drew between the animal, vegetable, and mineral kingdoms, according to which minerals were considered to grow like seeds in the earth and could be ripened and harvested like grain. Generation of the minerals took place in the same way that a kernel of grain grew: it first "rotted" in the matrix of the earth, returning to its *prima materia*, and then was regenerated.[111] Heat—fire, light, and the warmth of the sun—was necessary to all processes of change in nature, just as the light of Creation had separated day from night and set into motion the process of Time.

According to this understanding of the cosmos, art was the imitator of these natural processes. It could speed up or complete the processes of change that occurred in nature. Knowledge of these natural processes was gained by means of the imitation of nature in the art of the laboratory. Becher called nature an underground laboratory ("unter-Erdisches Laboratorium") that provided the model for art, the above-ground laboratory ("ober-Erdisches Laboratorium").[112] Theoretical knowledge of nature was gained by working with one's hands in the laboratory, and the fire of the laboratory furnaces—analogous to the warmth of the sun—was the primary way of bringing about generation and growth by art. For Becher, then, work in the laboratory represented a search for the principles of generation, and an attempt to imitate these natural processes by art.[113]

[109] This spirit, according to Becher's paraphrase of Hermes, was "Eine Feuchtigkeit; eine Feuchtigkeit/ sage ich/ in welcher aller Gestirn schwefflichte und saltzigte/ feurige und wässerige Influentzen und Einflüsse/ mit dem Band der allersubtilsten Erdenheit/ durch eine süsse Zäheit verknüpffet/ und überall zu finden seyn. Dann so wahr/ und solang ein Cörper erhalten wird; so wahr/ und solang/ dringet er mit diesem Wesen hervor: und so wahr die Sonn diese Welt bescheinet/ so wahr ist dieser lebliche Geist ein Brunnquell und Ursprung des Lebens/ und aller Erzeugung. Diß ist der jenige Geist/ der da in der Lufft wohnend/ auch alle Gewürme der Erden belebet/ dere Flüsse Wasser gähren macht . . . der in den Adern das Blut beweget und färbet; in den Mineren Metallen herfürbringt/ an *vegetabili*en und Erdgewächsen in die Blüt und Frucht außwächst: allen alles in allem: der in den Wolken donnert/ regnet/ schneyet/ in der Erden wächst/ blüet/ keimet; in den Thieren lebendig machet/ verändert/ *digerirt*; in den Mineren rachet/ durchdringet/ *figirt*; der/ durch Kunst angewendet/ das Leben erhält/ Kranckheiten heylet/ die Metallen verwandelt; in *Volati*lischen *volati*lisch/ in Fixen fix/ in Thieren thierisch in *Vegetabili*schen *vegetabili*sch; in Mineralischen mineralisch/ ein Philosophischer *Chamaeleon* in allen aber einer vollkommenen Natur/ einer gantz durchdringender Eigenschafft/ gantz subtilen Gehalts" (*Neue Chymische Prob*, pp. 81–82).

[110] Becher, *Natur-Kündigung*, pp. 170–75.

[111] For the clearest statement of this, see *Physica Subterranea*, pp. 30–39, 49–50, and passim.

[112] Ibid., p. 2.

[113] *Neue Chymische Prob*, chap. 5, proved the existence of this substance and "how one can obtain this substance through art" (p. 75).

The work of the laboratory was also a manner of philosophizing, one in which real, material things were manipulated. Becher considered this new manner of philosophizing to be a rediscovery of his own era. He explained that his own century was stranger than any other, for many new inventions and discoveries had been made. Kings had fallen and all of Europe had burned with the flames of war. The sciences had been renewed, and many different types of philosophizing ("varia Philosophandi genera") had developed. One of the methods rediscovered in this renewal was a manner of philosophizing even older than that of Aristotle. This was *Chymia*, articulated first by Hermes, the prince of philosophers, which dealt not in empty words, but in real things; not in chimerical terms or immaterial faculties, but in demonstrated effects and practical causes. It resulted in knowledge gained by "hearing, seeing, and touching."[114]

Becher contrasted the type of explanation gained by "Aristotelisch zu philosophiren" and "Chymisch zu philosophiren." The advantage of the latter was that one understood the causes of things (theory) and simultaneously gained knowledge of material things (practice), rather than simply spouting empty words, which Becher claimed was characteristic of Aristotelian philosophizing.[115] He considered chemical activity such an important method of philosophizing that he thought it should be taught in a special "Collegium Spagyricum" within a university, where "everything [will] be explained and discussed according to reason and experience in the auditorium as well as in the laboratory."[116]

This view of chemistry was also shared by Becher's contemporary, Nicolas Lefebvre, who stated that "Chymia is an effective and active [literally, "doing and working"] science of natural things" ("eine thuende und arbeitende Wissenschafft der natürlichen Dinge"). Although Lefebvre's chemical practice was largely confined to the art of the apothecary, his view of the material knowledge to be gained by this practice was as explicit as Becher's:

> The difference between a chemical physician and one who learned his physics in the higher schools is that the former, when asked the composition of an object, will not only answer your question with words, but also answer it by showing the parts of the object to your eyes and other senses; he will set out the parts that compose the object for you to taste, smell and touch.

In contrast, the schoolman would contentiously respond to a question about the composition of bodies with the answer "that such things are not yet completely decided [by disputations] in the schools."[117] The material, tangible results of

---

[114] *Institutiones Chimicae Prodromae*, Dedication to Francis de la Boë, Sylvius.

[115] *Oedipus Chymicus*, p. 154.

[116] "nach der Vernunfft/ und der Erfahrung/ sowol in dem *Auditorio* als dem *Laboratorio*, zu erklären/ und zu erörtern/ nichts erwinden lassen" (ibid., p. 156).

[117] "Daß solches in den Schulen noch nicht gantz beschlossen." From the German translation of the 1660 French text by Lefebvre, entitled *Chymischer Handleiter/ und Guldnes kleinod: Das ist:*

the chemist were here contrasted to the sterile and ineffective methods and results of the schools. As Becher saw it, it was clear to all that the Aristotelian philosophy "has as many doctors and masters as beggar children singing at night under the windows, and they do not make enough in a whole year with their philosophy to buy even a single meal."[118] It is revealing of Becher's later use of alchemy that he here measured the effectiveness of a method of philosophizing by its ability to produce hard cash.

Chemistry and alchemy gave an understanding of the material composition of natural objects and the processes that involved these objects. The significance of such a material understanding for the manufacture of things and the production of material wealth is made clear in a passage in Becher's Kunsthaus Referat. In discussing the glassworks where Venetian glass was to be produced, he stated that two things are to be considered in the production of this glass, the form and the material. The form is beautiful, but

> made in such a way that it cannot be communicated to this land except by a long period of apprenticeship, for it is an art and consists in work of the hand. If these Italians [who operated the glassworks] should die or go away, the art will go together with their hands, and this territory thus will not have been served. Therefore, it would be a good thing to find out [literally, "get behind"] the correct preparation of the material of the Venetian glass.[119]

Only through chemistry could one gain a knowledge both of material objects and of the principles of generation by which tangible, material things could be produced.

Alchemy and Commerce

The conceptions of generation and material productivity Becher developed in his (al)chemical work informed both his chemical projects in the laboratory and his commercial projects at court. They formed the backdrop to the commercial and alchemical reports he presented to the emperor in May 1674. A comparison of these two reports, the "Referat wie die Commercien . . . verschaffen seye" (Report on how commerce is constituted) and "Gutachten über Herrn Daniels Marsaly Process zur Tinctur" (Adjudication on Daniel Marsaly's preparation of

---

Richtige Anführung/ und deutliche Unterweisung/ so wol/ wie man die Chymische Schrifften/ welche von Chymischer Wissenschaft ins gemein handeln/ recht verstehen/ als/ wie man nach ihrer Ordnung/ solche Chymische Kunst/ durch wirckliche Operation, leicht und glücklich practiciren (Nuremberg: Christoph Endter, 1676), Zweyter Vorbericht, unpaginated. See Owen Hannaway's article on Lefebvre, *Dictionary of Scientific Biography*, and Metzger, *Les doctrines chimiques*.

[118] "Hat so viel *Doctores* und *Magistros*, als bey nah Bettelbuben Nachts bey den Fenstern singen/ und mit ihrer *Philosophia* ein gantzes Jahr nicht so viel gewinnen, daß sie nur darvon eine Mahlzeit zahlen können" (*Physica Subterranea*, p. 90).

[119] This glass could then be used for many types of products. Kunsthaus Referat, fol. 15v.

the tincture), makes clear Becher's manipulation of these conceptions in order to convince his patron of the importance of commerce and money.

Becher begins what I will call the Commercial Referat by listing the components of good "Policey" (i.e., good government):

> Next to preservation of religion, administration of justice, protection of the lands through sufficient soldiers, good relations with neighbors and foreigners, trade and commerce as well as the populousness and the sufficient sustenance of the subjects are the sole goal and basis of good government.[120]

Becher considered himself unfit to advise on the first four points, but the last two were germane to his "profession [medicine] and vocation [Commercien-Rath]" because they dealt with sustenance of the human population and trade in general. Thus he would concentrate in the Commercial Referat on these aspects of government.

The opening section of the Commercial Referat is remarkably similar to the opening of the second report, called here the Alchemical Gutachten; in it Becher summarized his thesis, expounded at greater length in the *Moral Discurs*, that because humans are made in the image of God, they take on five characteristics derived ultimately from the attributes of God: desire for perfection (derived from God's perfection), desire to live a virtuous life (from His complete virtue), the attempt to be learned in all sciences (from His omniscience), the desire for wealth and the power that flows from it (from His omnipotence), and the desire to live long and healthy lives (from His eternal existence).[121] Chemistry dealt with the last two attributes of humankind and thus constituted a natural and virtuous search for "Nahrung" (sustenance, livelihood) or "Reichthumb" (wealth) and "Gesundheit" (health).[122] Thus, alchemy itself was natural and virtuous because of its capacity to improve the *salus publici*, and, because it sought sustenance, health, and wealth, it could properly be called a part of the practice of healing in both politics and medicine. Both the Commercial Referat and the Alchemical Gutachten, then, draw on Becher's own idiosyncratic reading of the dictum "salus populi suprema lex esto" as the rule of the doctor and commercial advisor to pursue health and the furtherance of human welfare by the creation of material wealth.

Becher considered the cycle of production and consumption in commerce and alchemy to be the same, and both to result in material increase. The

---

[120] "Referat wie die Commercien . . . verschaffen seye . . ." (Ms. 12467, f. 2r; hereafter cited as Commercial Referat).

[121] "Gutachten über Herrn Daniels Marsaly Process zur Tinctur" (Ms. 11472, fols. 3v–4r; hereafter cited as Alchemical Gutachten).

[122] Becher referred the reader to his *Moral Discurs* (1669) for a full elaboration of his theory, and said that he only mentions this schema in an alchemical report in order to demonstrate that "unter Anderen vorgemelten Legibus natura, Reichthumb, und Gesundheit zu haben, und zu verlangen, an sich selbsten keine böse Sach, sonderen Eingewurtzelte Fünklein deß Göttlichen Ebenbildneß seyen" (Alchemical Gutachten, fol. 4v).

commercial report invoked the productive cycle of commerce by which society was sustained, and listed the ways in which the three productive estates comprising peasants, artisans, and merchants were improperly protected, supported, and administered by princes, as well as the ways in which the requisites of trade—markets, tolls, patents, and manufactures—were improperly overseen.[123] As with Becher's previous commercial projects, the purpose of the governmental regulation of commerce was to enable the peasant to "versilbern" his natural products.[124] In pursuing this aim, Becher believed that attention must first be directed toward foreign consumption of domestically manufactured goods and then toward domestic consumption. Both types of consumption would bring a maximum of money into the cycle among peasant, artisan, merchant, and ruler.[125] Becher took pains to establish the fact that consumption of material products actually increased the amount of money in this cycle of production. He gave a vivid illustration of the paradoxical nature of this process by relating a story about Queen Elizabeth and the English woolworkers. He recounted that the queen herself had to become a "Verläger" (putting-out merchant) in order to stop the export of raw wool out of England and the subsequent loss of bullion in the buying back of foreign-made woolen textiles. She bought up the raw wool, sold it to the weavers, then bought back the finished lengths from them. In time, the artisans had sold so many lengths to the queen, Becher claimed, that they became fearful that she would put a stop to production. In order to quell these fears, the queen had more than a million lengths of woven wool burned in a public square, saying, "consider these lengths as already consumed. Work industriously for me, and I will find the means."[126]

Becher's explanation of the process of alchemical transmutation in the alchemical report parallels this description of the process of commercial consumption. Transmutation was also a process of regeneration through destruction, and he compared it to the natural process by which a kernel of grain grew and multiplied into many more ripe kernels. The seed first disintegrated in the nutritive matrix of the earth into its *prima materia*. The universal generative force in nature then regenerated and ripened the kernel to grow into the stalk of

---

[123] Commercial Referat, fols. 12r–16r.

[124] Ibid., fol. 17r.

[125] Ibid., fols. 17r–18r. Becher explicitly stated that *Kleiderordnungen* should not limit luxury but rather the consumption of foreign products. It would be much better, he said, if everyone were allowed to wear silk clothes that had to be replaced four times a year, so long as the production of the silk and the manufacture of the clothes were domestic manufactures (fol. 18v).

[126] "Diese Tücher seind schon consumirt; Arbeitet mir fleißig darauf ich will schon Mittel finden" (ibid., fol. 44r). Becher's brother-in-law, Philipp Wilhelm von Hörnigk, in *Oesterreich über alles, wann es nur will* (publ. anonymously in 1684), pp. 168–69, used this example in a different way. He claimed that Elizabeth had raw wool burned in order to show the merchants of her own country and the artisans of other countries (who she hoped would migrate to England to work the wool) that she meant neither to create a personal monopoly of the wool nor to suggest that her resolve to ban the export of raw wool was to be taken lightly.

grain, and, finally, the heat of the sun ripened the stalk into a multitude of kernels. This natural process of regeneration, which resulted in material increase, was the basis of the agricultural labor that sustained human society. In the metals, too, the seeds of gold were destroyed by reduction to the *prima materia* before being regenerated and ripened by the philosophical tincture (the universal spirit). Finally, through the heat of fire, the augmentation of mature, corporeal gold was achieved.[127] This process of the generation of noble metal through primary destruction, or consumption, paralleled Queen Elizabeth's burning of the woven lengths. The consumption, and in this exemplary case, *destruction by fire*, of the worked wool led to a continued production of a nobler, refined material—bullion—that would ensure the maintenance of human civilization. This paradox of regeneration through consumption or destruction was redolent in biblical and natural imagery. The image of the redemption of the world lay behind these images of material increase: the single kernel of grain ripening into an entire harvest, the transmutation of base metals into valuable gold, and the raw wool being worked into the clothes of fallen humankind. Becher's interpretation of this image was not primarily at a religious level, but rather at the mundane and temporal level of material things, their production, and their place within the exchange economy. The religious imagery and the cosmic project of redemption resonated, however, at the Habsburg court. By talking about the paradoxical nature of commercial consumption in natural terms, and by juxtaposing this discussion with an explanation of the processes of alchemical consumption and regeneration, Becher sought to legitimate and make understandable the nature of artificial commercial wealth and profit. It was by the use of such images and the symbols contained within them that Becher made comprehensible to the emperor the world of objects, material production, and commercial profit.

In recounting the story of Queen Elizabeth and her woolworkers, Becher also sought to establish that the function of *Verläger* was suitable for those of noble blood, and that trade and commerce were honest sources of artificial wealth, worthy of a Christian ruler. He listed the king of France and the grand duke of Tuscany, as well as the States General of Holland as governors who had presided personally over the commerce of their countries.[128] Trade, Becher claimed, was "the correct means, in a legitimate way, to fish money and 'taxes' out of other people's lands. Holland and France know this very well, for up until now the whole world has paid 'taxes' to them."[129]

---

[127] Becher printed the second section (fols. 11r–55v) of the Alchemical Gutachten, entitled "Doctor Bechers Philosophisches Gutachten über die Philosophische Tinctur," as Articles 1–4 of "Doctor Bechers Philosophisches Gutachten" in the *Chymischer Glücks-Hafen*, pp. 26–73. Becher elaborated this process of alchemical generation on pp. 29–39. Hereafter, I refer to the pagination of the printed version in the *Chymischer Glücks-Hafen*.

[128] Commercial Referat, fols. 44r, 56r, 57r.

[129] "Der Rechte modus, Ehrlicherweiß, auß anderer Leuten Länder, gelt zu fischen, und contributiones zu nehmen, daß weiß Holland, und Frankreich wohl, welchen beyden bis dato noch die gantze Welt contribuirt hat" (ibid., fol. 57r).

In the same kind of language, Becher sought to show that alchemy too was an honest pursuit within the civic sphere. He began the alchemical report with an "Encomium Chymiae":

the most noble art of chymia preserves a healthy person from disease, cures the sick, rescues the pauper from poverty, assists nature, discovers hidden things, imbues the soul with true science, does harm to no one, benefits all, and leads to the very knowledge of God.[130]

Like commerce, this activity would injure no one, benefit the entire community, and was worthy of a prince. The intentions of the prince who pursued alchemy must be pure, and should not arise out of "greed, pride, carnal pleasures, oppression of the poor, unnecessary war, subjection of others," but must, rather, spring out of a desire for the

honor of God, preservation of the Catholic church, extension of Christianity, suppression of traditional enemies, liberation of Christian prisoners, relief of the subjects from heavy head and ground taxes, assistance of the poor, of the widowed, of orphaned and unmarried women, protection of the land and its people, and preservation of peace.[131]

Possession of the tincture would free the prince from all need to burden his subjects with heavy taxes. This noble goal was the precise aim of Becher's commercial program as well.

Moreover, both the commercial program of manufacturing and alchemy needed the direction of the prince, for merchants and guild craftsmen were as notoriously selfish as alchemists. In fact, if everyone had alchemical knowledge, society would completely break down, for it would make individuals independent of one another, and they would no longer be held together by the system of interlocking needs and dependencies that made up a society. Moreover, if everyone's time was spent in making gold, no one would attend to the trades necessary for civilized life, such as shoemaking and bread baking.[132]

As we have seen, Becher wrote the Commercial Referat primarily as an attempt to revive the Commercial Council. One of Becher's central efforts in resuscitating this body was obtaining for the council a hierarchy of officers

[130] "Nobilissima ars Chymia, hominem sanum a morbis praeservat, aegrum sanitat, restituit pauperem ab inopia, sublevat naturam, abdita eruit, Animum solida scientia imbuit, nulli iniuriam facit, omnibus prodest, et tandem ad ipsam Dei cognitionem adducit" (Alchemical Gutachten, fol. 14).

[131] "Geiz/ Hochmuth/ Wollust/ Unterdruckung der Armen/ unnöhtigen Krieg/ Beherrschung anderer" and "Ehren Gottes/ Erhaltung der Catholischen Kirch/ Erweiterung der Christenheit/ Unterdruckung des Erbfeinds/ Erlösung der Christlichen Gefangenen/ Erleichterung seiner Unterthanen von der schwären *Contribution*, Haußsteur/ Armen/ Witwen/ Waisen/ und Jungfrauen/ Beschützung Land und Leut/ auch zu Erhaltung gemeines Friedens/ und Ruhe" (*Chymischer Glücks-Hafen*, p. 26).

[132] Becher, *Psychosophia* (1705), pp. 130–32. The dialogue between the Philosopher and the Psychosopher (Becher) concerning alchemy occupies pp. 130–79.

responsible only for commerce, for the council shared its members with the Hofkammer at the time of his writing. In the Commercial Referat, Becher developed the argument that the officials of the Hofkammer were in fact unsuited to be members of the Commercial Council, for a particular "Studium und Erfahrenheit" (discipline and experience) was required by the commercial councillor that was different from that required by a treasury official.[133] Becher discussed the "kind of qualities belonging to a commercial advisor, and how he must differ from other faculties and must have a completely different profession than the cameral [i.e., treasury] profession."[134] He made it clear that the *Commercien-Rath* needed not only a completely different education, but also a different outlook and mentality from the treasury official. The commercial advisor must know about the trade, customs, useful inventions, and practices of other lands, as well as the "trade, geographical layout, type and nature" ("Handel und Wandel, Horizont, Art und Natur") of his own land. He must be familiar with general rights and laws in his land. Moreover he must be experienced enough with tradesmen and merchants to appreciate that they are always busy and on the move and cannot be kept waiting long in the antechamber.[135] Treasury officials, Becher claimed, did not appreciate the new "inventiones" presented to them by artisans and entrepreneurs, and had no idea of how to make use of them. The man of the Hofkammer either ignored these inventions, took them over for his own advantage, or made them common knowledge, so that the inventor could not profit and thus had no incentive to share his inventions with the court. Thus the treasury official did not encourage invention; indeed, he even hindered it.[136] Becher here complained that treasury officials had no idea how to build up a network of *Kundschaft* by which the inventions of artisans could be captured for the common good. Becher claimed further that treasury officials were not "well traveled and experienced in foreign lands," did not have "good correspondence [with other lands], nor do they desire to do things, rather than to hinder everything that cannot be their own. As soon as something proves profitable, they draw it to themselves and make a monopoly out of it."[137]

Thus, the qualities required by a commercial advisor were practical and

---

[133] Commercial Referat, fol. 28v.

[134] In a list of 95 points, point 92 was entitled "Was für Qualitäten zu einem *Commerci*en Rath gehören, und wie er von anderen facultäten unterscheiden, und eine gantz anderer als Cameral *profession* haben müßen" (ibid., fol. 27v).

[135] Ibid., fol. 28v.

[136] Ibid., fol. 29r.

[137] "Gereist, und in der Frembde erfahren" and "güte Correspondentz, und Lust . . . etwas zu Thuen, nicht alles hindern, was nicht ihnen eigen werden kann, oder so bald sich etwas Nutzliches herfür Thuet, also bald zu sich ziehen, und ein monopolium darauß machen" (ibid., fol. 53v). This last jab seems aimed at Georg Ludwig von Sinzendorf, who in fact did derive considerable profit from the silk manufacture (set up on his property). The *Hofkammerpräsident* also attempted to derive personal profit from the Kunst- und Werckhaus.

material, similar to those Becher himself possessed: he was widely traveled, claimed to have observed artisans and merchants at work, served as an intermediary between them and the court, had studied law, appreciated invention, and was himself an inventor of machines. Most important, because of his medical training and his position as commercial advisor (whose central tenets met so fortuitously in the dictum "salus populi suprema lex esto"), Becher promoted not his own interest and welfare, as a merchant or treasury official would have done in the same position, but the common good.

In alchemy, too, a lack of self-interest was important. Only a person of correct intentions could pursue this science. In the discussion of Marsaly's process for the transmutation of tin to silver that concluded the first section of the Alchemical Gutachten, Becher assured the emperor that he had hopes for the process itself, but believed that Marsaly was given too free a hand by the emperor, for he was young, ignorant in "politicis," inexperienced in "prudentia civili," and thus easily seduced into a life not befitting an adept of this "Venerabl[e] Scientz."[138] The practitioner of alchemy and chemistry, thus, must be disinterested and must pursue alchemy for the good it could do the whole society. Here we see Becher's fully developed view that the alchemist, like the commercial advisor, must be involved in civic life and the common goals of the polity.

Alchemy, like commerce, required practical experience as well as theoretical understanding if it was to produce material wealth. The remaining pages of the Commercial Referat were devoted to the practical details of maxims "by which to retain money within the territory,"[139] for example, the types of manufactures to introduce, where to obtain the necessary master craftsmen and journeymen, and how to finance the promotion of these industries. Throughout this report, Becher emphasized the capacity of the manufactures, by means of art and invention, to generate wealth. Manufacture was an artificial wealth, one that could be generated even from infertile soil, and did not need great tracts of land, but one that was part of the natural cycle of commerce, which enabled the peasant to "versilbern" his natural products.

The Alchemical Gutachten was also about the creation of material wealth by art—about the nature and generation of the most natural of artificial wealth, "gemachtes" gold. While the first section of the report comprised an adjudication of Marsaly's process, the second and longer portion explained the reality and preparation of the philosophical tincture. This tincture made possible the acceleration of the processes of nature through art, by which gold, a natural but

---

[138] Alchemical Gutachten, fol. 7v. Becher suggested that Leopold restrict Marsaly in some actions and not allow him so much "freyheit und Licentz." Becher maintained that in his treatment of Marsaly, the emperor appeared only to desire to avoid the reputation of being an ungenerous patron: "umb den Nahmen nicht zu haben daß sie einigen Philosophen im geringsten Hart Tractirten."

[139] "Daß Gelt im Land zu erhalten" (Commercial Referat, fol. 33v).

"made" wealth, could be produced. This section of the Alchemical Gutachten provided a schematic account of the goal and theory of alchemy for great lords who were involved in public life and so did not have time to read the many books of alchemical theory.[140] Becher portrayed alchemy as an imitation of natural processes and an example of material production by art. He emphasized its potential for fantastic material increase by producing a "manufactured" wealth not dependent on immovable property and land:

> The lover of this science must consider that he seeks the highest value in this world after piety, namely health and sufficient gold; gold in such a manner that no war or destruction can take it away from him, but rather, in all corners in the world the kitchen will waft it to him because in all places he will find enough metals to transmute. Thus he needs no letters of exchange because a little powder is enough to tincture a large amount. Thus the saying goes: "I carry all things with me" and the proverb of Paracelsus: "He who carries everything with him needs not the help of another." Not to mention the unceasing augmentation that one can give to each of his heirs, without disadvantage or division of the property, eternally, the entire substance of the Tincture. I will not say how precious it is to have such unassuming means without a bad conscience, without usury, without oppression, bitterness, and *Contribution*; means that can never be exhausted and through which no one can be burdened or robbed. How many thousand human beings are killed when one wants to seize a single fortification? But how much can this bring in, and how much is it, when reckoned against the Tincture? What is the greatest treasure chest of the world against a Lot of the true Tincture? [The true Tincture] continually multiplies itself, and increases many hundreds of times his capital both in quality and quantity. Compared to that, jewels and pearls lie dead and still, and the Tincture is multiplied that many thousand more times in its powers. Truly when one considers the great powers of the Tincture, one could easily doubt whether it is truly part of the nature of things, and because one knows for certain that such a thing is true, possible, and extant, why great lords do not leave everything standing to seek it. Indeed nowadays gold is the *nervus rerum gerendarum*, and to possess it so many unchristian acts are committed, when it could be gained completely scrupulously and legitimately by means of the Tincture.[141]

In this passage, Becher's remedy for the social and economic ills of post-1648 Germany is clear, although couched in the metaphor of alchemical transmutation. The alchemical tincture was capable of making wealth in a manner that contrasted sharply with the traditional "real" property of land. It produced an augmentation of wealth that could never result from the cultivation of land. This wealth allowed mobility and travel, by which the ruler could escape the destruction of war. If one possessed the tincture, one needed neither

---

[140] Becher, *Chymischer Glücks-Hafen*, p. 29.
[141] Ibid., p. 27.

land nor letters of exchange; one could move without impediment. It obviated the problems of primogeniture, division, and inheritance associated with the ownership of land. Although this wealth was "made," or artificial, it was at the same time paradoxically natural, for it was in the fires of the kitchen, the place of natural generation and sustenance, that this wealth was produced.[142] The ruler who possessed this secret of material increase need never face his subjects' displeasure, wrath, or rebellion.[143] The noble properties—land, fortifications, treasure chests, jewels, and pearls—could thus not be considered anything but dead when compared with the regenerative and creative capacity of the tincture. In this passage, the traditional real property and the ornamental wealth of the court have been completely overshadowed by the possibility of material augmentation by art, and by the potential of movable wealth.

Commerce, like alchemy, was a movable wealth that did not depend on land or the fruits of that land. Becher's commercial project, which he talked about here in an Alchemical Gutachten in the language of alchemy, was implicated in the dissonance created by the values of the landed nobility and the exchange economy of early modern Europe. He attempted to draw the prince and the entire realm of government into the world of money wealth and commercial transaction. The realm of the monarch and his court could no longer consist only in the land and the natural fruits of that land, but also had to participate in the world of the "made" thing and movable wealth. The proper activity of government and the prince was to be the creation of artificial wealth through the arts and inventions of manufacture and the movements of commerce.

Mercury / Hermes

The second page of the Alchemical Gutachten contains a drawing (figure 22), painted with vivid colors, entitled "Hieroglÿphische Figur Worinnen daß gantze Secret begriffen und vor augen gestellet wird" (Symbolic representation by which the entire secret is grasped and set before the eyes). It depicts the process by which alchemical transmutation takes place. In this drawing, Mercury, who is recognizable by the wings on his helmet and sandals, stands regnant on a mountain, a spring gushing beneath him. In his right hand he holds the caduceus and in his left hand, the orb of imperial power. Flanking him, on rocks one level lower around which the springwater flows, kneel a king and queen, arms outstretched, palms upturned, receptive of divine grace. Below

[142] It was also into the kitchen, where he sat by the fire, that Heraclitus invited the visitors disdainful of entering a place of manual work. In Aristotle's recounting of this anecdote, Heraclitus sat by an oven; in John Wilkins's seventeenth-century rendering, the oven had become a tradesman's shop.

[143] Becher, *Politischer Discurs*, 2d ed., p. 37: one rebellious subject is more dangerous than ten foreign enemies.

Figure 22. Mercury/Hermes. Alchemical Gutachten, 1674, fol. 2r.
Österreichische Nationalbibliothek, Handschriften-Abteilung, Vienna,
Ms. 11472.

them are two wells into which the streams disappear. Around each of these wells are five figures, dressed in clerical robes and kneeling in positions of prayer. This image could be read on three levels. As is clear from the inscription below the image, it was meant as religious allegory, in which Christ/Hermes presided over the salvation of the world. At the material level, this picture depicted mercury, the active ingredient of the tincture that caused transmutation. For the chemical adept the image would have evoked the processes of generation that occurred in metallic transmutation. At a third level, the image summoned up Hermes, the inventor of all the arts. The Habsburg emperor, for whom Becher had reproduced this carefully constructed emblem, would have been attuned to all the religious and alchemical levels of imagery.

This image might be read at a fourth level, one that Becher perhaps hoped would be educed by the emperor who received both a commercial and an alchemical report at the same time. The Commercial Referat included no image but it might have contained a portrayal of Mercury/Hermes, for Mercury could be construed not only as the agent of transmutation and salvation, but also as the bringer of good fortune, the god of persuasion and eloquence, and, most important, the patron of merchants and trade (figure 23).[144] His function as messenger between the world of the gods and the world of mortals corresponded to the movement, travel, and risk of trade. In explaining the "Kunst und Wissenschafft" of trade, Becher used the image of Mercury as an emblem to make clear his explanation.[145]

For Becher's contemporaries, Mercury was not only the most valuable agent of the alchemist, the god of trade, and the bringer of good fortune, but was also considered the patron of thieves.[146] The multivalent meanings with which the figure of Mercury was invested expressed perfectly the ambivalent attitude to the merchant and commerce.[147] Becher recognized this ambivalence, but he accounted for the juxtaposition of commerce and thievery by contending that the merchant could either ruin a society or bring it to a flourishing state, for if

[144] Hermes, the messenger of the gods, became Mercury, the Roman god of trade.

[145] The wings on Mercury's helmet symbolized "*theoria*," which was composed of "Verstand," and "*resolution*." The wings on his sandals were symbols for "*praxis*," one of which corresponded to freedom of trade, and the other to the capital needed for trade. The successful merchant must pay heed to these four components of trade, for they made up the whole science and art of commerce. *Politischer Discurs*, 2d ed., pp. 184–85.

[146] In *Praedones in Dialogi Huttenici* (Ebernburg, 1521), Hutten argued against merchants as a corrupted and corrupting influence in society, and said it was reflected in the fact that Mercury was the god of merchants and the god of thieves. Noted in Ferdinand August Steinhüser, *Johann Joachim Becher und die Einzelwirtschaft. Ein Beitrag zur Geschichte der Einzelwirtschaftslehre und des Kameralismus*, (Nuremberg: Verlag der Hochschulbuchhandlung Krische, 1931), p. 68.

[147] A contemporary of Becher, Philipp von Zesen, in describing the statue of Mercury that stood in the Townhall in Amsterdam, betrays his equivocal attitude to commerce. He described Mercury as a cunning thief, who taught the merchants the art of weighing and measuring, as well as an artificer who invented many useful arts, such as astronomy (*Beschreibung der Stadt Amsterdam* [Amsterdam: Joachim Nosch, 1664], pp. 264–65).

Figure 23. The frontispiece of the 1738 edition of *Oesterreich über Alles, wann es nur will* by Becher's brother-in-law, Philipp Wilhelm von Hörnigk, used Mercury to symbolize the trade that would save the Habsburg lands. This book, first published anonymously in 1684, developed many of Becher's commercial ideas and projects.

the merchant's activities were overseen and controlled by the prince, he would serve as a model of virtuous production for all others in the society.[148] If, on the contrary, commerce was not controlled by the prince, the merchant would destroy society completely with his greedy self-interest. Becher modeled his productive merchant on the *Verläger*, who not only provided a model of virtuous wealth-getting for the society, but even held the productive society in its cycle of sustenance. We might even regard Hermes as the inventor and articulator of the arts to coincide with the figure of the *Verläger*, who employed the arts to manufacture the goods of commerce.

Consider for a moment the parable of N. which Becher recounted to illustrate the cunning artifice of the alchemist. N. was an artist of deception and perhaps a thief. It is possible, however, to draw a parallel between his history and Becher's political program, exemplified by his submission of the commercial and alchemical reports at the same time. N.'s "transmutation" of his alchemical process into a glassworks was paralleled by Becher's representation of alchemy as the epitome of the projects by which the taxes on a monarch's subjects could be lessened. Becher had constructed both the commercial and alchemical reports around the common theme of material increase resulting in movable, "manufactured" wealth. Both commerce and alchemy resulted in material augmentation by a process of consumption and regeneration. In both reports, Becher advocated the manufacture of a natural wealth by art and invention. Alchemy represented, in a distilled form, the essence of commerce and manufacture, which was the creation of wealth by art (or, in N.'s case, by cunning artifice). N.'s easy transition from alchemy to glassworking, and Becher's movement from a report on the potential of alchemy for the production of material wealth to a report on the productive potential of manufacturing projects was an artifice worthy of the the mobility and persuasive skills of Mercury. Both N. and Becher desired to transfer the accepted symbolic significance of alchemy at the Habsburg court to a new material activity, that, like Mercury in another guise, employed, articulated, and described the arts, and that resulted in a material increase usually associated only with the destructive consumption of commerce and thievery.

The Practice of Alchemy and the *Praxis* of Ruling

In 1675, the year he transmuted lead into silver, Becher also published *Theses chymicae veritatem et possibilitatem transmutationis metallorum in aurum evincentes* (Chemical theses arguing the possibility of the transmutation of metals into gold), which set out the principles of metallic transmutation and

---

[148] *Politischer Discurs*, 2d ed., p. 188.

their importance for the prince.[149] This work formed one of three practical supplements to the *Physica Subterranea*. Becher had promised in the *Physica Subterranea* to publish a companion volume of practice (keeping to the principle of *Theoria cum Praxi*) and had even printed the contents of the future volume in the 1669 edition of the *Physica Subterranea*, but he never finished this second volume. Instead, he published three short "Supplements," all of which dealt with the generation and transmutation of metals, for he wished to demonstrate in practice that metals could actually be generated by art, in addition to proving the possibility of transmutation theoretically. In 1671 Becher had published *Experimentum Chymicum Novum, quo Artificialis & instantanea Metallorum* Generatio & Transmutatio *ad oculum demonstratur* (New chemical experiment by which the artificial and instantaneous generation and transmutation of metals is visibly demonstrated), which described a method of generating iron out of clay and linseed oil.[150] In 1680 he would bring out the *Experimentum Novum Curiosum de Minera Arenaria Perpetua sive Prodromus Historiae, seu Propositionis Praep. D. D. Hollandiae* (Curious new experiment of the perpetual

---

[149] (Frankfurt: Johann David Zunner). It described the process of transmutation in the three great realms as of two kinds: an essential change involving generation or putrefaction and a change of accidental properties involving digestion and penetration. Becher gave as an example of the first type the change of egg into chick and, as an example of the second type, sweet wine into sour. A transmutation in the mineral kingdom could only be classified as of the second type (p. 31) because gold was known only through its accidental qualities. The laws of the Holy Roman Empire defined gold by its fluidity, weight, malleability, color, fixity, and sound on hammering, and thus a transmutation achieving these accidental properties must indicate gold (p. 61). Transmutation takes place by making gold subtle enough to penetrate and merge completely with the metal being transmuted. This change in gold can only be achieved through treatment with the philosopher's mercury (p. 66).

[150] (Frankfurt: Johann David Zunner). Becher believed this experiment proved metals could be generated out of the earths (principles) that were contained in the clay (sulfurous/male) and linseed oil (mecurial/female). In this experiment, as in a transmutation, the metals had to be resolved into their *prima materia* so their seeds could mature out of it. The principles contained in the clay and linseed oil supplied the *prima materia* out of which the metal was generated. Leibniz, who saw Becher perform the test before the elector of Mainz in 1669 on his way to Holland to obtain a colony, reported to several correspondents that this experiment was genuine and illustrated the genesis of metals (Leibniz, *Sämtliche Schriften*, ser. 1, vol. 1, Leibniz to Gottlieb Spitzel, 3 October(?) 1670, pp. 100–102; Crafft to Leibniz, 11/21 December 1671, pp. 229–30). Leibniz described this experiment in detail to Henry Oldenburg, and Oldenburg assured him that the experiment would be tested in the meetings of the Royal Society (Leibniz, *Sämtliche Schriften*, ser. 2, vol. 1, Leibniz to Oldenburg, 11 March 1671 [new style], p. 90; 29 April/9 May 1671, p. 105; 8/18 June 1671, p. 124; and Oldenburg to Leibniz, 28 September/8 October 1671, p. 156. Leibniz also corresponded with Otto Tachenius about this experiment, 4 May 1671, pp. 100–101). The Royal Society later tested the experiment in its meetings and the *Experimentum Chymicum Novum* was reviewed in the *Philosophical Transactions*, no. 74, pp. 2232–33, on 14 August 1671. Leibniz was still wondering thirty-five years later about this experiment, when it was proposed by someone else to be performed before the Académie des sciences in Paris. Leibniz, *Leibnizens mathematische Schriften*, ed. C. I. Gerhardt (Berlin: A. Ascher, 1849), vol. 4, Leibniz to Varignon, Marquis de l'Hospital, 27 July 1705, pp. 127–31; and Varignon to Leibniz, 29 April 1706, p. 150.

mineral sand quarry or herald of the history of the proposition made to the States General in Holland), which described a process by which gold could be extracted from sand.[151]

In the dedication to the emperor that began the supplement of 1675, Becher defended alchemy against its detractors who objected that alchemy had nothing to do with "Staatskunst" (statecraft). In this defense, Becher criticized the "Staatsleute" (officials of the state) as bloodsuckers and servants of the god of war, whereas the chemists and chemistry served only the public good.[152] Court officials were only knowledgeable about how to raise armies, while the man who thought like a chemist knew how to bring great benefit to the state. Becher compared the useful arts invented by alchemy to the evils, not so much invented as worn out by the men of the Kammer such as "Contribution, impost, excise taxes, interest, toll, usury, tax and so on."[153]

In Vienna, the Hofkammer official was in fact instructed to make funding for the army and the border guards and the search for ever greater extraordinary revenues his main goals.[154] Thus Becher's charge that the officials of the treasury were educated only in war and taxation was not without foundation.

---

[151] (Frankfurt: Mauritius Georgius Weidmannus, 1680; and London: Marcus Pardoe, 1680). This was not, Becher claimed, a simple extraction of alluvial gold from sand, but rather a maturing of gold out of silver by heating together sand and silver. This process was first described in Becher's 1679 text, *Trifolium Becherianum Hollandicum oder . . . drey neue Erfindungen, bestehende in einer Seiden-Wasser-Mühle und Schmeltz-Wercke. Zum ersten mahl in Holland vorgeschlagen und werckstellig gemacht: Mit gründlicher Anweisung wie es mit denselbigen Sachen beschaffen ist. Auß der Niederländischen in die Hochteutsche Sprach übersetzet* (Frankfurt: Johann David Zunner). In these two practical works, Becher inhabited a safe middle ground between (bad) gold-making alchemy and (good and useful) mining and smelting. He distances himself in both these works from "alchemists." He was apparently called a "Goldmacher" when carrying out the trials of his process in Holland. He claimed in these works to be searching for a "Mineralische Krafft" in the sand, and if this was to be called "goldmachen," "so müssen alle Bergleute und Schmelzer Goldmacher seyn" (*Trifolium*, p. 6). Thus it was "keine Alchymisterey/ sondern ein Berg-Schmelz- und Scheid-Werck" (ibid., p. 22). However, this process was not a simple or common process of refining by separation or extraction of the metal already present in the sand. Rather it *was* alchemy insofar as it was a process of combining the components of gold, which were latent, but separate in the base metals. They did not have the form of material gold. These components were extracted by the art of alchemy, then joined, and thus yielded up real, material gold: "Utilitas ergo Alchymiae consistit in hoc, quod particulae aurum componentes, in Subjectis reperiantur divisim, & nondum conjunctae in formam Auri, quae Subjecta parum constent, ex quibus ope Artis Alchymicae extrahantur, conjungantur, & sic in Aurum Actuale, quod multi valet, reducantur, in hoc ergo consistit propriè Utilitas Alchymiae circa istam partem" (*Minera arenaria*, p. 59).

[152] "Chemistry has a goal that is much more useful to the fatherland and much more bearable for the subjects than those lazy statesmen and warmongers who draw blood and booty out of their war god. It is to be hoped that they would not do the common good so much harm with their warlike statecraft, but rather create as much fruit and use as the martial chemical philosophy" (*Philosophischer Beweisthum*, p. 9).

[153] Ibid., pp. 15–16.

[154] "Vor allem soll ein Hofkammerrat sein Augenmerk haben auf . . . die Verpflegung der Armee, die Bezahlung der ungrischen Grenzkosten und die Vermehrung ausserordentlicher Mittel

What Becher advocated was an entirely new sort of man for the treasury and a new way of thinking about the sources of income for the treasury; a way of thinking (and acting) that had more to do with practicing alchemy than with traditional methods of taxation.

Becher depicted the alchemist, in contrast to the treasury official, as helping his fellow man in "Gesundheit" (health), "Geld" (money), and "Gut" (property). This material aid was exactly the opposite of what the cameral men offered, for they only sucked wealth from the subjects, whereas the alchemist created new wealth.[155] Some might object that alchemy was risky, but certainly, Becher claimed, it was no riskier than mining, trade, agriculture, or artisanal work. There was, in fact, no science more honest and more useful to the prince, and less burdensome to the subjects than alchemy. Becher might here have substituted the word "manufacture" or "commerce" for "alchemy."

Unfortunately, Becher claimed, "money rules the world and no government can exist without it" ("Geld regiret die Welt/ ohne welches kein Regiment bestehen kan"); thus, in an age of money, it would be better for every prince to patronize alchemy rather than to employ harmful bureaucrats (who did not understand material wealth and its creation).[156] In patronizing alchemy, the monarch would be following the model government of the wisest and richest of kings, Solomon. Becher digressed at this point in his text to pass judgment on the controversy over whether Solomon had actually possessed knowledge about alchemy. Becher asserted blithely that it was obvious that only alchemy could have created the fabulous wealth of Solomon. While tradition held that Solomon had derived his wealth from the gold mines of Tyre and Ophir, Becher reminded his readers that the expeditions and voyages of the sixteenth century had turned up no traces of such mines. Becher believed that this misconception about the origin of Solomon's wealth had arisen because Solomon hid the source of his wealth from neighboring princes. When Solomon stated that his ships had made trips to the gold mines of Tyre and Ophir, they had, in reality, according to Becher, gone to his laboratories there.[157] It was typical, Becher concluded, that the source of this empty controversy over whether Solomon had possessed knowledge of alchemy was none other than a "Staats-Mann"; one of those who, as Becher had emphasized in his Commercial Referat, discouraged

---

zur Bestreitung der Ausgaben." A manuscript set of instructions for Hofkammer officials from Leopold I's reign, quoted in Wolf, "Die Hofkammer unter Leopold I.," 445.

[155] Becher, *Philosophischer Beweisthum*, p. 15. Becher added that even if the alchemist was not able to aid his neighbor, at least he did no harm to anyone but himself, a trait in stark contrast to those possessed by the men of the treasury.

[156] Ibid., p. 16.

[157] Becher claimed that at the same time, Solomon also continued to encourage trade and collect taxes in order to obscure further the sources of his wealth. Becher ended his discussion with the statement that even if Solomon did not know of alchemy, "es [ist] kein durchgehende Regel: Das sey alles unmöglich/ was Salomon nicht gekönnet" (it is no general rule that everything is impossible [to us today] that Solomon could not do) (ibid., p. 21).

invention, was self-interested, and had no new ideas for obtaining income for the territorial ruler. It was typical of the statesman, Becher said, that he did not genuinely appreciate invention and, indeed, even hid new sources of wealth. That was why, Becher concluded, "I do not have to do with statesmen, but with philosophers."[158]

Becher advocated here that a new sort of person should assist the prince in financing his court and administration, a person who had more in common with a hermetic philosopher than with a man of the Kammer. That this philosopher could not possibly be Aristotelian Becher had made clear when he pronounced that the man of the schools could not even get enough money together for a meal. The treasury official had a fundamentally mistaken approach to the sources of revenue for the state; he needed knowledge not about taxation and the traditional sources of cameral income, but instead about the principles of generation and about material things and their production by art. Alchemy stood for the material production and increase that could be brought about by the invention and understanding of the arts of manufacture. It epitomized as well the potential of personal mobility and movable wealth.

The person most qualified to teach the prince about the new sources of income was he who understood the principles of wealth generation personified in the image of Mercury as agent of the philosophers, inventor of the arts, and patron of the merchants. He knew the art by which he could imitate the productive capacity of nature and bring about material increase. Alchemy could convey an appreciation of this productive capacity, for it was an art that imitated nature directly, and its theory provided knowledge about the generation and growth of all things. It had the capacity to multiply artificial wealth as nature multiplied the natural seeds of grain sown by the farmer. Just as gold would be produced through a corruption and regeneration of its seeds in the tincture, so artificial wealth would be generated by the consumption of manufactured goods in commercial transactions. The man who knew how to "philosophize chemically" (Chymisch zu philosophiren) dealt in material things and achieved tangible effects. He would attain the "*Real*-Weisheit" of Erhard Weigel that came through the practice of the arts and could produce the material wealth and increase capable of reforming the world. Becher, the intermediary between words and things, between artisans and courtiers, and between symbols and material things, was one such qualified (and mobile) man. In both his vocation (commercial advisor) and his profession (medical doctor and chemist), he put into practice his understanding of the theory and practice of the (chemical) philosopher, for in both of these different spheres he needed an understanding of the theory of creation and generation as well as facility in the arts—habits of thought and action cultivated by a life in the laboratory.

By the end of his life, no distinction remained between Becher's vocation and

---

[158] "Ich hab nicht mit Staatsleuten zu thun/ sondern mit Philosophen" (ibid., p. 29).

his profession. Just as the four images of Hermes as agent of the alchemist, inventor of the arts, patron of merchants, and god of thieves collapsed into one another in the parable of N., so too did they in Becher's own work. He titled his last work of alchemy and chemistry *Chymischer Glücks-Hafen*. "Glückshafen" (literally, "harbor of fortune or safe port") also signified a lottery. In Becher's *Nachlaß* there is a printed pamphlet from Leipzig, dated May 1672, proclaiming a "Lotto oder Glücks-hafen."[159] Becher chose the name "Glücks-Hafen" for his great chemical "Concordanz"[160] because he regarded chemistry and commerce to be the same activity: the pursuit of productive knowledge that would create wealth by art for the treasury of the prince and his state. By unifying the realms of chemistry and commerce, Becher sought not only to draw the landed court world into the commercial republic but, more significantly, to draw practice and productive knowledge into the realm of the state— that is, the *praxis* of political life.

. . . . .

Becher's alchemical medallion of 1675 can be understood as the line of communication by which Becher sought the favor of the emperor in order to carry out his commercial projects; it was the means by which Becher could transmute the emperor's interest in alchemy into an interest for commerce. As a tangible object of display, the medallion established the power and eternal *fama* of the emperor, and by its creation, Becher hoped to establish his own space at court more firmly. But most important, it demonstrated the material productive po-

---

[159] Mss. var. 1(2), fols. 627r–634v. There were 22,000 tickets at one Reichsthaler each to be bought in this lottery for objects worth twenty thousand Reichsthaler. This was only one idea that Becher found in ephemeral printed literature—newspapers and pamphlets—that provided him with inventive new ways of increasing income for the territorial ruler and his state. Several different pamphlets are found in Mss. var. 1(2), fols. 627r–662r. According to Jacob and Wilhelm Grimm, *Deutsches Wörterbuch* (Leipzig: S. Hirzel, 1854–1960), "Glücks-Hafen" could mean the pot out of which the lots are drawn in a lottery or the entire structure of the lottery itself. It could signify as well "luck" or "harbor of fortune."

[160] The major part of the *Chymischer Glücks-Hafen* consists of recipes and processes Becher claimed he had collected during his life from different laboratories and chemists. By publishing them in the same place, he wished to form a "Concordantz" of chemistry, by which order would be imposed on chemistry. Understanding in any science, Becher stated, rested upon comprehension of its *"Principia"* and *"Axiomata,"* which arose out of *"Observation*en" and *"Experiment*en." These in turn, Becher claimed, had their origin in *"Combination*en" and *"Concordanti*en." In his book, the processes of different chemical authors would be compared, and truth extracted from the "Labyrinth" of opinions, processes, experiments and falsehoods. (Preface, p. ii verso.) In the index of Becher's books in *Opuscula Chymica Rariora*, ed. Friedrich Roth-Scholtz (Nuremberg and Altdorff: Johann Daniel Tauber, 1719), Friedrich Roth-Scholtz commented that if the empty processes that made up two-thirds of the *Chymischer Glücks-Hafen* were left out of the book, and the remaining third placed in a *"Glücks-Topff,"* the player-readers of this chemical lottery would not waste so much of their time and money (p. 17).

tential of the imitation of nature by art. The imitation of natural processes by the human action of art transmuted the made or artificial thing into a natural thing: gold made by alchemy became the equivalent of "Geld" made by manufacture. The possibility of transmutation made real by the medallion also demonstrated the advantages of movable wealth, common to both alchemy and commerce. Further, the medallion was evidence of a material transmutation that confirmed the truth and efficacy of the theories of consumption and regeneration that formed the basis for Becher's alchemy. It demonstrated the possibility of harnessing these principles of generation and their potential for material increase and profit. Finally, the medallion transmuted the alchemist into a commercial advisor, and the alchemist's knowledge of matter and manual skills into the requisite knowledge for the commercial advisor.

Becher's medallion also possessed a real, nonsymbolic exchange value. This exchange value would, Becher believed, in the real world save the German Empire and Habsburg lands from decay and destruction. In this small silver medallion, then, lies the essence of Becher's political program and its mediation through alchemy: it transmuted the symbols of power and of regeneration into the material objects of commerce, manufacture, and money, and it provided a means by which the sources of noble power—sources that once resided for the prince in natural generation, and which now resided in the world of the exchange economy—could be made material and manifest to the emperor.

INTERLUDE IN THE LABORATORY

Scaena: **The Laboratory**

THROUGHOUT his life Becher worked in the laboratory among the furnaces and their smoke, the bellows, the multitude of tiny glass vessels, bottles, alembics, crucibles, tools, chemicals, minerals, and metals. By the seventeenth century, this plethora of sooty instruments in greater or lesser states of disarray had come to symbolize the alchemist's work. The laboratory of Khunradt, where the alchemist prayed for divine revelation (figure 24), and the laboratory as a parable of greed (figure 25) and vain ambition (figure 26) gave way in Becher's work to the laboratory as the locus of practice, where the underground workshop of nature was imitated by *ars* to produce knowledge about nature.[1] It represented too a microcosm of artisanal society and its sphere of practical knowledge. The labor that the chemist undertook in the laboratory yielded many useful and profitable processes and materials.[2] The laboratories of Becher's Kunst- und Werckhaus formed the heart of his ambitious plan to reform revenue collection in the Habsburg lands by shifting the source of wealth to the practice of commerce and the manufacture of goods. The director's alchemical laboratory in the Kunsthaus exemplified all the levels at which Becher bound alchemy to this program of reform. The previous chapter treated Becher's attempt to portray for the prince a parallel between the regenerative capabilities of alchemy and commerce to bring about material increase. In the last decade of his life Becher formulated a specific plan for an alchemical laboratory that shows with clarity how the activity of the laboratory and workshop figured at several different levels in his plan of reform. This activity not only yielded goods of trade and so formed one component of the new sources of revenue, but also integrated the territorial ruler into the productive activity of artisans in their workshop. In this integration, however, the artisanal workshop was transformed, thus taking the sphere of Becher's reform beyond the simple production of goods to encompass as well the production of knowledge. Production of knowledge—knowledge that was productive—became the preserve of the natural philosopher and his patron, the territorial lord. Becher's laboratory plan allows us to view as well the transformation in

---

[1] Becher, *Chymisches Laboratorium*, pp. 2–3.

[2] Becher's vision of the laboratory here echoes Solomon's House in Francis Bacon's *New Atlantis*, Tommaso Campanella's vision of the laboratories in the *City of the Sun*, and the use of chemistry in Johann Valentin Andreae's ideal Christian society. All these utopias shared a vision of the use of natural knowledge and the practice of natural philosophy for the common good.

Figure 24. Oratorium and Laboratorium. Frontispiece from Heinrich Khunrath, *Amphitheatrum Sapientiae Aeternae*, 1609. With permission of Deutsches Museum, Munich.

the understanding of rational action and human control, for in his laboratory the "irrational" (for us) activity of alchemy becomes the "rational" activity of calculation and manufacture.

Becher's plan for the alchemical laboratory sets out a vision of the production of useful materials that reflected the order of productive town society. In the laboratory, as in the household of civic society, *ordo* was of first importance.[3] Becher sketched a picture of a workshop brought into disorder by its workers:

> If someone wants to take up working [*labori*ren] itself, there is nothing in the world that can bring him sooner into confusion than this, both because of the operations

---

[3] Becher quoted Xenophon," *Nihil utilius est hominibus, nihil pulchrius ordine*," and also Plato's *Laws*, "*Quicquid in Republica certo quodam continetur ordine*." See *Methodus didactica*, p. 59; cf. Mss. var. 1(1), fol. 684r–v.

as well as the instruments and the materials, which are abundant and diverse. If he has the misfortune to meet with a *Laborant* or assistant who is disorderly, messy, and lazy, inside a month the *Laboratorium* will look like the *Confusion* in Babylon. The used glass vessels have been smashed into bits so that they cannot be rinsed out. For each operation they take new crucibles and glasses just so that they do not need to clean the old ones. Whole things, broken bits, clean, dirty, new, used, prepared materials, raw materials, wooden, clay, and glass utensils are standing all mixed together. The windows, tables and floor are full. And nothing is labeled as to what it is. Tongs, ladles, hammers and other instruments lie strewn everywhere in such a way that when you want anything, you must search for a half hour. The stink from the furnaces, the soot and dust from the coals, the sand, water, and lime do not help the work so much as aid the confusion. Soon, the *Laborant* himself looks like a second Cyclops, who has just recently come from the grotto of Polyphemus or Trophonius, and who only washes on the first day of every new year. As the Poet well says:

> You who withstood the times of winter with unweakened chest,
> sodden by the falling rains and the smell of soot,
> blinded by smoke, burned by the thundering flames.

In this way the days and years disappear, as do the costs for materials, instruments, coals, and salary. In contrast, not only nothing remains in the crucible, but also the corporeal gold and silver become dirty and adulterated. When a year is over, you know nothing about what has been done, in fact you know less at the end than in the beginning, for all processes look very well on paper. But when they are tried, then, by the test of action, it comes to light whether the person who gave them to the laboratory—even if he gave his oath about their truth—ever worked them himself, or whether the person who worked them did not notice their falsities and impossibilities, or has not understood the content of the recipes properly. Which all makes alchemy as harmful as it is vexing. I have therefore taken it upon myself in this section to demonstrate a method by which alchemy can be practically treated with pleasure and in a useful way, so that a person is neither deceived nor robbed, and everything can be kept secret and in good order. Which in alchemy is not a small work, but nearly the most important work itself.[4]

To prevent such chaos, Becher set forth a detailed plan to order the laboratory and keep its secrets. In Becher's ideal laboratory the spaces and workers were separated according to the processes and operations of the great work.

---

[4] In the *Chymischer Glücks-Hafen*, Becher expanded the "Philosophisches Gutachten" presented to Leopold I in 1674 to include a section on the practice of alchemy. The original "Philosophisches Gutachten" corresponds to *Chymischer Glücks-Hafen*, pp. 25–73, and the section added, pp. 74–107. For this description of the laboratory, see pp. 74–75.

Dramatis Personae: **The Natural Philosopher**

In setting out the form of the productive society in his political work, Becher ordered civil society into estates based on the different work of each group, the different places where each group lived and worked, and the function of each group in the productive cycle. Becher separated human society into three estates—peasants, artisans, merchants—that formed an interlocking community of unceasing activity and production, all overseen by the prince. Becher's laboratory was also divided according to the chemical operation in which the worker participated, his place in the laboratory, and the function of his labor in the whole alchemical work. But in the laboratory the society of orders became a hierarchy of owners and laborers, in which the workers had control neither over their labor nor their product. As in his model polity, Becher's entire laboratory was overseen and regulated by the territorial prince.[5] The aim of the laboratory was the great work of alchemy: the ennoblement of base natural materials by art into noble and useful objects, such as gold, medicaments, and curiosities. This production of material things was fully integrated into the goals and concerns of the princely court and, most importantly, was controlled by a natural philosopher who united in himself both theory and practice. Becher's plan shows clearly how the natural philosopher, as the trusted counselor of the prince, both controlled the rude practitioners beneath him and reduced them to workers with neither independent skills nor knowledge. This plan reveals to us the way in which the production of natural philosophical knowledge came to depend upon the hierarchy of the noble court and the modes of commercial production.

The prince, at the center of the laboratory, although outside the community of workers, determined the existence of the laboratory and its order.[6] Surrounding him were the members of the first class of workers, the *Consilarii Laboratorii*, who had immediate responsibility to their lord. These were natural philosophers—"Naturkündiger"—who had long experience in "*Chymicis*," and who had performed operations in the laboratory themselves.[7] They were, in short, men of theory and practice. These advisors must be able to communicate with their lord in a fitting manner; they should be able to write a *consilium* (in Latin) about any process the prince gave to them.[8] This counsel would transform a vernacular (sometimes oral) recipe into a scholarly document. For the assistance of the counselor, Becher appended a model four-and-one-half page

---

[5] The spaces in his laboratory were divided among five different types of labor, which corresponded to the theoretical and practical operations of chemical processes. Each class of worker had its particular job in the whole, and each had a particular geographical place of work. *Chymischer Glücks-Hafen*, p. 75.

[6] Ibid., p. 81.

[7] Ibid., p. 76.

[8] The prince, too, must be able to demand information and advice in a fitting manner. Becher appends a model "Raths-Erholung" from a lord to his chemical counselors (ibid., pp. 87–88).

Figure 25. After Pieter Breughel the Elder, *The Alchemists in the Peasant's Kitchen*, sixteenth century, engraving. With permission of Deutsches Museum, Munich.

Figure 26. David Teniers the Younger, *The Alchemist*, 1640s (engraving by Pierre François Basan). The skulls and gutted candle on the wall as well as the hourglass symbolize the alchemist's vain pursuit of profit. His efforts literally go up in the smoke billowing out of the fireplace in the background. Courtesy Fisher Scientific.

consilium to his plan for the laboratory. This model set out in scholastic fashion a *consilium* on a three-line recipe (in the vulgar tongue) for ennobling base metals by smelting them with glass and a small amount of gold and silver.[9] The counsel contained a thesis (the recipe), the method, the *dubia* (the arguments against the method), and the theoretical and practical resolution of these doubts. Clearly these natural philosophical counselors of the laboratory must be men of theory in order to give authority to their counsel in their dealings with the court.

It was the counselors' task also to ascertain their lord's intention in the laboratory: whether he desired medicines, natural curiosities and principles of nature, or silver and goldmaking. The counselors were then to obtain processes suited to their lord's purposes.[10] To do this they had to know where to obtain good recipes and how to choose among them. In this they showed themselves men of practice as well, who not only were able themselves to do *Handwerk* and experiment, but could also converse with the *vulgus* thronging the doors of the laboratory. Being men of theory, however, they would be able to order the babble of the crowd, tame it, and draw out what was useful from it.

Becher set out general rules for the counselors of the laboratory they could follow in hunting up recipes and in dealing with the crowd. In general they should accept the principle that all recipe sellers were thieves, for if the sellers' processes were successful in making gold, they would not desire to sell them.[11] "The process hawkers lie in a marvelous manner. They swear to, and indeed use, all wonderful arts in doing alchemy, so that a person should first study a pickpocket, a cutpurse and a politician [court official] if he wants to differentiate these nasty fellows' machinations."[12] The *Consilarius* must carefully examine the life of the process seller, for if the seller is not virtuous, success in alchemy was impossible. In general, the counselor was directed to distrust sellers, but he could make an exception if he knew the seller had tried the process himself, or had it from a good source, or offered original manuscripts.[13]

Books of recipes, the other source of processes a counselor must examine, were faulty for the same reason:

> Much less are these things written down or printed and so indifferently set before the eyes of the world. If they had been, such great secrets would already long ago have been revealed to the world, for the many thousands of the world's *laboranten* who storm through all the recipe books would easily have found them, practiced them, and made them known.[14]

[9] Ibid., pp. 76–80.
[10] Ibid., p. 88.
[11] Ibid.
[12] Ibid., p. 91.
[13] Ibid.
[14] Ibid., p. 89.

Indeed, philosophers in past ages expressly said that the secrets of alchemy were to be found written down, but in such a way that they could only be understood by the learned. But the counselor cannot take this as a general rule in all cases because more recent philosophers have had different goals: "Because, however, today's gold-hungry world only wants processes, which can be understood literally, so the philosophers have accommodated themselves [to the market!] and have written plenty of processes that can be understood partly *æquivocè*, partly *analogicè*, and partly *ad literam*."[15] Becher believed some true processes could be understood literally and some old manuscripts could shed great light on the chemical work, so the counselor in examining printed processes could not always assume that "*ubi videris Recipe, cogita quod significet Decipe*" (where you see recipe [literally, receive], think, for it may signify deceive).[16] The counselor should look for true processes in manuscripts and, more specifically, in the concordances of those manuscripts. This involved the testing of processes and so was extremely time-consuming, as Becher claimed to know from the testing of six thousand processes himself. Such a concordance must begin from theory, that is, from the division of all the possible theoretical and practical operations of alchemical processes into logically ordered classes. All processes brought to the laboratory could then be compared with this list of operations in order to determine whether they conformed to the most basic characteristics of a true process.[17]

In addition to the concordance of manuscripts and books, a concordance of live experience should be assembled: "What is wanting is a *viva Correspondentia*, an oral conference and concordance of the processes and experiments."[18] As soon as word gets out that a lord has founded a splendid laboratory and spends something on it, all sorts of people will show up with secrets to tell. The counselor should "listen to all and scorn nothing."[19]

> Miners will come and bring all kinds of ore and materials and lie until the beams themselves bend. Ruined counts, knights, and colonels will come and on the basis of their reputation they will propose processes. They will turn out to be the worst deceivers, a thing that has often happened to me. These vagabonds do not want any learned commissioners [to examine their work]; indeed they are often such people as N.[20]

Thus the counselors should listen to all but trust no one. Even when the process seller does not seem to demand money or to work in his own interest, he may

---

[15] Ibid.
[16] Ibid.
[17] Ibid., p. 90.
[18] Ibid., p. 89.
[19] Ibid., p. 92.
[20] Ibid.

still plan a deceit, in the way that the alchemist N. deceived Becher at the court of the emperor. The counselors should bind the petitioners arriving at their laboratory by a civil contract and hold them as long in the laboratory as their processes seem to warrant, in order to get as much useful information out of them as possible.[21] However, the petitioners should quickly be shaken off if they proved useless, for "what one gives to alchemists and whores is the same thing, in that one cannot bring [the transaction] before the court, nor demand what one has given back again without loss of respect."[22] The form of the contract was of great importance, and Becher included in the laboratory plans a model contract that he had made with the counts of Pötting in 1672 in which he obligated himself to separate a ducat of gold from a mark of silver weekly, with no loss of silver. Becher promised to teach the process to the counts in return for 120 silver marks of capital each quarter and a third of the gold ducats produced. If Becher taught the counts the process to their mutual satisfaction, the counts promised to give Becher a certificate attesting to this fact and 62,400 gold ducats within ten years. Becher appends this contract to the laboratory plans in order to show "how honestly, even in alchemy, both sides can transact in a contract."[23] In this way, Becher transported the characteristic document of commercial society—the contract—into the workshop.

In addition to possessing knowledge about where to find processes and how to prove their truth, the counselors of the laboratory must know how to set up experiments investigating the nature, transmutation, maturation, and ennoblement of metals, and that find the great *Elixir* in both the dry and wet ways.[24] These learned men of theory should work in a space containing "a good alchemical library," in which they keep the *consilia* and contracts, together with the whole collection of recipes, and the finished products and reports of all the processes worked.[25]

The second class in the laboratory was the *Dispensator Laboratorii* or "Ober-*Laborant*en," who received instructions from the counselors for undertaking processes based on a deliberation of the *consilium* by the counselors. When the dispensators are given the process, they should not "tinker with it or add anything to it, but should perform it as it is written down and annotated in the *consilium*."[26] The dispensator should note in what circumstances the trial was made and how long it took. He should visit the *Laboranten* often, make a

---

[21] Contracting with alchemists had often been a part of Becher's duties (or strategies) in Mainz, Munich, and Vienna. See, for example, the contract with Colonel Boon discussed in Chapter 2.

[22] *Chymischer Glücks-Hafen*, p. 92.

[23] "wie redlich man auch in der *Alchymi* beederseits in *Contract*en umbgehen könne." Ibid., p. 86. The contract is on pp. 82–86.

[24] Ibid., p. 88.

[25] Ibid., p. 99.

[26] "Wann er nun einen *Process* bekommet/ so solle er an demselben nichts künstlen/ darvon/ oder darzu setzen/ sondern wie er geschrieben/ und von dem *Consilio* angemerckt/ treulich arbeiten lassen" (ibid., p. 99).

protocol of each process, and note carefully the volume and weight. When the trial comes to an end, he must retain the material obtained, label it, set it aside with its relevant process, and write a report of the trial to be given to the counselors. He is to obtain advice about problems in the process at any time from the counselors.[27]

The real task of this second class of worker, as its title suggests, was to divide each process into its proper operations and delegate it to the different types of laborers. Becher divided all processes into three main operations according to the mechanical action applied to the raw materials. The materials may either be pulverized, washed, and made into sludge; or soaked, evaporated, crystalized, and distilled; or dried and put to the fire.[28] These three sets of operations corresponded loosely to the natural processes of earth, water, and fire.

The dispensator's space in the laboratory was the "*Dispensation*-Cammer," where he dispensed the weighed materials to the other three laboratories. After each mechanical operation, the lower laborers would bring the refined material to the dispensator's room and he would send it on to its next operation in the appropriate laboratory. Thus his space contained a scale and balance and was filled with all the necessary chemicals and spirits. The dispensator was required every quarter to make an inventory of his space and to keep orderly bookkeeping to ensure the honesty of the workers. The amounts of materials taken from his shelves must be found to agree with the amounts used in the processes.[29] The dispensator's stock of materials was to be ordered and inventoried as in the workshop of an artisan or the warehouse of a merchant.

The dispensator must be loyal, close-mouthed, industrious, and orderly. His loyalty to the laboratory was essential for he looked after valuable materials and had to keep a true record of his stock and the course of the trials. In his relations with the three other groups of laborers, he had to be close-mouthed, for they must be kept in complete ignorance of one another's operations—indeed, if possible, of each other's existence. Naturally, he must never share the entire process with any of them.[30] He was in fact the last to see the whole process. He needed industry and order so that he could keep the materials from each operation moving on to the next operation with no confusion or slowing of the entire work.

The third chamber of the laboratory was the "*Triturir*-Cammer," the threshing/grinding room, in which materials were pulverized and made into sludge. This space would enclose a spring or a source of running water, a small mill that would run a grinding mill (*Trituratorium*), a stamp mill (*Excussorium*), and a shaker (*Conquassatorium*). Tools needed for these operations—sharpening stones, sieves, vats, and the like—would be kept in this chamber and inven-

[27] Ibid.
[28] Ibid., p. 100.
[29] Ibid.
[30] Ibid.

toried regularly.[31] The workers in the third chamber were "rough, strong people who should understand nothing else."[32] Operations with water were carried out in the fourth chamber of the laboratory, the *"Destillir*-Cammer." Here were located distillation vessels of glass and pottery, and furnaces for boiling, digestion, sublimation, and distillation. The inhabitants of this space were distillers and good *"Wasser-Brenner*, who, however, needed to know nothing further."[33] "Schmelzer" (smelters) and "Probirer" (assayers) worked in the fifth and final chamber, where they carried out the operations of the fire, dealing exclusively with dry materials. Their chamber was filled with furnaces for drying, reverberation, cementation, calcination, smelting, and other processes, as well as with fireproof instruments such as earthenware vessels, crucibles, ladles, and tongs.

The workers in the last three chambers would ideally be unable to read and write, and they must not be allowed paper or writing instruments. They were to be kept in ignorance of the entire set of operations carried out in the other parts of the laboratory so that they could neither attempt to imitate nor steal any of the processes for sale or private use outside the laboratory. The laborers were not to be allowed to handle any raw materials, but only those already prepared and dispensed by the dispensator. Further, the finished products they produced by their operations should be taken quickly from them so that they could not keep any samples. Becher believed if the laborers were not given raw materials and could not know of the other operations, they would have no notion of how they produced any given material. Even if at the end of the entire operation, the laborers of the fire produced gold and silver, they would have no idea how it had been done. Most important, the workers in the last three estates should not be allowed to talk, eat, or drink with each other, and, ideally, they should not even see or know of each other's existence. In the laboratory, they should only come in contact with the *Consilarius*, the dispensator, and the "Speißmeister," or cook.

Organized in this manner, Becher believed the whole work would proceed "philosophically": the counselor engrossed in his studies, the dispensator in his division of labor and materials, and the laborers in their unthinking toil. Each would progress, by constant repetition of single operations toward perfection of his job, and, because, as Becher stated in a burst of baroque pleonasm, "neither the processes, the operations, the materials, the instruments, nor the human beings come together, mix, confuse, collude, confer, communicate or—what is usual with the *Laboranten*—drink together," there will be perfect order and secrecy.[34]

---

[31] Ibid., p. 101.

[32] "Es gehören in diese Cammer grobe starcke Leuth/ die weiters nichts verstehen dörffen" (ibid., p. 101).

[33] Ibid.

[34] Ibid., p. 102.

Becher's laboratory contrasts sharply both with earlier notions of the alchemist's place of work and the traditional structure of the guild workshop, although it retains the aim of both these places: the production of valuable goods from raw material by the *Handwerk* of human art. The last three classes of workers were obviously hired laborers, rather than apprentices to be trained in guild secrets or journeymen to be confirmed in guild brotherhood with beery confraternity. While Becher's laboratory remains a center of production, akin to the guild workshop, he has transformed the manner in which the workers interact and the way in which the skills are reproduced. Keeping the secrets of the workshop has continued as a primary goal, but Becher has changed the way in which this is achieved from control of knowledge by the workers to its alienation from them. The counselor of the laboratory, whom Becher calls a natural philosopher, controls the secrets of productive knowledge, and puts them wholly at the service of the prince. Becher has here created a figure, who, much like himself, acts as an intermediary between the prince and the holders of productive knowledge, simultaneously distancing himself from both the charlatans who crowd the doors of the laboratory and the laborers who work within it.[35] Throughout the seventeenth and eighteenth centuries such projectors and natural philosophers appropriated the knowledge of artisans and came to control the processes that had once been held as guild secrets. This struggle over the control of knowledge paralleled the destruction of guilds in the same period by *Verläger* and princely intervention.[36] Pierre-Joseph Macquer would describe somewhat later in his *Dictionary of Chemistry* the typical chemist of the seventeenth century who worked to "discover and unravel the operations of workmen, who though not Chemists, exercised the most essential parts of Chemistry."[37] Becher's ordering of the laboratory brought these operations and their products more effectively under the control of the prince. The result of such organization, Becher believed, would make the laboratory a model of perfect industry, and the work done in it would result in a combination of theory,

[35] Recent work has focused on the way in which natural philosophers attempted to distance themselves from mechanics. J. A. Bennett, "Robert Hooke as Mechanic and Natural Philosopher," *Notes & Records of the Royal Society* 35 (1980–81): 33–48; Steven Shapin, "The House of Experiment in Seventeenth-Century England," *Isis* 79 (1988): 373–404; idem, "A Scholar and a Gentleman: The Problematic Identity of the Scientific Practitioner in Early Modern England," *History of Science* 24 (1991): 279–327; Michael Hunter and Simon Schaffer, eds., *Robert Hooke: New Studies* (Woodbridge, Suffolk: Boydell Press, 1989); Stephen Pumfrey, "Ideas above His Station: A Social Study of Hooke's Curatorship of Experiments," *History of Science* 29 (1991): 1–44.

[36] The crudest components of this struggle were set out in Boris Hessen's 1931 essay *The Social and Economic Roots of Newton's Principia* (ed. Robert S. Cohen, New York: H. Fertig, 1971), and in Edgar Zilsel, "The Sociological Roots of Science," *American Journal of Sociology* 47 (1941–2): 544–62. For a discussion of the fate of their Marxist interpretations in the subsequent history of science, see Pamela O. Long, "The Scholar and the Craftsman Revisited," paper presented at the annual meeting of the History of Science Society, Washington, D.C., December 1992.

[37] *A Dictionary of Chemistry*, trans. from the French (London: T. Cadell, 1771), pp. xiii–xiv.

practice, and civic virtue: "*Utile* [*sic*], *Honestum & Scientia* all together."[38]

Becher's Kunst- und Werckhaus centered on its chemical laboratories, and it can be inferred that Becher wished to set up these laboratories and the other workshops in the house on the model of his projected alchemical laboratory.[39] Economic historians have seen the organization and goals of Becher's Kunst- und Werckhaus as prefiguring the factory system of manufacture that emerged in the territories of the German Empire in the eighteenth century.[40] Becher's laboratory plans exhibit elements of a factory system, particularly in the division of labor. While it is tempting to draw a linear connection between Becher's plan and the manufacturing industries of later centuries, it is worthwhile to pay close attention to his use of the word *industria*. For Becher, this word connoted not industrial manufacture but civic industriousness and all that it involved. It is precisely through Becher's joining the form of his Kunsthaus to the notion of industrious activity that "industry" took on its modern meaning, but it is necessary to remember that he called it a "Kunst- und Werckhauß," not a "Manufakturhaus." For Becher, "industry" hovered in the space between artisanal guild town, *Verlag*, and manufactory. Like so many of his other ideas, we can see in it a moment of transformation. If one takes a sufficiently narrow sighting of this idea, it can be slotted into a modern understanding, but when the scope is broadened, we find that something as mundane as a chemical industry is occurring in a space as alien as an alchemical laboratory.

Becher linked the form of his Kunsthaus to the notion of *industria* as part of his attempt to integrate the court and commercial worlds. *Kunst* could evoke for the prince the *artificialia* of the Kunstkammer made by the artisans trained in the guild towns, as well as the human potential to imitate the creative principles of nature, whereas *industria* conjured up the productive cycle of the town world. Just as in the colony project, Becher had attempted to entice the count of Hanau to take on the values of the commercial republic by overseas commerce and colonization, so in the manufactures of the laboratory and the Kunst- und Werckhaus, he desired to persuade the emperor that industrious activity and civic virtue were values that could be brought under his control in a Kunsthaus.

Ludus Scaenicus: Industry in the Laboratory

The laboratory, a microcosm of human industry and the place of *ars*, became the stage where Becher completed the integration of court and commercial world. Becher began the discussion about the obligation of great lords to found

[38] *Chymischer Glücks-Hafen*, p. 103.

[39] Ibid., p. 102, states that illustrations of the laboratory are appended at the end of Article 4, but they were apparently never included.

[40] Hans J. Hatschek, *Das Manufakturhaus auf dem Tabor in Wien. Ein Beitrag zur österreichischen Wirthschaftsgeschichte des 17. Jahrhunderts* (Leipzig: Duncker & Humblot, 1886).

laboratories with a section on the proper end of the work. The prince's aim in founding a laboratory must be to enable him to exercise the traditional princely function as protector of his subjects. He must seek the ennoblement of materials in the laboratory with the aim of protecting his land and freeing his subjects from the burden of taxes:

> Great lords can never have too much money, and if they had too much, they have a hundred opportunities to use it; namely, to found churches, monasteries, schools, hospitals, and orphanages, to help poor children study and travel, to dower poor daughters, to improve common roads, to protect and fortify their land, to decrease the *Contribution* [head tax] of the subjects, to support the poor prisoners in Turkey, to spread the Christian religion in foreign places, and many more good works, all of which need means that are difficult to supply from the ordinary revenues of great lords. Therefore great lords should think about extraordinary means that are permissible and do not burden anyone.[41]

Such extraordinary means of income could legitimately only be found in the alchemical laboratory, for it was there that art demonstrated the regenerative capacity of nature, and the alchemist learned how to harness and direct this regenerative capacity. The fabulous profit to be gained in the alchemical laboratory had many advantages over the traditional forms of landed wealth:

> Such types of income only alchemy can supply, when even its most modest process is true, as, for example, granted that a mark of silver is worth ten Reichsthaler and equal to five [gold] ducats, this mark of silver can yield in only one week, by means of alchemy, one ducat of profit. That is in sum (reckoning in the decrease in silver) a 100 percent profit in eight weeks and a 1,000 percent profit in a single year. Thus the capital has been multiplied ten times. Where is there in the world a merchant's trade that can obtain such an interest on its capital? I will not mention how little even the best mines can produce. Who would bear to hazard his capital on an uncertainty and to put it outside of his own hand and power, especially when it is not necessary, when he could keep it in his laboratory out of danger and in his own house instead of investing it in his land, in mines or with the merchants, or lending it to princes or lords, which is burdensome, dangerous and not so useful? . . . Alchemy also has the advantage that its processes can be worked in different places and can be duplicated as often as needed, so that one's needs can be served in all places, which is necessary when one is driven from place to place in war. This is not possible with land [*Landgüter*] or the natural fruits of the land [*Früchte*]. For this reason, the Philosopher said: He who carries everything with him, needs not the aid of others. . . . When we daily see that many a bold man loses his freedom for a paltry thousand gulden [Becher's salary at the imperial court!], and must serve and wait on another with danger to life and limb; how much it would be worth to him to be his own lord! In addition to all this, one can pass this

---

[41] *Chymischer Glücks-Hafen*, p. 81.

science on to one's children as their inheritance, without diminution of the substance and always with preservation of the capital. It does not harm one brother when the other practices this art, too. This is the reason, then, that all great lords should aspire to make this art above all others a source of God-given extraordinary income, and not depend only upon direct taxes from their poor subjects, as an eagle remains sitting on a carcass.[42]

Becher here reiterates that the movable wealth supplied by alchemy is better than land, for even the natural "Landgüter" and "Früchte" of great lords do not have the capacity for generation and multiplication of alchemical processes. Moreover, real property, as well as creating dynastic disharmony and a burdensome and ultimately lethal system of taxes, cannot be carried into war or exile.

As a conclusion to his plan for the laboratory, Becher attached a proposal made to the emperor in 1674 shortly after submitting his Commercial Referat in which he advocated the manufacture of mineral dyes and materials in the Habsburg domain.[43] As with the Kunsthaus, this manufacture would create the means for founding and running the laboratory Becher had described so carefully. Thus "out of the *industria* of chemistry itself" would come the means for the laboratory project.[44]

It has been told to me at different times that Your Imperial Majesty is graciously inclined not only to alchemical, but also to other mathematical and philosophical sciences, inventions, rarities, and curiosities, and that you desire very much to support and protect their cultivators, not doubting that many rare and important things will come to light and be discovered. For, besides the usefulness, Your Imperial Majesty can extract much pleasure and contentment, especially because it is laudable when splendid arts and artists are maintained and put to work [*verlegt*] by high potentates. In these days, times and events have resulted in a shortage of money; in contrast to which the expenses are so great that one can hardly cover the necessary daily costs. At the same time, the subjects count every Kreutzer they are taxed and give as much attention to the application of their tax money. They quickly begin to murmur if, in their opinion, the money is not applied in the necessary places. But if some extraordinary means of income could be found, which is not connected with the taxes of the subjects and much less with the treasury of Your Imperial Majesty, but instead could be effected through industry for the good of the territory, Your Imperial Majesty would need have no misgivings about designating it for the maintenance and collecting of all kinds of arts and artists. Thus such means would be a fund out of which the necessary costs for these things could be taken.[45]

42 Ibid., pp. 81–82.
43 Ibid., pp. 104–7.
44 "auß *Industria* der *Chymi* selbsten" (ibid., p. 103).
45 Ibid., pp. 105–6.

In times when money was short and expenses great, Becher claimed, extraordinary income could be provided by the laboratory. In this proposal, however, the means would not be supplied by alchemy, but through industry, which would in turn produce the means to pursue alchemy. This new extraordinary form of revenue would allow the emperor to live in a style befitting his reputation, able to pursue his court diversions and patronize the arts and sciences. Not only would it allow him reputation, diversion, and pleasure, but would stabilize his power by removing the burden of taxation from his subjects, thus quieting this most dangerous of enemies.[46] All this could be brought about "for the good of the land through industry." This extraordinary means of income obtained through the industry of manufactures was similar to the extraordinary means that could result from the foundation of an alchemical laboratory. They both gave a high return on the funds invested, and provided a means of income entirely at the disposal of the noble lord that secured his rule.

Becher's *industria* had a moral and social significance as well, for it characterized the busy, productive cycle of sustenance in Becher's town model of human society. Its connection to alchemy is clear in Becher's words to the emperor about the alchemist, Daniel Marsaly:

> Marsaly's life lacks proportion to the venerable science [of alchemy]. Therefore it is desirable that he change it and live piously and modestly, so he will prostitute neither himself nor the science, nor make it public. Much is to be ascribed to his youth, his ignorance in *politicis*, his inexperience in *prudentia civili*, and to seduction; in particular to the freedom and license which Your Imperial Majesty permits him.[47]

The alchemist must be experienced in the active political life and in civil prudence, which for Becher meant understanding how to live in a "bürgerlich[e] Gesellschaft" (civil society),[48] and practicing a virtuous active life. The final goal of a civic society was "to be protected and served" ("beschüzt und bedient zu seyn").[49] These ends were accomplished by Becher's society of three estates, each of which served the other, while the prince watched over and protected them, by restraining them within the estate of humanity ("Stand der Menschheit"). As is clear from the Alchemical Gutachten, Becher claimed the alchemist should take part in the civil society and serve the other estates, as the peasants, artisans, and merchants served and protected one another. The alchemist must be part of the active life of "bürgerliche Nahrung," and conform to the needs of the common good. He must practice virtue, but ultimately it was the responsibility of the noble ruler to enforce his subjects' virtue. In his Alchemi-

---

[46] Becher, *Politischer Discurs*, 2d ed., p. 37, says that one rebellious subject is more dangerous than ten foreign enemies.

[47] Alchemical Gutachten, fol. 7v.

[48] Becher, *Psychosophia* (1705), p. 85.

[49] Ibid., p. 81.

cal Gutachten, then, Becher adjudicates not just the process of Daniel Marsaly, but also the virtue of the civil society and its relation to the noble ruler. The traditional sphere of the noble ruler, once external to civic industry, must come to encompass and direct the power of *Handwerk* and the virtue that can be produced by it.

But *industria* also connoted the *industria*, or *Fleiß*, practiced in the laboratory by the dispensator in his diligent, assiduous, and purposeful delegation of tasks and materials, and by the laborers in the repetition of their operations. It could also mean the accumulation of wealth by the industriousness of the merchant-*Verläger*, whose activities Becher considered a model both for princes and merchants. Becher's use of *industria* thus implied both the busy cycle of sustenance, as well as the *Verläger* and his manufacture.[50] Becher's reform of court revenue proposed to make the prince's reputation and power dependent on this *industria* that simultaneously combined the "manual work" of the artisan with the "manufacture" of the *Verläger*.

Becher has transformed the great work of the Paracelsian alchemical laboratory as a microcosm of human salvation into a model of civic *negotia* and manufacture. The alchemist must no longer be infused with divine powers but with the mundane virtue of action in the civil society. Salvation, so far as Becher considered it, was to come in the form of material increase and to be accomplished by a civic industry of manufactures directed by the prince.

Finis: Safe Port

The previous chapter noted that Becher's alchemical work, *Chymischer Glücks-Hafen*, took the name of the Leipzig lottery because both activities signified to Becher honest and ingenious means of increasing the flow of revenue into the treasury. If the noble ruler was attentive to these new means—commerce among them—he would gain authority and reputation, as well as the material surplus with which his power was sustained. If we look more closely at Becher's alchemical book, we find this verse on the title page:

Die Welt die ist ein Glückes-Topff/	The world is a lottery
Die stets herummer läufft/	that goes round and round.
Da gilt es eines jeden Kopff/	Each head counts equally.
Wann das Verhängnuß greifft:	When doom strikes
Es geht blind zu/ man sagt kein Wort/	it proceeds blindly, no word is said,
Nicht richtet/ niemand schreibt;	nothing directs, no one writes.
Gelückts/ so muß der König fort/	That's luck! So must the King away;
Der Esels-Treiber bleibt.	the donkey driver stays.

[50] Almost one hundred years later industry could be summed up as follows: " 'thereby is meant the active energy of free workers and of merchants, together with the so-called *savoir faire* or

"Glückshafen" (safe haven)—whether the new means of income like the lottery or the regenerative and creative means of commerce or alchemy–was not only a harbor of fortune, but a harbor *from* Fortune, a place to escape from the incessant vicissitudes of Fortune's wheel. It was the harbor in which the storms of fortune could be weathered.

Long before Becher's elaboration of this safe haven of alchemy and commerce, Marcellus Palingenius, Becher's sixteenth-century poet-guide and teacher, had equated virtue and possession of the philosophers' stone. Both provided protection from fortune's wheel. Palingenius had said that a rich man is not one who possesses real property but one who is virtuous, for this man can carry his wealth with him wherever he goes, as the man of real property cannot. Like the philosophers' stone, made from mobile mercury, virtue sustains and brings happiness, wherever *fortuna* may toss a man. Virtue and the philosophers' stone are one. For, as Marcellus phrased it, *"Vertue* true gives neuer place to Fortunes frowning spite," and:

> Then whiche no art more worthy is, the Heavenly Stone to frame,
> Which wicked people never knowe, nor can obtaine the same.
> And this whosoever doth enjoy may dwell in any land,
> Bothe free from feare of fortunes wheele, and force of robbers hand.[51]

The social virtue of civic industry and the creative industriousness of the alchemical laboratory could enable the noble ruler to overcome his uncertain *fortuna*. The Leipzig lottery was a game of chance, and those who entered it subjected themselves to the whims of fortune. Paradoxically, however, from this game of risk and gambling would come stability, for the prince who staged the lottery could subdue fortune. He and his state always won in this game of chance. Becher's use of the lottery as a means to control fortune parallels a transformation occurring in the understanding of other forms of risk, such as insurance. Begun as a form of gambling like the lottery, life insurance and annuity policies came to represent by the late seventeenth century a calculus of probabilities by which risk could be controlled.[52] Becher stood at a divide when

---

cleverness at extracting all possible gains from favorable opportunities. And in this sense, Industry is set in contrast with stable property and with land.'" Mack Walker, *German Home Towns: Community, State, and General Estate, 1648–1871* (Ithaca: Cornell University Press, 1971), pp. 121–22, quoting Johann G. Krünitz, *Oekonomische Enzyklopädie* (Berlin, 1783), p. 708ff.

[51] Marcellus Palingenius, *The Zodiake of Life*, trans. Barnabie Googe (London: Rause Newberie, 1576; fasc. repr. New York: Scholars' Facsimiles & Reprints, 1947), pp. 186, 188.

[52] See Hans Schmitt-Lermann, *Der Versicherungsgedanke im deutschen Geistesleben des Barock und der Aufklärung* (Munich: Kommunalschriften-Verlag J. Jehle, 1954); Lorraine Daston, *Classical Probability in the Enlightenment* (Princeton: Princeton University Press, 1988); Ian Hacking, *The Emergence of Probability* (London: Cambridge University Press, 1975). Ann Fabian, *Card Sharps, Dream Books, and Bucket Shops: Gambling in Nineteenth-Century America* (Ithaca: Cornell University Press, 1990), follows the dialectic between gambling and capitalism in a different setting.

the very bases of rationality and of rational action were being transformed by new economic practices and by a new understanding of the world. The revival in the late sixteenth century of Stoic doctrines that claimed the individual might triumph over fortune by a combination of will, virtue, and philosophical practice[53] flowered by the seventeenth century into a belief that this control of fortune might be exercised for the benefit of an entire territory, indeed even for society at large. Becher's gathering of statistics on the artisans in the Habsburg domains represents the very beginnings of a habit of applying the certainty of mathematical calculation to the inscrutable forces of fortune. Although Becher's own rise to favor may have been made possible by the whims of *fortuna* (or Providence), he helped to institute a concept of rationality that depended on prudent calculation and careful measurement of potential. In the same way, Becher's belief in the possibility of alchemical transmutation provided a bridge to what we believe to be the more "rational" practices of commercial manufacture and investment. This bridge stood rooted in the eternal verities of nature, however, for although Becher evinced interest in the Dutch forms of life annuities—*Lyf-Renten*—he still thought in terms of the processes of the natural world and their imitation by the human hand.[54] He attempted to make clear to the prince that by understanding and controlling the forces of nature, such as generation, creation, and material production—forces understood by the "*Real*-Weisheit" of the alchemist, mechanic, and artisan—the prince could overcome the uncertain returns to his treasury by harnessing the very sources of the creation of wealth.

[53] Gerhard Oestreich, *Geist und Gestalt des frühmodernen Staaten* (Berlin: Dunker & Humblot, 1969); Gotthardt Frühsorge, *Der politische Körper* (Stuttgart: J. B. Metzlersche Verlagsbuchhandlung, 1974).

[54] Mss. var. 1(2), fols. 636r–647v, contains a copy of Johann de Witt's pamphlet on life annuities: *Waerdye van Lyf-Renten naer proportie van Los-Renten* (The Hague: Jacob Scheltus, 1671).

FIVE

BETWEEN WORDS AND THINGS: THE COMMERCE

OF SCHOLARS AND THE PROMISE OF *ARS*

A S HE MOVED back and forth between the courts of the Holy Roman
Empire, Becher was accompanied throughout his life by a group of
men like himself, with whom he worked in the laboratory, projected,
and quarreled. These individuals were highly mobile and well traveled; they
usually combined the learned title of "Doctor" with an interest in the mechanical arts, and they competed for the favor of the prince in their pursuit of official
positions at court. Although immersed in the artifice of the baroque court, these
men usually came to court from (or identified themselves primarily with) the
republic of letters and they all had an interest in the new philosophy. This group
included the ubiquitous Johann Daniel Crafft, the Swedish projector, Bengt
Skytte, whom we know from the court of Hanau, and, eventually, Gottfried
Wilhelm Leibniz (1646–1716).

Historians usually do not speak of Leibniz as inhabiting the same world as
Becher, but an examination of Leibniz's interactions with Becher reveals that
despite his more conventional learned credentials, Leibniz was fascinated,
even obsessed, by Becher's activities, and saw no boundary between his own
sphere and that of Becher.[1] Indeed, if we investigate the reasons for Leibniz's
fascination with Becher, we find that they shared a number of assumptions and
understandings about the world, which they drew from a common vocabulary
of ideas and sources as well as from shared economic and political circumstances. Their understanding of the world and their actions based upon that
understanding helped shape a new notion of rationality, which, ironically, did
much to relegate a large portion of their own work to a space outside the
boundaries of that new rationality. Subsequent scholarship has chosen to give
more (in the case of Leibniz) or less (in the case of Becher) weight to those
aspects of their work which are now considered rational.[2] In recounting several

---

[1] An exception to those historians who regard Becher and Leibniz as belonging to separate
worlds is Herbert Breger, "Närrische Weisheit und weise Narrheit in Erfindungen des Barock,"
Aesthetik und Kommunikation 45–46 (October 1981): 114–22, and "Becher, Leibniz und die
Rationalität," Proceedings of a Becher Arbeits-Gespräch, 1987, to be published in *Wolfenbütteler
Forschungsreihe*, which he was kind enough to allow me to see in manuscript.

[2] Such judgments have been more evident in the history of science and intellectual history. One
notable exception is Rudolf W. Meyer, *Leibniz and the Seventeenth-Century Revolution* (1952;
New York: Garland Publishing, 1985). Recent studies of baroque literature, such as Wilhelm
Kühlmann, *Gelehrtenrepublik und Fürstenstaat* (Tübingen: Max Niemeyer Verlag, 1982); Gott-

interactions between these like-minded men, this chapter illumines the bases of reasonable action held to by Becher and his contemporaries and considers the transformation of their assumptions about rationality.

Scholars and Artificers

In the spring of 1677 Johann Daniel Crafft visited Gottfried Wilhelm Leibniz in Hanover where Leibniz had recently been called as historiographer and librarian to the duke of Hanover, Johann Friedrich. Among other news, Crafft told the court about the discovery by a certain Henning Brand in Hamburg of a new cold fire. It was a liquid white light called the *noctiluca* or the *lumen constans*. Leibniz communicated Crafft's news immediately to the *Journal des sçavans*, where he wrote that "if one rubs the face, the hands, and the clothes with the liquid, it lights them all up, which in good society by night brings very pretty effects. Furthermore, it has the good quality that the clothes are not ruined by it."[3] By July 1678 Leibniz had contracted with Brand in the name of the duke of Hanover to "communicate his fire, together with other curiosities that are known to him," and to correspond with other inventors so that he could inform the duke of any new curious objects and processes that came to his notice. In return the duke would pay him a monthly salary of ten Reichsthaler with an initial payment of sixty Thaler.[4]

Phosphorus promised something more than noble diversion, for it was produced from human urine that was distilled, crystallized, and fired in a retort. According to alchemical theory, the human body was the microcosm of the natural cosmos, and, as the natural distillate of the human body, urine held an important place in medicine. The cold fire, which contravened the paired qualities of hot and dry, cold and wet, and was produced from the human urine raised hopes that the much expected stone of the philosophers in the animal realm had been discovered. Leibniz believed further that the cold fire shed important light on the principles of chemistry because he believed it did not originate in the mercurial principle, but in the sulfurous one.[5]

This wondrous invention was the work of Henning Brand, who styled himself a doctor of medicine and was known for his ability in the laboratory. Johann

hardt Frühsorge, *Der politische Körper* (Stuttgart: J. B. Metzlersche Verlagsbuchhandlung, 1974); Wilfred Barner, *Barockrhetorik. Untersuchungen zu ihren geschichtlichen Grundlagen* (Tübingen: Max Niemeyer Verlag, 1970), and others try to map out the world in which Becher and Leibniz moved, although they generally do not deal with them.

[3] From *Journal des sçavans*, 2 August 1677, pp. 244–46, quoted in Hermann Peters, "Leibniz als Chemiker," *Archiv für die Geschichte der Naturwissenschaften und der Technik* 7 (1916): 87, n. 4. I follow Peters in the narrative of the phosphorous incident.

[4] Peters, "Leibniz," p. 88, n. 7.

[5] Ibid., p. 91.

Kunckel, another player in this drama, scornfully called him "a wrecked merchant who had applied himself to medicine," and a *"Doctor Teutonicus"* because he knew no Latin.[6] Kunckel too had dealt with Brand through Crafft. Kunckel recounts that he wrote to Crafft about his intention to offer Brand money for his secret, and Crafft immediately went to Hamburg and promised Brand two hundred Reichsthaler if he said nothing to Kunckel. Not suspecting Crafft's preemption, Kunckel traveled to Hamburg and questioned Brand, but Brand claimed to be unable to reproduce his first success, and Kunckel was thus unable to learn Brand's process until later, when Brand came to him, claiming to be disgusted with Crafft and ready to offer his secret to a new buyer.[7]

Leibniz and Kunckel were not alone in seeking out Brand for their patrons. Johann Joachim Becher, too, entered into the market fray developing around Brand and his curious invention. Becher had left the emperor's court with his brother-in-law Philipp Wilhelm von Hörnigk in early 1677 to enforce a ban on French imports into the free imperial cities, declared by the emperor as part of the German Empire's *Reichskrieg* against France.[8] This trip lasted through the autumn of 1677, when Becher and Hörnigk went their separate ways, neither of them returning to Vienna. Becher set off for Holland, and when he still had not returned to Vienna to make his report to the emperor by January 1678, the Hofkammer accused him of taking bribes and general incompetence.[9]

In the Netherlands Becher went first to Haarlem where he formed a company in February 1678 with five others, including among them Johann Daniel Crafft, the chemist-theologian Galenus from Amsterdam, and an architect cum glassmaker and lens grinder. This company had been granted a building and child labor from the orphanage by the city of Haarlem in order to set up and operate a winding instrument, invented by Becher, that wound spools of raw silk. This company was shortly thereafter dissolved and Becher turned to the extraction of gold from sand on the coast near Arnhem and Scheveningen. Before he could make even the small trial that was approved by the states of Holland and Westfriesland,[10] he left for Hamburg, where he came into direct competition

[6] Johann Kunckel, *Collegium Physico-Chymicum experimentale, oder Laboratorium Chymicum*, ed. Johann Caspar Engelleder (Hamburg and Leipzig: Samuel Heyl, 1716), pp. 660–63. Kunckel quotes Brand's Hamburg dialect to show his unlearned origins (p. 663). For additional information on Brand, see Herbert Breger, "Notiz zur Biographie des Phosphor-Entdeckers Henning Brand," *Studia leibnitiana* 19 (1987): 68–73.

[7] Kunckel, *Laboratorium Chymicum*, pp. 661–62.

[8] Leopold I declared the *Reichskrieg* in 1674 in an attempt to halt Louis XIV's expansion into Holland and Germany. Becher had always urged a ban on the import of luxuries as a crucial part of his economic program. For details of this trip, see Hassinger, *Becher*, pp. 216–30.

[9] Hassinger (*Becher*, p. 226) discusses these charges. In self-justification Becher wrote *Wohlgemeintes unvorgreiffliches Gutachten/ Wie das Reichs*-Edict *in* bannisierung der Frantzösischen Waaren in praxin *und zum* effect *zu bringen/* auch was dem gesammten Röm. Reiche und allen Ständen dran gelegen, and *Copia Eines Nohtwendigen Memorials* (Amsterdam: Jacob von Felsen, 1678).

[10] See *Trifolium Becherianum Hollandicum* and the contractual documents Becher reprinted there.

with Leibniz for Brand's knowledge (and for Brand himself) at the end of July 1678. Leibniz wrote to his patron, the duke Johann Friedrich of Hanover:

> Your Highness will perhaps remember that a few weeks ago I communicated to You that Brand possessed the very secret that Herr Arendt spoke so much about in Hanover. This secret was to be sold for colossal sums so it must really have brought out a considerable amount of gold in the silver mass. Brand assured me that he had tried it successfully and told me in detail about the extraordinary manner in which he had learned it. Many people assure me that there is really something in it and many reasons convince me that the above-mentioned Brand truly has it. . . . The only problem is that Brand, because he is in bad straits, will sell it for a small amount to the first bidder. I can judge according to the manner in which I had it from him yesterday: he treated with Dr. Becher, who came here from Amsterdam. The aforementioned Dr. Becher offered him 10 Reichsthaler weekly for his whole life and wanted him to work by himself in Boizenburg, a city on the Elbe belonging to the duke of Mecklenburg-Güstrow with whom Becher is involved in I do not know what business. I had the good fortune to thwart this agreement because I had information about him through intrigues that I had [set up] around Dr. Becher. I communicated to Brand that he would do better when he was employed by Your Highness to keep such an important subject to himself until he could ensure that it is true, and that he should place little value on the promises of Dr. Becher. He understood these reasons, but they were not enough for him without 20 Reichsthaler that I gave him in the hope Your Highness would approve it. Additionally I have given him hope that Your Highness would allow him to work on his light [phosphorus] and the process for it in Hanover, and if it is found to be genuine, he would be in a good position to be employed for the large-scale production. This is the only means to hinder him from selling his process here to everybody and perhaps also to Dr. Becher. I especially desire that not to happen because Dr. Becher is the man to proclaim it to all the world and to offer it for sale to all the powers on earth. In any case, if this process proves to be false, one only owes Brand the yearly 120 Reichsthaler for his light, and if it proves true, then Brand deserves to be employed in its application on a large scale and treated somewhat more generously. For, if for no other reason than it is enough that he keeps this secret hidden, which cannot be accomplished so long as he lives here in bad circumstances. Thus, I await the command of Your Highness, whether I should have him come as quickly as possible to Hanover?[11]

A month later Leibniz had succeeded in bringing Brand to Hanover and wrote jubilantly that he had rescued him from Becher's grasp:

> I am very happy to have brought Dr. Brand here because it broke up the negotiations with Dr. Becher, who undoubtedly, according to his manner, had made very

---

[11] Gottfried Wilhelm Leibniz, *Sämtliche Schriften und Briefe*, ed. Preussische Akademie der Wissenschaften et al. (Darmstadt: Otto Reichl et al., 1923–), ser. 1, vol. 2, Leibniz to Duke Johann Friedrich, 31 July/10 August 1678, pp. 63–65 (my translation from the original French).

favorable offers to the Duke of Güstrow in the expectation to have this man entirely at his disposal; but he is well ensnared now. I feared that Dr. Becher would get hold of him on his return to Hamburg. And, as far as I know Dr. Brand, one can bring him wherever one desires with a little money. And I had a meet reason in my dealings, namely, if Dr. Becher had Brand, he would certainly have learned from him that I planned to thwart his plans. And because he is quite an odd man [*homme tout à fait bizarre*], I do not want anything to do with him.[12]

To isolate Brand further, as well as give him access to large quantities of urine and wood with which to make phosphorus, Leibniz proposed to send him to the Harz Mountains. In two months however, Brand was back in Hamburg, where he and his wife Margaretha bombarded Leibniz with appeals for money and advances of salary. He threatened Leibniz with the prospect of Becher's greater generosity, and Margaretha wrote to Leibniz on behalf of her husband: "Dr. Becher is ever so honest and four weeks ago, as he left Hamburg for Amsterdam, he honored my husband with ninety-four Reichsthaler." Brand himself wrote to Crafft complaining that while Crafft had told him to trust Leibniz and to stay away from Becher, he had learned from experience that "Dr. Becher is as honest a man as I have met in all my days, while Leibniz is a fickle person, indeed very similar to a clown."[13] Brand not only threatened Leibniz with the specter of other buyers, but also attempted to use the credit he gained by being associated with the court in Hanover for other schemes. He wrote to Leibniz requesting a recommendation for a position with the Dutch East India Company where he could use his skills of smelting and assaying.[14]

In these dealings, as in so many others, Johann Daniel Crafft worked alongside and sometimes against Becher. No doubt he was the spy who enabled Leibniz to thwart Becher's negotiations with Brand. Like Becher, Crafft was a medical doctor, but after a professional stint in the Harz-Zellerfeld mines, he traveled widely in Europe and the New World. He served at the court of the elector in Mainz and as *Handelsrath* (trade advisor) in Saxony. It was Crafft who kept Leibniz abreast of Becher's doings throughout the 1670s. Leibniz had first become acquainted with Crafft at the court of the elector in Mainz between 1667 and 1671, when Leibniz was advising on judicial reform and Crafft was trade advisor,[15] and from the very beginning of their acquaintance, Leibniz probed Crafft for information about Becher.

In 1671, Crafft informed Leibniz about Becher's trip through Würzburg on his way to Amsterdam,[16] about his experiment performed before the elector of

---

[12] Ibid., Leibniz to Duke Johann Friedrich of Hanover, mid-September, 1678, pp. 68–70 (my translation from the original French).

[13] The whole series of letters from Brand to Leibniz is reprinted in Peters, "Leibniz," pp. 92–99.

[14] See letter from Brand to Leibniz, 5 March 1679, in ibid., p. 97.

[15] Rudolf Forberger, "Johann Daniel Crafft. Notizen zu einer Biographie," *Jahrbuch für Wirtschaftsgeschichte*, pts. 2–3 (1964): 63–79.

[16] Leibniz, *Sämtliche Schriften*, ser. 1, vol. 1, Crafft to Leibniz, 1/11 September 1671, p. 222; and 22 September 1671, pp. 222–23.

Mainz in which iron was drawn from linseed oil and clay,[17] and about the project for obtaining the million Reichsthaler credit for the emperor.

I have a little news about Dr. Becher's affairs in Holland (as Becher allowed himself to be understood in Würzburg), among which the principal is that he brought into being a million Reichsthaler for His Majesty, in such a way that His Majesty must pay 5 percent interest for forty years, after which time the capital will be his and no more will be owing. However, it is on condition that Cologne or Hamburg act as security for the forty-year interest. NB: [this project] is an example of Dr. Becher's judgment. I said to him and I am still of the opinion that this million will be coined in the kingdom [in America] of the Count of Hanau. Or perhaps the need for money or his greed drove [Becher] to contrive such a work so he would be sent to Hamburg and Cologne about their performance of the security, because he knows that besides a new deceit, he will have a rich allowance and respect from both places in carrying out his duties. The Emperor will have nothing but good words. Item: In Amsterdam [he said] there was a man who had 80,000 ounces of lead in the works and turned it into pure silver. [Becher] claimed to have learned this, but if he were really a *Physicus subterraneus*, he would have been able to do it already, or indeed [if] he were able to imitate it, he could make the million for the Emperor himself.[18]

The fact that Becher stood so highly in the emperor's favor seems to have rankled with Crafft, but at the same time he saw an opportunity to exploit Becher's situation at the imperial court to his own advantage. Late in 1672 he had reported to Leibniz that Becher had a laboratory and glassmaking workshop built in Vienna,[19] which must refer to the beginnings of the Kunst- und Werckhaus. In the middle of 1673, Crafft hoped to use the credit that this project had given to Becher for his own ends. He wrote to Leibniz:

From Dresden I travel to Vienna to put in order the steel and glass furnaces erected by Dr. Becher along with other things, from which several thousand yearly are to be expected. Above all else Dr. Becher stands very well with His Majesty, and, because of certain uncommon suggestions that will bring in millions, so well loved and in good credit that my planned journey will fall out for me on all sides excellently, which in the present situation seems to me right. In addition to these things there is the subject that another good friend, who for a certain reason I will not name, has invited me to [code: gold making], which comes out of [code: silver], with [code: great profit]. I have reason to believe that the process is genuine, about which I will send further notice, my Very Learned Sir. At another

---

[17] Ibid., Crafft to Leibniz, 1/11 September 1671, p. 222; and Crafft to Leibniz 11/21 December 1671, p. 230.

[18] Ibid., Crafft to Leibniz, 3/13 October 1671, pp. 224–25.

[19] Ibid., Crafft to Leibniz, 26 December 1672, p. 410.

place further news about the [code: lapis philosophorum] was found. Thus good things come all at once, which on this trip will complement each other.[20]

Becher could be both rival and valuable connection in Vienna. Leibniz's fear that Becher might uncover his intrigues in bringing Brand to Hanover indicated that Becher could indeed influence Leibniz's fate at the Viennese court, where Leibniz sought the position of *Reichshofrat*. When Leibniz was negotiating for a position with Christobal Rojas y Spinola (1626–94), the Franciscan bishop of Tinin, later bishop of Wiener Neustadt, and an important figure at Leopold's court, Leibniz expressly told Crafft, who was interceding with the bishop on his behalf, not to let Becher know of his intentions.[21]

After he left the court, Becher no longer posed a direct threat to Leibniz's interests there, but he remained in high standing with the emperor who contin-ued to show interest in his affairs. Leibniz also remained interested, indeed captivated by Becher's affairs. In 1679, when Becher had left Güstrow and was back in the Netherlands, pursuing his gold extraction scheme, Leibniz's search for news of Becher became almost frantic.[22] Leibniz was kept informed about Becher's affairs in Holland at this time by Christian Philipp, the elector of Saxony's resident minister in Hamburg, the publisher Daniel Elsevier,[23] the Dutch philologue Johann Georg Graevius, even Becher's printer, Johann David Zunner,[24] and, of course, Crafft.

Crafft first reported that Becher was back in Amsterdam in December 1679, when he claimed that Becher was seeking money from everyone.[25] When Leibniz obtained information (apparently from Crafft) that Becher's process for extracting gold from sand had succeeded in the small-scale trial, he believed he might be able to repeat it for his patron:

Here is one more matter, my Lord: I believe I spoke to Your Highness of a man in Holland who proposes to extract gold from sand. He claims that there will be

[20] Ibid., Crafft to Leibniz, 14/24 March 1673, p. 414. This is a particularly newsy letter in which Crafft also mentions Wilhelm von Schröder's affairs in England (where he was carrying out the instructions about commerce given him by the emperor) and the fact that he knows nothing at this time about Martin Elers.

[21] Ibid., Leibniz to Crafft, 24 May/2 June 1677, p. 272.

[22] Becher may have been back in Amsterdam as early as December 1678. His *Copia Eines Nohtwendigen Memorials* is dated the last day of 1678 in Amsterdam.

[23] Leibniz, *Sämtliche Schriften*, ser. 1, vol. 2, Elsevier to Leibniz, 11 March 1679, pp. 436–37; 25 March 1679, p. 449; and 3 June 1679, p. 483.

[24] Ibid., Johann David Zunner to Leibniz, 2/12 December 1678, p. 390. Zunner complains that Becher is planning to publish a larger edition of the *Politischer Discurs* with a printer in Rostock, something he has no right to do as Zunner was the first publisher of the book.

[25] Crafft to Leibniz, quoted in Peters, "Leibniz als Chemiker," pp. 284–85. In this letter Crafft says that he too had been caught up in Becher's scheme: "Ich bin auch in seine Netze geraten und fürchte, daß ich ohne Schaden nicht davon kommen werde." Christian Philipp wrote to Leibniz on 26 October/5 November 1678 that he had spoken with "the illustrious Mr. Becher" and had seen his

almost as much net profit in it as in the mines of Hungary. There is strong doubt about the event, but I learned from several letters that the experiment had succeeded in such a way as to make one hope for some success on a large scale. If that is the case I will tell to Your Highness a thing that I have not dared to speak about before because I doubted its truth. And that is that I know this person's secret, at least such as it was when he made the proposition to the States General in the past year, for if he has since found more I know nothing about it, nor do I believe it. One of his friends, a friend of mine, copied word for word a paper from the hand of this person. That which was copied was not a simple recipe or process, but a relation, well set out, of the experiments already done, which this person had put into writing when working in order to be reminded of the material and all the proportions and procedures. So that this makes me want to have it tried one day. Indeed Your Highness has a great advantage, for in your land there are all the things necessary for this operation.[26]

To Christiaan Huygens, however, Leibniz expressed himself a little more skeptically about what he knew of the process. He believed that gold had indeed resulted, but not necessarily out of the sand. In the autumn of 1679, Becher performed the large trial of the extraction, but the outcome was ambiguous.[27] After Becher published his *Trifolium Hollandicum*, Leibniz was still doubtful:

> The essays Becher published do not prove the reality of his proposition. At least they show that one can repeat the same operation up to fifty times with the same silver. For otherwise, all the silver of Europe would have to pass through his furnace before he would gain the million per year he promises.[28]

Late in 1679, Becher disappeared from view, and Leibniz sought information in vain. The Saxon elector's resident minister in Hamburg finally sent news in early 1680 that he had heard that "the affairs of Mr. Becher in Holland are finished like all his previous undertakings, and they are yet to see a single effect of his grand promises."[29] A few months later he had heard that "Mr. Becher, notwithstanding the cunning spirit of the Dutch, has succeeded in extracting a good sum of money and then disappeared afterward, but they are searching for him everywhere and will treat him most rigorously if he allows himself to be

new book "*Psychosophie*," and that Becher says he is traveling to Holland, "but you know, Sir, that his words are subjects of caution" (Leibniz, *Sämtliche Schriften*, ser. 1, vol. 2, pp. 377–78).

[26] Leibniz, *Sämtliche Schriften*, ser. 1, vol. 2, Leibniz to Duke Johann Friedrich, mid-June 1679, pp. 176–78.

[27] Ibid., Christian Philipp to Leibniz, 24 September/4 October 1679, pp. 518–19. Christian Philipp assumes that Leibniz has seen the news from the "gazettes," but adds that the outcome of the trial was disputed.

[28] Leibniz to Huygens, 8 September 1679: Christiaan Huygens, *Oeuvres complètes de Christiaan Huygens*, 22 vols. (The Hague: Martinus Nijhof, 1888–1950), *Correspondance*, vol. 8, letter no. 2192, and December 1679, no. 2205.

[29] Leibniz, *Sämtliche Schriften*, ser. 2, vol. 3, Christian Philipp to Leibniz, 21/31 January 1680, pp. 348–49.

found."[30] Finally, weeks later, Christian Philipp could inform Leibniz that Becher was said to be in England, "and there he has found his dupes as always."[31] Leibniz continued to seek informers about Becher's activities in England,[32] and in July 1680 Christian Philipp wrote to Leibniz that he had news from England that Becher finally "begins to lose all his credit."[33]

Artifice at Court

As we can see, Leibniz was fascinated by Becher, even asking one of his correspondents in code for news of Becher.[34] The phosphorous episode, as well as Leibniz's continuing interest in Becher, illustrates clearly that Leibniz and Becher, among others, competed with each other. They were rivals both for the artisan, Henning Brand, who made phosphorus, for his knowledge, and for favor at their respective courts. The patrons whom they represented in making the deal with Brand competed for the reputation and honor that would accompany the first large-scale production of the icy fire.

Leibniz and Becher were both projectors competing in a marketplace of ideas, machines, and the makings of spectacle for their princely patrons (who in their turn competed for *fama*, reputation, and power). The competition required a careful strategy and no small artifice. When in 1680 Leibniz finally made a determined effort to obtain a position as *Reichshofrat* at the imperial court, he drew up a meticulous plan of attack for his intermediary in the negotiations, Johann Daniel Crafft. This set of instructions illustrates how calculated this artifice could be. Leibniz began by deliberating on how he might best bring his schemes—of a commercial kind—quickly to the emperor's notice. First, a noble mediator was needed at the Viennese court; one who "has a great light and outstanding *judicium*, who can draw out exact information from all things, and who is happy to grant audiences."[35] This mediator would further their scheme and, most important, thoroughly inform His Majesty, the emperor, of everything. Leibniz settled on two possible noble mediators, the count of Pötting, who is "after the President, the first in the Bohemian Treasury," and the mar-

---

[30] Ibid., Christian Philipp to Leibniz, 27 March/6 April 1680, pp. 368–69.

[31] Ibid., Christian Philipp to Leibniz, 10/20 April 1680, p. 386.

[32] Leibniz received letters from several correspondents in England at this time clearly in reply to queries about Becher's whereabouts and affairs. Ibid., Edward Bernard to Leibniz, 23 September/3 October 1680, London, p. 430; Friedrich Adolf Hansen to Leibniz, 28 September/8 October, 1680, Oxford, pp. 431–33; Hansen to Leibniz, 17/27 October 1680, Oxford, pp. 436–39.

[33] Ibid., Christian Philipp to Leibniz, 17/27 July 1680, pp. 411–12. "on écrit d'Angleterre, que l'auteur [i.e., Becher] y commence à perdre tout son credit."

[34] Leibniz, *Sämtliche Schriften*, ser. 1, vol. 1, Leibniz to Johann Lincker, February 1674, p. 392.

[35] Beginning of July (?) 1680, draft by Leibniz for Daniel Crafft. Leibniz, *Sämtliche Schriften*, ser. 1, vol. 3, pp. 400–403; this quote, p. 400.

grave Hermann von Baden, a *Reichsfürst*. Leibniz favored the margrave because

> this proposal is very broad and stretches not only over the whole Habsburg lands,
> but also over the whole Empire of the German Nation, for the welfare and preserva-
> tion of which [the margrave] acts; indeed it stretches even further [than the sphere
> in which he acts]. Thus it seems to me that His Princely Highness, the Margrave
> Hermann von Baden, is a very apt instrument for it, because he is a *Reichs-Fürst*
> who is held in high consideration by His Imperial Majesty, whose zeal and good
> intentions are known, and also because Herr von Hörnigk has connections
> [*Kundschafft*] with him and could motivate him by a letter that will prick his
> appetite.[36]

Leibniz drafted a letter for Crafft to give to Philipp Wilhelm von Hörnigk
(Becher's brother-in-law and the second of Leibniz's intermediaries), who
would send it to the margrave. In this letter, Leibniz instructed Hörnigk to write
to the margrave and to tell him that he (Hörnigk) had come into contact with a
"certain Person" (i.e., Leibniz) for whose merit he could vouch. Hörnigk was to
write that:

> This person has elaborated wonderful concepts, which combine so aptly with
> mine, that I believe the right *arcanum* has been discovered, by which not only
> Germany as a whole can be restored, but the Imperial Majesty can be made
> fortunate and formidable, and his authority can be joined indissolubly with the
> public good. It is perhaps the only way that the House of Austria can rise again and
> that France can be held within its bounds. In sum it is an admirable harmony and
> union of the matters of state, war, and commerce.[37]

Leibniz instructed von Hörnigk to make clear his belief that his conversation
with the "certain person" must be regarded as "the finger of God" ("eine
sonderbare schickung Gottes"), which would bring honor and gratitude to all
those concerned with it. Hörnigk should mention that the person who had
proposed it was "not completely unknown at the Imperial court" and the concept would speak for his loyalty and good intentions. Hörnigk should caution
the margrave, however, that it would not be possible to reveal the particulars of
the project until it was clear that it would be carried out swiftly and directly
through the emperor. Otherwise the French faction at court would exploit it, or
others might make it the basis for intrigue and condemnation.

Leibniz planned to approach the count von Pötting from a different angle (and
only after the margrave had had a chance to mention the project to the emperor).
Leibniz believed they should "first sound out" the count to test his suitability for
this project. If "he manages the *Mercurial*-Werck" then they could use him in

---

[36] Ibid., p. 400.
[37] Ibid., pp. 400–401.

their scheme. But the meeting with Count Pötting would in any case have to wait until news reached them that the margrave had spoken to the emperor, for a proposition like theirs could only be discussed orally with the emperor. The modern reader can easily imagine Leibniz, von Hörnigk, and Crafft eagerly seeking news from their contacts and court gossip about the margrave's audiences with the emperor and the subject of conversation at those audiences. Impatient with the amount of time such intrigue could waste, Leibniz boldly concluded that it would be better to arrange a coincidental meeting between Crafft and the margrave to hasten the business. Leibniz explored this option in the instructions: von Hörnigk should write a letter to the margrave about the commercial schemes. Thus the margrave would be put into "a fully zealous mood" ("vollends stimmen und eifrig"), when he "coincidentally" ran into Crafft. Leibniz instructed Crafft to lead the margrave into a discussion of the scheme, and made clear how he should comport himself in this conversation. Leibniz believed that Crafft could "animate" the margrave by a "thousand things in commerce that conspire to this main business." Leibniz continued,

> I expect that my Very Learned Sir will keep this main scheme in mind and allow the greatest zeal to be manifest, and [I expect] that he will keep it secret from one and all, for it receives greater acclaim and happens with better style when my Very Learned Sir holds something in reserve, and puts it off for another person. It is all to be arranged in such a way that the full opening [i.e., to the emperor] at the Imperial court will be zealously sought, which we must attempt not only through the Margrave Hermann, but after him also through the Count von Pötting. . . . Therefore it is to be arranged so that the opening is made to the Emperor himself and submitted in writing and, that, in return for this, favor and a real position are promised.[38]

Leibniz emphasized that Crafft and von Hörnigk should make clear that only in return for "würcklichen *employ* und *commission*" (true employment and commission) would he investigate the entire German manufacture and commercial system ("*manufactur* und *commerci*en wesen") and assist the emperor's hereditary lands, as well as the most important German courts, in setting up manufactures and commerce. In pursuit of these ends, Leibniz advised Crafft to use a certain amount of exaggeration:

> As the opportunity arises with the Margrave, Count von Pötting and the Emperor himself, my Very Learned Sir will certainly know how to present with some exaggeration what can be expected from the person [i.e., Leibniz] in the introduction and powerful execution of uncommon things. At the same time, as the opportunity arises, it should be added that this person is competent and capable to take up employment in this negotiation as well as [to take up] the position in the [?] College with the emoluments that are to be stipulated. My Very Learned Sir should portray

[38] Ibid., p. 402.

the true state of cameral and commercial subjects and the associated advantages in the same way.[39]

Leibniz ended the instruction to Crafft by setting out the code they will use: d for the emperor, v for Hermann von Baden, a for Pötting, c for Abele (an imperial minister), b for Hörnigk, l for France, g for Spain, and the letters of the alphabet corresponding to a key that spelled out "labyrinthuscdefgkmopqwxz."[40]

Perhaps if Becher had still been at the imperial court in 1680, Leibniz would have approached him in his favor-seeking, but the rivalry between them would have made such an attempt risky for Leibniz, for Becher continued to stand in high credit with the emperor. Only the year before, the emperor had answered with a "placet" (i.e., approval) a proposition by Wilhelm von Schröder to take over Becher's Kunst- und Werckhaus for woolen manufacture, but at the same time the emperor had noted with his own hand that Schröder's activities should not "prejudice Dr. Becher and the Bishop of Tinin [Christobal Rojas y Spinola] who had first undertaken this *manufactur*."[41] In late 1679, Becher was still an important enough figure at the court for the emperor to ask his resident minister in The Hague to send news of him.[42] Thus Becher lingered in the emperor's favor even after he left Vienna. Leibniz could well have been jealous of the wielder of such artifice and the recipient of such favor, but Leibniz's interest in Becher went beyond competition and jealousy.[43] Becher's final publications shed light on the nature of this interest.

Art and Invention

When Becher reached England in 1680, he succeeded in finding patrons and continuing his work in chemistry and commerce. Edmund Dickinson, Oxford

[39] Ibid., pp. 402–3.

[40] Ibid., p. 403.

[41] "Referat deß Wilhelmb Schrötters weittere proposition, die introducirung der Engeländischen Wollinen Manufacturen betr.," undated, but ca. 1679: Vienna, Hofkammerarchiv, Verschiedene Vorschläge, Fasz. 7, fols. 21–28.

[42] Resident Minister Kramprich to Leopold, reported in a letter of 21 August 1679 in detail about Becher's contracts with the States General, even sending copies of the contract in Dutch and German. Kramprich assures Leopold that Becher entered into these contracts "privato nomine." On 10 November 1679, Leopold wrote back to Kramprich expressing his "gracious pleasure" at Kramprich's report, saying that Krampich had answered Becher wisely in their discourse, and that he wanted to hear more about any contracts Becher might undertake with the States General. Krampich to Leopold, Vienna, Haus-, Hof- und Staatsarchiv, Geheime Staatsregistratur, Rep. N., Karton 67; and a copy of Leopold to Kramprich, ibid.

[43] Even after Becher's death, Leibniz continued to discuss him with his correspondents. He was of the opinion that Becher knew much, although perhaps more from artisans than through his own abilities. However, his words could not be relied upon, and he was too much given to "Schriftstellerei" (writing books). He drew his knowledge from others and he had a terrible biting wit which drove both friends and patrons away. Leibniz, *Sämtliche Schriften*, ser. 1, vol. 8, Leibniz to

doctor and later personal physician to King Charles II, became his patron, as perhaps did Prince Rupert, Count Palatine and first lord of the admiralty, and Robert Boyle. Becher seems to have made contact with the Royal Society and he dedicated his work on a perpetual clock to it, but the society did not admit Becher to its ranks. He traveled to Cornwall to inspect the mines and applied for four patents for various machines.[44] While in England Becher published two works in the year of his death, 1682: the *Chymischer Glücks-Hafen*, and a book entitled *Närrische Weiszheit und Weise Narrheit: Oder Ein Hundert/ so Politische als* Physicali*sche/* Mechani*sche und* Mercantili*sche* Concept*en und* Proposition*en/ deren etliche gut gethan/ etliche zu nichts worden/ sammt den Ursachen/ Umständen und Beschreibungen derselben* (Foolish wisdom and wise foolishness, or one hundred political as well as physical, mechanical, and mercantile concepts and propositions, of which some succeeded and others came to naught, including their causes, circumstances, and descriptions). These two books give us an indication of the nature of Leibniz's fascination with Becher and point to the object of the competition between these two individuals.

We have already seen that in the *Chymischer Glücks-Hafen*, Becher extolled

---

Wilhelm Ernst Tenzel, 1692, p. 480; Leibniz to Crafft, 1697, quoted in Peters, "Leibniz," p. 281: "Ich der Dr. Becher gar wohl gekennet und zum öftern mit ihm conversiret, weiss allzu wohl, dass seine Worthe ganz kein Evangelium gewesen und dass es ihm an gründtlicher Wissenschaft in denen Dingen, so er ausgeben oft sehr ermangelt, welches sein guth Ingenium und scheinbare Worth, wenn man zur That kommen nicht zu ersetzen vermocht. Wenn er aber in den Schrancken blieben wäre und sich der geziemenden Bescheidenheit und Aufrichtigkeit gebraucht hätte, so hätte er viel Nützliches richten können." Leibniz discusses Becher at more length in "Historia Inventionis Phosphori," first publ. 1710 in *Miscellanea Berolinensia*, reprinted in Leibniz, *Opera Omnia*, ed. Ludovicus Dutens, 6 vols. (Geneva, 1768), 2:102–8.

[44] The Royal Society considered the work on the clock, *De nova temporis dimetiendi ratione, et accurata horologiorum constructione, theoria & experientia* (London: Marcus Pardoe, 1680), on 26 February 1679/80, and John Flamsteed, having "perused the book," asserted that "there was very little in it." True to form, Robert Hooke claimed that part of Becher's design merely imitated a pendulum clock that *he* had displayed at a meeting of the Society at Arundel House long before. Thomas Birch, *The History of the Royal Society of London* (London: A. Miller 1757), 4:16–17. Robert Hooke's diary entry for 28 February 1679/80 mentions that he missed Becher (Becker) while visiting at an acquaintance's house. *The Diary of Robert Hooke*, ed. Henry W. Robinson and Walter Adams (London: Taylor & Francis, 1935). Hooke's papers contain a sketch of a seal for Becher's "Psychosophic Society" (British Library, Sloane mss. 1039, fol. 166). A few of Becher's manuscripts (some later published by Friedrich Roth-Scholtz in the eighteenth century) ended up at the Bodleian Library, Oxford, and a beautifully bound manuscript collection of recipes in the British Library. One of the most interesting of his publications in England (and his only work published in English) was *Magnalia Naturae. . . . Published at the request, and for the satisfaction of several Curious, especially of Mr. Boyl, etc.* The four patents are an instrument for winding silk (no. 213, 2 Aug. 1681), a process for making pitch and tar from pit coals (no. 214, 29 Aug. 1681; see British Library, Sloane mss. 3299, fol. 41.), an engine to raise water from deep mines (no. 215, 29 Aug. 1681), and finally, floating (ship) mills for grinding grain (no. 217, 28 April 1682). Great Britain Patent Office, *Alphabetical Index of Patentees of Inventions 1617–1852* (London: Evelyn, Adams & McKay, 1969).

the promise and productive capabilities of alchemy as the imitator of nature. The fabulous productive power of alchemy represented what was possible by the practice of an art that imitated the natural processes of generation and resulted in mobile wealth. The practice of art resulted in legitimate and regenerative wealth, civic virtue, and a healthy body politic. As the phosphorous episode showed, both Becher and Leibniz saw the promise and power of art as productive knowledge. Because he respected Becher's *Kundtschafft*,[45] Leibniz believed Becher might have more direct access to that power. Art represented promise and power to these men at three levels: a personal level at which each man tried to establish his own position at court; a political level, in which productive knowledge yielded legitimate and regenerative wealth and the power that flowed from such wealth;[46] and, as Erhard Weigel's view of "*Real-Weisheit*" showed, a promise of material increase that would bring about economic prosperity and social harmony.

The second book published by Becher at the end of his life, the *Närrische Weiszheit* supplies the key to Leibniz's fascination with Becher. In this work, Becher set out to illustrate the *"donum Inventionis"* God had given to humankind. He praised his own gift of invention, and considered it to be the last bit of sustenance left to him after his enemies caused his exile and ruin. In his ability to recover from his fall, Becher compared himself with "his greatest enemy," Hofkammer President Georg Ludwig von Sinzendorf, who had fallen from favor and position in 1680. Such a typical cameral official had no gift of invention with which to pick himself up again.[47] The president's personal lack of invention was also reflected in his public persona, for in the affairs of the Hofkammer, Sinzendorf, like other cameral officials, had no imagination or invention with which to further the common good.

> During that time when I had been parted from all my means, one thing remained constant, which God had given to me, namely the gift of invention. And as it became worse for me and all appeared to be lost, God continued to strengthen [that gift], and the greater the persecution, the greater the grace He gave me. Seneca aptly said: anyone can be persecuted and fall, but not everyone can stand up again and help himself. Which we will now see with the Hofkammer President; whether he will stand up again as fast as he fell.[48]

---

[45] Leibniz, *Sämtliche Schriften*, ser. 1, vol. 8, Leibniz to Wilhelm Ernst Tenzel, 1692, p. 480: "Becher ist gewiß ein treflicher Kopff gewesen, und hat viel gewust, wiewohl mehr aus relation guter Artisten als eignem Grunde" (Becher was certainly a clever man, and knew much, but more from the relation of good artisans than from his own knowledge).

[46] This is very clear in an extraordinary fragment in Leibniz's papers from ca. 1672–76, entitled "Mechanica in Politicis," in which he claims that most politicians do not consider mechanics and mathematics although military and economic matters are the "nerves and veins of the civil body," and are supported by the principles of mechanical physics and mathematics. He points out that not even Machiavelli disdained military matters. Leibniz, *Sämtliche Schriften*, ser. 6, vol. 3, p. 375.

[47] Becher, *Närrische Weiszheit*, Vorrede, pp. A2v–A3r.

[48] Ibid.

Invention was precisely the trait that the Stoic and the man of chemistry and commerce possessed but that the man of the treasury decidedly lacked.

Becher began the *Närrische Weiszheit* with projects and inventions that appeared impossible or foolish, but proved themselves in practice to be useful and wise. His list commenced with the discovery of the magnet, the sailing trips that made known the New World, and Prince Rupert's beaver trapping company, but he passed quickly on to the technical inventions that made up the remaining forty-eight examples of foolish wisdom. Among these are canals, mills, pumps, perpetual motion machines, weaving machines, manufacturing processes, and various machines and instruments such as the thermometer, microscope, and telescope. All these attested to the productivity of the gift of invention and to the promise of art as productive knowledge.

In the second half of the book, Becher listed concepts that appeared workable in theory, but did not succeed in practice. These encompassed several colony projects, including his own, many trading schemes, and several inventions. Becher made clear that these inventions failed not from any problem inherent in the scheme itself, even though "they were held by the common man to be foolish and thoughtlessly proposed." More knowledgeable men would realize that these projects were not intrinsically foolish but that they had not been competently carried out or failed because of other external circumstances. In conclusion to this section, Becher reiterated his point:

> The Reader should know that [in this foolish wisdom] much wisdom is hidden, and what today did not reward this or that person by such and such a means, can perhaps succeed in another time, done by different people and by different means. From this we see God's omnipotence, the amazing ingenuity of humans, and the wondrous conjunction of things.[49]

Human ingenuity and invention (*ingenium* and *inventio*) were God's redeeming gifts to a fallen humankind, and humankind's exercise of those powers made clear its own peculiar place in Creation. The whimsical conjunction of things not only displayed God's free disposition of things, but also gave humans an opportunity to display their powers. Thus invention constituted an essential human activity by which humans could respond to the fortuitous conjunction of things after the Fall. Invention was the component of art by which knowledge and skill became productive. The method by which the artisan created valuable objects from raw materials was based on his ability to respond to the fortuitous circumstances of the material.[50] This knowledge (and power) lay behind the practice of the alchemist who had transmuted lead into gold in the professor's lectures. His parting shot, "Solve mihi hunc syllogismum," challenged the

---

[49] Becher, *Närrische Weizsheit*, p. 245.

[50] Mathematician/mechanics in sixteenth-century Italy also believed this to be the secret of their art. Paolo Rossi, *Philosophy, Technology, and the Arts in the Early Modern Era*, trans. Salvator Attanasio (New York: Harper and Row, 1970), p. 62.

professor to find the means by which the knowledge of scholars could become productive. Becher and Leibniz took up this challenge, eagerly seeking out artisans and attempting to induce them to "discover themselves," thereby betraying not only their techniques, but also the implicit knowledge that allowed them to manipulate nature by those techniques.

For Cicero, invention had meant finding suitable subject matter and arguments for one's oration, but by the sixteenth century, engineer/artisans, wanting to emphasize their learned credentials as well as their ability to create, transferred the notion of invention from the sphere of rhetoric to that of material things.[51] Becher too lodged invention and ingenuity in the sphere of material things. The artist displayed his material wit by adapting to the circumstances of the natural world, just as the courtier showed his verbal wit in extemporaneous conversation at the banqueting table. The artisanal ability to design projects and machines that were suited to the fortuitous circumstances of the natural world was the very essence of practice.[52] Becher had scorned the extemporaneous speech on salt by the French orator, and he had displayed his own ingenuity and invention by an unadorned, material discourse on the salt cellar. At table in Munich, Becher's verbal discourse of things attempted to capture the material understanding implicit in artisanal activity that could be gained by his method of material cognition. In the *Närrische Weiszheit*, Becher removed the notion of invention, too, from the sphere of words altogether and lodged it firmly in the material world of things. Leibniz also attempted to construct a material *"ars inveniendi"* that depended on observation and the study of artisanal methods.[53]

The power of material invention was the means by which the knowledge and techniques of the artisan could be reproduced outside the matrix of guild and guild town, thus allowing the man of the mobile world to assert himself over the town citizens who had excluded him from their walls. Becher's *Närrische Weiszheit* is a chronicle of his search for the essence of practice and the source of productive knowledge. Leibniz had watched his rival Becher's search closely and had kept his spies and correspondents alert for evidence of Becher's success.[54]

[51] Alex Keller, "Mathematical Technologies and the Growth of the Idea of Technical Progress in the Sixteenth Century," in *Science, Medicine and Society in the Renaissance*, vol. 1, ed. Allen G. Debus (New York: Science History Publications, 1972), p. 20; Keller, "Mathematics, Mechanics and the Origins of the Culture of Mechanical Invention," *Minerva* 23 (1985): 348–61; and Rossi, *Philosophy, Technology, and the Arts*, chap. 1.

[52] In a separate treatise appended to the *Närrische Weizsheit*, Becher discussed the nature and characteristics of water, and, based on this, the art of waterworks (waterwheels, mills, pumps, etc.). He said that *"Application"* of this theory in the actual machines must be left up to the *"Judicio und Verstand"* of the "vorsichtige[r] Wasser-Künstler," who must found his application on theory, but opportunity will provide the *praxis* for him ("und *Praxin* wird ihm die Gelegenheit weiter selbst an die Hand geben"; p. 279).

[53] See Cornelis-Anthonie van Peursen, "Ars Inveniendi bei Leibniz," *Studia Leibnitiana* 18 (1986): 183–94.

[54] Becher watched Leibniz also, although somewhat more jovially. In the *Närrische Weiszheit*, Becher claimed that Leibniz had invented a wagon that would travel from Hanover to Amsterdam in

Art and Artifice

The invention and ingenuity of the practitioner, then, had to do with production, but it also had to do with artifice. Becher and other seekers of material invention evinced particular fascination in the places where the practice of art took place. In their lives, they moved in and out of Kunstkammern, laboratories, and collections of natural objects such as Becher's *Theatrum Naturae et Artis*. In each of these places, art imitated nature, and the material products of artisanal invention could be found. Additionally, these places made clear the significance of artifice in artistry. Becher's *Theatrum Naturae et Artis* was to function as recreation for the prince and a re-creation of all the things of the world. The objects, labeled and still on their podia, were to stand in for real things; they were to deceive the eye in a way illustrations in books could not. The lifelike re-creations of animals and plants were to display, besides the wonders of art and nature, those of *artifice*. Rhetoricians were as much enamored of artifice in the baroque era as mechanics and projectors. Rhetoricians used Tacitean style and strove for metaphors that both awed and deceived,[55] while mechanical practitioners played with the relationship between art and nature to produce wonder.

In Becher's alchemical laboratory, for example, art imitated nature and industrious artistry brought virtuous wealth. Alchemy was both the quintessentially productive art and the source of much artifice. The agent of transmutation was, after all, Mercury, the paramount artificer who was the god of elegance, the patron of merchants, and the friend of thieves. The count of Hanau's Kunstkammer also displayed nature's artifice in its three realms, as well as artistic virtuosity in the imitation of nature (figure 27). The artifice of these cabinets produced wonder, but also emphasized the production of material wealth. This emerges in a contemporary description of a stone table inlaid with mother of pearl, in which the artisan had so artfully exploited the colors of the

---

six hours, which he judged to be a piece of wise foolishness. Becher said further, "This Leibniz is known through his literature as a very learned man. He wished to reform the system of laws, and he wrote his own philosophy, among other things, but I don't know who set him onto this Post wagon, from which he won't dismount although he has already sat on it for some years and sees that it will not go forward" (*Närrische Weiszheit*, pt. 2, no. 28). Becher's inclusion of Leibniz among the wise fools caused a short stir at the court in Hanover, and the Landgrave Ernst of Hessen-Rheinfels questioned Leibniz about his invention. See Leibniz, *Sämtliche Schriften*, ser. 1, vol. 3, Landgrave Ernst to Leibniz, 2/12 November 1682, pp. 273–75; Leibniz to Landgrave Ernst, 14/24 March 1683, pp. 276–80.

[55] The neo-Taciteans, especially in Spain (e.g., Gracián), took up Lipsius's neo-Stoicism. Kühlman, *Gelehrtenrepublik*; José Antonio Maravall, *Culture of the Baroque*, trans. Terry Cochran, (Minneapolis: University of Minnesota Press, 1986). The work of Emanuele Tesauro, especially *Il Cannocchiale Aristotelico* (1654), was especially influential in lands of the German tongue. See Emanuele Tesauro, *Il Cannocchiale Aristotelico* (Turin, 1670; facs. repr. Bad Homburg: Verlag Dr. Max Gehlen, 1968), particularly the introduction by August Buck, and Barner, *Barockrhetorik*, regarding Gracián translations (p. 42) and the influence of Tesauro (p. 358).

Figure 27. The artifice of nature crowned by the artifice of the human hand. Ornament crowning the Kunstschrank of Gustavus II Adolphus, 1630s. With permission of the University of Uppsala.

mother of pearl in portraying insects, flowers, and plants (*naturalia*) that his art (or artifice) could not be distinguished from nature:

> In this table made by art, nature and art play so wondrously through each other that we do not know which carries away the most praise. Indeed this table is so magnificent and precious that it deserves to stand in the most beautiful royal chamber. Its artwork attains such heights that the table is estimated to be worth several thousand Reichsthaler.

The admirer of this table was so taken with it that he composed verses upon its artifice:

> Sic Ars Naturam vicit: sic Arte novella
> Ars veterum jam nunc vincitur Artificum.
>
> Thus art conquered nature. Thus, by new art,
> the art of the old artists is conquered.[56]

Artifice was the perfect imitation of nature, in which nature itself was exploited to bring about the effect. This artifice gave evidence not only of the skill of the artisan but even the conquest of nature by art, for such artifice brought about ever greater power over nature and, finally, even progress in the arts. The scholar admiring the artifice in the artisan's table believed that material progress flowed from the artisanal power of invention.[57] Becher and Leibniz believed that as new philosophers and projectors they could capture this power of invention and thus control material progress.

Becher's theater, the count of Hanau's Kunstkammer, and the laboratory all held out the promise of art as productive knowledge and the possibility of material progress. These spaces were also designed to bring about wonder, admiration, and surprise by artifice. In *The Advancement of Learning*, Bacon named wonder as "the seed of all knowledge."[58] The motto of the Julian Academy proclaimed in the late seventeenth century: "Admiratio filia ingoratiae mater philosophiae" (Wonder is the daughter of ignorance, and the mother of philosophy).[59] Wonder, induced by artifice, led to the knowledge of nature and the practice of art.

---

[56] Philipp von Zesen, *Beschreibung der Stadt Amsterdam* (Amsterdam: Joachim Nosch, 1664), pp. 362–63, describing a German artisan resident in Amsterdam.

[57] In the battle of ancients and moderns, the moderns believed that the advent of the new philosophy and the advancement of technology exemplified the progress of knowledge and human society. See Rossi, *Philosophy, Technology, and the Arts*, chap. 2; Keller, "Mathematical Technologies"; Thomas DaCosta Kaufmann, *The School of Prague* (Chicago: University of Chicago Press, 1988); idem, *The Mastery of Nature* (Princeton: Princeton University Press, 1993). A recent work to treat the ancients/moderns debate is Joseph M. Levine, *The Battle of the Books: History and Literature in the Augustan Age* (Ithaca: Cornell University Press, 1991).

[58] Francis Bacon, *The Advancement of Learning*, 1605, bk. 1 in *The Works*, ed. James Spedding, Robert Ellis and Douglas Heath (Cambridge: Riverside Press, 1863), 6:95.

[59] Johann Andreas Schmidt, *Theatrum Naturae et Artis. Singulis semestribus novis machinis & experimentis augendum in Academia Julia curiosis B.C.D. pandet I.A.S.D.* (Helmstedt: Georgus-

Theatrum Mundi

Mundus vult decipi.
Qui nescit dissimulare nescit agere.

The quintessential location of such artifice in the seventeenth century was the stage. The baroque theater exemplified the spectacle and resulting wonder that human invention and ingenuity could produce.[60] While the theater functioned as recreation for potentates such as Leopold I and disseminated political[61] and religious[62] knowledge, it also recreated the world in microcosm. For example, the Spanish playwright Pedro Calderón de la Barca (1600–1681) set one of his dramas at God's heavenly court. The courtiers and the playmaster, God, prepare a play in which the world is the stage, all of humanity are the actors, and the play is life. In the final scene, death calls the actors off the stage. But they reenter one more time to have their performance judged by God, and those who acted well are invited to a heavenly banquet.[63] Such a play expresses a central organizing principle of sixteenth- and seventeenth-century society, the notion that all the world is a stage. Shakespeare's Globe Theater greeted the audience:

Wolfgangus-Hamius Acad. Typogr., ca. 1710), displays this motto on the frontispiece. It is not the motto, however, that Zedler in his *Encyclopedia* says adorned the faculty of philosophy at its founding in 1576. He claims the theological faculty's motto showed the Holy Ghost in the form of a dove between the sun and the moon with the caption, "Hic est filius meus dilectus, hunc audite." The juristic faculty's displayed a golden lion with a scepter in its paw and the caption, "Vae Vobis, si dictis bonum malum & malum bonum," while the medical faculty's motto showed a crowned ox under a star and "Altissimus de terra creavit medicinam" below. The philosophical faculty's had a lion strewn with rose petals, holding the sign of mercury in its paw, above the caption, "Vestigium Sapientiae." The change of motto to "Admiratio . . ." (if it is indeed a change) seems an apt baroque shift.

[60] August Buck points out that a scholar of the baroque such as Richard Alewyn in *Das große Welttheater: Die Epoche der höfischen Feste*, 2d ed. (Munich: Verlag C. H. Beck, 1985), regarded the theater as the emblem of the baroque era. August Buck, "Forschungen zur Romanischen Barockliteratur," in *Europäische Barock-Rezeption*, ed. Klaus Garber, 2 vols. (Wiesbaden: Otto Harrassowitz, 1991), 1:40. See also Barner, *Barockrhetorik*, passim; for discussion of the epigraph that opens this section, see p. 101.

[61] For example, the lavish spectacles put on by Elector Ferdinand Maria of Bavaria when Emperor Leopold I passed through Munich, or by the Viennese court when Leopold married his Spanish niece, Margarita Teresa, in 1667.

[62] Jesuit and Protestant drama aimed to transmit religious understanding as well as practice in Latin for schoolboys. Willi Flemming, *Geschichte des Jesuitentheaters in den Landen deutscher Zunge* (Berlin: Selbstverlag der Gesellschaft für Theatergeschichte, 1923); J. Müller, *Das Jesuitendrama in den Ländern deutscher Zunge vom Anfang (1555) bis zum Hochbarock (1655)*, 2 vols. (Augsburg, 1930). Although the dialogue was in Latin, the meaning was rendered clear by stage sets and action. See Robert Arthur Griffin, *High Baroque Culture and Theatre in Vienna* (New York: Humanities Press, 1972), p. 56.

[63] An English translation of "The Great Theater of the World" can be found in *Masterpieces of the Spanish Golden Age*, ed. Angel Flores (New York: Holt, Reinhart and Winston, 1957).

"totius mundus agit histrionem" (the whole world acts), and the Amsterdam stage proclaimed: "de wereld is een speeltooneel, elk speelt zijn rol en krijgt zijn deel" (the world is a stage, each plays his role and gets his share). While such a notion is a commonplace of twentieth-century life also, the theater of the world for a seventeenth-century person was simultaneously didactic, metaphorical, and an authentic representation of reality. The world was the site of the cosmic drama of redemption, but it was also the daily scene of petty deceit.[64] De la Barca's play encouraged the viewer to move between the material and the spiritual, between reality and appearance, and between the realms of eternal verities and human mortality.

Because the theater was such a multivalent medium, it was the perfect vehicle for an age obsessed with the relationship between words and things, theory and practice, and reality and artifice. The significance of nature, art, and artifice in theater and stage production is illuminated by the plays of sculptor, playwright, and scene maker Gian Lorenzo Bernini (1598–1680). Bernini wrote perhaps twenty plays in his long and very full life, all of which are now lost except a fragment of one, unfinished and unperformed, fittingly contained within the account books of his repairs to the Trevi Fountain. We have only partial descriptions of his other plays from those who passed through Rome. In the *Inundation of the Tiber* performed in 1638, Bernini set boats out to sail on a flooded stage. Suddenly the retainers holding back the water collapsed under the pressure and the water flooded toward the audience. The audience panicking and rising to flee before the onrushing waters were amazed to see barriers go up and the water drain off before their eyes. All the audience had experienced the flood, but not a single onlooker had got wet. Not long after this spectacle of deception, Bernini staged *The Fair* in which a torch bearer apparently accidently lit the scenery ablaze, but before the audience could quite trample each other to the doors, a rain storm began on stage and extinguished the flames.[65]

Bernini's one surviving (but fragmentary) script is set within the deceptions of court and artisanal intrigues, and considers deception, art, and the possibility of transforming words into things by the work of the hand. In an exemplary

---

[64] In the sixteenth and seventeenth century, the market as a metaphor for human life also gained currency. Jean-Christophe Agnew, *Worlds Apart: The Market and the Theater in Anglo-American Thought 1550–1750* (Cambridge: Cambridge University Press, 1986), shows how pervasive the metaphors of theater and market were, and how they overlapped in a work like *Confusion of Confusiones* (1688) by Joseph de la Vega. De la Vega described the stock market as a "Tower of Babel" and a drama: "Among the plays which men perform in taking different parts in this magnificent world theater, the greatest comedy is played at the Exchange. There, in an inimitable fashion the speculators excel in tricks, they do business and find excuses wherein hiding-places, concealment of facts, quarrels, provocations, mockery, idle talk, violent desires, collusion, artful deceptions, betrayals, cheatings, and even the tragic end are to be found . . . . Thus the whole stock exchange is represented in the drama" (quoted in Agnew, p. 144).

[65] Gian Lorenzo Bernini, *The Impresario (Untitled)*, trans. Donald Beecher and Massimo Ciavolella (Canada: Dovehouse Editions, 1985), introduction, p. 6.

passage, Graziano, the scene designer, explains his plans for a cloud machine to one of his workmen:

Graziano: I want it to appear completely natural.

Sepio: How do you mean, natural?

Graziano: By natural I don't mean a cloud stuck in place up there. I want my cloud standing out, detached against the blue, and visible in all its dimensions like a real cloud up in the air.

Sepio: Up in the air, eh? That's nothing but doubletalk. Detach it from up there, you'll more likely see a cloud on the floor than in the air— unless you suspend it by magic.

Graziano: Ingenuity and design constitute the Magic Art by whose means you deceive the eye and make your audience gaze in wonder, make a cloud stand out against the horizon, then float downstage, still free, with a natural motion. Gradually approaching the viewer, it will seem to dilate, to grow larger and larger. The wind will seem to waft it, waveringly, here and there, then up, higher and higher—not just haul it in place, bang, with a counterweight.

Sepio: Well, Messer Graziano, you can do these things with words but not with hands.

Graziano: Now look here. Before we're through, I'd like you to see what the hand can accomplish. Follow me, I'll explain how to go about it.

[*Exeunt*].[66]

While this dialogue lays bare the material bases of deception and questions the boundaries between reality and appearance, it also shows the concern with transforming words into things, out of which knowledge and power result. Becher, Bernini, Leibniz, and Crafft all sought to demonstrate how words could be transformed into things. They did this not only by hiring individual artisans and mechanics, but also by trying to discover the very art of the artisan's power by which he produced finished objects from raw material. Their discovery of the source of artisanal artifice would give them knowledge of how the artisanal skills could be reproduced outside the guilds and the guild town walls that incubated them. Perfect artifice and *admiratio* were marks of artisanal power, and they attempted to capture these in their search for knowledge.

[66] Bernini, *The Impresario*, p. 53. A German play of the same period involving artisans and the production of wonder is Andreas Gryphius's *Peter Squentz* (1663) about a group of artisans turned actors in order to gain favor (and cash) from their prince. The humor of this piece revolves around the artisans spectacular lack of success at inducing wonder. Gryphius rather clumsily takes the play within a play directed by Peter Quince in Shakespeare's *A Midsummer Night's Dream* as the basis of his play, but emphasizes the relationship of the players to the prince and their hope of material recompense for their absurd efforts.

Graziano claimed that it was his own abilities of "ingenuity and design" that constituted his artifice, and Becher and Leibniz also sought to transform words into things by their projects and designs. For Leibniz and Becher, the original meaning of "to project" was to effect alchemical transmutation by casting (or projecting) the philosophical powder, or stone, over the base metal. But they also began to use "project" to mean a plan, sketch, or concept that could be transferred onto the material world.[67] By the end of the century, "Projecten-macher" would go through one more transformation and come to mean deceptive artificer. In English, "projector" was already used in this manner in the early seventeenth century. For example, one of Ben Jonson's characters asked, "What is a Projector? I would conceive." He was answered: "Why, one Sir, that projects Wayes to enrich men, or to make 'hem great." And in 1691 in the *History of Air*, Robert Boyle wrote, "The women . . . think us still either projectors or conjurers."[68] In the eighteenth century, "project" and "projector" would come to take on this negative meaning still more strongly.[69]

During the eighteenth century, the notions of art and artifice, like those of project and projectors, would become polarized at opposite ends of a hierarchy of knowledge and rationality. Becher stood on the cusp of this transformation, and in the century following his death, he was considered the model of a useful, *practical* scholar and, simultaneously, the very archetype of a charlatan.[70] Alchemy, as well as commercial projections, would reflect this polarization of art and artifice in the eighteenth century. Alchemy was vehemently defended as productive art and just as fervently denounced as dangerously deceptive artifice.[71] Commercial projection entered government in the guise of cameralist

[67] One example among many of Becher's use of "project" is in Mss. var. 1(3), fols. 273r, 494v–496v. For later examples, Johann Heinrich Zedler, *Universal-Lexikon* (Halle and Leipzig, 1732–50), vol. 29, and Jacob and Wilhelm Grimm, *Deutsches Wörterbuch*, vol. 7 (Leipzig: S. Hirzel, 1854–1960).

[68] *Oxford English Dictionary*, s.v. "projector." Boyle's statement could refer either to an artificer or to the activity of an alchemist.

[69] Zedler, *Universal-Lexikon*: "Projectenmacher, heissen insgemein diejenigen, welche den Leuten dieses oder jenes Project, davon sie sich vor die Erfinder ausgeben, entdecken, und sie zu Ausführung unter scheinbahren Vorstellungen eines daraus zu erwartenden grossen Gewinnstes anermuntern." Zedler's long and proscriptive entry on "Projectenmacher" dating to the 1730s indicates that "projects" and "projectors" had become a subject of controversy in the generation after Becher. Grimm's nineteenth-century entry on "Project" is again short and not engaged in controversy.

[70] Urban Gottfried Bucher, *Das Muster eines Nützlich-Gelehrten in der Person Herrn* Doctor *Johann Joachim Bechers* (Nuremberg and Altdorff: Johann Daniel Tauber, 1722), and the negative view of Becher in Johann Christian Adelung, *Geschichte der menschlichen Narrheit, oder Lebensbeschreibungen berühmter Schwarzkünstler, Goldmacher, Teufelsbanner, Zeichen- und Liniendeuter, Schwärmer, Wahrsager, und anderer philosophischer Unholden*, 7 vols. (Leipzig: Weygandsche Buchhandlung, 1785–89), 1:141, 179.

[71] Becher's unpublished alchemical works were collected and printed by Friedrich Roth-Scholtz between 1717 and 1723, and many other alchemical collections appeared in the first half of the eighteenth century. At the same time, Adelung, *Geschichte*, and others denounced alchemy as pure

bureaucrats who would use projector as a synonym for charlatan. Thus were the seeds of the Enlightenment contained in the projects of the baroque. Where Becher had been able to use alchemy to talk about material increase, and where Leibniz saw nothing unusual in planning his artifice at court, the men of the Enlightenment turned against the multivalency of the baroque. They denounced deception, rejected metaphor and enigma,[72] and ridiculed the scholarship of the seventeenth century as charlatanry perpetrated by learned pedants.[73]

A multivalent vision of reality and of knowledge had been typical of the sixteenth and early seventeenth centuries. The ubiquitous emblem books of this period point to this, for emblems were not only favorite games, but also a method of revealing reality. The polysemic nature of an emblem constituted a more authentic representation of reality than could a representation that claimed to express a single objective truth.[74] An emblem thus was more real than, say, a microscopic observation, unless of course the microscope observation could be interpreted as an emblem. Interpretation was not the teasing out of a single meaning, but the revealing or discovering of all dimensions of reality including its significance for human society. Thus the collection of exempla and curiosities went both to illustrate and to order the complexity of the human and material worlds. In Becher we see both the collection of marvels as well as the beginning of the collection of "facts" that could result in certain knowledge.[75] But by the end of the seventeenth century truth had become univalent, and the previous century appeared filled with folly. The collection of facts—no longer as exempla but rather as discrete, visible proof—had become paramount. Alchemy became charlatanry, rather than potentiality; science became visible truth.[76]

---

charlatanry. See Dietlinde Goltz, "Alchemie und Aufklärung," *Medizinhistorisches Journal* 7 (1972): 31–48. Goltz discusses the Enlightenment collection of examples of irrationality on pp. 44–45.

[72] See Ernest B. Gilman, *The Curious Perspective: Literary and Pictorial Wit in the Seventeenth Century* (New Haven: Yale University Press, 1978).

[73] Leonard Forster, " 'Charlataneria eruditorum' zwischen Barock und Aufklärung in Deutschland," in *Res Publica Litteraria*, ed. Sebastian Neumeister and Conrad Wiedemann, 1:203–220; Conrad Wiedemann, "Polyhistors Glück und Ende. Von D. G. Morhof zum jungen Lessing," in *Festschrift Gottfried Weber*, ed. Heinz Otto Burger and Klaus von See (Bad Homburg: Verlag Gehlen, 1967), pp. 215–35. The view that the scholarship of the seventeenth century was marked by pedantry comes above all from Christian Thomasius. See Kühlmann, *Gelehrtenrepublik*.

[74] This is treated particularly by Barner, *Barockrhetorik*, pp. 99–109, and by Albrecht Schöne, *Emblematik und Drama im Zeitalter des Barock* (Munich: C. H. Beck Verlag, 1964).

[75] Lorraine Daston, "The Factual Sensibility," *Isis* 79 (1988): 466; idem, "Marvellous Facts and Miraculous Evidence in Early Modern Europe," *Critical Inquiry* 18 (1991): 93–124. See also Paula Findlen, *Possessing Nature: Museums, Collecting and Scientific Culture in Early Modern Italy* (Berkeley: University of California Press, 1994).

[76] Michel Foucault considered this change to have its roots in the relationship of language (signs) to the world (its signifier). The period he calls the Renaissance looked for similitudes, resemblances, correspondences, and identified language as having a profound and "natural"

In the new century, Becher's material theory of cognition and Leibniz's search for an *ars inveniendi* would give way to a full-blown effort to codify practice and material invention into a rational system. Practicing scholars ceased to need artifice when they possessed the rhetoric of a scientific method combining theory and experiment. Practice had thus been removed from the sphere of artisanal culture and taken outside the town walls and out of the realm of artifice, where it had previously been reproduced and nurtured. Once outside the town walls it was in the power of the territorial ruler and eventually in the sphere of the State, and, with time, came to be reproduced by means of a new "rational" system formulated by the mobile projectors of a culture called "science." Alchemy gave way to public utility, marvels and curiosities to facts, wonder to reason, and *fortuna* to human agency and state discipline.

---

relationship with that which it signified. The seventeenth century was a period of transition in which a crisis of representation was played out. For Foucault, Cervantes' figure, Don Quixote, epitomizes the onset of crisis which ended in a classical age when the relation of sign to signifier became artificial and univalent. The classification schemes of Linnaeus marked the full articulation of a new episteme. While Foucault's overarching concept of a episteme within which rationality was defined and practiced is important and useful, his intellectual grid for the epistemes of the Renaissance and classical ages is of such wide gauge as to be of little use. Michel Foucault, *The Order of Things* (New York: Random House, 1973). Subsequent studies of the baroque have followed Foucault in this periodization, for example, Timothy Hampton, ed., *Baroque Topographies: Yale French Studies*, 80 (1991).

EPILOGUE

PROJECTION

The Community Project

BECHER'S whole life was engaged in the projection of his own plan—formed from his diverse experiences—onto the world around him. He projected himself into the court and from there into the government of the state. This projection involved both art and artifice. Two of Becher's last concepts distill his attempt throughout his life to project this plan onto his world.

The first involves a plan for his own retirement from court life. In 1678, Becher had published *Psychosophia, das ist Seelen-Weiszheit* (Psychosophy, that is wisdom of the soul) which was meant not only to be an "essence" or distillation of all his works, but also the last of his public actions.[1] He planned to give up "Hofleben" (noble court life) to retire to a *"Retirada, tuguriolum, laboratorium, Eremitorium*, or whatever one wants to call it." Appended to the *Psychosophia* was a plan for an agricultural community that would have as its goal the creation of a place where people could live in "peace, still, and quiet," spending their time in devotions and virtuous activity, away from the business and busy-ness of the world ("Welt-Händel" and "Weitläufftigkeit").[2] Because housing, food, and clothing would be supplied to all members, they could spend their time bringing up their children in virtue and the sciences ("Tugend und Wissenschafften") and healing the sick. The members of the community would live simply, without "Geld-sorg" (money worries), and without external differences in rank such as clothing, but each could retain the rank, profession, and religion he or she had possessed before entering. Paradoxically, Becher believed only the busy commercial society of Holland could provide the right setting for this community.[3]

Members were to buy into the community, receiving a profit in proportion to

---

[1] *Psychosophia* (1705), Vorrede, unpaginated.

[2] "Entwurff/ oder Einladung/ einer Ruh-Liebenden und ihrem Nechsten zu dienen suchenden philosophischen Gesellschafft," unpaginated. In Mss. var. 1(2), fol. 609r–v, there is a draft in Becher's hand of a founding document for a society, undated. It begins: "Zu der Ehre Gottes und Beförderung Christlicher lieb auch zu aufferbawung *privat* nutzens haben wier endts underschribene eine *Compagnie* under folgenden *condition*en mit einander aufgerricht," after which follow fourteen articles, similar to those in the "Entwurff." In the manuscript version, however, there is greater attention paid to the division of profit, for example, that Becher, as founder of the company, receives three portions. The published "Entwurff" mentioned only that the profit would be divided in proportion to the capital invested by a member. There are no signatories to the manuscript version.

[3] *Psychosophia* (1705), p. 125.

their share, or they could sell themselves to the community as indentured servants. This share entitled them to all the necessities of life, but shareholders could also invest in the society without living in it. With the capital, land would be bought and a self-sufficient system constructed that would contain as its center a school of four grades. This school began with reading, writing, and arithmetic, moved on to the learning of Latin, the learning of the mechanical arts, and finally ended in the learning of all sciences ("Wissenschafften") by means of Becher's *Theatrum Naturae et Artis*. Eventually a school for the vernacular languages and for the exercise of the arts would be added. This school of practice would include a printing shop, library, mathematical and mechanical instruments, apothecary, and chemical laboratory. It would also carry on a correspondence with learned people all over the world.

Becher recognized that his society resembled communities formed in the past by religious groups. But he claimed that these communities had ended badly because they either became "fanatical" or the planners had really desired the labor or money that the members contributed rather than the members' common welfare.[4] Nevertheless, he praised such communal work, for it was evident "what great things they can do through such unions, companies, Mascopies, and societies."[5] Becher admired the radical sects because they approximated most closely the way of life in the early church.

> Others such as the Minists and the Quakers come closest to this Christian life, but they frighten others away and restrict Christian freedom, so that, because of their teachings, they have been the object of so much more suspicion and have been arrested, while because of their life, they have been loved and praised. . . . The Brotherhoods are next closest [to the Christian life], but the Münster war and the name of Anabaptist harmed them, just as the derisive name of Quaker and of Labadist for those in Friedland harmed the others.[6]

He feared his community plan might be mistaken for "Wiedertäufferisch" (Anabaptist), and he made clear that his society differed from the religious societies because his recognized a temporal government and allowed freedom of worship;[7] in fact, the society would be ratified and privileged by the government of the land.

While the corporate form of Becher's community would have been familiar to the members of his mother's hometown community, and the study of nature

---

[4] Becher himself had proposed a community or "colony" ten years earlier in which members would be completely equal and everyone would engage in agricultural work: *Moral Discurs,* pp. 209–14. In this work, Becher also discussed the bases for the value of money and lamented the need of it in the modern world (pp. 148ff.). He praised the peasant's estate as the true "first vocation" of humankind and therefore closest to God (pp. 244ff.).

[5] "Was grosse Sachen können sie durch solche Vereinigungen/ *Compagnien, Mascopien* und *Societ*äten thun."

[6] *Psychosophia* (1705), p. 47. Becher claimed that members of the Christian community of the early church used no money, worked with their hands, and served their neighbors (pp. 38–47).

[7] This was true even in the 1669 version of the agricultural society: *Moral Discurs,* p. 214.

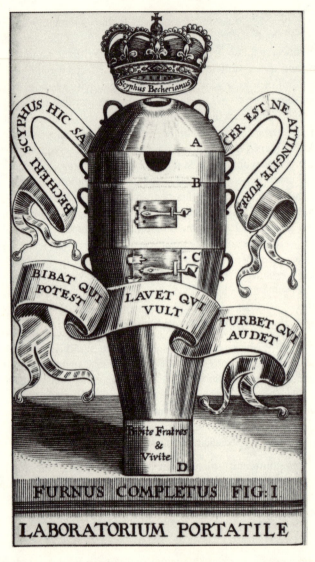

Figure 28. The Scyphus Becheri (the alchemical furnace) assembled. Adorned with an odd mix of captions, this "philosophical" furnace tells us much about Becher's trajectory through life. Crowned with the title, "Becher's beaker" (German *Becher*), the furnace appeals to the latinity of the late Renaissance man of learning, while the next caption, "this is sacred, thieves do not touch," seems to admonish the would-be infringer of his privilege. Beneath this stands the caption for an emblem Becher devised for himself long before: "Let he who is able drink, let he who wishes wash, and he who dares, stir up trouble." This call for order contains religious resonances, as do the crown over the chalicelike vessel, the *hic sacer est,* and of course alchemy itself. The base of the furnace brings out this significance, where the caption reads "Drink brothers and live." The connection with the wine of communion is more

obvious still in Becher's original early design for the emblem (see figure 30). While this later furnace continues to draw upon the emblem's religious symbolism, it more clearly displays Becher's economic concerns with mobility and movable wealth. In light of this multivalence, it is fitting that the archetypal soldier of fortune and count without lands, Prince Rupert, second son of the Winter King, purchased this portable furnace. *Tripus Hermeticus Fatidicus,* 1689. With permission of the Huntington Library, San Marino, California.

Figure 29. The Scyphus Becheri (the alchemical furnace) broken down. *Tripus Hermeticus Fatidicus,* 1689. With permission of the Huntington Library, San Marino, California.

Figure 30. Here the miracle of transubstantiation and the animating
essence of the chemical world are conflated. Becher devised this
emblem while still an alchemical projector seeking a patron, not
long after the religious war he blamed for making a comedy of faith.
Tripus Hermeticus Fatidicus, 1689. With permission of the
Huntington Library, San Marino, California.

and the arts would have been familiar to the religious reformers of his father's
generation, the shareholding company was a completely new element that
illuminates the course of events in Becher's generation. Becher's shareholding
community was embedded in the material world. It was to be situated at a port,
to make travel "in and out of the world" easier, and it was based on freedom of
religion. Becher was not concerned with the Last Days of the world, but with
the reform of his immediate society (and with his own retirement from the cares
of the courtly world). While his project illustrates how deeply the concern of
Paracelsus and Comenius with the things of nature and the material world had
influenced Becher, it also shows how fundamentally he differed from their
vision. Like his treatment of alchemy, which moved it from a metaphysical and
cosmic enterprise to one of mundane industry, Becher's projects were concerned with the material reform of his world by art and the human manipulation
of things, rather than with the unfolding of the cosmic plan.[8] Becher's community was to be firmly tied to the temporal world by submission to a territorial
ruler's power. Finally, the use of money in the community and the fact that
Becher imposed the structure of a shareholding company upon the community

---

[8] In his novels, Christian Weise also exhibits a belief that the true sphere of action and of concern
is the temporal world, and that the stage of reform is the state. See Arnold Hirsch, "'Politischer'
Roman und 'politische' Lebensführung," in *Deutsche Barockforschung. Dokumentation einer
Epoche*, 2d ed., ed. Richard Alewyn (Cologne and Berlin: Kiepenheuer & Witsch, 1966), pp. 211–

indicate how thoroughly the forms of the exchange economy and commerce had entered into the concepts of reform and salvation in Becher's own generation.

"Mobiliora, Nobiliora": The Portable Furnace

Becher began life in travel, carrying with him certain possessions, books, ideas, and the intellectual and social baggage of his mother's and father's worlds.[9] In the course of his life, he continued his restless travels, unpacking this baggage along the way to form a particular vision of the world around him and the possibility of its reform. In this vision, alchemy represented the promise of nature, art, mobility, and artifice. By means of the theory and practice of alchemy, Becher created a space for his experience in the sphere of government and attempted to transmute money and commerce into objects of virtue. By alchemy, he transported them from the sphere of self-interest into the public sphere of the common welfare, and he attempted to graft the mobile sphere of the merchant and commerce onto the natural values of the landed court. Becher remained concerned with mobility until the end. One of his last projects was the construction of a portable alchemical furnace (figures 28–30),[10] which could be broken down into many smaller pieces, carried as baggage, and reassembled as needed.

---

13. Instances of what John Bossy has called "migrations of the holy" are especially to be found in attitudes to alchemy. See Robert Jan Van Pelt, "The Utopian Exit of the Hermetic Temple; or, A Curious Transition in the Tradition of the Cosmic Sanctuary," in *Hermeticism and the Renaissance*, ed. Ingrid Merkel and Allen G. Debus (Washington D.C.: Folger Shakespeare Library, 1988) pp. 400–423; Herbert Breger, "*Elias Artista*—A Precursor of the Messiah in Natural Science," in *Nineteen Eighty-Four: Science between Utopia and Dystopia*, ed. Everett Mendelsohn and Helga Nowotny (New York: D. Reidel, 1984), pp. 49–72; and John Bossy, *Christianity in the West, 1400–1700* (Oxford: Oxford University Press, 1985).

9 "Mobiliora, Nobiliora" comes from the dedication of Sigismund von Birken, *Hoch Fürstlicher Brandenburgische Ulysses: oder Verlauf der Länder Reise, welche der Durchleuchtigste Fürst und Herr, Herr Christian Ernst, Marggraf zu Brandenburg . . . durch Teutschland, Frankreich, Italien und die Niderlande, auch nach den Spanischen Frontieren, hochlöblichst verrichtet: Aus denen mit Fleiss gehaltenen Reis-Diariis zusammen getragen und beschrieben* (Bayreuth, 1661), quoted in J. Bientjes, *Holland und der Holländer im Urteil Deutscher Reisender, 1400–1800* (Groningen: J. B. Wolters, 1967), p. 250.

10 "Laboratorium Portatile cum Methodo verè spagyricè, sc. juxta exigentiam Naturae, laborandi," in *Tripus Hermeticus Fatidicus, pandens Oracula Chymica* (Frankfurt: Johann Georg Schiele, 1689). In the preface, Becher claimed he had the movable furnace built by the "Blech-Schmied" Holdin in St. Martin Street, London, who then constructed ovens according to Becher's design for Edmund Dickinson, Robert Boyle, and Prince Rupert (costing twelve pounds each). Becher's original sketch for the emblem (see Figure 30) is in Mss. var. 2, fol. 657r (in papers dated 1656). Becher's sketch differs slightly from the engraving and contains an additional tag: "In silentio & spe erit fortitudo mea."

BIBLIOGRAPHY

ARCHIVES

Mainz, Germany, Stadtarchiv.

Munich, Germany, Bayrisches Hauptstaatsarchiv (abbreviated as BHA).

Stockholm, Sweden, Riksarchivet.

Vienna, Austria, Haus-, Hof-, und Staatsarchiv.

Vienna, Austria, Hofkammerarchiv.

MANUSCRIPTS BY BECHER

Becher's *Nachlaß*, covering the period from ca. 1657 to 1678, is bound into four volumes—Mss. var. 1(1), 1(2), 1(3), and 2—in the Special Collections of the University library in Rostock, Germany.

Before 1664: "Genealogica Botanica." Handschriften B100, Sächsische Landesbibliothek, Dresden.

1674: "Doctor Johann Joachim Bechers Römischer Kayserl. Mayt. Commercien Raths Referat Wie die Commercien, auch gemeiner Handel und Wandel, gegenwärtig in Ihro Kayl. Mayt. Erblanden, verschaffen seye, auch wie solchem, durch restabilirung eines Commercien Collegÿ könnte geholffen werden, daß sie den Kayl. Erblanden, zur Ehr und nutzen besser florirten." 11 May 1674, Hs. 12467, Handschriften-Abteilung, Österreichische Nationalbibliothek, Vienna.

"Doctor Johann Joachim Bechers, Römischer Kayl. Mayt. Rath Gutachten Über Herrn Daniels Marsaly Process zur Tinctur." 11 May 1674, Hs. 11472, Handschriften-Abteilung, Österreichische Nationalbibliothek, Vienna.

1676: "Referat, oder gründliche Beschreibung was in dem Kunst- undt Werckhauß sambt beyliegenden Schmeltz- Undt Glaßhütten, gethan und operirt wirdt, auch wie selbige angeordnet seye." 19 March 1676, Hs. 8046, Handschriften-Abteilung, Osterreichische Nationalbibliothek, Vienna.

1681: Becherus, Opera varia *Can. Misc. cxxii*, Bodleian Library, Oxford. This material contains manuscript versions of the supplements to the *Physica subterranea*, as well as material published in *Tripus Hermeticus Fatidicus*, 1689.

ca. 1673–1682: Sloane Mss. 2867, British Library. An unfinished codex by Becher, containing chemical recipes and manufacturing processes, some of which are contained in *Närrische Weiszheit* and *Chymischer Glücks-Hafen*.

PUBLISHED WORKS BY BECHER

The following list includes first editions only, unless the works were translated or expanded by Becher in subsequent editions. More information on Becher's bibliography is in Herbert Hassinger, *Johann Joachim Becher 1635–82. Ein Beitrag zur Geschichte des Merkantilismus* (Vienna: Adolf Holzhausen, 1951); in a list of Becher's writings attached by Roth-Scholtz to Friedrich Roth-Scholtz, ed., *Opuscula Chymica Rariora* (Nuremberg and Altdorff: Joh. Dan. Tauber, 1719); and in a 1680 "Catalogus Librorum & Scriptorum" attached by Becher to his *De nova temporis dimetiendi ratione* (London: Marcus Pardoe, 1680). The works listed here reflect only those still extant and listed in the *Gesamtverzeichnis des deutschsprachigen Schrifftums*. In his 1680 *Catalogus*, Becher claimed to have written many more works.

1654: Solini Saltzthals Regiomontani Discurs von der Großmächtigen Philosophischen Universal-Artzney/ von den Philosophis genannt Lapis Philosophorum Trismegistus. No place of publishing. In 1661, this work, translated into Latin as *Discursus Solini Saltztal Regiomontani De Potentissima Philosophorum medicina universali Lapis philosophorum trismegistus dicta*, was included in the sixth volume of the *Theatrum Chemicum*, edited by Johann Joachim Heilmann, pp. 675–94. Strasbourg: Eberhard Zetzner, 1661.

1658: Olitor Opportunus, hoc est, Simiplex narratio, de nobilissima quadam Medicina tribus sui natura optimis principiis, Auro, Zacharo & spiritu vini philosophice junctis. Frankfurt: Schönwetter's Heirs. Published anonymously.

1661: Character pro Notitia Linguarum Universali. Inventum steganographicum Hactenus inauditam quo quilibet suam legendo vernaculam diversas imò omnes linguas, unius etiam diei informatione, explicare ac intelligere potest. Frankfurt: Joh. Wilh. Ammon & Wilh. Serlin.

Natur-Kündigung der Metallen. Frankfurt: Joh. Wilh. Ammon & Wilh. Serlin.

1662: Panegyricus Atlanti Medico, seu Magno Lexico Medico D. Ludovici de Hornigk. Frankfurt: Serlin.

Parnassus Medicinalis Illustratus. Ulm: Joh. Görlin, 1662–63.

1663: Aphorismi ex Institutionibus Medicis Sennerti, Frankfurt: Balthasar-Christ. Wust.

1664: Institutiones Chimicae Prodromae i.e. . . . . Oedipus Chimicus. Obscuriorum Terminorum & Principiorum Chimicorum, Mysteria Aperiens & resolvens. Frankfurt: Herman a Sande, 1664. Translated by Becher in 1680 as *Oedipus Chymicus, oder Chymischer Rätseldeuter/ worinnen derer verdunckelten Chymischen Wortsätze Urhebungen und Geheimnissen offenbahret und aufgelöset werden.* N.p.

1667: Bona Becheri. Das ist: Handleytung zu dem Himmel/ Begreiffend den Kern der Lehre der H. H. Vätter/ und alten Weltweisen. Erstlich in Latein beschriben/ durch den Hochwürdigen Herrn D. IOANN BONA. Munich: Johann Wilhelm Schell.

1668: Methodus didactica, das ist: Gründlicher Beweiß/ daß die Weg und Mittel/ welche die Schulen bißhero ins gemein gebraucht/ die Jugend zu Erlernung der Sprachen/ insonderheit der Lateinischen zuführen/ nicht gewiß/ noch sicher seyen/ sondern den Reguln und Natur der rechten Lehr und Lern-Kunst schnurstracks entgegen lauffen/ derentwegen nicht allein langweilig/ sondern auch gemeinigliche unfruchtbar und vergeblich ablauffen. Sambt Anleitung zu einem besseren. Munich:

Maria Magdalena Schellin. A second edition with slightly different title was published in Frankfurt: Johann David Zunner, 1674.

Politischer Discurs von den eigentlichen Ursachen deß Auf- und Abnehmens/ der Städt/ Länder und Republicken. Frankfurt: Johann David Zunner. Second edition including much extra material published in 1673, and reprinted in 1688. Facsimile reprint of this 1688 ed., Glashütten im Taunus: Verlag Detlev Auvermann, 1972.

1669: Appendix practica über seinen Methodum Didacticam. Frankfurt: Johann David Zunner.

Methodi Becherianae Didacticae Praxis, Ejusdemque Liber seu annun primus, primam Vocabulorum connexionem continens. Frankfurt: Johann David Zunner.

Moral Discurs von den eigentlichen Ursachen deß Glücks und Unglücks. Frankfurt: Johann David Zunner.

Actorum Laboratorii Chymici Monacensis, seu Physicae Subterraneae libri duo. Johann David Zunner. Becher translated this into German in 1680 as *Chymisches Laboratorium oder Unter-erdische Naturkündigung.* Frankfurt: Johann Haaß, 1680. This translation included a translation of the three practical supplements.

Gründlicher Bericht von Beschaffenheit und Eigenschafft/ Cultivirung und Bewohnung/ . . . deß in America . . . Strich Landes. Frankfurt: Wilhelm Serlin. Published anonymously in 1669; included in 1673 edition of *Politischer Discurs.*

1670: Novum, breve, perfacile, & solidum Organum pro Verborum copia, in quavis materia, expedite acquirenda, omni scriptioni & dictioni perutile. Munich: Sebastianus Rauch. A second edition with a slightly different title was published in Frankfurt: Johann David Zunner, 1674.

1671: Experimentum Chymicum Novum, quo Artificialis & instantanea Metallorum Generatio & Transmutatio *ad oculum demonstratur. Loco* Supplementi *in Physicam suam subterraneam et* Responsi *ad D. Rolfincii Schedas de non Entitate Mercurii corporum.* Frankfurt: Johann David Zunner. Translated by Becher in 1680 as Experimentum Chymicum Novum: *Oder Neue Chymische Prob, worinnen die künstliche gleich-darstellige* Transmutation, *oder Verwandelung/ derer Metallen/ augenscheinlich dargethan: An statt einer Zugabe/ in die* Physicam subterraneam: *Und Antwort auff D. Rollfinken Schrifften von der Nicht-Wesenheit des* Mercurii *derer Cörper.* Frankfurt: Johann Haaß, 1680.

1673: Anmerckungen über die Schrifft, welche im Nahmen Ihrer Königl. Majestät in Frankreich, Robertus de Gravel . . . übergeben. N.p., published anonymously.

1675: Theses chymicae veritatem et possibilitatem transmutationis metallorum in aurum evincentes. Frankfurt: Joh. Dav. Zunner. Translated by Becher in 1680 as *Nochmalicher Zusatz über die Untererdische Naturkündigung . . . Philosophischer Beweisthum: Oder Chymische/ die Wahr- und Mögligkeit derer Metallen Verwandelung in Gold bestreitende Lehr-Sätze.* Frankfurt: Johann Haaß, 1680.

*Machiavellus Gallicus, Das ist: Verwandelung und Versetzung der Seele Des Machiavelli in Ludovicum XIV. . . . * N.p., published anonymously.

1677: Commentatio orationis ex S.S. Patribus congesta, atque ad promovendum orationis studium luci exposita. N.p., 1677.

1678: Wohlgemeintes unvorgreiffliches Gutachten/ Wie das Reichs-Edict in bannisierung der Frantzösischen Waaren in praxin und zum effect zu bringen/ auch was dem gesammten Röm. Reiche und allen Ständen dran gelegen, and *Copia Eines Memorials/ welches der Röm. Kayserl. Majest. Cammer- und Commercien-Raht* D. Johan Joachim Becher, *An Ihro Hoch-Fürstl. Gnaden Herrn* Marquarden, *Bischoffen zu Aichstet/ und Kayserl.* Plenipotentiarum *auf dem Reichstag zu Regenspurg/ unterthänigst und wohlmeinend geschrieben. Betreffend die* fundierung eines Reichs Ærarii. Amsterdam: Jacob von Felsen.

Psychosophia, das ist/ Seelen-Weiszheit. Güstrow: Christian Scheippel. A slightly revised edition was published in Frankfurt in 1683, and reprinted in 1705.

1679: Trifolium Becherianum Hollandicum oder . . . drey neue Erfindungen, bestehende in einer Seiden-Wasser-Mühle und Schmeltz-Wercke. Zum ersten mahl in Holland vorgeschlagen und werckstellig gemacht: Mit gründlicher Anweisung wie es mit denselbigen Sachen beschaffen ist. Auß der Niederländischen in die Hochteutsche Sprach übersetzet. Frankfurt: Johann David Zunner.

1680: Experimentum Novum Curiosum de Minera Arenaria Perpetua sive Prodromus Historiae, seu Propositionis Praep. D. D. Hollandiae. Frankfurt: Maritius Georgius Weidmannus. Published as supplement 3 to *Physica Subterranea.*

Minera Arenaria Perpetua: sive Prodromus Historiae, seu Propositiones Prae. D. D. Statibus Hollandiae ab Authorae Factae, circa Auri Extractionem, mediante Arena Littorali, per modum minerae Perpetuae seu Operationis Magnae Fusoriae cum Emolumento. London: Marcus Pardoe.

De nova temporis dimetiendi ratione, et accurata horologiorum constructione, theoria & experientia. London: Marcus Pardoe.

Magnalia Naturae or, The philosophers-Stone lately expos'd to publick Sight and Sale. Being a true and exact account of the Manner how Wenceslaus Seilerus the late famous Projection-maker, at the Emperours Court, at Vienna, came by, and made away with a very great Quantity of Powder of Projection, by projecting with it before the Emperor, and a great many Witnesses, selling it, etc. for some years past. Published at the request, and for the satisfaction of several Curious, especially of Mr. Boyl, etc. London: Thomas Dawks. (Considered by Hassinger, *Becher,* to be spurious.)

1682: Chymischer Glücks-Hafen/ Oder Grosse Chymische Concordantz und Collection/ von funffzehen hundert Chymischen Processen. Frankfurt: Georg Schiele. Facsimile reprint, Hildesheim: Georg Olms, 1974.

Närrische Weiszheit und Weise Narrheit: Oder Ein Hundert/ so Politische als Physicalische/ Mechanische und Mercantilische Concepten und Propositionen/ deren etliche gut gethan/ etliche zu nichts worden/ sammt den Ursachen/ Umständen und Beschreibungen derselben. Frankfurt: Johann Peter Zubrodt.

1689: Tripus Hermeticus Fatidicus, pandens Oracula Chymica. Frankfurt: Johann Georg Schiele.

1698: Published under Becher's name: *Kluger Hauß-Vater/ verständige Hauß-Mutter/ vollkommner Land-Medicus.* Leipzig: Friedrich Groschuff.

1700: Published spuriously under Becher's name: *Des Hochberühmten Becheri Medicinische Schatz-Kammer/ darinnen zu finden/ wie man die Kinder-Kranckheiten/ mancherley alters/ glücklich und geschwind curiren kan. Uns desses hinterlassenen raren Manuscriptis mit Fleiß zusammen getragen von H.I.I.* Leipzig: Christoff Hülfens.

1706: Domini Doctoris Becheri Pantaleon Delarvatus, pp. 106–22, in Johann Michael Faustus, *Philaletha Illustratus, sive Introitus Apertus ad occlusum regis palatium, novis quibusdam Animadversionibus explanatus cum nova praefatione qua vita pariter ac Scripta, tum edita tum inedita, Aeyrenaei Philalethae breviter exponuntur. Accessit his Narratio de Vita et Scriptis Starckii, Nec non Dn. Doct. Becheri Pantaleon delarvatus. Opera Joh. Michaelis Faustii, Medic. Doct. Reiquepublicae Francofurtensis ad Moenum Physici Ordinarii.* Frankfurt, Joh. Philipp Andrea.

1717: Published under Becher's name: Friedrich Roth-Scholtz, ed., *Chymischer Rosen-Garten.* Nuremberg: Johann Daniel Tauber.

1719: Friedrich Roth-Scholtz, ed., *Opuscula Chymica Rariora, addita nova Praefatione ac Indice locupletissimo multisque Figuris aenis illustrata.* Nuremberg and Altdorff: Johann Daniel Tauber, 1719. This book is a compilation of several of Becher's tracts not published during his lifetime, with some additions by Roth-Scholtz.

Published under Becher's name: Friedrich Roth-Scholtz, ed., *Bericht von Polychrest Pillen samt Hrn. Joh. Can. Gohls Gedancken.* Nuremberg: Johann Daniel Tauber.

Published under Becher's name: Friedrich Roth-Scholtz, ed. and trans., *Mineralisches ABC oder vier und zwanzig Chymische Theses.* Nuremberg and Altdorff: Johann Daniel Tauber.

WORKS CONSULTED

Aarsleff, Hans. "Comenius." In *Dictionary of Scientific Biography.* Edited by Charles C. Gillispie. New York: Scribner, 1970–.

Abel, Günter. *Stoizismus und Frühe Neuzeit.* Berlin: Walter de Gruyter, 1978.

Adelung, Johann Christian. *Geschichte der menschlichen Narrheit, oder Lebensbeschreibungen berühmter Schwarzkünstler, Goldmacher, Teufelsbanner, Zeichen- und Liniendeuter, Schwärmer, Wahrsager, und anderer philosophischer Unholden.* 7 vols. Leipzig: Weygandsche Buchhandlung, 1785–89.

Agnew, Jean-Christophe. *Worlds Apart: The Market and the Theater in Anglo-American Thought 1550–1750.* Cambridge: Cambridge University Press, 1986.

Ahonen, Kathleen Winnifred Fowler. "Johann Rudolph Glauber: A Study of Animism in Seventeenth-Century Chemistry." Ph.D. diss., University of Michigan, Ann Arbor, 1972.

Åkerman, Susanna. *Queen Christina of Sweden and Her Circle.* Leiden: E. J. Brill, 1991.

Albineus, Nathan. *Bibliotheca Chemica*. 1653.

Alewyn, Richard. *Das große Welttheater. Die Epoche der höfischen Feste*. 2d ed. Munich: Verlag C. H. Beck, 1985.

———, ed. *Deutsche Barockforschung. Dokumentation einer Epoche*. 2d ed. Cologne and Berlin: Kiepenheuer & Witsch, 1966.

Alpers, Svetlana. *The Art of Describing: Dutch Art in the Seventeenth Century*. Chicago: University of Chicago Press, 1983.

Apfelstedt, Heinrich. "Staat und Gesellschaft in J. J. Bechers Politischen Discursen." Ph.D. diss., Giessen, 1926.

Apostolidès, Jean-Marie. *Le Roi-Machine. Spectacle et politique au temps de Louis XIV*. Paris: Minuit, 1981.

Aretin, Christ. von. *Des großen Kurfürsten Maximilian I. von Baiern Anleitung zur Regierungskunst*. Bamberg and Würzburg: Goebhardtische Buchhandlung, 1822.

Arico, Denise. *Il Tesauro in Europa*. Bologna: Collana del Dipartimento di Italianistica, Università degli Studi di Bologna, 1987.

Aristotle. *De partibus animalium*. Translated by D. M. Balme. Oxford: Clarendon Press, 1972.

———. *Nicomachean Ethics*. Translated by H. Rackham. Loeb Classical Library. Cambridge, Mass.: Harvard University Press, 1982.

———. *Politics*. Translated by H. Rackham. Loeb Classical Library. Cambridge, Mass.: Harvard University Press, 1977.

Arnheim, Fritz. "Freiherr Benedikt Skytte (1614–1683), der Urheber des Planes einer brandenburgischen 'Universal-Universität der Völker, Wissenschaften und Künste.'" In *Festschrift zu Gustav Schmollers 70. Geburtstag. Beiträge zur brandenburgischen und preußischen Geschichte*, edited by Verein für Geschichte der Mark Brandenburg, pp. 65–99. Leipzig: Duncker & Humblot, 1908.

Bacon, Francis. *The Advancement of Learning*. 1605. Book 1. In *The Works*, vol. 6, edited by James Spedding, Robert Ellis, and Douglas Heath. Cambridge: Riverside Press, 1863.

Ballauff, Theodor, and Klaus Schaller. *Pädagogik. Eine Geschichte der Bildung und Erziehung, Vom 16. bis zum 19. Jahrhundert*. Vol. 2, *Orbis Academicus. Problemgeschichten der Wissenschaft in Dokumenten und Darstellungen*. Freiburg and Munich: Verlag Karl Alber, 1970.

Barner, Wilfred. *Barockrhetorik. Untersuchungen zu ihren geschichtlichen Grundlagen*. Tübingen: Max Niemeyer Verlag, 1970.

Bauer, Alexander. *Chemie und Alchymie in Oesterreich bis zum beginnenden 19. Jahrhundert*. Vienna: R. Lechner, 1883.

Becker, Marvin. *Civility and Society in Western Europe, 1300–1600*. Bloomington: Indiana University Press, 1988.

Bennet, J. A. "The Mechanics' Philosophy and the Mechanical Philosophy." *History of Science* 24 (1986): 1–28.

———. "Robert Hooke as Mechanic and Natural Philosopher." *Notes & Records of the Royal Society* 35 (1980–81): 33–48.

Bérenger, Jean. "Public Loans and Austrian Policy in the Second Half of the Seventeenth Century." *Journal of European Economic History* 2 (1973): 657–69.

Bernini, Gian Lorenzo. *The Impresario (Untitled)*. Translated by Donald Beecher and Massimo Ciavolella. Carleton Renaissance plays in translation, vol. 6. Canada: Dovehouse Editions, 1985.

Bessel, Christian Georg. *Faber Fortunae Politicae, Monitis ad vitam politicam admodum necessariis & saluberrimis*. Hamburg: Johannes Naumann & Georgius Wolff, 1673.

Biagioli, Mario. *Galileo Courtier*. Chicago: University of Chicago Press, 1993.

———. "Galileo the Emblem Maker." *Isis* 81 (1990): 230–58.

———. "Galileo's System of Patronage." *History of Science* 28 (1990): 1–62.

———. "The Social Status of Italian Mathematicians, 1450–1600." *History of Science* 27 (1989): 41–95.

Bientjes, J. *Holland und der Holländer im Urteil Deutscher Reisender, 1400–1800*. Groningen: J. B. Wolters, 1967.

Birch, Thomas. *The History of the Royal Society of London*. 4 vols. London: A. Miller, 1757.

Black, Antony. *Guilds and Civil Society in European Political Thought from the Twelfth Century to the Present*. Ithaca: Cornell University Press, 1984.

Blumenberg, Hans. *Die Legitimität der Neuzeit*. 2d ed. Frankfurt am Main: Suhrkamp, 1988.

Boccalini, Trajano. *De' ragguagli di Parnaso*. 1613. Translated as *Advices from Parnassus in Two Centuries*. London, 1706.

Bolton, Henry C. *The Follies of Science at the Court of Rudolf II*. Milwaukee: Pharmaceutical Review Publishing, 1904.

Borrichius, Olaus. *De Ortu, et progressu chemiae dissertatio*. Copenhagen: Mathias Godicchenius, 1668.

Bossy, John. *Christianity in the West, 1400–1700*. Oxford: Oxford University Press, 1985.

Boyle, Robert. *The Works of the Honourable Robert Boyle*. Edited by Thomas Birch. 6 vols. London: J. & F. Rivington, 1772.

Braudel, Fernand. *The Wheels of Commerce*. Vol. 2 of *Civilization and Capitalism: The 15th to 18th Century*. Translated by Sian Reynolds. New York: Harper & Row, 1982.

Breger, Herbert. "Becher, Leibniz und die Rationalität." *Wolfenbütteler Forschungsreihe*, forthcoming.

———. "*Elias Artista*—A Precursor of the Messiah in Natural Science." In *Nineteen Eighty-Four: Science between Utopia and Dystopia*, edited by Everett Mendelsohn and Helga Nowotny, pp. 49–72. New York: D. Reidel, 1984.

———. "Närrische Weisheit und weise Narrheit in Erfindungen des Barock." *Aesthetik und Kommunikation* 45–46 (October 1981): 114–22.

———. "Notiz zur Biographie des Phosphor-Entdeckers Henning Brand." *Studia Leibnitiana* 19 (1987): 68–73.

Brückner, Jutta. *Staatswissenschaften, Kameralismus und Naturrecht. Ein Beitrag zur Geschichte der Politischen Wissenschaft im Deutschland des späten 17. und frühen 18. Jahrhunderts*. Munich: C. H. Beck, 1977.

Brunner, Otto. *Adeliges Landleben und europäischer Geist. Leben und Werk Wolf Helmhards von Hohberg, 1612–1688*. Salzburg: Otto Müller, 1949.

———. "Das 'ganze Haus' und die alteuropäische Ökonomik." In *Neue Wege der Sozialgeschichte*. Göttingen: Vandenhoeck & Ruprecht, 1956.

———. *Land and Lordship: Structures of Governance in Medieval Austria*. Translated by Howard Kaminsky and James Van Horn Melton. Philadelphia: University of Pennsylvania Press, 1992.

———, ed. "Johann Joachim Bechers Entwurf einer 'Oeconomia ruralis et domestica.'" *Sitzungsberichte der österreichischen Akademie der Wissenschaften* 226, pt. 3 (1949): 85–91.

Bucher, Urban Gottfried. *Das Muster eines Nützlich-Gelehrten in der Person Herrn Doctor Johann Joachim Bechers*. Nuremberg and Altdorf: Johann Daniel Tauber, 1722.

Buck, August. "Forschungen zur Romanischen Barockliteratur." In *Europäische Barock-Rezeption*, 2 vols., edited by Klaus Garber, 1:15–44. Wiesbaden: Otto Harrassowitz, 1991.

Buck, August, et al., eds. *Europäische Hofkultur im 16. und 17. Jahrhundert*. 3 vols. Wolfenbütteler Arbeiten zur Barockforschung, vols. 8, 9, 10. Hamburg: Dr. Ernst Hausmedell, 1981.

Burke, Peter. *The Fabrication of Louis XIV*. New Haven: Yale University Press, 1992.

Calvinus, Ioannis. *Lexicon Iuridicum*. 3d ed. Hannover: Wechelian, Impensis Daniel & David Aubriorum & Clemens Schleichius, 1619.

Campanella, Tommaso. *The City of the Sun*. Translated by Daniel J. Donno. Berkeley: University of California Press, 1981.

Cardanus, Hieronymus. *Arcana politica sive de Prudentia civili*. Leiden: Elzevier, 1656.

Carsten, F. L. *Princes and Parliaments in Germany from the Fifteenth to the Eighteenth Century*. Oxford: Clarendon Press, 1959.

Cicero, Marcus Tullius. *De republica, De Legibus*. Translated by C. W. Keyes. Loeb Classical Library. London: W. Heineman, 1988.

Cole, Charles Woolsey. *French Mercantilist Doctrines before Colbert*. New York: Richard R. Smith, 1931.

Coleman, Donald Cuthbert, ed. *Revisions in Mercantilism*. London: Methuen, 1969.

Comenius, Jan Amos. *Orbis sensualium pictus*. Nuremberg: Endtner, 1658.

Conrads, Norbert. *Ritterakademien der frühen Neuzeit. Bildung als Standesprivileg im 16. und 17. Jahrhundert*. Göttingen: Vandenhoeck & Ruprecht, 1982.

Coudert, Allison. "Some Theories of a Natural Language from the Renaissance to the Seventeenth Century." *Studia Leibnitiana*, Sonderheft 7, 56–118. Wiesbaden, 1978.

Court, Jan de la. *Consideratien van Staat ofte Polityke weegschaal*. Amsterdam, 1661. Translated by Christophorus Kormarten into German as *Consideratien van Staat oder politische Wag Schale mit welcher die allgemeine Staa[t]s-Angelegenheiten Haupt-Gründe und Mängel aller Republicken*. Leipzig and Halle: Fickischer Buchladen, 1669.

———. *Politike discoursen handelende in Ses onderscheide Boeken van Steeden, Landen, Oorlogen, Kerken, Regeeringen, en Zeeden*. Amsterdam: van der Gracht, 1662.

Court, Pieter de la. *Interest van Holland, ofte gronden van Hollands-welvaren*. Amsterdam: vander Gracht, 1662. Translated as *Interesse von Holland oder Fondamenten von Hollands-Wohlfahrt*. N.p., 1665.

Daston, Lorraine. *Classical Probability in the Enlightenment*. Princeton: Princeton University Press, 1988.

———. "The Factual Sensibility." *Isis* 79 (1988): 452–70.

———. "Marvellous Facts and Miraculous Evidence in Early Modern Europe." *Critical Inquiry* 18 (1991): 93–124.

Dear, Peter. "Jesuit Mathematical Science and the Reconstitution of Experience in the Early Seventeenth Century." *Studies in the History and Philosophy of Science* 18 (1987): 133–75.

———. "*Totius in Verba*: Rhetoric and Authority in the Early Royal Society." *Isis* 76 (1985): 145–61.

Debus, Allen G. *The Chemical Philosophy*. 2 vols. New York: Science History Publications, 1977.

Denzer, Horst. "Samuel Pufendorfs Naturrecht im Wissenschaftssystem seiner Zeit." In *Samuel von Pufendorf. 1632–1982. Ett rättshistoriskt symposium i Lund 15–16 Januari 1982*, pp. 17–30. Lund: Bloms Boktryckeri, 1986.

Dictionary of Scientific Biography. Edited by Charles C. Gillispie. 18 volumes. New York: Scribner, 1970–.

Dittrich, Erhard. *Die deutschen und österreichischen Kameralisten*. Darmstadt: Wissenschaftliche Buchgesellschaft, 1974.

Dobbs, Betty J. T. *Alchemical Death and Resurrection: The Significance of Alchemy in the Age of Newton*. Washington, D.C.: Smithsonian Institution Libraries, 1990.

———. *The Foundations of Newton's Alchemy*. Cambridge: Cambridge University Press, 1975.

Doeberl, Michael. "Innere Regierung Bayerns nach dem dreissigjährigen Krieg." *Forschungen zur Geschichte Bayerns* 12 (1904).

Dollinger, Heinz. *Studien zur Finanzreform Maximilians I. von Bayern in den Jahren 1598–1618. Ein Beitrag zur Geschichte des Frühabsolutismus*. Göttingen: Vandenhoeck & Ruprecht, 1968.

Doppelmayr, Johann Gabriel. *Historische Nachricht von den Nürnbergischen Mathematicis und Künstlern*. Nuremberg: Peter Conrad Monath, 1730.

Dreitzel, Horst. *Protestantischer Aristotelismus und absoluter Staat*. Wiesbaden: Franz Steiner Verlag, 1970.

Ehalt, Hubert C. *Ausdrucksformen absolutistischer Herrschaft. Der Wiener Hof im 17. und 18. Jahrhundert*. Munich: R. Oldenbourg Verlag, 1980.

Elias, Norbert. *The Court Society*. Translated by Edmund Jephcott. New York: Pantheon Books, 1983.

———. *The Development of Manners*. Vol. 1 of *The Civilizing Process*. 1939. Translated by Edmund Jephcott. New York: Urizen Books, 1978.

———. *Power and Civility*. Vol. 2 of *The Civilizing Process*. 1939. Translated by Edmund Jephcott. New York: Pantheon Books, 1982.

Elliott, J. H. "Self-Perception and Decline in Early Seventeenth-Century Spain." *Past and Present* 74 (1977): 41–61.

Evans, R.J.W. *The Making of the Habsburg Monarchy*. Oxford: Clarendon Press, 1984.

———. *Rudolf II and His World*. Oxford: Clarendon Press, 1973.

Fabian, Ann. *Card Sharps, Dream Books, and Bucket Shops: Gambling in Ninenteenth-Century America*. Ithaca: Cornell University Press, 1990.

Feingold, Mordechai. *The Mathematicians' Apprenticeship*. Cambridge: Cambridge University Press, 1984.

Fellner, Thomas, and Heinrich Kretschmeyer. *Die österreichische Zentralverwaltung. Von Maximilian I. bis zur Vereinigung der österreichischen und böhmischen Hofkanzlei (1749)*. Vol. 1. Vienna: Adolf Holzhausen, 1907.

Ferguson, John. *Bibliotheca Chemica*. 2 vols. London: Derek Verschoyle, 1954.

Ferrari, Giovanni. "Public Anatomy Lessons and the Carnival in Bologna." *Past and Present* 117 (1987): 50–106.

Findlen, Paula. "The Economy of Scientific Exchange in Early Modern Italy." In *Patronage and Institutions: Science, Technology, and Medicine at the European Court, 1500–1750*, edited by Bruce Moran, pp. 5–24. Woodbridge, Suffolk: Boydell, 1991.

―――. *Possessing Nature: Museums, Collecting and Scientific Culture in Early Modern Italy*. Berkeley: University of California Press, 1994.

Fix, Andrew. "Radical Religion and the Age of Reason." In *Germania Illustrata*, Sixteenth Century Essays and Studies, vol. 18, edited by Andrew C. Fix and Susan C. Karant-Nunn, pp. 35–55. Kirksville, Mo.: Sixteenth Century Journal Publishers, 1992.

Flemming, Willi. *Geschichte des Jesuitentheaters in den Landen deutscher Zunge*. Berlin: Selbstverlag der Gesellschaft für Theatergeschichte, 1923.

Flores, Angel, ed. *Masterpieces of the Spanish Golden Age*. New York: Holt, Reinhart and Winston, 1957.

Forberger, Rudolf. "Johann Daniel Crafft. Notizen zu einer Biographie (1624 bis 1697)." *Jahrbuch für Wirtschaftsgeschichte*, pts. 2–3 (1964): 63–79.

Forster, Leonard. "'Charlataneria eruditorum' zwischen Barock und Aufklärung in Deutschland." In *Res Publica Litteraria. Die Institutionen der Gelehrsamkeit in der frühen Neuzeit*, 2 vols., edited by Sebastian Neumeister and Conrad Wiedemann, vol. 1, pp. 203–20. Wiesbaden: Otto Harrassowitz, 1987.

Foucault, Michel. *The Order of Things*. New York: Random House, 1973.

Freyberg, Max von. *Pragmatische Geschichte der bayerischen Gesetzgebung und Staatsverwaltung*. 4 vols. Leipzig: Friedrich Fleischer, 1836–39.

Friedrichs, Christopher R. *Urban Society in an Age of War: Nördlingen, 1580–1720*. Princeton: Princeton University Press, 1979.

Frühsorge, Gotthardt. *Der politische Körper. Zum Begriff des Politischen im 17. Jahrhundert und in den Romanen Christian Weises*. Stuttgart: J. B. Metzlersche Verlagsbuchhandlung, 1974.

Gagliardo, John. *Germany under the Old Regime, 1600–1790*. London: Longman, 1991.

Garin, Eugenio. *Italian Humanism: Philosophy and Civic Life in the Renaissance*. Translated by Peter Munz. New York: Harper and Row, 1965.

―――. *Science and Civic Life in the Italian Renaissance*. Translated by Peter Munz. New York: Doubleday, 1969.

Geertz, Clifford. "Centers, Kings, and Charisma: Reflections on the Symbolics of Power." In *Local Knowledge*, pp. 121–46. New York: Basic Books, 1983.

Gilman, Ernest B. *The Curious Perspective: Literary and Pictorial Wit in the Seventeenth Century*. New Haven: Yale University Press, 1978.

Goldammer, Kurt. *Paracelsus: Natur und Offenbarung*. Hanover: Theodor Oppermann Verlag, 1953.

Golinski, Jan Victor. "Language, Method and Theory in British Chemical Discourse, c. 1660–1770." Ph.D. diss., University of Leeds, 1984.

Goltz, Dietlinde. "Alchemie und Aufklärung." *Medizinhistorisches Journal* 7 (1972): 31–48.

Goodman, David C. *Power and Penury: Government, Technology and Science in Philip II's Spain*. Cambridge: Cambridge University Press, 1988.

Goslinga, Cornelis Ch. *The Dutch in the Caribbean and on the Wild Coast, 1580–1680*. Gainesville: University of Florida Press, 1971.

Gouk, Penelope. *The Ivory Sundials of Nuremberg, 1500–1700*. Cambridge: Whipple Museum of the History of Science, 1988.

Grafton, Anthony. *Defenders of the Text: The Traditions of Scholarship in an Age of Science 1450–1800*. Cambridge, Mass.: Harvard University Press, 1991.

———. "The World of the Polyhistors: Humanism and Encyclopedism." *Central European History* 18 (1985): 31–47.

Gratarolo, Guglielmo. *Verae Alchemiae Artisque Metallicae, citra Aenigmata, Doctrina*. 1561.

Great Britain. Patent Office. *Alphabetical Index of Patentees of Inventions 1617–1852*. London: Evelyn, Adams & MacKay, 1969.

Greenblatt, Stephen. *Renaissance Self-Fashioning from More to Shakespeare*. Chicago: University of Chicago Press, 1980.

Griffin, Robert Arthur. *High Baroque Culture and Theatre in Vienna*. New York: Humanities Press, 1972.

Grimm, Gunter E. "Muttersprache und Realienunterricht." In *Res Publica Litteraria. Die Institutionen der Gelehrsamkeit in der frühen Neuzeit*, 2 vols., edited by Sebastian Neumeister and Conrad Wiedemann, 1:299–324. Wiesbaden: Otto Harrassowitz, 1987.

Grimm, Jacob and Wilhelm Grimm. *Deutsches Wörterbuch*. 16 vols. Leipzig: S. Hirzel, 1854–1960.

Habermas, Jürgen. *Strukturwandel der Öffentlichkeit. Untersuchungen zu einer Kategorie der bürgerlichen Gesellschaft*. 6th ed. Ulm: Luchterhand, 1974.

Hacking, Ian. *The Emergence of Probability*. London: Cambridge University Press, 1975.

Hadamowsky, Franz. *Barocktheater am Wiener Kaiserhof 1625–1740*. Vienna: Verlag A. Sexl, 1955.

Hahnzog, Ferdinand. "Das Hanauer 'tolle Jahr' 1669." *Hanauer Geschichtsblätter* 20 (1965): 147–71.

———. "Einige unbekannte Figuren im Spiel um Hanauisch-Indien." *Neues Magazin für hanauische Geschichte* 3 (1958): 69–84.

Haitsma Mulier, Eco O. G. *The Myth of Venice and Dutch Republican Thought in the Seventeenth Century*. Translated by Gerard T. Moran. Assen: Van Gorcum, 1980.

Hampton, Timothy, ed. *Baroque Topographies: Yale French Studies*. 80 (1991).

Hannaway, Owen. *The Chemists and the Word: The Didactic Origins of Chemistry*. Baltimore: Johns Hopkins University Press, 1975.

Hartmann, Peter Claus. *Geld als Instrument europäischer Machtpolitik im Zeitalter des Merkantilismus*. Munich: Kommission für bayerische Landesgeschichte, 1978.

Haskett, Miriam. "Wilhelm Freiherr von Schröder: Economic Thought and Projects for Fiscal Reform in Austria in the Reign of Leopold I." Ph.D. diss., University of California at Los Angeles, 1960.

Hassinger, Herbert. "Die erste Wiener orientalische Handelskompagnie, 1667–1683." *Vierteljahrschrift für Sozial- und Wirtschaftsgeschichte* 35, no. 1 (1942): 1–53.

————. *Johann Joachim Becher, 1635–82. Ein Beitrag zur Geschichte des Merkantilismus.* Veröffentlichungen der Kommission für neuere Geschichte Österreichs, vol. 38. Vienna: Adolf Holzhausen, 1951.

————. "Johann Joachim Bechers Bedeutung für die Entwicklung der Seidenindustrie in Deutschland." *Vierteljahrschrift für Sozial- und Wirtschaftsgeschichte* 38, no. 3 (1951): 209–46.

————. "Johann Joachim Bechers Kampf gegen Frankreich und die Gründung einer Wollmanufaktur in Salzburg im Jahre 1677." *Mitteilungen der Gesellschaft für Salzburger Landeskunde* 78 (1938): 168–82.

————. "Wien im Zeitalter des Merkantilismus." *Nachrichtenblatt des Vereines für Geschichte der Stadt Wien*, n.s., 3 (1941): 1–17.

Hatschek, Hans J. *Das Manufakturhaus auf dem Tabor in Wien. Ein Beitrag zur österreichischen Wirthschaftsgeschichte des 17. Jahrhunderts.* Staats- und sozialwissenschaftliche Forschungen, vol. 6, no. 1. Leipzig: Duncker & Humblot, 1886.

Hecksher, Eli F. *Mercantilism.* Translated by Mendel Shapiro. 2 vols. London: George Allen & Unwin, 1935.

Held, Felix E. *Christianopolis: An Ideal State of the Seventeenth Century.* Oxford: Oxford University Press, 1916.

Herr, Otfried. "Johann Joachim Becher über das Verhältnis von Staat und Wirtschaft in seinen wirtschaftlichen Schriften." Ph.D. diss., Heidelberg, 1936.

Hessen, Boris. *The Social and Economic Roots of Newton's* Principia. 1931. Edited by Robert S. Cohen. New York: H. Fertig, 1971.

Heubaum, Alfred. "Johann Joachim Becher. Ein Beitrag zur Geistesgeschichte des 17. Jahrhunderts." *Monatsheft der Comeniusgesellschaft* 9 (1900): 154–74.

Hintereicher, Margarete. *Georg Christian von Hessen-Homburg (1626–1677).* Quellen und Forschungen zur hessischen Geschichte, vol. 58. Darmstadt and Marburg: Selbstverlag der Hessischen Historischen Kommission Darmstadt und der Historischen Kommission für Hessen, 1985.

Hintze, Otto. "Der Commissarius und seine Bedeutung in der allgemeinen Verwaltungsgeschichte." In *Gesammelte Abhandlungen zur allgemeinen Verfassungsgeschichte*, edited by Fritz Hartung, 1:232–64. Leipzig: Koehler & Amelang, 1941.

————. "Der österreichische und der preußische Beamtenstaat im 17. und 18. Jahrhundert." In *Gesammelte Abhandlungen zur allgemeinen Verfassungsgeschichte*, edited by Fritz Hartung, 1:311–48. Leipzig: Koebler & Amelang, 1941.

Hirsch, Arnold. "'Politischer' Roman und 'politische' Lebensführung." In *Deutsche Barockforschung. Dokumentation einer Epoche*, 2d ed., edited by Richard Alewyn, pp. 205–66. Cologne and Berlin: Kiepenheuer & Witsch, 1966.

Hirschman, Albert O. *The Passions and the Interests: Political Arguments for Capitalism before Its Triumph.* Princeton: Princeton University Press, 1977.

Hobbes, Thomas. *Leviathan.* London, 1651.

Hooke, Robert. *The Diary of Robert Hooke.* Edited by Henry W. Robinson and Walter Adams. London: Taylor & Francis, 1935.

Hooykaas, R. *Humanisme, science et réform. Pierre de la Ramée (1515–1572).* Leiden: E. J. Brill, 1958.

[Hörnigk, Philipp Wilhelm von]. *Oesterreich über alles, wann es nur will.* N.p., 1684.

Houghton, Walther E., Jr. "The History of Trades: Its relation to seventeenth-century Thought." *Journal of the History of Ideas* 2 (1941): 33–60.

Hulshof, Abraham. "Een duitsch econom in een over ons land omstreeks 1670." *Onze eeuw 10* 4 (1910): 65–96.

Hunter, Michael. *Establishing the New Science: The Experience of the Early Royal Society.* Woodbridge, Suffolk: Boydell, 1989.

Hunter, Michael, and Simon Schaffer, eds. *Robert Hooke: New Studies.* Woodbridge, Suffolk: Boydell, 1989.

Hutchison, Terence. *Before Adam Smith: The Emergence of Political Economy, 1662–1776.* Oxford: Basil Blackwell, 1988.

Hüttl, Ludwig. *Caspar von Schmid (1622–1693), ein kurbayerischer Staatsmann aus dem Zeitalter Ludwigs XIV.* Miscellanea Bavarica Monacensia, supplement 29. Munich: Kommissionsbuchhandlung R. Wölfle, 1971.

Huygens, Christiaan. *Oeuvres complètes de Christiaan Huygens.* 22 vols. The Hague: Martinus Nijhoff, 1888–1950.

Impey, Oliver, and Arthur Macgregor, eds. *The Origins of Museums: The Cabinet of Curiosities in Sixteenth- and Seventeenth-century Europe.* Oxford: Clarendon Press, 1985.

Jaeger, C. Stephen. *The Origins of Courtliness: Civilizing Trends and the Formation of Courtly Ideals 939–1210.* Philadelphia: University of Pennsylvania Press, 1985.

Jaeger, F. M. "Over Johan Joachim Becher en zijne Relatie's met de Nederlanden." *Economisch-Historisch Jaarboek* 5 (1919): 60–135.

Jantzen, Heinrich. "Johann Joachim Becher als theoretischer und praktischer Privatökonom." Ph.D. diss., Cologne, 1925.

Jeanneret, Michel. *A Feast of Words: Banquets and Table Talk in the Renaissance.* Translated by Jeremy Whiteley and Emma Hughes. Chicago: University of Chicago Press, 1991.

Jöcher, Christian Gottlieb. *Allgemeines Gelehrten-Lexicon.* 4 vols. Leipzig, 1750–51.

Johnson, F. R. "Thomas Hood's Inaugural Address as Mathematical Lecturer of the City of London (1588)." *Journal of the History of Ideas* 3 (1942): 94–106.

Kamil, Neil. "War, Natural Philosophy and the Metaphysical Foundations of Artisanal Thought in an American Mid-Atlantic Colony: La Rochelle, New York City and the Southwestern Huguenot Paradigm, 1517–1730." Ph.D. diss., Johns Hopkins University, 1988.

Karpenko, V. "Coins and Medals Made of Alchemical Metal." *Ambix* 35 (1988): 65–76.

Kauder, Emil. "Johann Joachim Becher als Wirtschafts- und Sozialpolitiker." Ph.D. diss., Friedrich-Wilhelm-Universität zu Berlin, 1924.

Kaufmann, Thomas DaCosta. *Drawings from the Holy Roman Empire 1540–1680.* Princeton: Princeton University Press, 1982.

———. *The Mastery of Nature: Aspects of Art, Science, and Humanism in the Renaissance.* Princeton: Princeton University Press, 1993.

———. *The School of Prague.* Chicago: University of Chicago Press, 1988.

Kelbert, Heinz. "Johann Joachim Becher. Ein Beitrag zur Erforschung des berufspädagogischen Erbes." *Studien zur Geschichte der Berufsausbildung,* ser. 23, 1 (1954): 7–55.

Keller, Alex. "The Age of the Projectors." *History Today* 16 (1966): 467–74.

———. "Mathematical Technologies and the Growth of the Idea of Technical Progress in the Sixteenth Century." In *Science, Medicine and Society in the Renaissance,* vol.

1, edited by Allen G. Debus, pp. 11–27. New York: Science History Publications, 1972.

———. "Mathematics, Mechanics and the Origins of the Culture of Invention." *Minerva* 23 (1985): 348–61.

Kern, Arthur, ed. *Deutsche Hofordnungen des 16. und 17. Jahrhunderts.* 2 vols. Denkmäler der deutschen Kulturgeschichte, pt. 2. Berlin: Weidmannsche Buchhandlung, 1907.

Kertzer, David I. *Ritual, Politics, and Power.* New Haven: Yale University Press, 1988.

Kettering, Sharon. "Gift-giving and Patronage in Early Modern France." *French History* 2 (1988): 131–51.

———. *Patrons, Brokers, and Clients in Seventeenth-Century France.* Oxford: Oxford University Press, 1986.

Kiesel, Helmuth. *"Bei Hof, bei Höll." Untersuchungen zur literarischen Hofkritik von Sebastian Brant bis Friedrich Schiller.* Tübingen: Max Niemeyer Verlag, 1979.

Kindleberger, Charles P. *A Financial History of Western Europe.* London: George Allen & Unwin, 1984.

Kircher, Athanasius. *Mundus Subterraneus in XII Libros.* Amsterdam: Joannes Janslonius a Waesberge & Elzaeus Weyerstraet, 1665.

Klapsia, Heinrich. "Daniel Neuberger: Beiträge zur Kunsttätigkeit am österreichischen Kaiserhofe im 17. Jahrhundert, III." *Jahrbuch der Kunsthistorischen Sammlungen in Wien* 45 (n.s., 9) (1935): 223–48.

Koenigsberger, H. G. *Politicians and Virtuosi: Essays in Early Modern History.* London: Hambledon Press, 1986.

Kolb, A. "Johann Joachim Becher in Bayern." Ph.D. diss., Munich, 1941.

Kopp, Hermann. *Die Alchemie in älterer und neuerer Zeit.* Heidelberg: Carl Winter Universitätsbuchhandlung, 1886.

Krauth, Wolf-Hagen. *Wirtschaftsstruktur und Semantik. Wissenssoziologische Studien zum wirtschaftlichen Denken in Deutschland zwischen dem 13. und 17. Jahrhundert.* Soziologische Schriften, vol. 42. Berlin: Duncker & Humblot, 1984.

Krieger, Leonard. *The Politics of Discretion: Pufendorf and the Acceptance of Natural Law.* Chicago: University of Chicago Press, 1965.

Kruedener, Jürgen Freiherr von. *Die Rolle des Hofes im Absolutismus.* Stuttgart: Gustav Fischer Verlag, 1973.

Kühlmann, Wilhelm. *Gelehrtenrepublik und Fürstenstaat.* Tübingen: Max Niemeyer Verlag, 1982.

Kunckel, Johann. *Collegium Physico-Chymicum experimentale, oder Laboratorium Chymicum.* Edited by Johann Caspar Engelleder. Hamburg and Leipzig: Samuel Heyl, 1716.

Larner, John. "Europe of the Courts." *Journal of Modern History* 55 (1983): 669–81.

Laspeyres, Etienne. "Mitteilungen aus Pieter De La Courts Schriften, ein Beitrag zur Geschichte der niederländischen Nationaloeconomik des 17ten Jahrhunderts." *Zeitschrift für die gesammte Staatswissenschaft* 18 (1862): 330–74.

Lefebvre, Nicholas. German translation of the 1660 French text, *Chymischer Handleiter/ und Guldnes kleinod: Das ist: Richtige Anführung/ und deutliche Unterweisung/ so woll wie man die Chymische Schrifften/ welche von Chymischer Wissenschaft ins gemein handeln/ recht verstehen/ als/ wie man nach ihrer Ordnung/ solche*

Chymische Kunst/ durch wirckliche Operation, leicht und glücklich practiciren. Nuremberg: Christoph Endter, 1676.

Le Goff, Jacques. *Time, Work, and Culture in the Middle Ages.* Translated by Arthur Goldhammer. Chicago: University of Chicago Press, 1980.

Leibniz, Gottfried Wilhelm. *Leibnizens mathematische Schriften.* Edited by C. I. Gerhardt. Berlin: A. Ascher, 1849.

——. *Miscellanea Berolinensia.* Reprinted in Leibniz, *Opera Omnia*, edited by Ludovicus Dutens. 6 vols. Geneva, 1768.

——. *Sämtliche Schriften und Briefe.* Edited by Preussische Akademie der Wissenschaften et al. 6 series. Darmstadt: Otto Reichl et al., 1923–.

Levine, Joseph M. *The Battle of the Books: History and Literature in the Augustan Age.* Ithaca: Cornell University Press, 1991.

The Life of Leopold, Late Emperor of Germany. . . . London, 1706.

Lipowsky, Felix Joseph. *Des Ferdinand Maria . . . Churfuerstens . . . Lebens- und Regierungs-Geschichte.* Munich: Jakob Giel, 1831.

Long, Pamela O. "The Scholar and the Craftsman Revisited." Paper presented at the annual meeting of the History of Science Society, Washington, D.C., December 1992.

Lux, David S. *Patronage and Royal Science in Seventeenth-Century France.* Ithaca: Cornell University Press, 1989.

Macquer, Pierre-Joseph. *A Dictionary of Chemistry.* Translated from the French. London: T. Cadell, 1771.

Maier, Hans. *Die ältere deutsche Staats- und Verwaltungslehre.* 2d ed. Munich: C. H. Beck, 1980.

Maravall, José Antonio. *Culture of the Baroque.* Translated by Terry Cochran. Minneapolis: University of Minnesota Press, 1986.

Marin, Louis. *Portrait of the King.* Translated by Martha M. Houle. Theory and History of Literature, vol. 57. Minneapolis: University of Minnesota Press, 1988.

Martin, Julian. *Francis Bacon, the State, and the Reform of Natural Philosophy.* Cambridge: Cambridge University Press, 1992.

Mauss, Marcel. *The Gift.* 1950. Translated by W. D. Halls. New York and London: W. W. Norton, 1990.

McGuire, J. E., and P. M. Rattansi. "Newton and the 'Pipes of Pan.'" *Notes and Records of the Royal Society of London* 21 (1966): 108–43.

Meinel, Christoph. "De praestantia et utilitate Chemiae. Selbstdarstellung einer jungen Disziplin im Spiegel ihres programmatischen Schrifttums." *Sudhoffs Archiv* 65 (1981): 366–89.

——. "Reine und angewandte Chemie." *Berichte zur Wissenschaftsgeschichte* 8 (1985): 25–45.

——. "Theory or Practice? The Eighteenth-Century Debate on the Scientific Status of Chemistry." *Ambix* 30 (1983): 121–32.

——, ed. *Die Alchemie in der europäischen Kultur- und Wissenschaftsgeschichte.* Wolfenbütteler Forschungen, vol. 32. Wiesbaden: Otto Harrassowitz, 1986.

Memmert, Leonhard. "Die öffentliche Förderung der gewerblichen Produktionsmethoden zur Zeit des Merkantilismus in Bayern." *Abhandlungen aus dem Staatswissenschaftlichen Seminar an der Universität Erlangen* 7 (Leipzig, 1930).

Mendelsohn, J. Andrew. "Alchemy and Politics in England 1649–1665." *Past and Present* 135 (1992): 30–78.

Merk, Walther. *Der Gedanke des gemeinen Besten in der deutschen Staats- und Rechtsentwicklung*. 1934. Reprint. Darmstadt: Wissenschaftliche Buchgesellschaft, 1968.

Metzger, Hélène. *Les doctrines chimiques en France du début du XVIIe à la fin du XVIIIe siècle*. Paris: Albert Blanchard, 1923.

Meyer, Rudolf W. *Leibniz and the Seventeenth-Century Revolution*. 1952. Reprint. New York: Garland Publishing, 1985.

Middelfort, H. C. Erik. "Curious Georgics: The German Nobility and Their Crisis of Legitimacy in the Late Sixteenth Century." In *Germania Illustrata*, Sixteenth Century Essays and Studies, vol. 18, edited by Andrew C. Fix and Susan C. Karant-Nunn, pp. 217–42. Kirksville, Mo.: Sixteenth Century Journal Publishers, 1992.

Mintz, Sidney W. *Sweetness and Power: The Place of Sugar in Modern History*. New York: Viking Penguin, 1985.

Montgomery, John Warwick. *Cross and Crucible: John Valentine Andreae (1586–1654)*. The Hague: Martinus Nijhoff, 1973.

Moran, Bruce T. *The Alchemical World of the German Court: Occult Philosophy and Chemical Medicine in the Circle of Moritz of Hessen (1572–1632)*. Sudhoffs Archiv. Supplement 29. Stuttgart: Franz Steiner Verlag, 1991.

———. "German Prince-Practitioners: Aspects in the Development of Courtly Science, Technology, and Procedures in the Renaissance." *Technology and Culture* 22 (1981): 253–74.

———, ed. *Patronage and Institutions: Science, Technology, and Medicine at the European Court, 1500–1750*. Woodbridge, Suffolk: Boydell, 1991.

Morgenstern, Philipp, ed. *Turba Philosophorum*. Basel: Ludwig König, 1613.

Müller, Günther. "Höfische Kultur." In *Deutsche Barockforschung. Dokumentation einer Epoche*, 2d ed., edited by Richard Alewyn, pp. 182–204. Cologne and Berlin: Kiepenheuer & Witsch, 1966.

Müller, J. *Das Jesuitendrama in den Ländern deutscher Zunge vom Anfang (1555) bis zum Hochbarock (1655)*. 2 vols. Schriften zur deutschen Literatur, vols. 7–8. Augsburg, 1930.

Müller-Jahncke, Wolf-Dieter, and Joachim Telle. "Numismatik und Alchemie. Mitteilungen zu Münzen und Medaillen des 17. und 18. Jahrhunderts." In *Die Alchemie in der europäischen Kultur- und Wissenschaftsgeschichte*, edited by Christoph Meinel, pp. 229–75. Wolfenbütteler Forschungen, vol. 32. Wiesbaden: Otto Harrassowitz, 1986.

Multhauf, Robert P. *The Origins of Chemistry*. New York: F. Watts, 1967.

Nadler, Josef. "Das bayerisch-österreichische Barocktheater." In *Deutsche Barockforschung. Dokumentation einer Epoche*, 2d ed., edited by Richard Alewyn. Cologne and Berlin: Kiepenheuer & Witsch, 1966.

Neue deutsche Biographie. 16 vols. Berlin: Duncker & Humbolt, 1953–.

Neumeister, Sebastian, and Conrad Wiedemann, eds. *Res Publica Litteraria. Die Institutionen der Gelehrsamkeit in der frühen Neuzeit*. 2 vols. Wiesbaden: Otto Harrassowitz, 1987.

Newman, William R. *The Summa Perfectionis of Psuedo-Geber*. Leiden: E. J. Brill, 1991.

————. "Technology and Alchemical Debate in the Late Middle Ages." *Isis* 80 (1989): 423–45.

Nutton, Vivian, ed. *Medicine at the Courts of Europe, 1500–1837*. London and New York: Routledge, 1990.

Oestreich, Gerhard. *Geist und Gestalt des frühmodernen Staates*. Berlin: Duncker & Humblot, 1969.

Oldenburg, Henry. *Correspondence*. Edited by A. Rupert Hall and Marie Boas Hall. 13 vols. Madison: University of Wisconsin Press, 1965–86.

Olson, Richard. *Science Deified and Science Defied*. 2 vols. Berkeley: University of California Press, 1982–90.

Ong, Walter J. *Ramus, Method, and the Decay of Dialogue: From the Art of Discourse to the Art of Reason*. Cambridge, Mass.: Harvard University Press, 1983.

Ovitt, George. *The Restoration of Perfection: Labor and Technology in Medieval Culture*. New Brunswick, N.J.: Rutgers University Press, 1987.

Pagel, Walter. *Das medizinische Weltbild des Paracelsus. Seine Zusammenhänge mit Neuplatonismus und Gnosis*. Wiesbaden: Franz Steiner Verlag, 1962.

————. *Joan Baptista Van Helmont: Reformer of Science and Medicine*. Cambridge: Cambridge University Press, 1982.

————. *Paracelsus: An Introduction to Philosophical Medicine in the Era of the Renaissance*. 2d ed. Basel: Karger, 1982.

Palingenius, Marcellus. *The Zodiake of Life*. Translated by Barnabie Googe. London: Rause Newberie, 1576. Reprint. New York: Scholars' Facsimiles & Reprints, 1947.

Parry J., and M. Block, eds. *Money and the Morality of Exchange*. Cambridge: Cambridge University Press, 1989.

Partington, J. R. *A History of Chemistry*. 4 vols. London: Macmillan, 1961–70.

Peters, Hermann. "Leibniz als Chemiker." *Archiv für die Geschichte der Naturwissenschaften und der Technik* 7 (1916): 85–108, 220–74, 275–87.

Peursen, Cornelis-Anthonie van. "Ars Inveniendi bei Leibniz." *Studia Leibnitiana* 18 (1986): 183–94.

Pocock, J. G. A. *The Machiavellian Moment: Florentine Political Thought and the Atlantic Republican Tradition*. Princeton: Princeton University Press, 1975.

————. *Virtue, Commerce, and History*. Cambridge: Cambridge University Press, 1985.

Prag um 1600: Kunst und Kultur am Hofe Rudolfs II. 2 vols. Freren/Emsland: Luca Verlag, 1988.

Press, Volker, ed. *Städtewesen und Merkantilismus in Mitteleuropa*. Städteforschung, vol. 14. Cologne and Vienna: Böhlau Verlag, 1983.

Pumfrey, Stephen. "Ideas above His Station: A Social Study of Hooke's Curatorship of Experiments." *History of Science* 29 (1991): 1–44.

Quercetanus, Josephus (Joseph du Chesne). *Ad veritatem Hermeticae medicinae ex Hippocratis veterumque decretis ac Therpeusi. . . .* Paris: Abrahamus Savgrain, 1604.

Raeff, Marc. *The Well-Ordered Police State: Social and Institutional Change through Law in the Germanies and Russia 1600–1800*. New Haven: Yale University Press, 1983.

Ranum, Orest. "Courtesy, Absolutism, and the Rise of the French State, 1630–60." *Journal of Modern History* 52 (1980): 426–51.

Rattansi, P. M. "Paracelsus and the Puritan Revolution." *Ambix* 11 (1963): 24–32.

Rausch, Wilhelm, ed. *Die Städte Mitteleuropas im 17. und 18. Jahrhundert.* Beiträge zur Geschichte der Städte Mitteleuropas, 5. Linz and Donau: Der Arbeitskreis, 1981.

Redlich, Oswald. *Weltmacht des Barock. Österreich in der Zeit Kaiser Leopolds I.* 4th ed. Vienna: Rudolf M. Rohrer Verlag, 1961.

Reinhard, Wolfgang. "Staatsmacht als Kreditproblem. Zur Struktur und Funktion des frühneuzeitlichen Ämterhandels." In *Absolutismus*, edited by Ernst Hinrichs, pp. 214–48. Frankfurt: Suhrkamp, 1986.

Revel, Jacques. "The Uses of Civility." In *A History of Private Life*, vol. 3, edited by Roger Chartier, pp. 167–205. Cambridge, Mass.: Harvard University Press, 1989.

Rink, E. G. *Leopolds des Grossen Röm. Kaysers wunderwürdiges Leben und Thaten.* Cologne, 1713.

Rohr, Julius Bernhard von. *Einleitung zur Ceremoniel-Wissenschaft der großen Herren.* 2d ed. Berlin: Johann Andreas Rüdiger, 1733.

Rolfinck, Guerner. *Chimia in artis formam redacta, sex libris comprehensa.* Jena: Samuel Krebs, 1661.

Rood, Wilhelmus. *Comenius and the Low Countries.* Amsterdam: Van Gendt, 1970.

Roscher, Wilhelm. *Geschichte der National-Oekonomik in Deutschland.* Geschichte der Wissenschaften in Deutschland, vol. 14. Munich: R. Oldenbourg, 1874.

Rossi, Paolo. *Philosophy, Technology, and the Arts in the Early Modern Era.* Translated by Salvator Attanasio. New York: Harper and Row, 1970.

———. *Francis Bacon: From Magic to Science.* Translated by Sacha Rabinovitch. London: Routledge & Kegan Paul, 1968.

Ryan, Michael T. "Assimilating New Worlds in the Sixteenth and Seventeenth Centuries." *Studies in Society and History* 23 (1981): 519–38.

Sacks, David Harris. *The Widening Gate: Bristol and the Atlantic Economy 1450–1700.* Berkeley: University of California Press, 1991.

Schaffer, Simon. "Making Certain." Essay review of *Probability and Certainty* by B. J. Shapiro. *Social Studies of Science* 14 (1984): 137–52.

Schaller, Klaus. *Die Pädagogik des Johann Amos Comenius und die Anfänge des pädagogischen Realismus im 17. Jahrhundert.* Heidelberg: Quelle & Meyer, 1962.

———. "Die Pädagogik des Johann Joachim Becher. Psychosophia contra Pansophiam." *Wolfenbütteler Forschungsreihe*, forthcoming.

———. *Studien zur systematischen Pädogogik.* 2d ed. Heidelberg: Quelle & Meyer, 1969.

Schama, Simon. *The Embarrassment of Riches: An Interpretation of Dutch Culture in the Golden Age.* Berkeley: University of California Press, 1988.

Scheel, Günter. "Leibniz, die Alchimie und der absolute Staat." In *Theoria cum Praxi. Zum Verhältnis von Theorie und Praxis in 17. und 18. Jahrhundert. Akten des III. Internationaler Leibnizkongresses, 1977.* Vol. 1. *Studia Leibnitiana Supplementa* 19 (1980): 267–83.

Schlögl, Rudolf. "Der Bayerische Landtag von 1669." *Zeitschrift für bayerischer Landesgeschichte* 52 (1989): 221–54.

Schlosser, Julius. *Kunst- und Wunderkammern der Spätrenaissance.* 2d ed. Braunschweig: Klinkhardt & Bierman, 1978.

Schmidt, Friedrich. *Geschichte der Erziehung der Bayerischen Wittelsbacher von den frühesten Zeiten bis 1750*. In Monumenta Germaniae Paedagogica, vol. 14, edited by Karl Kehrbach. Berlin: A. Hofmann, 1892.

Schmidt, Johann Andreas. *Theatrum Naturae et Artis. Singulis semestribus novis machinis & experimentis augendum in Academia Julia curiosis B.C.D. pandet I.A.S.D.* Helmstedt: Georgus-Wolfangus-Hamius Acad. Typogr., ca. 1710.

Schmitt-Lermann, Hans. *Der Versicherungsgedanke im deutschen Geistesleben des Barock und der Aufklärung.* Munich: Kommunalschriften-Verlag J. Jehle, 1954.

Schnapper, Antoine. "The King of France as Collector in the Seventeenth Century." In *Art and History: Images and Their Meaning*, edited by Robert I. Rotberg and Theodore K. Rabb, pp. 185–202. Cambridge: Cambridge University Press, 1986.

Schneppen, Heinz. *Niederländische Universitäten und Deutsches Geistesleben.* Münster: Aschendorffsche Verlagsbuchhandlung, 1960.

Schöne, Albrecht. *Emblematik und Drama im Zeitalter des Barock.* Munich: C. H. Beck, 1964.

Schrohe, Heinrich. *Johann Christian von Boineburg, Kurmainzer Oberhofmarschall.* Mainz: Joh. Falk 3 Söhne, ca. 1926.

———. "Johann Joachim Becher in Mainz." *Zeitschrift für die Geschichte des Oberrheins*, n.s., 42 (1929): 444–50.

Schwartz, Stuart B. "The Voyage of the Vassals: Royal Power, Noble Obligations, and Merchant Capital before the Portuguese Restoration of Independence, 1624–1640." *American Historical Review* 96 (1991): 735–62.

Scriba, Christoph J. "The Autobiography of John Wallis, F.R.S." *Notes and Records of the Royal Society* 25 (1970): 17–46.

Shapin, Steven. "The House of Experiment in Seventeenth-Century England." *Isis* 79 (1988): 373–404.

———. "Pump and Circumstance: Robert Boyle's Literary Technology." *Social Studies of Science* 14 (1984): 481–519.

———. "A Scholar and a Gentleman: The Problematic Identity of the Scientific Practitioner in Early Modern England." *History of Science* 24 (1991): 279–327.

Shapin, Steven, and Simon Schaffer. *Leviathan and the Air-Pump: Hobbes, Boyle and the Experimental Life.* Princeton: Princeton University Press, 1985.

Shapiro, Barbara J. *Probability and Certainty in Seventeenth-Century England.* Princeton: Princeton University Press, 1983.

Sicher, Erwin. "Leopold I of Austria: A Reappraisal." Ph.D. diss., University of Southern California, 1970.

Slaughter, M. M. *Universal Languages and Scientific Taxonomy in the Seventeenth Century.* Cambridge: Cambridge University Press, 1982.

Small, Albion W. *The Cameralists: The Pioneers of German Social Polity.* New York: Burt Franklin, 1909.

Smith, Pamela H., "Alchemy, Credit, and the Commerce of Words and Things: Johann Joachim Becher at the Courts of the Holy Roman Empire, 1635–82." Ph.D. diss., Johns Hopkins University, 1990.

Soliday, Gerald Lyman. *A Community in Conflict: Frankfurt Society in the Seventeenth and Early Eighteenth Centuries.* Hanover, N.H.: Brandeis University Press, 1974.

Solomon, Howard M. *Public Welfare, Science, and Propaganda in Seventeenth Century France.* Princeton: Princeton University Press, 1972.

Sombart, Werner. *Luxus und Kapitalismus*. 2d ed. Munich: Duncker & Humblot, 1922.

Spielman, John P. *Leopold I of Austria*. New Brunswick, N.J.: Rutgers University Press, 1977.

Srbik, Heinrich von. "Abenteuer am Hofe Kaiser Leopold I." *Archiv für Kulturgeschichte* 8 (1910): 52–72.

———. *Wilhelm von Schröder. Ein Beitrag zur Geschichte der Staatswissenschaften*. Sitzungsberichte der Kais. Akademie der Wissenschaften in Wien, vol. 164. Vienna: Alfred Hölder, 1910.

Stahl, Georg Ernst, ed. *Actorum Laboratorii Chymici Monacensis, seu Physicae Subterraneae libri duo. Joh. Joachimi Beccheri . . . Physica subterranea profundam subterraneorum genesin, è principiis hucusque ignotis, ostendens. Opus sine pari, primum hactenus & princeps, editio novissima. Præfatione utili præmissa, indice locupletissimo adornato, sensuumque & rerum distinctionibus, libro tersius & curatius edendo, operam navavit & Specimen Beccherianum fundamentorum, documentorum, experimentorum, sujunxit Georg. Ernestus Stahl*. Leipzig: J. L. Gleditsch, 1703.

Steensgaard, Niels. "The Seventeenth-Century Crisis." In *The General Crisis of the Seventeenth Century*, edited by Geoffrey Parker and Lesley M. Smith, pp. 26–56. London: Routledge & Kegan Paul, 1979.

Steinhüser, Ferdinand August. *Johann Joachim Becher und die Einzelwirtschaft. Ein Beitrag zur Geschichte der Einzelwirtschaftslehre und des Kameralismus*. Nürnberger Beiträge zu den Wirtschaftswissenschaften, vols. 24–25. Nuremberg: Verlag der Hochschulbuchhandlung Krische, 1931.

Störmer, Wilhelm. "Wirtschaft und Bürgertum in den altbayerischen Städten unter dem zunehmenden absolutistischen Einfluss des Landesfürsten." In *Die Städte Mitteleuropas im 17. und 18. Jahrhundert*, edited by Wilhelm Rausch, pp. 237–66. Beiträge zur Geschichte der Städte Mitteleuropas, 5. Linz and Donau: Der Arbeitskreis, 1981.

Stolleis, Michael, ed. *Hermann Conring (1606–1681). Beiträge zu Leben und Werke*. Berlin: Duncker & Humbolt, 1983.

Straub, Eberhard. *Representatio Maiestatis oder churbayerische Freudenfeste*. Miscellanea Bavarica Monacensia, vol. 14. Munich: Kommissionsbuchhandlung R. Wölfe, 1969.

Strich, Michael. *Das Kurhaus Bayern im Zeitalter Ludwigs XIV und die europäischen Mächte*. 2 vols. Munich: Verlag der Kommission, 1933.

———. "Kurfürstin Adelheid von Bayern." *Historisches Jahrbuch* 47 (1927): 63–96.

Strong, Roy. *Art and Power*. Woodbridge, Suffolk: Boydell, 1984.

———. *Splendor at Court*. Boston: Houghton Mifflin, 1973.

Stroup, Alice. *A Company of Scientists*. Berkeley: University of California Press, 1990.

Struever, Nancy S. *Theory as Practice: Ethical Inquiry in the Renaissance*. Chicago: University of Chicago Press, 1992.

Sturm, Johann Christoph. *Collegium Experimentale, sive Curiosorum in quo Primaria hujus seculi inventa & experimenta Physico-Mathematica . . . Phaenomena & effecta. . . .* Nuremberg: Wolfgang Maurice Endter & Johannes Andrea Endter, 1676.

Suhling, Lothar. "'Philosophisches' in der frühneuzeitlichen Berg- und Hüttenkunde: Metallogenese und Transmutation aus der Sicht montanistischen Erfahrungswissens." In *Die Alchemie in der europäischen Kultur- und Wissenschaftsgeschichte*, edited by Christoph Meinel, pp. 293–313. Wolfenbütteler Forschungen, vol. 32. Wiesbaden: Otto Harrassowitz, 1986.

Teich, Mikuláš. "Interdisciplinarity in J. J. Becher's Thought." *History of European Ideas* 9 (1988): 145–60.

Tesauro, Emanuele. *Il Cannocchiale Aristotelico*. Turin, 1670. Reprint. Bad Homburg: Verlag Dr. Max Gehlen, 1968.

Troitzsch, Ulrich. *Ansätze technologischen Denkens bei den Kameralisten des 17. und 18. Jahrhunderts*. Schriften zur Wirtschafts- und Sozialgeschichte, vol. 5. Berlin: Duncker & Humblot, 1966.

Trunz, Erich. "Der deutsche Späthumanismus um 1600 als Standeskultur." In *Deutsche Barockforschung. Dokumentation einer Epoche*, 2d ed., edited by Richard Alewyn, pp. 147–81. Cologne and Berlin: Kiepenheuer & Witsch, 1966.

Turnbull, G. H. *Hartlib, Dury and Comenius: Gleanings from Hartlib's Papers*. London: Hodder & Stoughton, 1947.

———. "Johann Valentin Andreaes Societas Christiana." *Zeitschrift für deutsche Philologie* 74 (1955): 151–85.

———. *Samuel Hartlib*. Oxford: Oxford University Press, 1920.

Ullrich, Konrad. *Dr. Johann Joachim Becher. Der Erfinder der Gasbeleuchtung*. Munich: R. Oldenbourg, 1935.

Van Leeuwen, Henry G. *The Problem of Certainty in English Thought 1630–1690*. The Hague: Martinus Nijhoff, 1963.

Van Pelt, Robert Jan. "The Utopian Exit of the Hermetic Temple; or, A Curious Transition in the Tradition of the Cosmic Sanctuary." In *Hermeticism and the Renaissance*, edited by Ingrid Merkel and Allen G. Debus, pp. 400–423. Washington, D.C.: Folger Shakespeare Library, 1988.

Vives, Juan Luis. *De tradendis disciplinis*. 1531. Reprint. Translated by Foster Watson. Totowa, N.J.: Rowman and Littlefield, 1971.

Volberg, Heinrich. *Deutsche Kolonialbestrebungen in Südamerika nach dem Dreißigjährigen Kriege insbesondere die Bemühungen von Johann Joachim Becher*. Cologne and Vienna: Böhlau-Verlag, 1977.

Walker, Mack. *German Home Towns. Community, State, and General Estate, 1648–1871*. Ithaca: Cornell University Press, 1971.

Webster, Charles. *From Paracelsus to Newton: Magic and the Making of Modern Science*. Cambridge: Cambridge University Press, 1982.

———. *The Great Instauration: Science, Medicine, and Reform 1626–1660*. London: Gerald Duckworth, 1975.

———. "Macaria: Samuel Hartlib and the Great Reformation." *Acta Comeniana* 26 (1970): 147–64.

———, ed. *The Intellectual Revolution of the Seventeenth Century*. London: Routledge & Kegan Paul, 1974.

Weczerka, Hugo. "Entwicklungslinien der schlesischen Städte im 17. und in der ersten Hälfte des 18. Jahrhunderts." In *Die Städte Mitteleuropas im 17. und 18. Jahrhundert*, edited by Wilhelm Rausch, pp. 119–42. Beiträge zur Geschichte der Städte Mitteleuropas, 5. Linz and Donau: Der Arbeitskreis, 1981.

Weigel, Erhard. *Gesammelte pädagogische Schriften*. Edited by H. Schüling. Gießen: Universitätsbibliothek, 1970.

————. *Tertius interveniens mit einem allgemeinen Friedens-Mittel.* 1673(?). Reprinted in Erhard Weigel, *Gesammelte pädagogische Schriften*, edited by H. Schüling. Gießen: Universitätsbibliothek, 1970.

————. *Vorstellung der Kunst- und Handwercke/ nechst einem kurtzen Begriff des Mechanischen Heb- und Rüst-Zeugs. Samt einem Anhang/ Welcher Gestalt so wohl der gemeinen Leibes-Nothdurfft/ als der Gemüths-Wohlfarth und Gelehrsamkeit selbst/ durch die Wissenschafft der Mechanischen Künste geholffen werden möge. Auf veranlassung im Mertzen dieses Jahrs erschienenen Neuen Cometen unmassgeblich entworffen.* Jena: Johann Jacob Bauhofer, 1672.

Westfall, Richard S. "Scientific Patronage: Galileo and the Telescope." *Isis* 76 (1985): 11–30.

Westman, Robert S. "The Astronomer's Role in the Sixteenth Century: A Preliminary Study." *History of Science* 18 (1980): 105–47.

Weyer, Jost. *Chemiegeschichtsschreibung von Weigleb (1790) bis Partington (1970).* Hildesheim: Verlag Dr. H. A. Gerstenberg, 1974.

Whigham, Frank. *Ambition and Privilege: The Social Tropes of Elizabethan Courtesy Theory.* Berkeley: University of California Press, 1984.

Whitney, Elsbeth. *Paradise Restored: The Mechanical Arts from Antiquity through the Thirteenth Century.* Transactions of the American Philosophical Society, vol. 80. Philadelphia: American Philosophical Society, 1990.

Wiedemann, Conrad. "Polyhistors Glück und Ende. Von D. G. Morhof zum jungen Lessing." In *Festschrift Gottfried Weber*, edited by Heinz Otto Burger and Klaus von See, pp. 215–35. Bad Homburg: Verlag Gehlen, 1967.

Wiesner, Merry E. *Working Women in Renaissance Germany.* New Brunswick, N.J.: Rutgers University Press, 1986.

Wilentz, Sean, ed. *Rites of Power: Symbols, Rituals, and Politics since the Middle Ages.* Philadelphia: University of Pennsylvania Press, 1985.

Wilkins, John. *Mathematical magick.* London, 1648.

Witt, Johann de. *Waerdye van Lyf-Renten naer proportie van Los-Renten.* The Hague: Jacob Scheltus, 1671.

Wolf, Adam. "Die Hofkammer unter Kaiser Leopold I." *Sitzungsberichte der kaiserlichen Akademie der Wissenschaften* 11 (1853): 440–84.

Wollgast, Siegfried. *Zur Stellung des Gelehrten in Deutschland im 17. Jahrhundert.* Berlin: Akademie-Verlag, 1984.

Wunder, Bernd. "Hof und Verwaltung im 17. Jahrhundert." In *Europäische Hofkultur im 16. und 17. Jahrhundert*, edited by August Buck et al., 9: 199–204. Wolfenbütteler Arbeiten zur Barockforschung, vols. 8, 9, 10. Hamburg: Dr. Ernst Hauswedell, 1981.

Yates, Frances A. *The Art of Memory.* Chicago: University of Chicago Press, 1966.

————. *Giordano Bruno and the Hermetic Tradition.* Chicago: University of Chicago Press, 1964.

————. *The Rosicrucian Enlightenment.* London: Routledge & Kegan Paul, 1972.

Zedler, Johann Heinrich. *Grosses vollständiges Universal-Lexikon aller Wissenschaften und Künste.* 64 vols. Halle and Leipzig: Johann Heinrich Zedler, Verleger, 1732–50. Reprint. Graz: Akademische Druck- und Verlagsanstalt, 1961.

Zesen, Philipp von. *Beschreibung der Stadt Amsterdam.* Amsterdam: Joachim Nosch, 1664. Reprint. New York: Peter Lang, 1988.

Zetzner, Lazarus, et al. *Theatrum Chemicum*. 6 vols. Strasbourg, 1602–61.

Zilsel, Edgar. "The Sociological Roots of Science." *American Journal of Sociology* 47 (1941–42): 544–62.

Zincke, Georg Heinrich, ed. *D. Johann Joachim Bechers politischer discurs von den eigentlichen ursachen des auf- und abnehmens der städte und Länder. Oder gründliche anleitung zur stadt-wirtschaft und policey der teutschen staaten . . . neue hauptstücke von denen . . . wahrheiten des ganzen stadt-, policey- und cämmerey-, manufactur-, commercien- und haushaltungs-wesens, das erste mahl für jetzige umstände . . . brauchbarer gemacht und verbessert von d. Georg Heinrich Zincken.* Frankfurt and Leipzig: G. C. Gsellius, 1754.

Zorn, Wolfgang. "Humanismus und Wirtschaftsleben nördlich der Alpen." In *Humanismus und Ökonomie*, edited by Heinrich Lutz, pp. 31–60. Mitteilung der Kommission für Humanismusforschung, vol. 8. Weinheim: Acta humaniora, 1983.

INDEX

Académie des sciences, 4, 222n
academies, 39, 191, 192; Academia naturae
    curiosorum, 4, 39; Académie des sciences,
    4; Accademia dei lincei, 44; Accademia del
    Cimento, 39; Julian Academy (Helmstedt),
    4, 265; Royal Society, 4, 39
Agricola, Rudolph, 35
alchemical furnace, 274–77
Alchemical Gutachten, 209–20, 244
alchemical transmutation, 174–76, 211–12,
    215–17, 222–23; adjudicator of, 78, 185,
    187; of Becher, 173–74, 221–22; contracts
    for, 72, 236; and metallurgy, 182; and "N.",
    183–84; and piety, 182, 185, 199; in
    Vienna, 179–86, 198–99. *See also* alchemy
alchemists, 174; as self-interested, 213, 215;
    in Vienna, 181–85
alchemy: and civic life, 120n, 204, 213, 215,
    243–44; and commerce, 209–17, 221; con-
    cordance of processes in, 226, 235; in
    eighteenth century, 269–70; at Habsburg
    court, 198–99; as knowledge of genera-
    tion, 8, 202–4, 225, 241–42; in Kunst-
    und Werckhaus, 191–98; as a language, 8–
    9, 50; as movable wealth, 52–54, 216–17,
    225, 241–42; patronage of, 179–80, 182,
    189; theory and practice in, 45, 50; and vir-
    tue, 53–54, 182, 210, 213, 243, 245. *See
    also* alchemical transmutation
Alsted, Johann Heinrich, 30, 34
Althusius, Johannes, 42, 123
Amalie Elisabeth (landgravine of Hessen-
    Kassel), 144
Amsterdam, 146–61
anatomy, 73, 85, 86n
Andreae, Johann Valentin, 30, 37, 228n
Anhalt-Dessau, 143
Aristotle, 37n, 46, 64, 120n, 206, 208–9,
    217n; and organization of knowledge, 47–
    48; political thought of, 42–43, 122
ars inveniendi, 262, 271
art: and artifice, 263–65; human, 5, 7, 260,
    267–68; as imitation of nature, 7, 40, 89,
    128, 169, 207, 225, 227, 263–65; as pro-
    ductive knowledge, 9, 45, 50, 56, 91, 92,
    239, 260–61, 263, 276; as *technē*, 48

artifice, 255–58, 263–65, 268–71
artisans, 8, 34, 41, 91, 264–65; Becher's net-
    works of, 70–80; culture of, 7; as an "es-
    tate," 120–21, 211; *hofbefreite*, 27, 145;
    method of, 9, 40, 49, 261–62, 268; and
    natural philosophers, 239; and new philos-
    ophy, 5; in Ramist reform, 35; and travel,
    50; and vulgar tongue, 81; workshops of,
    36–37, 228, 239

Bacon, Francis, 31, 37, 39, 228n, 265
Becher, Joachim, 29–30
Bernini, Gian Lorenzo, 267–69
Besoldus, Christoph, 69n
Bewindheber, 155–62
Boccalini, Trajano, 45–47, 49
Bodin, Jean, 42, 123
Boë (Sylvius), Francis de la, 208n
Boeckler, Johann, 41n, 43
Boehme, Jacob, 31, 39, 40
Boineburg, Christian von, 59, 60n, 81n, 131–
    32, 145n, 146n
Boschart, Samuel, 41n
Boyle, Robert, 38, 61, 62, 74, 259, 269,
    277n
Brand, Henning, 18, 248–51, 255
Brand, Margaretha, 251
Breslau, 51, 52
Buno, Johannes, 51n, 83
bureaucracy: in Bavaria, 98–99; of the court,
    98, 106; in Vienna, 177–78

Cain, Abraham, 151, 156
Calderón de la Barca, Pedro, 266
cameral matters of the treasury, 70, 75, 111,
    115, 119
cameral officials, 127–28, 165, 214–15,
    223–24, 269–70
cameral science, 19, 20
Campanella, Tommaso, 228n
canals, 118, 261
Cardano, Jerome, 70n, 120n
centralization of power, 3, 5, 119, 125; in
    Bavaria, 95–102
charlatanry, 269–70
Charlemagne, 95